TOBRUK

Ex Libris
J.E. JENNINGS
2012

TOBRUK

THE GREAT SIEGE
1941-42

WILLIAM F. BUCKINGHAM

First published 2008
This edition published 2009

The History Press
The Mill, Brimscombe Port
Stroud, Gloucestershire, GL5 2QG
www.thehistorypress.co.uk

© William F. Buckingham, 2008, 2009

The right of William F. Buckingham to be identified as the Author
of this work has been asserted in accordance with the
Copyrights, Designs and Patents Act 1988.

British Library Cataloguing in Publication Data.
A catalogue record for this book is available from the British Library.

ISBN 978 0 7524 5221 0

Typesetting and origination by The History Press.
Printed in Great Britain

Contents

Introduction   7

1   Lines in the Sand and Black Shirts: Egypt, Libya   10
     and the Horn of Africa, c.200 BC – 1940

2   Down the Slippery Slope, Ready or Not: Italy's   30
     Entry into the Second World War,
     September 1939 – September 1940

3   Stroke and Counter-Stroke: The Italian Invasion   56
     of Egypt and Operation COMPASS,
     June 1940 – December 1940

4   Tobruk Captured: The British Advance into   86
     Libya, December 1940 – January 1941

5   COMPASS Concluded: The Conquest of   116
     Cyrenaica and the Battle of Beda Fomm,
     22 January 1941 – 9 February 1941

6   Tobruk Menaced: The Arrival of the *Deutsches*   140
     Afrikakorps in Libya and the British Retreat from
     Cyrenaica, 7 February 1941 – 8 April 1941

7   Tobruk Invested: 8 April 1941 – 12 April 1941   173

8   Tobruk Attacked: 12 April 1941 – 18 April 1941   215

9   Tobruk Assailed: 19 April 1941 – 4 May 1941   240

10 Tobruk Besieged: 4 May 1941 – 25 October 1941   270

11 Tobruk Relieved: 303
    25 October 1941 – 10 December 1941

12 Epilogue: Tobruk Taken: 319
    10 December 1941 – 21 June 1942

Notes   325

List of Illustrations   339

Bibliography   341

Index   344

Introduction

The Libyan port of Tobruk occupies a key place in the history of the Second World War in North Africa, largely due to the two hundred and forty day siege endured by the garrison composed of British, Australian, Indian and Polish troops between April and December 1941. This was the longest siege in British military history, and included a complete garrison relief carried out by sea in the face of overwhelming German and Italian airpower. Moreover, the series of deliberate attacks on the port by Rommel's newly arrived *Afrika Korps* between 11 April and 2 May 1941 was the first time the German *blitzkrieg* technique employing Panzers and close air support had been held and successfully repulsed by defenders holding fixed defensive positions. The fact that the rebuff was delivered by an inexperienced and relatively poorly equipped Allied force made the event all the more noteworthy.

The defence of Tobruk was also one of very few bright spots in the dark days of 1941. At that time the German triumph in continental Europe and the Dunkirk evacuation were very fresh in mind, and German invasion of Britain seemed a very real possibility. The Blitz was at its height and the Axis tide of victory seemed unstoppable after the humiliating series of Allied reverses in Holland, Belgium, France, Greece and Crete. Tobruk thus joined the Battle of Britain and the stalwart defence of the Mediterranean island of Malta as a beacon of hope for the beleaguered British public, and the relief of the port in December 1941 was greeted with much jubilation. Its importance became unfortunate when on 21 June 1942, Tobruk's new South African-led garrison surrendered to Rommel after less than a day of fighting with the loss of 30,000 Allied prisoners of war. Occurring a mere six months after the end of the great siege, the shock of this event was rendered all the more intense.

Published works on Tobruk tend to focus, to a greater or lesser extent, on the great siege and this event from the Allied perspective, with some more recent works covering matters from the Axis perspective as part of a wider examination. While these provide perfectly adequate and in some instances very detailed coverage, most focus narrowly on the siege and subsequent Axis recapture of Tobruk and thus do not fully address the crucial role the port played in a wider sense. The Desert War swung back and forth along a coastal strip running for a thousand miles of Egypt and the Italian colonial provinces of Cyrenaica and Tripolitania. Operations were restricted to this narrow cockpit by the Mediterranean to the north and impassable terrain to the south, and Tobruk played a vital role in this operational ebb and flow, not only when the fighting came close by. The port was located virtually astride the road and rail links that ran through the coastal strip, which in turn meant that neither side could afford the luxury of ignoring it whether it lay in the immediate battle area or suddenly far to the rear of the fighting front as was often the case. Possession of Tobruk thus became a major preoccupation for both sides, and this imperative exerted a clear and overriding influence on the conduct of operations in the Western Desert throughout the whole of the period between September 1940, when the Italians launched their ill-fated invasion of Egypt, and the final German defeat at El Alamein in November 1942.

A second major omission in works on Tobruk concerns the portrayal of the Italian contribution which, wittingly or otherwise, tends to echo British and German wartime attitudes. The British view was shaped largely by wartime propaganda, with seemingly endless lines of Italian prisoners of war marching happily into captivity being among the most iconic images from the war. The German view is well illustrated by Rommel, who made no secret of his contempt for his Italian allies and took every opportunity to denigrate and humiliate them. As a result, the current casual reader could be forgiven for not realising that Tobruk was actually located inside an Italian colony, or that the Italian armed forces actually provided the bulk and backbone of the Axis effort at Tobruk and indeed North Africa generally. Without them Rommel would have been hamstrung: he was dependent on Italian logistical resources and Italian military units, which were largely less mobile but more numerous, to pin down his British opponents and guard the flanks of the fast moving armoured operations with which he is associated. Even more importantly, the Australian acquisition of Tobruk in January 1941 also involved a siege, for the Italians had invested much time and treasure in constructing the port's defences. The quantity and quality of those defences is not only readily apparent from the effort which was required to overcome them. That those same defences played a key role in the subsequent Allied defence of Tobruk against Rommel is frequently overlooked, as is the fact that a British survey to establish a shorter defensive perimeter discovered that Italians had not only occupied the only feasible line of defence, but had done so with good deal of tactical expertise.

This work will therefore address these omissions as part of a wider and properly rounded account, that not only tells the story of the epic siege of Tobruk using official documentation, captured German records and participant accounts, but also provides the background that shaped events at Tobruk, thus placing the latter in its proper context. There will also be a deliberate emphasis on the Italian perspective in Libya, elsewhere in Africa and the Mediterranean region, again to set matters in their proper context and attempt to compensate for the neglect of this important angle in other accounts.

Finally the author would like to thank Jonathan Reeve at Tempus Publishing for once again tolerating a sometimes elastic approach to deadlines, and the members of the Tanknet Internet Military Forum who provided invaluable help and advice, often at short notice.

William F. Buckingham
Bishopbriggs, Glasgow, February 2008

1
Lines in the Sand and Black Shirts: Egypt, Libya and the Horn of Africa, c.200 BC – AD 1940

At 17:30 Hours on 4 November 1942 *Generalfeldmarschall* Erwin Rommel ordered his *Panzerarmee Afrika* to commence a general withdrawal from Egypt along the coast road running west toward the Libyan frontier. The withdrawal was prompted by Operation SUPERCHARGE, the second of two major British attacks that made up what has become known as the Battle of El Alamein. The first attack, codenamed Operation LIGHTFOOT, began on the night of 23–24 October 1942 after an intensive deception effort and preparatory artillery barrage. A two-pronged infantry assault, LIGHTFOOT was intended to breach the extensive Axis minefields and push the fighting into back into their carefully sited defensive zone. There the defenders could be worn down, a process referred to as 'crumbling', and Rommel's mobile reserves drawn into the fight. With this achieved SUPERCHARGE was launched on the night of 1–2 November, aimed at the junction between the *Deutsches Afrika Korps* and the less well equipped Italian forces occupying the southern portion of the Axis line.

By 3 November SUPERCHARGE was exerting such pressure that Rommel issued a preliminary withdrawal order, but this was countermanded by Hitler via one of the grandiloquent statements that were to become increasingly common as the war tilted against Germany. Rommel was ordered to '...stand fast, yield not a yard of ground and throw every gun and every man into the battle.'[1] During the morning of 4 November the pressure finally became too much. While elements of the British 1st Armoured Division fought German armoured units around Tel el Aqaqir at the northern end of the attack frontage,[2] elements of the British 7th and 10th Armoured and 2nd New Zealand Divisions found their way through the Axis line at the south-west corner of the salient created by SUPERCHARGE. British armour swiftly cut the main Axis supply line, known as the Rahman Track, overran the *Deutsches Afrika Korps* battle headquarters complete with its commander *Generalleutnant* Wilhelm Ritter von Thoma and began pushing north and west into the Axis rear areas. Facing the imminent encirclement and destruction of his *Panzerarmee*, Rommel appealed to Hitler to rescind his no retreat order. When the Führer reluctantly agreed in the late afternoon Rommel immediately ordered a withdrawal to Fuka, almost fifty miles west of the fighting front.

Anxious to avoid giving their provenly resilient foes the opportunity to regroup, the British began a pursuit operation at dawn on 5 November. While this failed to yield the complete encirclement envisaged, it nonetheless prevented the retiring Axis forces from more than pausing at Fuka and extended Rommel's initial withdrawal to Mersa Matruh, a further fifty miles or more to the west. The fuel-starved remnants of the 21 Panzer Division fought a successful delaying action just east of Mersa on 6 November. A series of similar actions were fought all the way along the North African coast, at Sollum and Halfaya on 11 November, just west of Tobruk two days later and near Derna on 15 November. The port of Benghazi fell five days after that, on 20 November 1942. The pace of the Allied advance then slackened as Axis resistance stiffened and the supply lines from Egypt lengthened. It took just under four weeks, from 25 November to 13 December, to overcome Axis defences near El Agheila and a similar period ending on 16 January 1943 to deal with a more extensive blocking position west of Buerat. Thus was *Panzerarmee Afrika* harried west out of Egypt, across the breadth of Libya and halfway into Tunisia before finally coming to a stop behind the Mareth Line, three months and over a thousand miles after Rommel had ordered the Axis withdrawal from El Alamein.

The remainder of the fighting in North Africa up to the final defeat and surrender of the Axis forces there in May 1943 was distinct in nature and geography from the earlier fighting in the Western Desert. In addition, with the exception of the short-lived Allied foray into Greece and subsequent debacle on Crete in 1941, the Western Desert campaign in Libya and Egypt was the sole focus of British and Commonwealth ground operations in the west from the evacuation of France in June 1940 until the TORCH landings in Algeria in November 1942. The campaign swung back and forth along a thousand-mile coastal strip of Egypt and Libya, trammelled by a combination of largely featureless and indefensible terrain and logistical limitations. The port of Tobruk played a crucial role in this operational ebb and flow. It was the principal logistic hub for the initial Italian invasion and occupation of western Egypt that sparked the campaign in 1940. More famously the port was also the scene of three separate sieges, one of which being not only unbroken but also, at 242 days, the longest in British and Commonwealth military history. Unsurprisingly therefore, possession of Tobruk was a major preoccupation for both sides that exerted a clear and distinct influence on the conduct of their operations. Consequently, while it may not have been apparent at the time, the Axis withdrawal past Tobruk on 12 November 1942 not only marked the point where the port sank back into military obscurity, but also ended a distinct chapter in the history of the Second World War.

The circumstances that led to the conflict which raged around Tobruk in the early 1940s went back the better part of a century, to the period of colonial expansion into Africa by the European Great Powers in the latter half of the nineteenth century. Egypt was an Ottoman province until 1805, when civil war permitted Muhammad Ali Pasha to seize control. After gaining Ottoman approval for his semi-autonomous rule, Muhammad Ali launched a series of

military campaigns into Arabia and Libya and embarked on a series
of domestic reforms aimed at improving the Egyptian economy.
These included establishing state monopolies over key commodities
and manufacturing, and the cultivation of cotton in the fertile Nile
Delta. International trade was also encouraged and the new regime
actively promoted Egypt as a conduit for the transport of goods
between Europe and India, through the ancient Mediterranean port
of Alexandria, down the River Nile and overland to the Red Sea.
The construction of a canal linking Alexandria to the Nile ordered
by Muhammad Ali in 1819 was intended to assist this trade route.

   Muhammad Ali died in 1849 but his successors continued his
reforms and their associated development. In 1854 the French engineer and diplomat *Vicomte* Ferdinand Marie de Lesseps approached
Said Pasha with the idea of constructing a new canal between the
Mediterranean and the Red Sea; a similar link had been constructed
in the thirteenth century BC and maintained with varying degrees
of success until finally falling into disrepair in the eighth century
AD. International financial backing for the new project was secured
via the Egyptian-owned *Compagnie Universelle du Canal Maritime de
Suez* in 1858, with Egyptian and French backers owning most of
the stock. Construction began on 25 April 1859 and was completed
on 17 November 1869 at a cost of $100 million, the finished Canal
running for just over a hundred miles from Suez at the head of the
Gulf of the same name in the south to Port Said in the north. It did
not follow the shortest route but instead linked three existing bodies
of water, the Bitter Lakes, Lake Manzilah and Lake Timsâh, in order
to minimise excavation. Construction was further simplified and
speeded by the fact that the course of the Canal was virtually level,
which meant there was no need for locks to carry the watercourse
over topographical elevations.

   However, by the time the Canal was complete Egypt was heading for a financial crisis. Said Pasha was succeeded by Ismail the
Magnificent in 1863, who became Khedive in 1867. Ismail paralleled
construction of the Suez Canal with an ambitious civil engineering
programme that included extending the breakwater at Alexandria

and modernising the harbour at Suez, improving coastal navigation with additional lighthouses and extending railway and telegraph networks across the country. The work was initially financed with profits from the sale of Egyptian cotton, which boomed when the American Civil War interrupted supply from the US southern states in the 1860s. By the end of the decade, however, this windfall was running out, foreign investors were becoming wary of extending additional credit to the Egyptian government and Ismail began to accrue a formidable national debt. As a result the financial burden of Ismail's extensive reforms began to fall disproportionately on the impoverished general population. The overall result was to render Egypt increasingly vulnerable to external interference.

The British initially opposed the construction of the Suez Canal, and their objections delayed finalisation of the agreement between Said Pasha and de Lesseps for two years. They also exploited the situation to gain favourable concessions for the British-owned Eastern Telegraph Company and the establishment of a British-influenced Bank of Egypt. The completion of the Canal increased British interest, for it offered a way of avoiding the lengthy voyage around Africa to reach India and other British colonies in the Far East. This was not merely a matter of length of journey, for the passage could also be extremely hazardous, as shown by the example of HMS *Birkenhead*. One of the Royal Navy's first iron-hulled vessels, the *Birkenhead* was carrying troops from Portsmouth to Algoa Bay in the Western Cape when she struck an uncharted rock in the early hours of 26 February 1852. The ranking officer aboard, Lieutenant-Colonel Seton of the 74th Regiment of Foot, mustered the personnel on deck and ordered them to stand fast as the few boats available were loaded with dependants. The soldiers obeyed the order as the ship broke up under them, and only 193 of approximately 640 souls aboard survived, the remainder being drowned in the rough sea or taken by sharks. The incident inspired Rudyard Kipling's poem about the 'Birken'ead Drill', and it is also widely acknowledged as the root of the maritime tradition of women and children first in times of emergency.

Egypt's financial straits gave the British the opportunity to make up for their earlier disinterest in the Suez Canal and to extend their involvement in Egyptian domestic affairs. In 1875 Ismail was obliged to sell Egyptian shares and thus control of the Canal to the British for £976,582, and within four years Egypt was being governed by an Anglo-French partnership labelled Dual Control. The latter forced Ismail from power as Khedive in favour of his son Tawfiq in 1879.[3] A short period of relative stability degenerated into widespread unrest against foreign interference in Egyptian affairs led by an Egyptian Army officer named Ahmed Urabi. The British, concerned for their huge investments in Egypt, sought support for military action from the French and Italians and when the latter declined, decided to go it alone. On 11 July 1882 Royal Navy vessels bombarded the Egyptian gun batteries at Alexandria and the port itself in an effort to quell an open revolt. The exchange cost the British two ships, and a large naval landing party only succeeded in occupying the city two days later after fierce resistance. The episode prompted Tawfiq to seek British protection, leaving Ahmed Urabi as the de facto ruler of Egypt, and persuaded British Prime Minister William Gladstone to despatch an expeditionary force to restore the situation.

The British assembled a 24,000 strong force on Cyprus and Malta, commanded by Lieutenant-General Sir Garnet Wolseley. Wolseley was not only a veteran of the Crimea, the Indian Mutiny and numerous other colonial campaigns but had also been instrumental in Cardwell's Army reforms in the early 1870s. His successful campaign against the Ashanti in what is now Ghana in 1873–74 won him promotion, the GCMG and KCB, a grant of £25,000 and made him a household name in Victorian Britain; the term 'all Sir Garnet', referring to his painstaking preparations for the Ashanti campaign also became a national catchword for efficiency and competence. As Urabi's forces were blocking the western route from Alexandria, Wolseley opted to approach the Egyptian capital Cairo from the east via the Suez Canal instead. The force from Cyprus and Malta thus entered the Port Said end of the Canal while an additional 7,000 strong force despatched from India via Aden did the same at the

Suez entrance, all supported by forty Royal Navy warships. Landings at Ismailia, roughly midway along the Canal and just under a hundred miles east of Cairo, began on 20 August 1882.

On 26 August a British force seized Kassassin, twenty miles from Ismailia, to secure fresh water supplies and captured seven Krupp guns and a large quantity of stores at a cost of five dead and twenty-five wounded. After two unsuccessful attempts to retake Kassassin the Egyptians fell back to a blocking position at Tel-el-Kebir on 10 September 1882. After a careful reconnaissance Wolseley decided on a dawn surprise attack with a night approach march beginning on the night of 12–13 September. The force was guided across the open desert by Royal Navy Commander Wyatt Rawson using the stars and his naval navigation training. This succeeded in placing the attack force undetected within 300 yards of the Egyptian positions, and the attack began as dawn broke at 05:40 on 13 September 1882. The resulting battle lasted under an hour and ended with an Egyptian collapse but was nonetheless hard-fought, costing the lives of 2,000 Egyptians and 480 of Wolseley's men.[4] British cavalry entered Cairo the on 14 September and Khedive Tawfiq was restored to power twelve days later. Ahmed Urabi was captured, tried and sentenced to death, subsequently commuted to banishment to Ceylon. Direct British involvement in Egypt was supposed to be short-term, but control of the area proved simply too important to British Imperial interests. Thus Egypt became a British Protectorate in 1914 and when the Protectorate ended on 28 February 1922 and Egypt became a nominally independent state again, the British retained control of defence and Imperial communications among other specific responsibilities. In the event, direct British involvement in Egypt did not end until 1956, after the ill-fated invasion of the country with the French prompted by the nationalisation of the Suez Canal by Egyptian President Gamal Abdel Nasser.

The beginning of British involvement in Egypt coincided with the arrival of Italy on the European imperial stage, following the unification of the country brought about by the events of the *Risorgimento* (Resurgence) between 1859 and 1871. As possession of overseas colonies was then a major indicator of great power status, the new Italian state displayed an understandable interest in joining the 'scramble for Africa', focussing attention on the Red Sea coast where Italian merchants had been plying their trade for some time. In 1885, with the tacit consent of the British, Italian forces occupied the Red Sea port of Massawa and began to extend their influence into Eritrea. Local opposition was not especially formidable; in March 1885 an Italian force used balloons to throw a body of tribesmen into panic, and on another occasion a night attack on Italian troops was routed with electric searchlights, to the amusement of the troops involved. Events did not always end with such merriment, however. In January 1887 an Italian force moving to relieve a besieged garrison was ambushed and wiped out at Dogali, losing 430 dead and eighty-two wounded from a force of 550. Nonetheless, by the end of the decade Italy was the proud possessor of the colonies of Eritrea and Italian Somaliland in the Horn of Africa.

Their colonial appetite suitably whetted, the Italians set about extending their control over the neighbouring and independent Kingdom of Abyssinia, later known as Ethiopia, ruled by King Menelik II from his capital at Addis Ababa. On 2 May 1889 the Italians succeeded in obtaining Menelik's signature to the Treaty of Wichale. However, the wording of the Abyssinian Amharic language version differed significantly from the Italian. The former bound Menelik to nothing more than the option of voluntary co-operation with the Italians at his discretion, whereas the latter effectively made him an Italian vassal; Menelik was understandably less than impressed on discovering the Italian duplicity and began planning to overturn his agreement with them. A premature Abyssinian invasion of Eritrea was repulsed and Italian forces took the opportunity to pursue the retreating invaders into Abyssinia; their occupation of a number of towns then sparked what became known as the First Abyssinian War. The Italians appear to have assumed that the Abyssinians could also be cowed with balloons and electric spotlights, but their new adversaries turned out to be rather more resilient and sophisticated. King Menelik had spent the first half of the 1890s obtaining modern small-arms and rifled artillery for his army; ironically his armoury included 2 million rounds of small-arms ammunition obtained from the Italians as a bribe for earlier co-operation.

The Italian Governor of Eritrea, General Oreste Baratieri, travelled to Rome to receive parliamentary plaudits for his invasion of Abyssinian territory, and somewhat rashly promised to not only finish the job, but to also capture King Menelik and parade him in a cage, before returning to Eritrea to supervise operations. As the Abyssinians lacked a regularised supply system to complement their modern weaponry, Baratieri's initial strategy was to wait until they had denuded the area around their camp of food before moving against them.[5] This took rather longer than expected, however, and by early 1896 a combination of his own failing supplies and political pressure from Rome obliged Baratieri to make the first move. On the night of 29 February – 1 March 1896 a force of 10,600 Italian infantrymen and 7,100 native Askari,[6] divided into four brigades and with fifty-six artillery pieces embarked on a six mile march from their base at Sauria to secure high ground overlooking the Abyssinian positions at Adowa.

They covered around two miles before running into a force of around 196,000 Abyssinians, around half of whom were equipped with modern firearms including magazine rifles. By the late morning Baratieri was obliged to order a retreat that swiftly degenerated into a rout, and by nightfall his force had been annihilated, losing 3,207 Italian and 2,000 Askari dead, 1,428 combined wounded and 954 missing. Abyssinian losses are estimated at 7,000 dead and 10,000 wounded. 700 Italian soldiers and 1,800 Askari were captured; seventy of the former and 230 of the latter were tortured to death before Menelik personally intervened. The surviving prisoners were later released for a ransom of 10 million *Lire*, although 800 of the captured Askari had their right hands and left feet amputated in the traditional local punishment for disloyalty. Baratieri's force also lost all fifty-six of its guns, 11,000 rifles and all its transport and supplies. Baratieri himself escaped but was relieved of his command and tried for dereliction of duty. The resultant furore also brought down the Crispi government, while Menelik shrewdly refrained from invading Eritrea and thus turning the Italian setback into an excuse for a national crusade for revenge. On 26 October 1896 the new Italian government signed the Treaty of Addis Ababa that ended the First Abyssinian War and recognised the continuing autonomy of Menelik's kingdom. Adowa remains the greatest military defeat inflicted on a Western power by an indigenous native force, and 1 March is the National Day for Abyssinia's successor state Ethiopia.[7]

The humiliation meted out in Abyssinia did not cure the Italian hankering for African colonies, it merely shifted the focus further west. The ancient North African territories of Cyrenaica and Tripolitania belonged originally to the Greeks and Phoenicians respectively and fell to the Romans in the second century BC, who were in turn supplanted by Islamic Arab invaders in the decade following AD 640. In the sixteenth century a temporary power vacuum resulted in the Libyan coastline becoming a haven for the Barbary pirates until the Ottoman Turks occupied Tripoli 1551 and spread their influence across the region. The Ottomans divided their new acquisition into three provinces based on Algiers, Tunis and Tripoli, and a semi-autonomous Pasha was appointed to govern the area from Tripoli in 1565. Ottoman control was far from rigid, however. The activities of the Barbary pirates were still tolerated to an extent and the Ottoman authorities operated a profitable sideline charging foreign traders protection money. In 1801 this practice rebounded on Pasha Yusuf Karamanli when he tried to raise the charge agreed with the newly independent United States of America in 1796. The Americans not only refused but retaliated by blockading Tripoli, as commemorated in the line of the US Marine Corps Hymn referring to the 'Shores of Tripoli'; the resulting war ended with a treaty signed on 10 June 1805.

More importantly for the future, the decentralised and haphazard nature of Ottoman rule also permitted the Senussi to establish a strong presence in the desert hinterland of Cyrenaica and Tripolitania. The Senussi was an Islamic political order established in Mecca by

Sheikh Muhammad bin Ali al Senussi in the 1830s, which mobilised the indigenous desert tribesmen against Ottoman rule. By the
1880s the Senussi were virtually running a state within a state, complete with a capital at the oasis town of Kufra in the far southeast of
Cyrenaica and a network of religious teaching establishments that
spanned the Sahara. Despite their best efforts the Senussi were unable to totally expel the Ottomans and the territories remained part
of the Ottoman Empire until 1911, when the Italians arrived on the
scene.

The Italian claim to Tripolitania and Cyrenaica went back to an
Anglo-French appropriation of Ottoman territory via the 1878
Congress of Berlin, with the French giving tacit approval for a future
Italian seizure of Tripoli as a *quid pro quo* for their occupation of
Tunisia. In the event the Italians did not act until 1911, when political agitation resulted in considerable support for an invasion among
the Italian public based on the twin assumptions that it would be
easy and that the value of Libyan resources were worth the effort.
The Italian government thus issued the Ottoman authorities with
an ultimatum on the night of 26–27 September 1911 and, ignoring
Ottoman proposals for a peaceful transfer of power, declared war
two days later. Italian warships bombarded Tripoli on 3 October
1911, a 1,500 strong naval landing party secured the city and a 20,000
man Italian Army expeditionary force arrived on 10 October. The
Cyrenaican capital of Derna and port of Tobruk were rapidly seized,
but the port of Benghazi proved a tougher nut to crack and Ottoman
resistance stiffened thereafter.

As in Abyssinia fifteen years earlier, the subsequent campaign
proved a little more difficult than the Italians had envisaged. An
Italian force was almost surrounded near Tripoli on 23 October, and
an outright defeat at Tobruk on 22 November wiped out a large
portion of the original expeditionary force and obliged a reinforcement to expand it to 100,000 men. The war then developed into a
positional stalemate, with the Italians holding Tripoli and a number
of besieged enclaves along the coast. Italian attempts to carry the
conflict into the Aegean and Dardanelles had little effect, and the

stalemate continued until Turkey was distracted by the outbreak of the First Balkan War at the beginning of October 1912. The Italians seized the opportunity to press their advantage and a treaty ceding control of Tripolitania and Cyrenaica to Italy was signed at Lausanne on 18 October 1912. Given that the conflict had cost the Italians over 3,000 dead and around 80 million lira per month, it is ironic that the terms of the Treaty were virtually identical to those the Ottomans had offered at the outset.

However, the treaty was not recognised by the Senussi, who continued their struggle against foreign domination with some success. By the outbreak of the First World War the Italians had failed to quell the unrest in Cyrenaica and were obliged to restrict their presence to coastal areas and the ports of Benghazi, Derna and Tobruk, leaving the bulk of the territory to the Senussi. A truce that recognised this de facto separation brought a measure of peace in 1917, and on 25 October 1920 the Italians regularised the arrangement with the Agreement of Ar-Rajma. This conferred the title of Emir of Cyrenaica upon the Senussi leader, Sheikh Sidi Idris, and recognised his authority over Kufra and the other oasis towns in the interior of the territory. The peace was short-lived, however, once the 1923 Treaty of Lausanne removed the Ottoman Turkish claim to their North African territories. This was a welcome development for Mussolini's Fascist government, newly installed following his March on Rome in October 1922. *Il Duce* was an enthusiastic proponent of Italian imperial ambitions and authorised his military commanders to take advantage of the situation. Italian troops thus occupied Senussi territory near Benghazi in early 1923, sparking the Second Italian-Senussi War. Emir Idris fled to Egypt, leaving an experienced commander, Sheikh Omar Mukhtar, to lead the resistance.[8]

Troops under *Generale* Pietro Badoglio, a veteran of the Italian campaign of 1911–1912, quickly brought northern Tripolitania under control and gradually extended Italian control into the south of the territory. Cyrenaica proved more difficult than envisaged however, and bands of Senussi waged a successful guerrilla campaign against Italian supply lines, outposts and isolated units until a short-lived truce was established on 3 January 1918. The following year Badoglio was promoted to Governor of Libya and military command in Tripolitania and Cyrenaica passed to *Generale* Rudolfo Graziani, who according to one account made being permitted to operate unfettered by Italian or international law a condition of accepting the command. Thereafter the campaign assumed a far more ruthless and brutal character. Italian motorised columns supported by aircraft ranged far and wide searching for the bases used by the Senussi bands, backed up by a concerted effort to cut their sources of supply. This included sealing wells, slaughtering livestock and clearing the population from the arable Jebel Akhdar region in the north of Cyrenaica; over 100,000 inhabitants were incarcerated in camps at Suluq and El Agheila where thousands died. In 1930 the blockade was extended to cut the Senussi off from external support, with the construction of a 320 kilometre barbed wire barrier running along the Egyptian border from the Mediterranean coast to the oasis at Al Jaghbub. The barrier was patrolled by armoured vehicles and aircraft, which were authorised to attack anyone approaching the barrier or even spotted in the vicinity. All this had the desired effect. Kufra, the last Senussi stronghold, fell to the Italians in 1931 and Omar Mukhtar was captured on 15 September the same year. His execution by hanging before an assembled crowd of 20,000 at Benghazi effectively marked the end of Senussi resistance.

Flushed with success, Italians turned their attention to similarly unfinished business in the Horn of Africa, where the drubbing they had received at the hands of the Abyssinians at Adowa in 1896 still rankled. The Italo-Abyssinian Treaty signed on 2 August 1928 was supposed to guarantee friendship and co-operation for twenty years and fix the border between Abyssinia and Italian Somaliland. However, the Italians then repeated their trick of reinterpreting the terms of the Treaty, this time to shift the new border further into Abyssinian territory; and in 1930 an Italian military garrison was established at the Walwal oasis inside the disputed zone. A survey of the border by the Anglo-Abyssinian Border Commission at the end of November 1934 was abandoned when it happened upon the fort at Walwal; a subsequent clash there at the beginning of December cost a total of 200 casualties, three-quarters of them Abyssinian. The latter appealed to the League of Nations for arbitration on 3 January 1935 but this proved of little practical benefit as the League merely exonerated both parties of blame for the incident after eight months of deliberation. The Italians, meanwhile, had put this hiatus to good use, securing French non-involvement in return for a pledge to support the latter against resurgent Germany, while moving 100,000 troops into Eritrea and Italian Somaliland.

The Italians attacked without a formal declaration of war on 3 October 1935, earning a censure from the League of Nations in the process. The initial invasion was carried out by a 125,000 strong force equipped with aircraft, armour and motor vehicles under *Maresciallo* Emilio De Bono, which advanced south from Eritrea. Within three days Adowa was in Italian hands but the town of Mekele, only seventy-five miles from the Eritrean border, was not secured until 8 November. The Abyssinians had mobilised around 500,000 men, but this vast host was poorly equipped; many warriors were armed with firearms that dated back to the First Abyssinian War, and others were reliant on spears and bows. Given favourable conditions they were still capable of inflicting serious damage on the invaders, however. On 15 December 1935 a 1,000 strong force of Eritrean troops supported by nine Italian CV33 light tankettes pulling back from a threatened forward position at Mai Timkat ran into a large Abyssinian blocking force at the Dembeguina Pass. An attempt to force the pass with the tanks failed when the vehicles ran into impassable terrain and their accompanying infantry were overrun and wiped out by a pursuing force of Abyssinians; the latter then eliminated the tanks and killed their crews after disabling their running gear and machine-guns. An Italian relief column with a further ten CV33s was ambushed and bottled up by the simple but effective expedient of rolling large rocks onto the trail in front and behind the column. Attempts to manoeuvre around the roadblock led to some tanks slipping off the trail and down a steep slope where they overturned; two vehicles that made a stand permitting some of the accompanying infantry to escape were finally knocked out by Abyssinian warriors climbing onto their rear deck and setting fire to their fuel tanks.[9]

Such outcomes were more the exception than the rule, however, and the Italians had no intention of retiring as they had done in 1896. De Bono was relieved for his tardiness on 6 November 1935. He was replaced by former Libyan Governor Badoglio, whose former Libyan subordinate Graziani led a second invasion of Abyssinia from Italian Somaliland six days later, and once again the conflict rapidly assumed a more brutal complexion. Mussolini had authorised the use of poison gas in October 1935 in defiance of Italy's signature to the Geneva Protocol of 1925, and Badoglio's forces began dropping mustard gas bombs and spraying the gas from the air onto Abyssinian troops, civilian villagers and Red Cross encampments from December 1935. This was subsequently augmented by a deliberate terror campaign authorised by Mussolini in June and July 1936 that included firebombing villages and towns, executing prisoners, taking and executing civilian hostages and forcing the civilian population into labour camps. 1936 opened with a series of military engagements. Graziani's forces destroyed a large Abyssinian force at Ganale Dorya between 7 and 10 January, and the Italians inflicted 8,000 casualties on another Abyssinian force at Tembien thirteen days later. An Abyssinian counter-attack was defeated with heavy casualties at Amba Aradam on 10 February, and another clash at Tembien ended with the same result on 27 February.

The end came at Maychew on 31 March 1936, when the Italians annihilated a 40,000 strong Abyssinian force led by Emperor Haile Selassie in person. The Italians emphasised their ascendancy with a concerted drive on the Abyssinian capital. The 'March of the Iron Will' saw a 12,500 strong force mounted in 1,785 vehicles including tanks and motorised artillery advance 200 miles in ten days, although the bulk of the opposition came from bad weather and the terrain rather than the Abyssinians.[10] Addis Ababa was occupied on 5 May 1936, Abyssinia was officially annexed two days later, and King Victor Emmanuel was its proclaimed Emperor two days after that on 9 May. The territory was merged with Eritrea and Italian Somaliland on

1 June 1936 to become Italian East Africa, but this did not mark the end of the fighting. An Abyssinian force unsuccessfully attempted to liberate their capital on 28 July 1936, leading to the execution of the Archbishop of Dessie for alleged complicity, and the surrender of an Abyssinian force on 18 December led the Italians to declare the territory pacified. This did not prevent an attempt on Graziani's life as he was made Viceroy of the new colony on 19 February 1937, which led to an estimated 30,000 executions. The final clash in the field took place on the same day near Lake Shala, when Italian forces destroyed the last remnants of Haile Selassie's army and killed two of the three surviving resistance leaders; the third was captured and executed five days later.

Back in North Africa the Italians spent the 1930s consolidating their grip on Tripolitania and Cyrenaica. In 1934 the territories were reorganised into the new province of Libya, which was sub-divided into the provinces of Benghazi, Darnah, Misratah and Tripoli; a fifth area in the south-west dubbed South Tripolitania remained under military control. The new colony was governed by a civilian Governor-General, a post retitled First Consul in 1937, via a General Consultative Council that included Arab representation. The focus of the Italian colony also diverged markedly over this period, in comparison with what had gone before and with its Egyptian neighbour. As we have seen, the British presence in Egypt was essentially strategic in nature, being concerned largely with maintaining control over Imperial communication links with India and other British colonies in the Far East. Some Italian development work in Libya was carried out in the same vein. For instance in March 1937 Mussolini opened the *Via Balbia* in person, a tarmac road running the entire 935 mile length of the Libyan coast from Egypt to Tunisia. Primarily, however, the new colony was seen as a solution to overpopulation and unemployment in Italy proper via a process referred to as demographic colonisation, the ultimate goal of which was to transplant half a million Italians to Libya by the 1960s. Libya was thus to become Italy's 'Fourth Shore' in the Mediterranean and the settlers were given access to the most fertile land and government assistance via the state-run Libyan Colonisation Society, which provided credit and oversaw the necessary civil engineering work. The first 20,000 settlers, dubbed the *ventimilli*, arrived en mass in October 1938 and by 1940 their numbers had swollen to 110,000, comprising around twelve per cent of the total Libyan population.

Thus by the late 1930s, Italy had succeeded in attaining the overseas colonies it had sought since the latter half of the Nineteenth Century. Italian East Africa dominated the Horn of Africa, dwarfing and virtually surrounding British Somaliland and thus dominating much of the southern shore of the Red Sea and access to the Suez Canal. Farther west Libya, nestling between French North Africa and the British Mandate of Egypt, provided Italy with its 'Fourth Shore' in the Mediterranean and an outlet for Italy's surplus population. Opposition to all this was restricted largely to protests and ineffective sanctions from the League of Nations, as the attitude of the other major European colonial powers, Britain and France, was rather more ambivalent. The latter actively co-operated to limit the scope of the anti-Italian sanctions and unsuccessfully attempted to appease the Italians by offering them Abyssinian territory, most notably via the secret Hoare-Laval Pact of 1935. Named for the British and French foreign ministers that drew it up, the Pact conceded two-thirds of Abyssinian territory to the Italians without troubling to consult with the Abyssinians themselves but was stymied when the details became public knowledge in December 1935, in part via publication in a French newspaper. The subsequent scandal caused some embarrassment to the British and French governments, prompted the resignation of both foreign ministers and led to the abandonment of the Pact.

However, finally meeting Italy's long-held colonial aspirations was not an end in itself, but merely part of a wider, ongoing process. This is clear from Mussolini's personal definition of Fascism published in the Italian Encyclopaedia in 1932: '...For Fascism, the growth of Empire, that is to say the expansion of the nation, is an essential manifestation of [national] vitality, and its opposite a sign of decadence.' It was this Darwinian impulse that shaped and drove Mussolini's domestic and foreign policy. In the former sphere, the prestige afforded by colonial success bolstered Fascist standing in Italy proper, where the irreligious nature of Fascism sat uneasily with the devout Catholicism of the bulk of the populace, and supported Mussolini's long-term aim of displacing and superseding the Italian crown. In the foreign policy sphere, warfare was the preferred method of generating and demonstrating national vitality and spreading Fascist ideology, and a new outlet appeared just as military operations in Abyssinia were winding down.[11]

On 17 July 1936 years of political unrest in Spain sparked a military revolt by right-wing Nationalists, led by General Francisco Franco, against the government of the Spanish Second Republic. While the bulk of the army rallied to Franco, the Spanish navy and air force remained loyal to the government. This presented the Nationalists with a serious problem, for large numbers of their troops were stationed in North Africa and other overseas garrisons. Franco thus appealed separately to Rome and Berlin for assistance, simultaneously providing Mussolini with the opportunity to support political fellow-travellers and to establish a friendly power on France's western border. A volunteer *Avazione Legionaria* drawn from the *Regia Aeronautica* landed in Spain on 27 July 1936, and a *Luftwaffe* detachment arrived the following day. The transport mission lasted until September, during which the latter alone lifted almost 9,000 men, forty-four artillery pieces and well over a hundred tons of ammunition and other equipment.[12] The aircraft involved were also configured as bombers, and Italian aircraft began bombing Republican forces on the island of Majorca from 16 August 1936, while the transport mission was still underway. Neither was the bombing restricted to military targets. Attacks began on Madrid shortly thereafter, and air attacks on the Spanish capital became a regular occurrence; a *Luftwaffe* raid on 27 October 1936 killed sixteen civilians and wounded a further sixty.

Franco's initial plan was to seize Madrid and Nationalist troops reached the outskirts of the city at the beginning of November 1936. They then launched a series of abortive attacks supported by

Italian aircraft dropping leaflets urging the inhabitants to rally to the Nationalist cause or face the consequences. The fighting petered out in mutual exhaustion on 23 November, and the Nationalists began redrawing their plans for a longer war of attrition. This prompted Mussolini to commit Italian ground troops to Spain, following a conference with his senior military commanders on 12 December 1936. The first detachment of 3,000 volunteers from the *Regio Esercito* landed at Cadiz eleven days later, and by February 1937 the force had grown to 44,000 organised into four divisions, the fully motorised Army division *Littorio* and three partly motorised *Camicie Nere* (Blackshirt) or CCNN divisions made up of regular soldiers and volunteers from the *Fasci di Commbattimento* militia. Renamed the *Corpo Truppe Volontarie* or CTV at the end of February, the force was fully supported with tank, armoured car and field, anti-tank and anti-aircraft artillery units. The CTV played a major role in the battle of Guadalajara in March 1937 and subsequent fighting until Franco's Nationalists finally triumphed in February 1939, and at its peak deployed 50,000 men. Mussolini thus achieved his aim, but at considerable cost in lives, material and treasure. Of the 78,500 Italian volunteers that served in Spain, 3,819 were killed and a further 12,000 wounded, and all the military equipment deployed including 120 tanks, 760 aircraft and 6,800 motor vehicles, was written off. The equipment loss costed between six and eight and a half billion *lire*, which equated to between fourteen and twenty per cent of annual Italian government spending over the period.[13]

Mussolini's involvement in Spain had a another, further reaching consequence. Before 1933 the relationship between the Italian dictator and Adolf Hitler was one of mutual admiration. The successful Fascist March on Rome in October 1922 that put Mussolini in power was the inspiration for Hitler's less successful Munich *Putsch* in November 1923, and Mussolini supported Hitler's rise in the early 1930s in the press and among his Fascist contemporaries. Relations cooled drastically after Hitler's unsuccessful attempt to bring Austria into the National Socialist fold via a coup in July 1934, which prompted Mussolini to mass troops on the Brenner

Pass. They warmed again after following the League of Nations imposition of economic sanctions on Italy following the latter's invasion of Abyssinia, when Hitler increased coal exports to Italy to offset their impact on Italian industrial activity; these tripled from twenty-three per cent of Italian consumption in 1933 to sixty four per cent by 1936.[14] The relationship became increasingly close thereafter. A formal alliance, dubbed Rome–Berlin Axis, was concluded in November 1936 and Italy joined the German-Japanese Anti-Comintern Pact a year later, on 25 November 1937. On 22 May 1939 the Italian and German foreign ministers, Count Galeazzo Ciano and Joachim von Ribbentrop, signed the Pact of Steel that bound the signatories to render immediate military support to one another in the event of war. With hindsight, co-operation in Spain can be seen as the beginning of a process that drew Italy into increasingly closer co-operation and ultimately a subordinate relationship with Hitler's Germany. The final step came with Ciano's signature of the Tripartite Pact on 27 September 1940, alongside that of Hitler himself and the Japanese ambassador to Berlin, Saburo Kurusu. By that time Italy had been at war with Britain for just over four months, and the port of Tobruk had been acting as the main supply conduit for *Maresciallo* Graziani's invasion of Egypt for fourteen days. It is doubtful that anyone at the time fully appreciated the crucial role the port was to play in unfolding events.

2
Down the Slippery Slope, Ready or Not: Italy's Entry into the Second World War, September 1939 – September 1940

At 04:40 on 1 September 1939 *Luftwaffe* aircraft began bombing targets inside Poland, marking the beginning of the German invasion codenamed *Fall Weiss* (Plan White). Planning for this had begun on Hitler's order immediately after the dismemberment and occupation of Czechoslovakia in March 1939. By 5 September the three-pronged German attack had thoroughly penetrated the Polish border defensive zone, and three days later elements of one German unit had reached the outskirts of the Polish capital Warsaw, after an advance of 140 miles. Ground attacks on the city began on 9 September, and by 13 September the city was surrounded and besieged. The Battle of Bzura, a Polish counter-attack west of Warsaw on 9 September, ended after ten days with the encirclement and destruction of the Polish force; German dive-bomber units alone expended almost 400 tonnes of ordnance in the course of the battle.[1] The effective end came on 17 September when Soviet forces invaded Poland from the east, as agreed in a secret protocol to the Molotov-Ribbentrop Pact signed only seven days before Hitler launched *Fall Weiss*. The Poles nonetheless fought on doggedly for another nineteen days; the last operational Polish unit surrendered near Lublin on 6 October 1939.

The reaction of the Western Allies to all this was swift and une-
quivocal, particularly given their previous appeasing behaviour
when Hitler had re-militarised the Rhineland, carried out *Anschluss*
with Austria and annexed Czechoslovakia. After delivering an
ultimatum, Britain and France declared war on 3 September. The
reaction of Hitler's Axis partner was more circumspect. Although
Article III of the Pact of Steel stipulated that the signatories were
to come to each other's assistance in the event of war, Mussolini
proclaimed Italy a non-belligerent power on 2 September 1939 and
remained aloof. This was in line with a specific exclusion to the Pact
should any conflict involve Britain and France, not least due to the
latter's ability to sever Italy's vital overseas trade links. Mussolini's
appetite for new territory may also have been sated somewhat by
his recent conquest of Albania. In March 1939 the Italians presented
King Zog of Albania with a list of impossible demands, which were
duly rejected on 6 April 1939. The following day the Italian fleet
appeared off the Albanian coast and landed an expeditionary force
under *Generale* Alfredo Guzzoni at Durazzo, St. Giovanni de Medua
and Valona. Further landings were carried out on 8 April, prompting
King Zog to flee to Greece the same day, and the Albanian state and
crown were incorporated into Italy on 16 April 1939. More importantly, in September 1939 Italian public opinion was opposed to war
and King Victor Emmanuelle III forced Mussolini into declaring
non-belligerence by exercising his veto over political decisions on 1
September 1939.[2] While Mussolini styled himself *Il Duce*, his regime
nonetheless remained subordinate to the Italian crown.

However, in practical terms a key factor in Mussolini's wish to
avoid conflict with Britain and France was the condition of the
Italian armed forces. Mussolini was well aware that Italian forces
were poorly prepared to fight a full-scale war against a first-rank foe,
and that the situation would take at least three or four years to rectify.
Indeed, this was the understanding on which the Pact of Steel was
signed, and it was also cited to Hitler in as an explanation for Italy's
declaration of non-belligerence; Mussolini reinforced the point by
appending a huge list of the materials and equipment the Italian

armed forces required in order to go to war with any prospect of success.[3] Planned measures for the three- to four-year period included expanding the Army by a further 500,000 men, totally modernising its artillery arm, building a further six battleships and modernising existing units. Given all this, it might be illuminating at this point to examine the Italian military in a little more detail.

Superficially, the Italian armed forces appeared to be the perfect tool to support Mussolini's conflict-oriented Fascist ideology, and Fascist propaganda made much of the image of a modern, well equipped, highly efficient and ruthless military machine. There was an element of truth in this portrayal. Italian equipment was generally equal to that produced elsewhere in the inter-war period, and world class in some instances. The tri-motor Cant Z506 established eight separate world records for range, payload and altitude in 1936 and 1937, for example, and the Breda Ba88 *Lince* set two world speed records in April 1937. The Italian military could also be innovative in employing their technology, and proved capable of learning from experience. The deployment of largely motorised forces like the CTV in Spain, for example, was novel for the time. Even more so was the large scale use of motor vehicles in difficult terrain, such as the 1,785 assorted vehicles deployed in the 1936 advance on Addis Ababa, and the experience thus gained led to the formation of an experimental all-arms *Regimento Misto Motorizzato* (Mixed Motorised Regiment) in Libya, consisting of motorcycles, tanks, infantry and heavy weapons.[4] The Italians were also pioneers in the development of airborne forces, after perfecting the *Salvatori* static line parachute. Thus equipped, Italian troops carried out the world's first collective parachute drop at Cinisello airfield near Milan on 6 November 1927. The paratroopers were graduates of the world's first formal parachute training school, established earlier that year, and by the end of the 1930s the Italians fielded a number of parachute battalions, which participated in manoeuvres in Libya in 1937 and 1938.[5] The Italian airborne force thus preceded that of the Soviets by several years, of the Germans by almost a decade, and the British and Americans by over a decade.

However, the reality behind the propaganda images was somewhat different, and these examples were largely the exception rather
than the rule. In part this was due to a paucity of funding. Although
Italian military expenditure in the inter-war period was greater than
that of France and three quarters that of Britain, it represented only
a small fraction of Italy's gross national product and peaked at only
twenty-three per cent of the latter in 1941.[6] More important, however, were the shortcomings of Italian weapon manufacturers and
Italian industry in general. The Fascist regime nationalised between
a fifth and a quarter of Italian heavy industry during the Great
Depression, more than any other Western state. At the same time
the Fascist authorities permitted, if not openly encouraged domestic
manufacturers to establish an unchallenged monopoly in weapon and
equipment manufacture. The deleterious effects of this ideologically
driven policy were exacerbated by industry preference for artisanal
methods rather than mass production and corrupt, inefficient procurement procedures that vastly inflated costs; Italian manufactured
steel cost four times the world market price, and warship production costs were at least double those of other national shipbuilders,
for example. At best, all this resulted in poorly framed specifications,
stultifying bureaucrat approval processes, extended delays between
prototype approval and mass production, and long production runs
of equipment optimised to suit the manufacturer rather than the end
user. At worst it resulted in the Italian military being supplied with
sloppily manufactured aero engines that routinely failed in flight,
armour plate with falsified proof tests, poorly manufactured naval
propeller shafts with covertly welded cracks and tank armour that
shattered like glass when struck by projectiles.[7] As one writer on the
subject succinctly summed up, 'Italy's weapons and weapon systems
were the least effective, least numerous, and most overpriced produced by a major combatant in the Second World War'.[8]

These were serious handicaps by any standard, but they might have
been offset to at least an extent with some of the dynamic thinking and energetic action extolled as virtues by the Fascist regime.
Unfortunately these attributes were not particularly noteworthy in

the Italian military, and especially with regard to largest of the three services, the *Regio Esercito*. Indeed, the army's general philosophy can be summed up as consisting of three assumptions, namely that men were more important than machines, mind would invariably triumph over matter, and sheer numbers counted for more than quality. At the top the army's main preoccupation appeared to be creating jobs for the largest number of officers possible, in part as a reaction to cuts in the size of the officer corps in the early 1920s. One scheme implemented in 1938–39 addressed this and the preoccupation with numbers by simply reducing the strength of divisions from three to two component regiments; this not only allowed a near doubling of the number of divisions in the Army's order of battle, but also created numerous additional command and staff posts. The War Ministry was also a rich source of less than onerous posts for officers, not least because the Ministry reverted to ending the working day at 2:00pm in July 1940, only a month after Italy's declaration of war on Britain and France. Many of the officers employed in the Ministry were involved in adding an additional set of obstacles to the design and procurement process, via a tortuous procedure that required every new weapon and piece of equipment to be approved individually by the Army General Staff training section, the Ministry secretariat, the appropriate Ministry department, the relevant service branch technical office, and the relevant branch inspectorate. Modifications at any stage required the item to undergo the whole protracted process all over again.[9]

Predictably, the decisions reached via this process created problems further down the chain of command, with small-arms providing perhaps the clearest examples. The Army's standard issue rifle, the bolt-action 6.5mm calibre Mannlicher-Carcano M1891, was a reliable and robust weapon but experience in the First World War and Abyssinia suggested that the cartridge lacked stopping power. A modified version in 7.35mm calibre, the M1938, was therefore approved, but the programme was far from complete in June 1940 and War Ministry was obliged to switch production back to the earlier weapon. The resultant issuing of two virtually identical rifles in different calibres was only part of the picture. The variety of Italian service pistols on issue used at least three different calibres of ammunition, the Beretta M1938 sub-machine-gun was issued in two calibres, and the situation was compounded by the presence of large numbers of 8mm Schwarzlose medium machine-guns in the Italian inventory, obtained from Austria-Hungary as reparations after 1918.

The domestically designed automatic weapons approved by the War Ministry complicated matters yet further. Unlike foreign contemporaries like the French M1924/29 or British Bren, the 6.5mm Breda Model 30 light machine-gun featured a permanently attached twenty-round box magazine with an integral cartridge oiler to ease extraction. The idea of loading the magazine with rifle stripper clips was laudable insofar as it meant that ammunition could be sourced from ordinary riflemen. However, this was a slow process, much more so than other contemporary weapons, and damage to the magazine rendered the weapon totally unusable. In addition, the cartridge oiler was a magnet for dust and grit in desert conditions, with obvious consequences for reliability, and the quick change barrel was difficult to operate when hot because it lacked a handle. The 8mm Fiat-Revelli M1935 also used a cartridge oiler, and while the fifty-round stripper clips were an improvement on the Model 30's attached box magazine the fact it used a closed bolt made it prone to rounds spontaneously detonating in the breech after prolonged firing, an occurrence commonly known as a 'cook off'. The stripper clip was later modified with a more conventional belt feed. The 8mm Breda Model 37 heavy machine-gun used a cartridge oiler too, and was utilised yet another atypical loading system with twenty-round stripper clips. This weapon replaced the spent cartridge cases back in the clips after firing, a sensible idea for peacetime range conditions, but which obliged the gun crew to strip them out again before they could be refilled on the battlefield. The Model 37 also fired from a closed bolt and thus also suffered from cook offs.[10]

Less than optimum procedures also intruded into the way the Italian military was organised and run. The *Regio Esercito* was a conscript force, with fit males liable for call up at the age of twenty-one for between twelve and eighteen months service, after which they reverted to the reserve until age thirty-two. Conscripts were mixed between at least two different regions before being allocated to a regiment elsewhere in the country, a measure dating from the late nineteenth century intended to promote national cohesion and stymie regional factionalism. Service conditions were poor by any measure. Rations were adequate at best and frequently less so; when Allied prisoners of war held in Italy were fed on the Italian Army ration scale it prompted complaints to the International Red Cross.[11] Barracks were frequently unheated, in poor repair and too few in number, resulting in many conscripts being routinely housed under canvas. The mobilisations of autumn of 1939 and spring 1940 saw large numbers of recalled reservists sleeping in the streets. Unsurprisingly all this prompted resentment among the army's rank and file, which was exacerbated by the clear privileges enjoyed by their officers and the stiff and formal relationship the latter maintained with their men. Basic training was carried out at regimental depots and, as there was no overarching training programme or oversight, the standard was generally low at best. Potential junior NCOs were selected and trained at this stage, although most elected to leave with the rest of their intake at the end of their compulsory service period, due to the poor pay, conditions and future employment prospects. This system resulted in a general shortage of competent NCOs throughout the Army, which was not helped by the practice of employing the few career NCOs and warrant officers available in officer training or bureaucratic posts.

All this was somewhat at odds with the Army's mantra that manpower was its most vital resource, and the same could be said of the Army's largest single branch. Infantry training revolved almost exclusively around drill and route marching with full kit, live firing was rare due to budgetary constraints, and a lack of regimental officers along with the dearth of long-service NCOs cited above not only precluded anything more sophisticated, but also remedying basic training deficiencies. Consequently tactical training involved little more than teaching the troops to advance *en masse* along clearly defined axes of attack, and combined arms training frequently consisted of little more than learning how to co-ordinate such advances with the artillery. Despite the lessons of Abyssinia and Spain joint training with armoured vehicles was unusual, and most infantrymen had never seen such a tank before meeting one on the battlefield.[12]

All this presents a highly unflattering portrait of Italian military efficiency and preparedness, and of a force oriented toward re-fighting the conflict of 1915–1918 rather than a modern mechanised war. However, when viewing the Italian example in isolation it is easy to fall into the trap of assuming that all these shortcomings were somehow unique to the Italian armed forces, which was simply not the case. The gap between officers and the rank and file was probably not much if any worse than in the contemporary French, British or indeed German armies for example; combined arms training was notable by its absence in most contemporary armies and some of the latter also fielded equally poorly designed and performing weapons. Japanese small-arms, and especially the Imperial Japanese Army's machine-guns, provide a clear and relevant case in point. It is thus pertinent to note that for all its shortcomings, the Italian military under Mussolini succeeded in conquering a colonial empire in the arduous conditions of North Africa, and played a major role in defeating a much better equipped enemy in Spain. The question was how they would fare against a first-rank foe, and Hitler was determined to see it answered sooner rather than later.

The ease of the German victory over Poland and the subsequent quiescence of the British and French through the so-called 'Phoney War' in the winter of 1939–40 doubtless caused Mussolini to question the wisdom of his non-belligerence policy. Hitler played on the point at his meeting with Mussolini near the Brenner Pass on 18 March 1940, by holding out the prospect of Italian dominion throughout the Mediterranean in return for support in a war against Britain and France. Although he stuck by his reluctance to enter a long war, Mussolini appears to have been stung by Hitler's inference that continued non-involvement would condemn Italy to the status of a second-rate power. He therefore agreed to enter the conflict on the proviso that the German attack on France was successful. For all his wooing of Mussolini, Hitler was somewhat blasé about keeping him informed, and the Italian dictator only learned of Hitler's invasion of Denmark and Norway after the event, from the Italian ambassador to Berlin. Codenamed *Weserübung*, the invasion began in the early hours of 9 April 1940, ostensibly to protect them from Allied aggression. German ground forces crossed the Danish border at 04:15, while *Luftwaffe* paratroops seized the bridge linking Copenhagen with the Gedser ferry terminal, the airfield at Aalborg in the north of Denmark, and the airfields at Oslo – Fornebu and Stavanger – and Sola in Norway; these were the world's first operational parachute operations.[13] Troops were then landed by sea at Copenhagen and key points in Norway including Oslo, Bergen, Trondheim and Narvik. Faced with imminent bombing of civilian areas by circling *Luftwaffe* aircraft the Danish government surrendered at 09:20.on 9 April. The fighting in Norway went on for two months, and ended with the withdrawal of Allied troops from Narvik in the north of the country on 9 June 1940. Without external support and with most of the country occupied by German troops, the Norwegian government had little option but to formally capitulate the next day.

Hitler began his assault in the West while the fighting was still going on in Norway, and with another airborne first. At first light on 10 May twenty DFS 230 troop-carrying gliders landed atop the Belgian fortress of Eben Emael and alongside three bridges over the nearby Albert Canal. This opened the way for a German advance across the breadth of Holland, preceded by more airborne troops seizing airfields and water crossings.[14] Within four days German troops were at the Belgian border, and the Dutch surrendered on 14 May after the Germans fire bombed Rotterdam and threatened to destroy Utrecht and Amsterdam the same way. Successful as it was, the attack into Holland was merely a feint to distract attention from the main German attack by *Heeresgruppe* B in the Ardennes, spearheaded by three *Panzer Korps*. German units reached the River Meuse in the afternoon of 12 May, forced three crossings the next day, and the Panzers reached the French coast at Boulogne on 21 May, effectively splitting the Allies. With the bulk of the British Expeditionary Force (BEF) trapped in the Pas de Calais, the British launched a hasty improvised evacuation, codenamed Operation DYNAMO, on 26 May. DYNAMO ended on 4 June, after between 315,567 and 338,226 British and other Allied personnel had been lifted under fire from Calais, Dunkirk and nearby beaches; the remainder of the BEF was lifted from ports in north and western France by 20 June.[15]

With his condition of French defeat met, Mussolini declared war on France and Britain at 16.45 on 10 June 1940, with a particular eye on annexing French territory and colonies. That this was his motive is clear from a comment made to Chief-of-Staff *Maresciallo* Pietro Badoglio at the time: 'I only need a few thousand dead to ensure that I have the right to sit at the peace table in the capacity as a belligerent'.[16] To this end *Gruppo Dell'Esercito Ad Ovest* (Army Group West) under the heir to the Italian throne, Prince Umberto of Savoy, was detailed to invade France. Consisting of the Italian 1° and 4° *Armatas*, commander by *Generale* Pietro Pintor and *Generale* Alfredo Guzzoni respectively, the Italian force consisted of thirty-two divisions, totalling around 300,000 men. They were faced by a much smaller French force, the *Armée des Alpes*, which had only six divisions and which had been further weakened by the removal of many specialist mountain troops for the expedition to Norway. The Italians attacked ten days after Mussolini's declaration of war, with a two-pronged advance, into the Alps in Savoy, and into Provence along the Mediterranean coast toward Nice. The advance toward Savoy was stopped cold by French fixed defences, which were a mountainous version of the Maginot Line to the north and the weather, with an Italian attack into the Little St. Bernard Pass being paralysed by heavy snowstorms. The attack along the *Côte d'Azur* toward Nice fared little better, penetrating only five miles into French territory toward Menton by 25 June when the armistice brought hostilities to an end; according to one account, the Italian advance was held up at one point by a single French NCO and seven men.[17] The five days fighting cost the Italians 1,247 killed and missing, 2,361 wounded and a further 2,151 men were hospitalised with frostbite. This was sufficient to gain Mussolini his place at the peace table, although that afforded him rather less than he might have expected because Hitler was keen not to provoke the French into renewing hostilities. Italian gains were thus restricted to control of Nice and Savoy, which the French had exchanged for control of Lombardy via the 1860 Treaty of Turin.

Mussolini's initial attempt to cement the Pact of Steel with military action against France was thus somewhat underwhelming. The same can be said of his attempt to join in the Axis fight against Britain directly, prompted in part by RAF night bombing raids against targets in northern Italy immediately following the Italian declaration of war. On the night of 11–12 June thirty-six Whitley bombers from RAF No. 10 Squadron flew from Guernsey to bomb the Fiat works at Turin, and Wellingtons from Nos. 99 and 149 Squadrons made two similar raids from a forward base at Salon in southern France before being withdrawn to Britain on 17 June.[18] Mussolini responded with the *Corpo Aereo Italiano* (CAI). Formed at Milan on 10 September 1940 and consisting of two fighter and two bomber units, the CAI moved to Belgium later that month. 13° and 43° *Stormos BT*, equipped with Fiat BR.20 bombers, arrived at their bases at Moelsbroek and Chièvres respectively on 25 September 1940, although several aircraft forced landed en route as a result of technical problems and bad weather. Their fighter support, 18° *Gruppo CT* equipped with Fiat CR.42 biplanes and 20° *Gruppo CT* flying Fiat G.50 monoplanes were based at Moldegchen and Usel; a support unit equipped with Cant Z1007 reconnaissance aircraft and Caproni Ca.133 transports, 172ª *Squadriglia*, was also based at Chièvres.

After a period of training and familiarisation the CAI carried out its first operation, a raid on Harwich and Felixstowe on the night of 24–25 October 1940 involving eighteen BR.20s. Not all the raiders located their targets, one crashed on take-off and two more ditched in the sea after running out of fuel. Undaunted, the Italians then turned to daylight attacks, beginning with a raid on Ramsgate involving fifteen BR.20s escorted by seventy-three fighters on 29

October; the raiders returned with only three bombers damaged by anti-aircraft fire. They fared less well when faced with the RAF, however. In the early afternoon of 11 November 1940 British radar vectored Hawker Hurricanes from No.257 Squadron onto a formation of approximately fifteen BR.20s heading for Harwich, escorted by a mixed force of Fiat CR.42s and G.50s. According to some accounts the Italians had abandoned their mission due to bad weather but the Hurricanes intercepted them nonetheless, later reinforced by more from Nos.17 and 46 Squadrons. They shot down at least six and possibly nine Italian machines at a cost of two Hurricanes damaged. Three of the BR.20s and three CR.42s came down on British territory, with one of the latter being repaired and evaluated by the RAF. Four more bombers had to make forced landings in friendly territory and two fighters were written off on landing, with a further eight suffering damage. Two more CR.42s were lost in a fight with Spitfires on 23 November, and thereafter the CAI restricted its activities to night bombing in the East Anglia area. The bomber units and 18° *Gruppo* were withdrawn in January 1941, and 20° *Gruppo* followed three months later in April 1941. The Italians might have been rather less diligent than their north European friends and foes and the impact of their involvement may have been negligible at best, but the CAI had nonetheless put up a gallant performance. Going up against heavily armed monoplane fighters like the Hurricane and Spitfire in machines like the Fiat CR.42 biplanes must also have taken considerable courage.[19]

Be that as it may, Italian forces met with more success in Africa. The Duke of Aosta, Governor-General of Italian East Africa, had a force of around 280,000 troops at his disposal. This included two *Regio Esercito* infantry divisions (the 40° *Cacciatori d'Africa* and 65ᵗʰ *Granatieri Savoia*), a battalion of *Alpini* mountain troops, a *Bersagliari* light infantry battalion and several units of *Camicie Nere* (Black Shirt) militia, equipped with tanks, armoured cars, over 800 assorted artillery pieces and supported by over 300 aircraft. This force outnumbered that of their immediate British and French opponents, which numbered approximately 30,000 and 7,000 respectively with similarly smaller numbers of armoured vehicles and aircraft, but the Italians had to spread their force to cover four possible fronts in Kenya, Sudan and British and French Somaliland. Despite this, the Duke of Aosta took the initiative from the outset, initially from the sea and air.

Italian bombers crossed the Gulf of Aden to attack the British base of the same name on the two days following their declaration of war on 10 June 1940, and on 13 June three Caproni Ca.133s from 31ª *Squadriglia BT* attacked the British airbase and fort at Wajir in Kenya just as Hawker Hardy biplanes from No.237 (South Rhodesian) Squadron were warming up for their own dawn patrol. The Italian raiders badly damaged two Rhodesian aircraft, destroyed the airfield's fuel dump, killed two members of the fort's garrison and wounded eleven more. In the north raids were carried out against the capital of British Somaliland, the port of Bera Bera, on 14 June and Italian ground forces launched an attack into French Somaliland four days later. Intended to forestall a French attack, the Italian effort was fought to a standstill by 20 June, after which they contented themselves with bombing raids on Djibouti. The Italians fared less well at sea, due to the mismatch between the British Far Eastern Fleet and the *Flotilla Del Mare Rosso*; based at Massawa on the Red Sea, the latter numbered only seven destroyers, the same number of assorted torpedo boats, eight submarines, two gun boats and a minelayer. By the end of June 1940 the *Flotilla* had lost half its submarine strength in return for the sinking of a single tanker and a RN patrol vessel, and the loss of the destroyer HMS *Khartoum* to an internal explosion while in action against the submarine *Evangelista Toricelli*. Subsequent operations were constrained by shortages of fuel and spare parts, although the submarine *Guglielmo* sank another tanker on 6 September. The Flotilla fought its largest combined action on 20–21 October, when the surviving destroyers and submarines unsuccessfully attacked Convoy BN7 en route to the Suez Canal, losing the destroyer *Francesco Nullo* in the process.

Ground operations were the major focus, however, and after the French surrender on 25 June 1940 removed one front from the equation the Duke of Aosta embarked on a two-stage strategy against the British. The first stage began with simultaneous ground attacks into Kenya and Sudan on 4 July. The Kenyan attack captured the border town of Fort Harrington, subsequently renamed Moyale, after heavy fighting and ended three weeks later when the Italians halted near the villages of Buna and Debel, sixty miles from the border. The attack into the Sudan was somewhat wider in breadth. Small Italian forces captured the fort at Gallabat and two smaller posts at Karora and Kurmuk, around two hundred and fifty miles to the north and south respectively. The largest operation took place two hundred miles north of Gallabat, where an Italian force including tanks and armoured cars attacked Kassala, twenty miles inside Sudan. Situated on the River Gash and the Sudan Railway line, Kassala was defended by two companies of the Sudan Defence Force, but the Italians secured the town at a cost of 117 casualties after an all day fight; the defenders withdrew twenty miles up the railway line to Butana Bridge. All this left the Italians in control of the best avenues of attack into their territory from Kenya and Sudan, while possession of Kassala cut British rail communications with the south and provided a useful staging post for further operations. The town was thus given a brigade-size garrison that set about preparing fixed defences.

With his southern and eastern flanks secure the Duke of Aosta was free to launch an invasion of British Somaliland as the second stage of his strategy. The invasion was assigned to *Generale di Corpo d'Armata* Guglielmo Nasi and a force of just under 35,000 men, the equivalent of a corps, supported by a squadron of Fiat armoured cars, twelve CV35 tankettes, twelve M11/39 medium tanks and a reinforced heavy artillery battalion. Nasi divided his force into three. An eastern column, commanded by *Generale di Brigata* Bertello, was assigned the task of capturing the border town of Odweina, after which it was to advance to Burao and then on to the coast at Bera Bera via the Sheikh Pass. *Generale di Corpo d'Armata* Bertoldi's western column was tasked to mask French Somaliland by advancing north through the Jirreh Pass to the coastal town of Zeila, after which a detachment was to advance down the rough coastal tracks to Bera Bera. The central column, commanded by *Generale di Divisione* Carlo de Simone, was the strongest, consisting of three colonial brigades and all the armour and artillery. De Simone was tasked to advance along the main road to Bera Bera that ran through Hargeisa, across the Tug Argan, a gap in the rugged hills that paralleled the coast, and on through Laferug.

Opposing them was a much smaller British force commanded by newly promoted Brigadier Arthur Reginald Chater RM. It consisted of the partly motorised Somaliland Camel Corps and four infantry battalions; the 1st Battalion The Northern Rhodesian Regiment, the 1st Battalion, 2nd Punjab Regiment, the 2nd (Nyasaland) Battalion The King's African Rifles, the 3rd Battalion, 15th Punjab Regiment, and the 1st East African Light Battery RA, equipped with four 3.7-inch howitzers. Air defence was provided by two 3-inch guns detached from 23 Battery, Hong Kong and Singapore Brigade RA based at Aden. In total the British force numbered approximately 4,000 men, which was too small to cover the whole border, but Chater correctly anticipated Italian intentions and made his dispositions accordingly. The Camel Corps established a screen to monitor and harass any Italian advance and the $1^{st}/2^{nd}$ Punjab Battalion was despatched to cover the Sheik Pass, while Chater concentrated on blocking the main road to Bera Bera. A detachment from the Camel Corps, reinforced with elements from the North Rhodesian Battalion, occupied the town of Hargeisa, approximately forty miles from the border. The main blocking position was set up roughly midway between Hargeisa and Bera Bera, where the road crossed a dry watercourse called the Tug Argan. The Northern Rhodesians occupied a row of five hills that straddled the road and overlooked the crossing, while the King's African Rifle's set up on another hill overlooking a the road four miles further back, with a detachment blocking the Jerato Pass through the Assa Hills to the east. Chater's HQ was established just to the rear near Barkasan, and the $3/15^{th}$ Punjab Battalion remained in reserve at Bera Bera.

The Italian invasion force crossed the border on 3 August 1940, supported by aircraft operating from forward airstrips around Diredawa.

As the British screening force had orders to fall back in the face of the Italian ground advance, most of the action over the first few days of the invasion took place in the air. Three SM.81 bombers hit Bera Bera on the day the invasion began, and one was damaged by a Gladiator fighter, one of a Flight of four detached to the port from No. 94 Squadron in Aden under Squadron-Leader W.T.F.Wightman. Italian bombing prompted the redeployment of two Gladiators to a forward airstrip at Laferug, but when the Flight's two remaining aircraft at Bera Bera were destroyed on the ground in a strafing attack by Italian fighters on 8 August they were withdrawn to Aden. The lack of facilities and anti-aircraft defences at Bera Bera obliged the Blenheim equipped Nos. 8, 11, 39 and 203 Squadrons to operate from their bases in Aden throughout. Despite the distance penalty of 400 miles per sortie this entailed, the RAF bombers carried out raids on the invasion force and targets deeper in Italian territory, and fighter-configured machines from No. 203 Squadron maintained a standing patrol over Bera Bera. They were unable to prevent Italian aircraft bombing the port on 5 August, however, while others struck at Aden, Burao and Zeila in support of Bertoldi's approaching force. The same day No. 8 Squadron Blenheims were engaged in strafing elements of de Simone's centre column on the approaches to Hargeisa, losing one machine shot down to a Fiat CR.32 from 410ᵃ *Sezione CT Autonomo*.

On the ground, Bertoldi's western column reached and secured Zeila without a fight on 5 August, and despatched a two battalion force with some artillery along the coast toward Bera Bera as planned, commanded by *Generale* Passerone. To the east Bertello's column reached Odweina on 6 August but then veered north-west toward Adadle and the centre column route, instead of continuing on toward Burao and the Sheikh Pass. This deviation may have been ordered, for de Simone's centre column had become embroiled with the British blocking force Hargeisa. The latter stopped the initial Italian advance and destroyed a number of vehicles on 5 August, but were then forced to withdraw to Tug Argan by a more determined Italian attack supported by tanks. Having secured the town de Simone then paused to reorganise and build up his supplies, as the road back to the border had been badly affected by the unaccustomed volume of traffic and heavy rain.

By this point it was apparent that the Italian attack was a full-scale invasion rather than another border skirmish like Fort Harrington or Kassala, and Lieutenant-General Sir Archibald Wavell, the British Commander in Chief Middle East, began to organise reinforcements. The 5th Indian Division, which was in the process of moving from India to Egypt, was instructed to load its troopships to permit an infantry battalion and support elements to be unloaded at Bera Bera en route. An RA Field Regiment from the 4th Indian Division located in the Western Desert was directed to Bera Bera via a special convoy, along with a Section of two 2-Pounder anti-tank guns prompted by the appearance of Italian armour at Hargeisa. As a stop gap a 3-Pounder saluting gun and three man crew offered by the cruiser HMAS *Hobart* was rushed forward to the Tug Argan, where it was emplaced on a mounting made from an oil drum. The 2nd Battalion, The Black Watch were also despatched from Aden, where they had been stationed in readiness to reinforce French Somaliland. Finally, the expanding force received a more senior commander and Major-General A.R. Godwin-Austen, who was en route to east Africa to take command of the 2nd African Division, was directed to take over command from Chater. He was also ordered to prepare a confidential evacuation plan.

Under pressure from Nasi, de Simone's column resumed the advance from Hargeisa on 8 August, just as the 2nd Black Watch disembarked in Bera Bera and replaced the 3/15th Punjab Battalion as Chater's reserve; the Indian unit redeployed forward to the Tug Argan. It took the Italians two days to cover the fifty miles to the Tug Argan and reconnoitre the British positions, and once again much of the action took place in the air. In that period two Blenheims were lost in a collision and a third damaged by a CR.42, while AA fire from HMAS *Hobart* damaged another Italian fighter over Bera Bera. The five day battle at the Tug Argan began on 11 August, with Italian attacks on both sides of the main road to Bera Bera. The Rhodesians to the north held firm but by the time Major-General Godwin-Austen arrived to take command in the evening the Italians had gained a foothold on a feature on the south side called Punjab Ridge, driving back a company from the 3/15th Punjab in the process. Heavy fighting continued the following day, and the Italians expanded their foothold on Punjab Ridge to include the Mirgo Pass, which opened out onto the Bera Bera road behind the Rhodesian's positions. They also captured the hill nearest the northern side of the road, dubbed Mill Hill, in the late afternoon along with two of the 1st East African Light Battery's 3.7-inch howitzers. On 13 August further Italian frontal assaults on the Rhodesian were rebuffed, but Italian infiltrators using the Mirgo Pass attacked a supply convoy en route to the rearmost Rhodesian position on Castle Hill.

By 14 August the Italians were on the verge of cutting the Bera Bera road and isolating the Rhodesians holding out at the Tug Argan, and the danger grew more acute with the failure of a counter-attack by the King's African Rifles to regain Punjab Ridge. With the prospect of being overrun and destroyed piecemeal becoming a certainty, Godwin-Austen asked HQ Middle East whether he was to fight to the end in place or implement his evacuation plan. Permission to evacuate was granted at midday on 15 August, and Godwin-Austen immediately ordered the establishment of a rearguard position at Barkasan, sixteen miles from the Tug Argan, with a second at Nasiyeh, twenty-five miles from Barkasan and seventeen from Bera Bera. Both were to be manned by the Black Watch, reinforced with elements of the King' African Rifles and the 1/2nd Punjab. The decision came none to soon, for in the early evening the Italians took Observation Hill, the height closest to the south side of the main road. Despite this the Rhodesians and the survivors of the East African Light Battery successfully withdrew from their positions after dark, and made their way back to Bera Bera with the 3/15th Punjab. The evacuation was already underway, with HMAS *Hobart* orchestrating the effort of thirteen vessels including cruisers, destroyers and a hospital ship. Over three nights this little fleet successfully lifted over 5,000 military personnel, 23 Battery's two 3-inch AA guns and a thousand civilians to the safety of Aden.

The evacuation force was assisted by Italian tardiness, for de Simone paused again at Tug Argan and did not reach Barkasan until 17 August. The ferocity of the British response when he got there, which included at least one bayonet charge by the Black Watch, prompted another pause that rendered the second British rear-guard position at Nasiyeh superfluous; the Black Watch were able to withdraw the whole forty or so miles to Bera Bera after dark on 17 August, where they embarked in the early hours of 18 August. The Italians did not resume their advance until the next day, and their forward elements finally entered Bera Bera that evening. The British ground forces lost thirty-eight dead, 102 wounded and 120 missing, most at the Tug Argan, while RAF losses totalled twelve dead, two wounded, seven aircraft destroyed and ten badly damaged. Italian losses were somewhat higher, totalling just over 2,000 includ-ing 465 killed. Although something of a sideshow in the grand scale of things, the Italian seizure of British Somaliland was noteworthy because it was the only unassisted victory they achieved over the Allies throughout the war.

The real cockpit for Anglo-Italian hostilities was the border between Libya and Egypt, in the area the British dubbed the Western Desert, and events there unfolded somewhat differently. Like the Duke of Aosta in Italian East Africa, the Italian forces in Libya were commanded by a competent and charismatic individual. An early convert to Fascism, *Maresciallo d'Italia* Italo Balbo was one of the key organisers behind the October 1922 March on Rome that led to Fascist rule in Italy, and played a leading role in the development of the *Regia Aeronautica* after being appointed Secretary of State for Air in 1926. Despite knowing nothing of flying on appointment, he took a crash course of instruction and subsequently led two pioneer-ing trans-Atlantic flights using formations of flying boats. The first, involving a dozen aircraft flying from Italy to Rio de Janeiro, was carried out between 17 December 1930 and 15 January 1931. The second, a round trip flight from Rome to the Centre of Progress International Exposition in Chicago involving twenty-four aircraft, was carried out between 1 July and 12 August 1933. The feat earned

Balbo a lunch invitation from US President Franklin D. Roosevelt, honorary adoption by the Sioux as 'Chief Flying Eagle' and having a Chicago street was renamed in his honour, while in Italy 'balbo' became colloquial shorthand for any large flight of aircraft. Appointed Governor General of Libya later the same year, Balbo was behind the improvements to the colony's infrastructure such as the 935 mile long *Via Balbia* opened by Mussolini in March 1937, and the colonisation effort aimed at turning Libya into an economically viable destination for Italy's surplus population, 110,000 of whom were resident in Libya by the outbreak of war in 1940.

Balbo also commanded Libya's military garrison. The ground component was reorganised when war broke out between Germany and the Allies in September 1939, at which time Balbo informed Mussolini in person of his reservations about aligning Italy with Hitler's Germany. This was not the first time Balbo had expressed such sentiments. His appointment as Governor General of Libya in 1933 had followed similarly outspoken comments, compounded by suggesting that an alliance with Britain was more in Italy's interests, and he is reputed to have presciently warned that Italy would end up shining Germany boots following the signing of the Rome–Berlin Axis in November 1936.[20] He reacted in a similarly forthright manner on being ordered to prepare plans for invasions of Tunisia and Egypt, pointing out that his existing force lacked motor transport and that such operations would require eight additional divisions including at least two airborne formations and a concomitant increase in air support. The manpower requirement was addressed to an extent by the arrival of 80,000 reinforcements in March 1940, and the effective removal of the French from the equation at the hands of the Germans after 10 May alleviated it yet further.

Thus when Mussolini announced Italy's declaration of war on the Allies on 10 June 1940 Balbo's command consisted of a *Regia Marine* detachment made up of a squadron of destroyers, a squadron of torpedo boats, two squadrons of submarines and a number of auxiliary vessels in Libyan bases, while the *Regia Aeronautica* deployed one ground-attack, two fighter and four bomber *Stormos* along with a number of reconnaissance units in the colony, totalling between 151 and 350 aircraft, depending on the source cited.[21] The ground component numbered in the region of a quarter of a million men, organised into between thirteen and fifteen divisions, again depending on the source.[22] Nine were *Regio Esercito* units, three or four were Fascist *Milizia Volontaria per la Sicurezza Nazionale* (MVSN) divisions and the remaining one or two were made up of Libyan native troops, all reinforced by a number of artillery regiments, tank battalions and other support units. Commanded from Tripoli, this force was divided into two armies; 5° *Armata*, commanded by *Generale d'Armata* Italo Gariboldi, was stationed in Tripolitania while 10° *Armata* under *Generale d'Armata* Mano Berti faced the Egyptian border in Cyrenaica. However, whilst this was impressive on paper, in Balbo's opinion his ground forces were ill equipped to take on a first-rank foe like the British. This is clear from a letter he wrote to Mussolini immediately after the Italian declaration of war, warning that his force lacked modern field artillery and anti-tank and anti-aircraft weapons. When Mussolini ignored this and ordered him to invade Egypt forthwith, Balbo responded with an itemised list that included communications equipment, sufficient tanks to equip two armoured divisions, a thousand motor vehicles and 200 water tankers.[23] The latter were perhaps the most vital items, for the invasion would be reliant on supplies brought overland from Tripoli, Benghazi or the port of Tobruk, which was almost a hundred miles from the frontier.

Balbo's demands for additional equipment mirrored a general feeling of inferiority on the part of the Italian forces in Libya *vis-à-vis* their British counterparts across the border in Egypt. Perhaps the clearest example of this was the widespread tendency to overestimate British strength. Claims that they were facing a '100,000 strong Anglo-Egyptian Army' backed up by other British troops in the 'Near East' inflated the true figure by around two thirds,[24] although *Comando Supremo* was doubtless misled to some extent by inaccurate reports from Italian supporters in Egypt too. There was certainly no shortage of the latter, given that British official estimates numbered

Italian residents in Egypt at around 80,000 in the mid-1930s.[25] For their part the British did their utmost to reinforce the Italian sense of inferiority on the outbreak of hostilities by seizing and holding the initiative on sea, air and land. Within eight hours of the Italian declaration of war the bulk of Admiral Sir Andrew Cunningham's Eastern Mediterranean Fleet, including the battleships *Warspite* and *Malaya* and the aircraft carrier *Eagle*, was carrying out a sweep that cut access to Libyan ports, bombarded some and passed within 120 miles of the Italian mainland. While Cunningham's force was steaming west twenty-six RAF Blenheims were bombing the major Italian airfield at El Adem, twenty miles south of Tobruk and seventy miles inside Libya. That raid and a daylight follow-up attack destroyed eighteen *Regia Aeronautica* machines on the ground for the loss of three Blenheims, and an attack on Tobruk at dawn the next day damaged the Italian cruiser *San Giorgio* at anchor in the port. The real damage to Italian confidence was done on the ground, however, by roving British armoured patrols that raided Italian installations and ambushed road traffic up to fifty miles inside the Cyrenaican border.

It is unclear to what extent if any Balbo shared his countrymen's attitude, for his attitude toward the war and invasion of Egypt is usually ascribed to a mixture of his overt enthusiasm for all things British and a realistic grasp of Italian military capabilities. Certainly his energies in the run up to and immediately after the outbreak of war were directed toward preparing to ward off an expected British attack, principally by organising the defences of Bardia and Tobruk. By the end of June 1940 planning for the invasion of Egypt had thus not proceeded far beyond the demands for additional resources cited above. At that point, however, Balbo simply ran out of time. On 28 June 1940 he conducted a reconnaissance flight over Sidi Barrani and Maaten Baggush in Egypt in his personal Savoia Marchetti SM.79 tri-motor before heading for Tobruk. Unfortunately the port had again been on the receiving end from RAF Blenheims since dawn and when Balbo's aircraft approached it was mistaken for yet another attacker and hit by AA fire, most likely from the damaged *San Giorgio*. An accompanying aircraft escaped but Balbo's machine crashed and burned, killing everyone on board. The circumstances of the incident and Balbo's undisguised antipathy toward Mussolini led perhaps inevitably to suspicions of a conspiracy, which were fanned by Mussolini's refusal to visit Balbo's grave on a subsequent visit to Libya. Eye-witness testimony suggests that it was simply a case of mistaken identity however, and Balbo was buried at Tripoli on 4 July 1940. His passing was also marked by his opponents with a chivalrous gesture reminiscent of the First World War; Air Chief Marshal Sir Arthur Longmore, RAF commander in the Mediterranean and Middle East, arranged for an aircraft to drop a wreath and note of condolence near the crash site at Tobruk. Not to be outdone, the Italians performed a similar act in early August, by dropping a list of their British POWs and notification that one who had died of wounds in captivity had been buried with full military honours.[26]

Balbo was swiftly replaced by *Maresciallo* Rodolfo Graziani, who had been serving as *Regio Esercito* chief of staff in Rome, and who had been instrumental in finally pacifying Libya a decade earlier. His arrival coincided with more specific instructions originally intended for Balbo, which ordered the invasion of Egypt to commence on 15 July 1940; the date was supposed to coincide with the German invasion of Britain. After reviewing his forces Graziani informed *Comando Supremo* that such an operation would not only require all the equipment Balbo had requested but significant aerial reinforcements too, for *Regia Aeronautica* strength in Libya had been reduced to around sixty serviceable machines in the twenty days or so since hostilities had commenced.[27] This was allegedly due to the RAF being equipped with more modern fighter aircraft, a claim that illustrates the degree of ascendancy the British had established and the Italian tendency to exaggerate their enemy's strength. The RAF's fighters were not only outnumbered by two to one, but their Gloster Gladiator biplane fighters were slightly inferior in performance in comparison with Fiat CR.42, a ratio and criteria that also applied to the RAF bomber force.[28] The response from Rome was not encouraging. A proportion of the requested reinforcements including a number of medium tanks were en route, but Graziani was to strip the remainder from the 5th *Armata* facing the now dormant border with French North Africa. Furthermore, the 15 July start date was not negotiable.

Graziani therefore consulted with his staff and by 5 July had drawn up a plan for a limited advance to seize the town of Sollum, just a few miles from the frontier, which would then be converted into a support base for further operations. In the event the 15 July deadline passed without an attack or censure from Rome, presumably because the German invasion of Britain did not materialise on that date and because the two ships carrying the additional equipment did not dock in Tripoli until 27 July either. Furthermore, Mussolini and *Comando Supremo* were dissatisfied with the limited nature of Graziani's proposed operation, which led to Graziani being summoned to Rome for a conference on 5 August where he agreed to extend the scope of his offensive, albeit to an unspecified degree. The final shape of the Italian offensive finally emerged on 11 August, when Graziani ordered *Generale* Berti's 10° *Armata* to be ready to commence operations by 27 August. The initial objective was again Sollum and the surrounding plateau. The final objective was Sidi Barrani, sixty miles inside Egypt, with the caveat '…should maximum exploitation be achievable.'[29]

The task of carrying out the invasion was assigned *Generale* Lorenzo Dalmazzo's 21° *Corpo d'Armata*. The original plan had been to push the *Marmarica* and *Cirene* Divisions east along the coast road, covered by a parallel but independent advance to the south by *Generale* Pietro Maletti's *Raggruppamento Maletti*, a mechanised force that included two armoured battalions equipped with M11/39 medium tanks and L3/35 light tanks, supported by two Libyan formations, the 1st and 2nd *Libica* Divisions.[30] Maletti was a veteran of the mechanised operations in Abyssinia and was considered something of a firebrand. However, the plan was revised when Mussolini insisted the operation commence on 9 September, due to a shortage of motorised transport and rumours of a large British armoured force lurking to the south. The two Libyan divisions were thus placed at the forefront of the advance down the coast road, supported by the 1st MVSN

(23 *Marzo*) Division and the *Marmarica* and *Cirene* Divisions took up a following role. *Raggruppamento* Maletti was still tasked to screen the advance from the south, but at closer range and under direct 10° *Armata* control. Even then, the operation did not commence on 9 September as ordered. The 1ˢᵗ and 2ⁿᵈ *Libica* Divisions took much longer than planned to assemble at their designated concentration area near Fort Capuzzo, and *Raggruppamento* Maletti became so badly lost en route to its concentration area near Sidi Omar that aircraft had to be despatched to find them.

The invasion finally opened on 13 September 1940 with the bombardment and seizure of Musaid, followed by Sollum and a nearby airfield. The British covering force, consisting of a reinforced battalion from the Coldstream Guards, could do little more than harass the invaders with artillery and demolitions and began to withdraw in the afternoon. By nightfall the 1ˢᵗ *Libica* and *Cirene* Divisions were approaching the Halfaya Pass that cut through the Sollum Escarpment and provided access to the coastal strip to the east. Movement through the Pass began on the morning of 14 September, and over the next three days the British fought a series of delaying actions at Buq Buq, Alam Hamid, Alam-el-Dab and Sidi Barrani, in the face of a slow but steady Italian advance. The British plan was to withdraw to prepared defences at Mersa Matruh, 120 miles from the frontier, before attacking from the south with their as yet uncommitted armour.[31] The Italians had other ideas, however. In the early evening of 16 September the lead elements of the 1ˢᵗ MVSN Division entered Sidi Barrani, before pushing on to set up a protective screen at Maktila, fifteen miles to the east. Over the next few days the remainder of Graziani's force closed up and came to a halt at Sidi Barrani, having achieved 'maximum exploitation' as planned, sixty miles or so inside Egypt. They then set to work repairing the damage wrought by the British during their withdrawal, and constructing a surfaced road and water pipeline from Sollum to Sidi Barrani. At the front the invasion force busied itself constructing a chain of fortified positions running south for the twenty-five miles between Sidi Barrani and Bir Enba on the edge of the high ground paralleling the coast, and then west along the escarpment for a further twenty miles. And there they remained, under the watchful eyes of British reconnaissance troops and aircraft.

3
Stroke and Counter-Stroke: The Italian Invasion of Egypt and Operation COMPASS
June 1940 – December 1940

On the surface, Mussolini's Italy was firmly in the ascendant in the Middle East by the second half of 1940. In the Horn of Africa, the conquest of British Somaliland by the Duke of Aosta's forces presented a potential threat to British sea traffic accessing the southern end of the Suez Canal, and Italian forces also occupied key locations in northern Kenya and Sudan. To the west, the Italian forces in Libya were poised to invade Egypt; in conjunction with their incursion into Sudan this raised the prospect of a concerted attack seizing the Suez Canal and thus severing the most direct British line of communication with India, the Far East and the Antipodes. In addition, Italian air and ground forces in both locations were more numerous than their British and Commonwealth opponents, and also better equipped in many instances.

The reality was somewhat less positive, however. A combination of British naval superiority and geography meant that Italian East Africa's isolation from reinforcement or outside assistance outweighed the threat it presented to British Imperial communications, and the same could be said of the Italian occupation of the

Egyptian coastal border zone. The latter appears to have been driven less by strategic vision or desire for further colonial expansion than Mussolini's feelings of inferiority and consequent desire to match Hitler's achievements and keep his place as a belligerent at future peace tables. This explains his insistence that the Italian move into Egypt coincide with the German invasion of Britain, to which all other considerations were subordinate; on 10 August 1940 he explicitly made this point the paramount concern of the senior Italian commander in Libya, *Maresciallo* Rodolfo Graziani, in a letter that stated 'The invasion of Great Britain has been decided on, its preparations are in the course of completion and it will take place...the day on which the first platoon of German soldiers touches British territory, you will simultaneously attack. Once again, I repeat there are no territorial objectives, it is not a question of aiming for Alexandria, nor even for Sollum. I am only asking you to attack the British forces facing you. I assume full personal responsibility for this decision of mine.'[1]

With such poor to non-existent strategic direction from the top Balbo and Graziani's tardiness in embarking on an invasion of Egypt is arguably excusable and certainly understandable, and this also goes some way to explaining the relative incompetence and lack of push displayed by the Italian forces in British Somaliland and subsequently in Egypt. All this ought to have made the Italians relatively easy meat for a competent opponent, but the British were initially unable to capitalise upon them. The key factor was simply numbers, for the Army and RAF contingents in both locations were simply too badly outnumbered to offer more than token resistance, as the fighting in British Somaliland had clearly shown. This was a puzzling and serious omission given the importance of the region to the efficient running of British Imperial trade and communications, and it is therefore germane to establish how such a state of affairs came about before moving on to examine the British reaction to the attacks on their territory.

As we have seen, while the Italians saw their Libyan colony as an extension of their domestic territory, the British presence in

Egypt was focussed primarily on safeguarding the Suez Canal as a communications link between Britain and the Empire.

Consequently, prior to the emergence of Italy as a regional threat, the principal role of the British ground and air forces stationed in Egypt and across the wider Middle East was imperial policing. Operations of this type are frequently regarded as something of a soft option, but the reality was somewhat different. Dissident tribesmen and indigenous populations were just as capable of inflicting death and injury as conventional military forces, and service in the reaches of the Empire also involved coping with extremes of geography and climate as a matter of course. Carrying out even the most basic of military operations under such conditions thus required a high level of operational competence and flexibility.

Troops operating in the Western Desert, for example, had to contend with extreme heat by day and near-freezing cold by night as a matter of course, as well as sandstorms that reduced visibility to zero and the *khamsin*, a hot wind blowing from the Sahara between February and June that routinely raised the temperature to in excess of 104 degrees Fahrenheit; according to local lore murder was justified when the *khamsin* blew.[2] Even routine tasks like patrolling in the arid, largely featureless terrain required strict water discipline and navigational skills of a high order. Keeping weapons and equipment functioning amidst the ever-present sand and gritty dust required constant and diligent cleaning, and mechanisation increased the maintenance load manifold. The dust shortened the life of engines even when equipped with special filters, and the rough terrain took a similarly heavy toll on suspension components, tyres and tracks. Vehicle and aircraft maintenance was complicated yet further by the paucity of sheltered facilities; an RAF report on air operations in the Western Desert noted that it took up to twenty-four hours' work to restore aircraft on forward bases to a flyable condition after sandstorms, with instrument intakes and constant speed propeller mechanisms being especially troublesome.[3]

Relations between the Air Ministry and War Office in the interwar period and Second World War were frequently acrimonious at best, not least because the RAF had justified its existence after 1918 by cutting into the Army's traditional function to create an imperial policing role for itself by '...substituting air power for land power in the more inaccessible corners of the British Empire.'[4] After contributing an eight-aircraft strong detachment codenamed Z Squadron to suppressing the 'Mad Mullah' in Somaliland in 1919–20, the Air Ministry was given responsibility for Iraq on 1 October 1922.[5] However the practical limitations of Air Control, as the policy was labelled, rapidly became apparent when the RAF were obliged to form a ground support unit equipped with Rolls Royce armoured cars.[6] In fact, Air Control had always been something of a fiction, given that there had been a substantial Army involvement alongside Z Squadron and that the then Secretary of State for War and Air, Churchill, who had played a major role in the implementation of Air Control, nonetheless considered that policing Iraq would also require at least 14,000 Army troops.[7] Despite this, the inter-service hostility diminished with distance from London, if only for reasons of pragmatism and operational necessity; hence the comment from Sir Gifford Martel, one of the British Army's armour pioneers, while serving in India in the 1930s: 'the Air Force is a good show out here; I wish the Army was as progressive.'[8]

The result was an extremely high level of co-operation between the Army and RAF at the operational level in the Empire. The evacuation of casualties by air began with Z Squadron, which deployed the world's first custom-built air ambulance, and rapidly became a staple feature of British imperial policing operations. Over 200 men were airlifted from Kurdistan for treatment in Baghdad following a serious outbreak of dysentery in 1923, and by the mid-1930s an average of 120 patients per year were being airlifted to hospitals in Egypt, Palestine and Iraq. There was also a regular medical shuttle to Port Said and Jaffa for cases requiring repatriation to Britain by sea.[9] Aircraft were also pressed into service for more routine military transport tasks. In September 1920 two Handley Page o/400s lifted a dismantled mountain gun complete with crew and ammunition from Heliopolis to Almaza in Egypt, and a complete company of infantry was lifted from Baghdad to Kirkuk in May 1924 in response to an outbreak of civil disorder.[10] A similar operation from Palestine to Cyprus in October 1931 was the world's first troop airlift over the open sea, and the following year the RAF mounted its largest airlift in the interwar period, using twenty-five Vickers Victoria aircraft to move a complete infantry battalion the 800 miles from Egypt to Iraq in the period 22–27 June 1932.[11] By the late 1930s such large-scale operations were routine; during the Waziristan campaign a total of 5,750 troops and 400 tons of supplies were lifted in the period between November 1936 and May 1938.[12]

However, operational co-operation and flexibility were of little use against a threat arguably more insidious than desert dust or inter-service rivalry. Government fiscal parsimony toward the British Armed Forces was and remains something of a perennial, as demonstrated by the debate about overstretch and equipment shortages in Afghanistan and Iraq at the time of writing. The root of the problem at the beginning of the Second World War dated back to the military drawdown immediately after the First World War. In August 1919, within a month of the signing of the Treaty of Versailles, a Government memo declared that 'non productive employment of manpower and expenditure, such as is involved by naval, military and air effort, must be reduced within the narrow limits consistent with national safety.'[13] This policy resulted in a series of military budgets that were barely sufficient to cover the Service's existing commitments. The Army had its budget reduced every year between 1919 and 1932 despite a parallel raise in its commitments, for example, and pay cuts prompted by a £5 million cut in the Royal Navy's budget in 1931 sparked a mutiny in the Atlantic Fleet at Invergordon.[14] The situation continued until the mid-1930s, when a Government statement in Parliament admitted that the situation was 'approaching a point when we are not possessed of the necessary means of defending ourselves against an aggressor.'[15] As events in 1939 and more especially 1940 were to show, subsequent measures to reverse the situation came barely in the nick of time. That was of little immediate solace to those charged with safeguarding the Empire, for Home defence requirements were the first priority and the former were thus obliged to accept whatever of modern equipment or obsolescent hand-me-downs could be spared.

This was not initially seen as a matter for concern because Italy was not considered a threat to British interests in the Middle East, and this remained the case even when Mussolini embarked on an extensive re-armament programme in 1933 and invaded Abyssinia two years later. Although the British Mediterranean Fleet was substantially reinforced in September 1935 in anticipation of enforcing League of Nations sanctions against Italy for her aggression, Italian vessels carrying supplies and munitions for their forces in Abyssinia were still permitted to transit the Suez Canal, in line with the 1888 Treaty of Constantinople that guaranteed access to the Canal for all and prohibited warlike activity within three miles of the Canal's entry points. Indeed, the possibility of conflict with Egypt itself was a more pressing concern, as relations had been ambiguous between the abolition of the British Protectorate over Egypt in 1922 and the signature of the Anglo-Egyptian Treaty in August 1936. The Treaty bound the British to withdraw from Cairo within four years, to restrict its military presence in the country to the area immediately adjacent to the Suez Canal and the RAF airfield at Abu Sueir, seventy miles from Cairo, and to train and equip the Egyptian Army and Air Force. In return the Egyptian government was to improve and/or increase road and rail links, permit British military training in designated areas and provide unlimited access to all Egyptian facilities in time of war. In return the British sponsored Egypt's election as an independent member of the League of Nations in May 1937.

In the meantime relations with Italy had deteriorated, and the British initially tried to address the situation with diplomacy, leading to the Anglo-Italian Joint Declaration signed in Rome on 2 January 1937. Popularly dubbed the 'Gentlemen's Agreement', the Treaty debarred both parties from interfering with the sovereignty of states in the Mediterranean area and guaranteed mutual free movement in the Eastern Mediterranean. However, the Declaration quickly failed to live up to expectations, and the British government was obliged to extend its policy of military renovation to the Middle East from July 1937, beginning with a modernisation programme for port defences in the Mediterranean and Red Sea. Limited measures to counter possible Italian attacks were also authorised, with the caveat that they should be discrete and unprovocative.

British concerns initially centred on naval matters, and specifically secure basing for the Mediterranean Fleet. Traditionally this had been provided from Gibraltar and Malta, but the former was too distant from the likely seat of future operations in the Eastern Mediterranean, and Malta was too close to the Italian mainland. Alexandria was selected as the best option in April 1937, not least because it had undergone modernisation during the Abyssinian Crisis in 1935, and permission was obtained from the Egyptian government to extend docking and repair facilities. The situation was more serious with regard to air and land defence, for most of the army units were based away from the Libyan border and were significantly under their official War Establishment strength, while there were no RAF fighters or army anti-aircraft units based in Egypt at all. Nonetheless, the British were able to mount some semblance of defence during the Sudeten Crisis in September 1938 with the army occupying defensive positions at Mersa Matruh, two thirds of the way between Alexandria and the Libyan border, and the RAF deploying to forward airfields in support. By that time some of the more glaring deficiencies had been addressed, at least to an extent. An anti-aircraft brigade equipped with twenty-four 3-inch guns and the same number of searchlights had been despatched from Britain in December 1937 along with a battalion of light tanks. This was followed by a twenty-one strong squadron of Gloster Gladiators and twelve Bristol Blenheims in February 1938. More reinforcements followed. The 11th Indian Infantry Brigade arrived in Egypt in July 1939, followed by a New Zealand brigade in February 1940, and the Indian presence was expanded to form the 4th Indian Division by the arrival of a second brigade eight months later.

By the outbreak of war with Italy in June 1940 the British were thus in a better, if not comfortable position to defend Egypt. At the top, the clumsy and arguably unworkable triumvirate system created in June 1939, which relied on the local Commander in Chiefs of the three Services to co-operate voluntarily whilst beholden to their individual Chiefs of Staff and Ministries in Whitehall, had been modified with the appointment of a Commander-in-Chief Middle East on 15 February 1940.[16] The officer selected to fill the new post was Lieutenant-General Sir Archibald Wavell, who had been commanding the army's Middle East Command from July 1939.[17] Wavell was a highly experienced and competent soldier who had seen service in the Boer War, India and as an observer with the Russian Army before 1914; during the First World War he served initially in a Staff position, was wounded and lost an eye at Ypres in 1915, was seconded to the Russian Army in Turkey as a liaison officer the following year, and ended the war on General Allenby's staff in Palestine.[18] The RAF contribution to defending the Libyan frontier was No. 202 Group, commanded by then Air Commodore Raymond Collishaw DSO and Bar, DSC, DFC. A Canadian by birth and also a First World War veteran, Collishaw had begun his career flying fighters with the Royal Naval Air Service and was the third highest scoring British ace at the end conflict, with sixty victories. No. 202 Group consisted of six squadrons, the Gladiator equipped No. 33 Squadron, Nos. 45, 53, 113 and 211 Squadrons equipped with Blenheims, and No. 208 Army Co-Operation Squadron equipped with Westland Lysanders.[19] The army contingent in Egypt numbered 36,000 men, but not all were organised into complete formations, and the formations that did exist were understrength in addition to overall shortages of artillery, transport and ammunition. The Western Desert Force tasked with defending the border with Libya was commanded by Major-General Richard O'Connor, who arrived from Palestine to take over on 8 June 1940. O'Connor's Force consisted of the understrength 7th Armoured and 4th Indian Divisions; the former lacked two of its constituent armoured regiments and the latter a complete infantry brigade, although this was offset to some extent by the presence of the 6th Infantry and 22nd Guards Brigades.[20]

This was a fairly respectable force, but not in comparison with the Italian 10° *Armata* facing them across the border in Libya. However, there was more to the matter than bald numbers, and the British possessed a qualitative advantage that to an extent offset Italian numerical superiority. There were two aspects to this advantage. The first went back to 1935, when elements of the Cairo Cavalry Brigade were formed into a Mobile Force and began training for mechanised desert operations. This was a new concept and thus very much a matter of trial and error. At the beginning it took a squadron from the 11th Hussars three days to reach the oasis at Baharia, 200 miles south of their base at Cairo, thanks to navigation difficulties, vehicle suspension failures, flat tyres and bogging in soft sand, and it took a further two days of intensive maintenance before the return trip could begin. Within ten months the same unit was capable of sallying forth south across the coastal plain from Mersa Matruh to the Siwa Oasis on the rugged plateau that separated the plain from the Great Sand Sea and back in the same time, a round trip of almost 400 miles as the crow flies. The experience garnered in the process was converted into a formalised training programme for all British mechanised units in Egypt that taught the importance of vehicle loading, field maintenance and repair, desert driving techniques, how to use the terrain for movement and concealment, and navigation by the sun and stars as well as with the magnetic compass.[21] The end result was a number of units capable of operating in the harsh conditions of the Western Desert as a matter of routine. The second aspect was turning these trained units into a cohesive mechanised force, and that was down to the involvement of Major-General Percy Cleghorn Stanley Hobart DSO MC.

Hobart was commissioned into the Royal Engineers in 1904 and after service on the Western Front and in Mesopotamia during the First World War, transferred to the Royal Tank Corps in 1923. A disciple of Colonel J.F.C. Fuller and an armoured theorist in his own right, he was promoted to command the 2nd Battalion, Royal Tank Corps in 1928. In 1933 he became Inspector Royal Tank Corps, and after promotion to Brigadier the following year formed and commanded the 1st Tank Brigade, the first armoured formation of that size in the British Army. A single-minded and difficult character,

Hobart made more than his fair share of enemies in the army establishment, but avoided being edged out of the army like his fellow armour pioneers Fuller and Liddell Hart and was appointed Director of Military Training at the War Office in 1937, on the understanding that he would be given a command more in line with his expertise in the event of war. That circumstance came with the Munich Crisis, and Hobart was despatched to form an armoured division in Egypt on 25 September 1938. His appointment was not universally popular as his difficult reputation appears to have preceded him; the General Officer Commanding-in-Chief, Lieutenant-General Sir Robert Gordon-Finlayson, greeted him with the immortal words 'I don't know what you've come here for, and I don't want you anyway.'[22]

Despite this inauspicious start, Hobart set to work reorganising and expanding the Mobile Force into the Mobile Division at his base at Mersa Matruh. The new formation consisted of three parts. The Light Armoured Brigade was created by the simple expedient of renaming the Cairo Cavalry Brigade, which was made up of the 7th Queen's Own Hussars equipped with a variety of Light Tanks, the 8th King's Royal Irish Hussars making do with 15 cwt Ford trucks in lieu of tanks, and the 11th Hussars mounted in Rolls Royce Armoured Cars. The Heavy Armoured Brigade consisted of the 1st and 6th Battalions, Royal Tank Corps, the former equipped with Light Tanks and the latter with a mixture of Light and Medium. The third part, dubbed the Pivot Group, was intended to provide the armoured striking force with infantry and artillery support. It consisted of 1st Battalion, The King's Royal Rifle Corps (KRRC), and the 3rd Regiment, Royal Horse Artillery (RHA) equipped with 3.7-inch howitzers. Hobart also managed to form a divisional HQ with personnel located through his parallel responsibility for Garrison Troops in Cairo, including increments from the Royal Corps of Signals and a complete company from the Royal Army Service Corps (RASC). The latter proved invaluable in locating supplies of ammunition and spare parts, and more modern replacement equipment slowly became available over the winter of 1938–39; this permitted the 6th Royal Tank Regiment to replace some of its venerable Mk. II Medium Tanks for more modern A9 Cruisers, and the 3rd RHA to re-equip with 25-Pounder guns. In parallel with all this Hobart instructed and drilled his command until its disparate components were capable of operating smoothly together in offensive and defensive manoeuvres.[23] By the end of 1939 Hobart had largely achieved his mission, as is clear from Major-General O'Connor's comment that the Mobile Division was the best trained division he had ever seen.[24]

In the event, Hobart did not get to see the fruits of his labour in action. In July 1939 Gordon-Finlayson was replaced as General Officer Commanding-in-Chief by Lieutenant-General Henry Maitland Wilson, who had attended the same course as Hobart at the Staff College at Camberley in 1920.[25] Initially their relationship was good, and Wilson praised the performance of the Mobile Division after attending the final phase of a week long exercise at the end of July. Things deteriorated rapidly following another divisional exercise three months later however, when a series of misunderstandings and missed communications ended in a stand up argument and a public dressing down for Hobart.[26] Wilson followed this up on 10 November 1939 with a request that Hobart be relieved, and Wavell complied after a personal interview with Hobart four days later; he was replaced by Major-General Michael O'Moore Creagh MC. The news does not appear to have gone down well with Hobart's men, for according to his biography they lined the road from Hobart's HQ and cheered him all the way to the airstrip where he began his journey back to Britain.[27]

The relief of such a technically proficient officer during such perilous times was certainly curious, and Hobart's biography suggests that it was the upshot of long standing grudges against Hobart in the army's upper echelons, and that it was accomplished via improper use of confidential competence reports. While Wavell's decision is far more likely to have been motivated by the need for harmonious working relationships than resentment over an incident during an exercise in 1934,[28] subsequent events do support the grudge theory to some extent. Despite assurances to the contrary from the Chief of Imperial General Staff General Sir Edmund Ironside, Hobart was retired from the army with effect from 9 March 1940, and interestingly the British Official History published in 1954 makes no mention of Hobart at all. Be that as it may, this was clearly a waste of talent and expertise, but fortunately it was not the end of the story. In August 1940, while serving as a Lance-Corporal in the Chipping Camden detachment of the Local Defence Volunteers, Hobart took a position with the Ministry of Supply linked to tank production. He came to Prime Minister Winston Churchill's attention at a conference at Chequers, and by early 1941 he had been returned to the army active list and given the task of forming the 11th Armoured Division. He was then given the same task with regard to the 79th Armoured Division in March 1943, and oversaw the development of a host of specialised armoured vehicles that played an important role in the D-Day invasion on 6 June 1944.[29]

Wavell's plan in the event of war with Italy was to seize the initiative from the outset by using the Western Desert Force to attack Italian border posts in Libya and dominate the border zone as far west as practicable. This was intended to forestall or at least delay any Italian attack into Egypt, with the object of denying it the coastal town of Mersa Matruh, which housed the terminus of the coastal railway to Cairo. Thus the 7th Armoured Division, as the Mobile Division had been renamed on 16 February 1940, had been deployed in the area of Mersa Matruh and Maaten Baggush, where O'Connor had established Western Desert Force HQ on 8 June 1940. The division had been expanded, and its constituent formations had also been renamed and reorganised. The Light and Heavy Tank Brigades had become the more balanced 4th and 7th Armoured Brigades, made up of the 7th Hussars and 6th Royal Tank Regiment (RTR) and 8th Hussars and 1st RTR respectively. The Pivot Group, renamed the Support Group, was made up of the 1st KRRC, the 2nd Battalion, The Rifle Brigade and the 4th RHA, while the 3rd RHA and 11th Hussars were grouped together as Divisional Troops.

As soon as news of the Italian declaration of war was received O'Connor ordered the 11th Hussars up to the border, followed at around a forty mile interval by the 7th Hussars Light and Cruiser Tanks and the Support Group. At around the same time Collishaw moved No. 202 Group HQ up to one of his forward airfields and ordered all aircraft to be made ready, but confirmation came too late to commence operations before nightfall on 10 June 1940. Dawn sorties by reconnaissance Blenheims from No. 211 Squadron to the major *Regia Aeronautica* base at El Adem found aircraft parked in the open, and eight Blenheims from No. 45 Squadron made the first of several attacks shortly afterward. By the end of the day the RAF had destroyed or damaged eighteen Italian aircraft for the loss of two Blenheims and three damaged.[30] On the ground the 11th Hussars reached the border in the evening of 11 June, and their Rolls Royce and Morris armoured cars crossed the border at four points between Forts Capuzzo and Fort Maddalena, after breaching the Italian concertina wire by the simple expedient of flattening the picket posts with their vehicles and then dragging the wire aside or churning it into the sand. At 02:00 on 12 June a small detachment from B Squadron guarding one of the gaps shot up an Italian truck on the path paralleling the border, capturing fifty-two very surprised Italians who had not been informed that hostilities had commenced; the occupants of another truck captured near Fort Capuzzo told a similar story.

This set the tone for the next few days and nights and once the Support Group closed up and took responsibility for dominating the area immediately inside the Libyan border, the 11th Hussars pushed their activities further into Italian territory in company with elements of the 7th Hussars. On 14 June the Italian posts at Fort Maddalena and Fort Capuzzo were captured, the former without a fight by A Squadron, 11th Hussars; the garrison of five Italians and thirteen Libyans ran up the white flag on their approach. Fort Capuzzo also surrendered after an RAF attack that failed to actually hit the Fort and a few of the 7th Hussars' Cruiser Tanks had put some 2-Pounder armour piercing rounds through the walls. The heaviest fighting of the day took place at Sidi Azeiz, the target of a subsidiary probe by a mixed force from the 7th and 11th Hussars supported by an RHA battery. The 11th Hussars tanks successfully overran outlying Italian infantry positions protecting the post but ran into a mine-field that knocked out three tanks and stranded several more, which then came under accurate Italian artillery fire. When the accom-panying RHA battery proved unable to suppress the Italian guns, which were deployed on the reverse slope of a ridge, the British force withdrew in the afternoon. While all this was going on six Italian CV33 tankettes approached a screening position held by ele-ments of B Squadron, 11th Hussars, but retired at speed when one of their number was knocked out with a Boys anti-tank rifle, leaving the crew to be made prisoner.

By 16 June the 11th Hussars had expanded their marauding to the north, and C Squadron had set a successful ambush on the stretch of the *Via Balbia* linking Tobruk with Bardia using a felled telegraph pole as a roadblock. Over the course of the morning this netted a number of Italian trucks and a Lancia car carrying *Generale di Corpo* Lastucci, senior engineer officer to the 10° *Armata*, his *aide-de-camp* and two female companions, one of whom proved to be pregnant. Lastucci carrying detailed plans of the Italian defences at Bardia and, in one of those curious coincidences of war, was also a personal acquaintance of Major-General O'Connor; the latter saw Lastucci briefly en route to captivity along with his pregnant companion, who subsequently gave birth in Alexandria. The same day saw the largest engagement of the period at Nezuet Ghirba, south-west of Fort Capuzzo, when C Squadron 11th Hussars ran into an Italian col-umn of thirty trucks, four artillery pieces and twelve CV33 tankettes divided equally between the front and rear of the column. According to orders subsequently found on the body of the Italian commander, a *Colonello* D'Avenso, the column was part of a force – another larger column had also been spotted by British scouts – tasked to 'destroy enemy elements which have infiltrated across the frontier, and give the British the impression of our decision, ability and will to resist', but things did not turn out quite that way.[31]

On being somewhat impetuously attacked by two Rolls Royce armoured cars after a communications failure, the Italians made no attempt to find cover or occupy defensible terrain but simply formed their trucks into a square formation with their artillery pieces at the corners while the CV33 tankettes patrolled outside. The formation came as something of a surprise to Lieutenant-Colonel John Combe, the commander of the 11th Hussars, when he arrived on the scene and was presumably a drill developed to counter unsophisticated colonial enemies. Whatever its provenance, the tactic proved of little value against better armed and more adept opponents and having summoned tank and artillery reinforcements, the British went on the offensive. The Italians may have been tactically inept but they were not short of courage. Three CV33s had been knocked out in the initial stages of the action, and seven of the remainder mounted a counter charge to protect their infantry from the oncoming British tanks, but their inadequate armour was not up to the task and they were knocked out in quick succession. When the Italian square broke under the British assault the last surviving CV33 was destroyed in an attempt to ram an A9 Cruiser tank and the Italian artillerymen also fought to the last, being machine-gunned as they tried to bring their guns to bear on the British tanks. Only around a hundred Italians and a dozen trucks survived to be escorted back through the frontier wire to captivity in Egypt; their opponents did not incur a single casualty.

O'Connor's men thus achieved Wavell's objective of throwing the Italians off balance and dominating the Libyan side of the frontier, but the operational tempo soon began to tell on machines and especially men alike. According to the history of the 11th Hussars the first two weeks of hostilities were considered by some to be the most intensive of the entire war.[32] The lack of sleep, insufficient water and short and monotonous rations were bad enough in themselves; it was not unusual for exhausted crewmen to simply collapse to the floor of their vehicles, and bully beef and biscuits were literally the only rations available for days on end.[33] All this was exacerbated by the onset of the *khamsin* on 19 June, with 25 June being recorded as the hottest day the 11th Hussars had experienced to date. The heat was so intense that the armoured cars were too hot to touch, and the unfortunate crews were obliged to dismount and seek shelter beneath them. The severity of the conditions is well illustrated by an episode involving the second-in-command of the 4th Armoured Brigade who, during a reconnaissance for a joint operation to take the Italian-held oasis at Jarabub, refused to subject his tanks to such furnace-like conditions and insisted that they made operations impossible; the same officer collapsed later when informing Lieutenant-Colonel Combe that he intended to get the armoured car unit withdrawn.[34]

By July the strain was becoming too much, and when C Squadron 11th Hussars lost four men dead and fourteen captured in an abortive action O'Connor intervened. The 11th Hussars were thus ordered to reduce their activities to allow half its strength to be resting on the coast at Buq Buq, while the 4th Armoured Brigade was rotated out of the frontier zone in its entirety and replaced by the 7th Armoured Brigade. Thereafter the screening force reverted to a watching brief, and kept the British commanders informed of the Italian reoc-cupation of Fort Capuzzo, and their pre-invasion build-up and reconnaissance activity in the vicinity of the latter, Sidi Omar and Bardia. This prompted a further reorganisation to face the develop-ing threat, and on 13 August all the British armour was withdrawn to Mersa Matruh, leaving responsibility for the frontier zone to the 7th Armoured Division's Support Group, commanded by Brigadier W.H.E. Gott; the latter was instructed to maintain close watch on the enemy, especially in the area between Sollum and Maddalena. To achieve this, the Support Group had received reinforcements includ-ing the 3rd Battalion The Coldstream Guards, the 3rd RHA, a section from the 25/26th Medium Battery R.A., two anti-tank batteries, a detachment of Royal Engineers and the 7th Hussars' Cruiser Tank Squadron.[35]

The reorganisation was in line with O'Connor's defensive plan, which required the Support Group to conduct a fighting with-drawal to Mersa in preparation for an armoured thrust from the desert to the south against the Italian's flank, to cut off and hope-fully starve their vanguard into submission.[36] This was a little less wishful than it appears, for on 10 August 1940 the War Office had presented Churchill with a list of the units and equipment allocated for despatch to Egypt as soon as shipping and escorts could be procured. The list included forty-eight 2-Pounder anti-tank guns, the same number of 25-Pounders, twenty Bofors guns and over million assorted rounds of ammunition. Perhaps more importantly, the list also included the 3rd King's Own Hussars and the 2nd and 7th Royal Tank Regiments, equipped with Light, Cruiser and Infantry Tanks respectively.[37]

O'Connor was obliged to put his plan into effect at dawn on 13 September 1940, when Graziani finally launched his invasion. It began with the bombardment and seizure of Musaid via the gaps torn in the frontier wire by the 11th Hussars on the night of 11–12 June, followed by an advance on Sollum and the adjacent airfield. All this was observed by a platoon from the 3rd Battalion The Coldstream Guards which primed mines emplaced along the tracks leading east as it withdrew, and in Sollum proper the Royal Engineer detachment attached to the Support Group busied themselves demolishing buildings and supply dumps. The damage inflicted by the mines was compounded by the RHA, which accurately dropped salvos of shells on the advancing Italian transport using the reflections from their windscreens as a target indicator. British artillery also shelled the large traffic jams that built up on the trails leading down to the Halfaya Pass that cut through the Sollum Escarpment and provided access to the coastal plain to the east. The 1st *Libica* and *Cirene* Divisions were occupying the approaches to the Pass by nightfall, and began to move through it on the morning of 14 September. By the afternoon Italian troops were occupying the 11th Hussars rest and recuperation site at Buq Buq, almost forty miles from the border. On 15 September the Support Group's fighting withdrawal toward Mersa Matruh continued, although the RHA batteries exhausted their supply of 25-Pounder ammunition in the early afternoon, and the 7th Armoured Division's armour was moving west in readiness to begin their counter-attack on 17 or 18 September.

The slow but seemingly unstoppable Italian advance continued on 16 September, and by the early evening lead elements of the

1st MVSN Division entered Sidi Barrani where, at least according to Italian propaganda broadcasts, non-existent trams were still running. A defensive screen was pushed out as far as Maktila, fifteen miles to the east, but there the advance stopped. Over the next few days the remainder of Graziani's force closed up in the region of Sidi Barrani, having achieved 'maximum exploitation' as planned sixty miles or so inside Egypt. At first the British assumed that the halt was temporary, but a close reconnaissance by a Sergeant from the 11th Hussars revealed the construction of permanent defences, and aerial observation noted the construction of a surfaced road and water pipeline between Sollum and Sidi Barrani and the arrival of large amounts of supplies.[38] With that the 7th Armoured Division's tank formations were recalled and deployed to cover the approaches to Mersa Matruh; according to O'Connor they considered their with-drawal to be 'rather a disappointment'.[39] The Support Group was also withdrawn for a well earned rest, and the 11th Hussars took up their watching brief once again.

On the Italian side Mussolini was soon badgering Graziani to push on, but the latter was intent on modernising and strengthening his logistic links to Libya before resuming the offensive, and then only as far as Mersa Matruh. It was at this point that the Germans made their first, brief foray into events in North Africa. Following a meeting with his senior land and air commanders Hitler had cancelled the invasion of Britain, codenamed Operation *Seelöwe* (Sealion), on 17 September 1940. As a result the *Oberkommando der Wehrmacht* (OKW) began to consider the possibility of deploying an armoured force to assist their Italian allies in Libya, and with Hitler's approval despatched *Generalmajor* Wilhelm Ritter von Thoma to Libya to investigate the possibilities. In the meantime the 3 Panzer Division was warned of possible North African service, and Hitler formally offered Mussolini assistance at their Brenner Pass meeting on 4 October 1940. Von Thoma's report was not encouraging. The situation was judged 'thoroughly unsatisfactory', largely due to the poor road net and resultant logistical difficulties. As the presence of a German mechanised force would compound the latter severely, von

Thoma therefore counselled against any deployment until Mersa Matruh was in Italian hands. Hitler accepted the report, 3 Panzer Division was stood down and the whole idea was placed on the back burner.[40]

In the meantime the British had no intention of allowing Graziani to make his preparations unmolested, and thus reverted to harassing the Italians. RAF Blenheims destroyed three Italian bombers on the ground at Benina airfield near Benghazi on 17 September, and sixty day and night sorties were carried out against Italian road convoys and forward positions between 16 and 21 September alone.[41] The RAF in Egypt was also receiving more modern aircraft; by the end of September No. 202 Group had re-equipped No. 33 Squadron with Hawker Hurricane monoplane fighters and No. 113 Squadron with Blenheim Mk. IVs, and had operational control of the Vickers Wellington equipped No. 70 Squadron from Middle East Command.[42] However, their effectiveness was offset by the loss of the forward landing areas in the vicinity of Sidi Barrani. This reduced the effective range of Nos. 6 and 208 Army Co-Operation Squadron's reconnaissance aircraft, a mixture of Lysanders and Hurricanes, by around a hundred miles and also obliged Blenheims to operate at extreme range to reach the port of Benghazi, through which much of Graziani's materiel was passing. It also removed the possibility of shuttling fighters from Egypt to Malta, and curtailed air cover for RN vessels operating further west than Sidi Barrani.[43] This was offset to an extent by the activities of the latter. Fleet Air Arm aircraft from HMS *Illustrious* mined the approaches to Benghazi and sank the destroyer *Borea* and two cargo ships on 17 September, and nearer the front destroyers and the gunboats *Aphis* and *Ladybird* bombarded targets of opportunity along the coast from Sollum to Sidi Barrani. The damage was not all one-way, however. On the night of 17–18 September the cruiser HMS *Kent* was attacked by SM.79 torpedo bombers from 240ª *Squadriglia Aerosiluranti* whilst en route to shell Bardia; *Tenente* Carlo Emanuele Buscaglia scored a hit on the cruiser's stern which damaged the vessel to the extent it had to return to Britain for dockyard repair after a temporary fix at Alexandria.[44]

On the ground the 11th Hussars continued to penetrate deep into Italian controlled territory, but the strain of virtually non-stop operations was taking a barely sustainable toll that manifested itself in unreliable and worn-out vehicles and a lengthening list of battle casualties at the hands of the increasingly adept Italians. The Hussars were reinforced in October 1940 with No. 2 Armoured Car Squadron RAF from Palestine,[45] but in the meantime a stopgap response was the formation of small all-arms units equipped with artillery, anti-tank and anti-aircraft weaponry to protect the Hussars as they went about their business. Named 'Jock Columns' after the inventor of the concept, Lieutenant-Colonel J.C. 'Jock' Campbell RA and drawn largely from the Support Group, these units were tasked to support the 11th Hussars from the end of October. They also engaged in operations on their own, including surveying Italian defences and general harassment including attacking installations and transport in the Italian rear areas. This was all in line with the Support Group's mission to dominate the seventy miles that separated the main forces between Maktila and Mersa Matruh, to which end the latter's units also engaged in raiding on their own account. On 23 October 1940, for example, troops from the 2nd Battalion The Queen's Own Cameron Highlanders supported by tanks from the 8th Hussars attacked a fortified Italian camp near Maktila. Unfortunately, the Italians were forewarned courtesy of poor security in Cairo, and the attackers were greeted by the *Marmarica* Division in its entirety. Despite this a platoon of Highlanders penetrated the camp and succeeded in taking prisoners and destroying a number of motor vehicles before escaping in a commandeered truck; unfortunately the truck was shot up by friendly anti-tank fire and the prisoners escaped in the confusion.[46]

Wavell had been looking for an opportunity to attack the Italians since before the invasion of Egypt, and had ordered a study into the possible problems presented by an advance into eastern Libya as early as 11 September 1940.[47] After Graziani's force had been immobile around Sidi Barrani for a month he ordered Lieutenant-General Wilson to begin planning for a rapid, limited attack involving the 7th Armoured Division, the 4th Indian Division and the Mersa Matruh garrison. By this time the Italians had four divisions and *Raggruppamento* Maletti ensconced in a chain of ten fortified positions located roughly on a line running south for the thirty-odd miles between Maktila and Bir Enba on the edge of the coastal escarpment, and then west along the escarpment for a further twenty miles to Sofafi. Starting at the coast, Sidi Barrani was held by the 4° MSVN Division, with the 1° *Libica* Division holding Maktila and a fortified camp to the east of the town. The 2° *Libica* Division occupied three camps around Tummar, *Raggruppamento* Maletti one at Nibeiwa, and the remaining four at Rabia and around Sofafi were held by the *Cirene* Division. Further west, the *Catanzaro* Division was concentrated near Buq Buq, the *Marmarica* west of Sofafi and around Halfaya, and the 1st and 2nd MSVN Divisions were located near the border at Sidi Omar and the Sollum-Fort Capuzzo region respectively.

The information painstakingly gathered by the 11th Hussars and Jock Columns showed that while the Italian camps were generally well constructed and laid out, frequently with protective minefields, anti-tank ditches and wire, they were too far apart to provide mutual support. This was especially the case in the centre of the Italian line where the camps at Nibeiwa and Rabia were separated by almost twenty miles, an opening dubbed the Enba Gap. Graziani later claimed to have brought this to the attention of the commander of 10° *Armata* in November 1940, but whether that was *ex post facto* justification or not, nothing was done. Initial planning discussions involved only Wilson, his Chief-of-Staff, Lieutenant-General O'Connor and Major-General Creagh, in part because the raid on the Maktila camp had stressed the importance of tight security. The resulting scheme, codenamed Operation COMPASS, was largely O'Connor's and envisaged a two-pronged attack. The northern prong involved an advance along the coast road to attack the 1st *Libica* Division at Maktila and thus distract Italian attention from the Enba Gap, by a 1,800 strong force drawn from the troops holding Mersa Matruh. Christened 'Selby Force' after its commander Brigadier A.R. Selby, it was made up of the 3rd Battalion The Coldstream Guards, three companies drawn from the Northumberland Fusiliers, the South Staffordshire Regiment and Cheshire Regiments respectively, a detachment from the Durham Light Infantry, and tanks from A Troop, 7th Hussars.

The main blow was to be delivered from further south. The 7th Armoured and 4th Indian Divisions were to carry out a sixty mile approach march to a concentration area approximately fifteen miles south-east of Nibeiwa. They would then attack through the Enba Gap, with the 4th Armoured Brigade heading north toward Azziziya, midway between Buq Buq and Sidi Barrani. Its running mate, the 7th Armoured Brigade, was to form a screen between the Gap and the Italian camps at Rabia and Sofafi, and act as an exploitation reserve. While the armour was rampaging around the Italian rear areas as Hobart had envisioned the 4th Indian Division would attack the Italian camps around Tummar from the rear. Supplies for the operation were to be stockpiled in two large dumps forty miles west of Mersa Matruh from 5 November, well inside the disputed zone between the two armies. Field Supply Depot No. 3 was located near the Sidi Barrani–Mersa road ten miles from the coast, and No. 4 Field Supply Depot a further fifteen miles to the south, a hundred mile round trip across difficult terrain for the transport units tasked to shuttle the materiel forward from dumps near Qasaba. Each Depot was stocked with sufficient fuel, ammunition, hard scale rations and water for personnel and vehicle cooling systems to last for five days, the period of the attack.[48] Thereafter the forces involved were to withdraw and revert to their former defensive posture.

The plan may have been straightforward, but preparations proved to be less so. Wavell had originally intended to keep knowledge of COMPASS from an increasingly impatient Churchill until the planning and preparation was complete, to avoid raising unrealistic expectations and long-range micromanagement from London.[49] This strategy succeeded until the Italians invaded Greece on 28 October 1940, for the effort to assist the Greeks threatened to remove aircraft, troops, anti-aircraft guns and transport needed for COMPASS. Ironically, this placed Wavell in virtually the same predicament as his opposite

number Graziani; on 5 November Mussolini informed the latter
that he ought to be attacking in Egypt to tie up British forces that
might otherwise be sent to Greece.[50] In order to avoid having the
forces allocated to COMPASS stripped away Wavell therefore revealed
the operation to Secretary of State for War Anthony Eden when the
latter visited the Middle East on Churchill's orders on 8 November;
the latter was becoming increasingly dissatisfied with what he per-
ceived as Wavell's failure to make the best use of his reinforcements.
Churchill reacted with characteristic aggression on learning of COM-
PASS, insisting that any success should be exploited to the full, and his
dissatisfaction with Wavell was reinforced when he saw the content
of a cable from him to Chief of Imperial General Staff Field Marshal
Sir John Dill pointing out that 'undue hopes [were] being placed
on this operation which was designed as a raid only. We are greatly
outnumbered on ground and in air, have to move over 75 miles of
desert and attack enemy who has fortified himself for three months.
Please do not encourage optimism.' Churchill's response was equally
forthright, expressing shock and the opinion that Wavell was 'playing
small' and thus failing to rise to the occasion in the spirit required.[51]
This may have been the driver for a memo Wavell sent to Wilson
while the COMPASS force was moving to its jump off positions, which
acknowledged that it was 'possible that an opportunity may offer
for converting the enemy's defeat into an outstanding victory', and
asking that if so all ranks be 'prepared morally, mentally and adminis-
tratively to use it to the fullest'.[52]

Be that as it may, it was too late for Churchill to interfere for
good or ill as COMPASS was scheduled to begin on 9 December 1940.
Security remained tight, and the Western Desert Force's senior commanders were not informed of the plan until 2 November 1940;
Wavell briefed the senior commanders in Kenya and the Sudan the
same day. O'Connor issued strict instructions that nothing was to be
committed to paper until shortly before the attack commenced, and
the troops were not to be informed until they were en route to their
assembly areas.[53] The latter thus had no idea that Training Exercise
No.1 carried out near Mersa Matruh on 25–26 November was

actually a full-scale rehearsal for COMPASS, and that Training Exercise No.2 was in fact the opening stages of the Operation. The first unit to move was the 7th RTR, which reached Field Supply Depot No.4 en route to an 'exercise' area in the vicinity of Bir el Kenayis, forty miles south west of Mersa Matruh, on Thursday 5 December. Having only been in Egypt for two months, this was the unit's first foray into what desert veterans referred to as 'the blue', and its early start was necessary because the forty-five Tank, Infantry, Mk.IIs with which the unit was equipped were only capable of eight miles per hour cross country. Despite this the unit was O'Connor's ace in the hole, and not merely because the Italians were unaware of its presence in Egypt. The twenty-six ton Matilda, as the vehicle was popularly known, weighed over twice as much as the Italian M11/39, and the former's 78mm cast armour was not only twice as thick but also impervious to Italian anti-tank weapons.[54] The 4th Indian Division, commanded by Lieutenant-General Sir Noel Beresford-Peirse, followed on 6 December, and remained dispersed around Bir el Kenayis for thirty-six hours, to give the impression of routine training; an Italian reconnaissance aircraft flew overhead during a well attended church parade on 7 December.

The 7th Armoured Division, commanded by Brigadier J.R.L. Caunter in lieu of a temporarily hospitalised Creagh, left its nearby harbour area for the forward concentration area on 7 December; as this was only fifteen miles from Nibeiwa the division went into hard routine on arrival, with no fires or unnecessary movement. The air preparation for COMPASS began the same night, with a raid by eleven Malta-based Wellingtons that destroyed or damaged twenty-nine Italian aircraft at Castel Benito airfield near Tripoli. The following night a mixed force of Wellingtons and Blenheim Mk.IVs destroyed ten more at Benina, while other Blenheims attacked Italian forward airfields. Even obsolete Bristol Bombay bomber/transports from No. 216 Squadron were pressed into service to bomb the Italian forward positions. No. 202 Group's fighter contingent were employed in creating and maintaining air superiority over the COMPASS ground forces; almost 400 fighter sorties were made in the first week of the

Operation, with some pilots carrying out four in a single day. In the process they claimed thirty-five Italian machines shot down and a further twelve possibles for a loss of six RAF aircraft and three pilots.[55]

That lay in the future, however, and by the late afternoon of 8 December the 4th Indian Division had also reached the concentration area near Nibeiwa and O'Connor had set up his forward HQ nearby at a location codenamed 'Piccadilly Circus'. This was no mean feat in itself, involving as it did moving some 36,000 men and in excess of 5,000 vehicles undetected across sixty miles of open desert. The move may not have gone totally unnoticed, for an Italian reconnaissance pilot reported 400 vehicles at various points approximately forty miles south-east of Nibeiwa at around midday on 8 December, but no account appears to have been taken of his report.[56] O'Connor's force carried out its final preparations and moves up to start lines under cover of darkness on the night of 8–9 December. The 7th Armoured Division moved up into the Enba Gap, and sent back guides to direct 7th RTR and 11th Indian Brigade to their jump off positions for the opening attack on the Nibeiwa camp. To the north the noise of Selby Force moving into position was concealed by Royal Navy gunfire. A Bombarding Force consisting of HM Monitor *Terror*, the minesweeper *Bagshot* and the gunboats *Aphis* and *Ladybird* had sailed from Alexandria at 20:00 on 7 December. *Terror* and *Aphis* were to concentrate on Italian strongpoints and transport parks, while *Ladybird* was to shell gun positions and troop tents just to the west at Sidi Barrani; the latter was intended as cover for a Commando raid against Italian communications and pipelines, but the landing was prevented by heavy seas that also prostrated the raiders with seasickness. The bombardment began at 23:00 on 8 December and lasted for ninety minutes, although dust and misdropped flares from supporting Fairey Swordfish from HMS *Illustrious* made spotting difficult.[57]

The Italian camp at Nibeiwa was occupied by *Generale* Pietro Maletti's *Raggruppamento*, with a battalion of M11/39 medium tanks, a battalion of L3/35 Light Tanks and 2,500 Libyan infantry. The camp measured a mile by a mile and a half and was protected by a perimeter wall, an anti-tank ditch and berm, barbed wire and a perimeter minefield. However, on the night of 7–8 December a reconnaissance patrol from the 2nd Battalion, The Rifle Brigade located a gap in the defences at the north-western corner of the camp where supply columns passed back and forth; approximately twenty tanks, mostly M11/39s, were deployed outside the camp in a screen to protect this weak point. The action began shortly before 05:00 on Monday 9 December with an hour long diversion against the eastern side of the camp, followed by a light shelling on the south-east corner of the camp at 07:00. The main attack commenced at 07:15 with a simultaneous artillery concentration from seventy-two guns on selected targets within the perimeter and attack by two Squadrons of the 7th RTR against the north-western gap. The vehicles in the protective tank screen were unmanned, and the Matildas proceeded to pick them off at leisure before advancing into the camp proper, followed at 07:45 by the 2nd Battalion The Queen's Own Cameron Highlanders and the 1st/6th Rajputana Rifles.

As at Nezuet Ghirba back in June, some of the Italians attempted to make up for operational incompetence with raw courage. Artillery men fired ineffectually at the Matilda IIs at point blank while others attacked the armoured behemoths with hand grenades, and the British were obliged to bring up artillery pieces to reduce some stubborn groups of defenders. Most were simply overawed by the speed and surprise of the assault, however, and by 10:40 Nibeiwa camp had been secured at a cost of fifty-six British and Indian casualties.[58] Italian losses are unclear, but the dead included *Generale* Maletti and his *aide-de-camp* son, who had been cut down as they emerged from the tent where they had been awaiting breakfast. The British captured between 2,000 and 4,000 prisoners and twenty-three tanks along with numerous transport vehicles, water and supplies.[59] The latter included large numbers of dress uniforms and associated accoutrements, freshly made beds and a positive cornucopia of food and drink. According to a journalist on the spot, the latter included freshly baked bread, fresh vegetables, jars of liqueurs, hundreds of cases of *Rocoaro* brand mineral water, huge amounts of spaghetti and macaroni and Parmesan cheeses the size of wagon-wheels.[60]

While this was going on the 4th Armoured Brigade was forging northward. Elements of the 11th Hussars reached the Sidi Barrani-Buq Buq road at 09:00, and within a few moments had captured eight trucks and fifty POWs. They were joined by the rest of the Brigade shortly thereafter, which had taken another 400 POWs at Azziziya when the garrison surrendered without firing a shot. With Sidi Barrani thus cut off from reinforcement the 11th Hussars began probing to the west while the 7th Hussars crossed the road and patrolled north toward the coast. Back to the south-east the 5th Indian Brigade had attacked the next camp in the chain, Tummar West, with the arrival of the 7th RTR at around 11:00, although the latter had lost six Matilda IIs immobilised by mines leaving Nibeiwa. Preparations were complicated by a sandstorm and the arrival of the *Regia Aeronautica*, which scattered bombs randomly into the dust cloud. However the Matildas and infantry from the 1st Battalion, The Royal Fusiliers attack finally went in through another gap in the defences at 13:30.

The Tummar West garrison put up stiffer resistance and the Fusiliers were obliged to fight through with grenades, bayonets and rifle-butts; one group of dug-outs in the centre of the camp held out until Matildas were brought in to crush the shelters under their tracks. By 16:00 the surviving defenders had been pinned down in the south-east corner of the camp, and they surrendered after negotiations by an Italian general and thirteen senior officers, putting another 2,000 POWs into the British bag. The garrison of the Tummar East camp had been reduced substantially when two M11/39 tanks, six trucks and a large number of infantry sallied forth to assist their neighbours and unwittingly traversed the frontage of the 4th/6th Rajputana Rifles and a machine-gun detachment from the 1st Northumberland Fusiliers. The tanks were knocked out with Boys anti-tank rifles and the infantry driven back into their camp, leaving 400 dead and wounded behind them. The 7th RTR's sixteen running Matilda IIs redeployed and penetrated Tummar East in the early evening but the attack was called off due to the onset of darkness and a thickening of the ongoing sandstorm.

Word of events at the Tummar camps was carried by survivors to the main Italian force engaged with Selby Force east of Sidi Barrani. The senior Italian officer there, *Generale di Corpo* Sebastiano Gallina, had informed Graziani that afternoon that the entire area of his command was 'infested' with British mechanised forces against which he had no effective counter.[61] The commander of the infestation came forward to 4th Indian Division's HQ near Nibeiwa at 17:00 and expressed his pleasure with progress. Although nothing had been heard of Selby Force, the fact that 4th Armoured Brigade had been left largely unmolested astride the Sidi Barrani-Buq Buq road suggested that the Italian garrison at Sidi Barrani and Maktila were being kept occupied, while the camps at Rabia and Sofafi had also remained passive. O'Connor therefore instructed the 7th Armoured Division to despatch the 8th Hussars to a blocking position west of Sofafi, and ordered the 4th Indian Division to reduce the remaining camps at Tummar East and Point 90 the next day, and to send its reserve formation, the attached 16th Infantry Brigade commanded by Brigadier C.E.N. Lomax, north to join the 4th Armoured Brigade in preparation for an attack on Sidi Barrani; Lomax moved off on receipt of the order and covered part of the distance during the night.

Operations on 10 December were again hampered by sand storms but began well with the surrender of the Tummar East camp at dawn without a fight. The 16th Infantry Brigade was on the move by 06:00, prompted in part by Italian artillery fire on its exposed night position. After a stiff fight involving the 1st Battalion, The Argyll and Sutherland Highlanders at Alam el Dab, eight miles or so east of Azziziya, the Brigade was in position across the routes running west and south from Sidi Barrani by 13:30. Eager to press his advantage, Beresford-Peirse engaged in some hasty reorganisation. The 4th Armoured Brigade was ordered to cover the 16th Infantry Brigade's left flank with the Cruiser-equipped 2nd RTR and to send the 6th RTR to reinforce Selby Force, and the 7th RTR's remaining serviceable Matilda IIs were assigned to assist Lomax as well. That done, the 16th Infantry Brigade was ordered to launch an attack on Sidi Barrani, which began with a divisional artillery concentration at 16:00 hours. Within thirty minutes the attackers had passed right through the town in spite of a severe sandstorm, and at 17:15 the 6th RTR overran the Italian defences east of the town. The action cost the 16th Infantry Brigade 277 casualties but left the remnants of the 1° and 2° *Libica* and 4° MVSN Divisions trapped against the sea in a pocket ten miles long and five miles deep, bloodied but as yet unbowed; a subsequent attack at around midnight by the 6th RTR was rebuffed, largely due to the efforts of Italian artillerymen, and reduced the unit's strength to twelve tanks.[62]

Thus by the end of the second day of Operation COMPASS the Italian camps north of the Enba Gap and Sidi Barrani itself were in British hands. The exception was the camp at Point 90, where elements of the 2nd *Libica* Division continued to hold out. The impact of all this on the Italians only became apparent on the third day, 11 December. The Italian troops bottled up east of Sidi Barrani began to give up as soon as the British renewed the attack at dawn, the 1st *Libica* Division formally surrendering by 13:00, and the 4th MVSN Division by nightfall. To the south, patrols from the Support Group found that the *Cirene* Division had abandoned the camps at Rabia and around Sofafi during the night. The last to give in were the 2nd *Libica* holdouts at Point 90. When the Italian commander responded to demands for surrender by saying that he intended to fight to the death, a deliberate attack was organised by the 3rd/1st Punjab Regiment, supported by seven Matilda IIs from the 7th RTR, two of which turned up at the last moment after hasty repair, and two RA Field Regiments. They found 2,000 Libyan troops waiting patiently to surrender complete with packed luggage, the fight to the death threat being merely a face saving ploy by their commander.[63] By nightfall on Wednesday, 11 December 1940 the British had captured between 20,000 and 38,300 prisoners, seventy-three tanks, 237 guns and over 1,000 transport vehicles. The fighting cost the British and Indians 624 killed, wounded and missing, with 153 of these coming from the 1st Battalion, The Argyll and Sutherland Highlanders.[64] Operation COMPASS had therefore far exceeded expectations for a limited raid within three days. In the process the military situation on Egypt's western border was totally recast, prompting a shift in British thinking.

4
Tobruk Captured: The British Advance into Libya December 1940 – January 1941

By nightfall on Tuesday 10 December 1940, with three of the four Italian camps north of the Enba Gap and the town of Sidi Barrani in British hands, it was clear that Operation COMPASS was far exceeding expectations. Major-General O'Connor therefore implemented measures to comply with last-minute orders from Commander-in-Chief Middle East Lieutenant-General Sir Archibald Wavell to expand the scope of COMPASS from a raid to general westward exploitation should the opportunity arise.[1] O'Connor ordered Brigadier H.E. Russell's 7th Armoured Brigade, which had held as the 7th Armoured Division's reserve near Nibeiwa, to move north to Buq Buq with all possible speed to prevent any Italian withdrawal toward Sollum and the Libyan border. He also ordered the 7th Armoured Division's Support Group to move against the Italian camps south of the Enba Gap at Rabia and around Sofafi as per the original COMPASS plan, supported by the 4th Armoured Brigade once the latter had reorganised after the fighting at Sidi Barrani. The wisdom of this reorientation was confirmed on 11 December when the Support Group discovered that the *Cirene* Division had withdrawn from the Sofafi area during the night. Armoured cars from the 11th Hussars scouting ahead of the Support Group located and began harassing the retreating Italians during the morning, but were forced to disengage at around midday by strafing attacks from Italian fighter aircraft.

O'Connor had originally ordered the 4th Indian Division to move south and assist the Support Group in overcoming the camps around Sofafi, but this was countered by the removal of the Indian formation from the Western Desert Force with immediate effect at dawn on 11 December; Wavell had decided to despatch the Indian Division to the Sudan for operations against Italian East Africa, and in exchange O'Connor was given the 6th Australian Division. This was a far from satisfactory substitution, for although the Australian Division had begun concentrating in the Middle East from February 1940, its training had been slowed by equipment shortages. As a result only the 16th Australian Brigade was considered fully battle worthy, and that formation was located sixty miles or more behind the current fight, at Mersa Matruh where it was acting as the Western Desert Force's reserve formation. O'Connor was therefore less than impressed at having his fighting power halved at a stroke even allowing for Wavell permitting him to retain control of the 16th Infantry Brigade, which had been attached to the 4th Indian Division. However, while the removal of the Indian Division made little sense from O'Connor's operational perspective, it was perfectly logical at the strategic level. The Italian presence in the Horn of Africa, and especially the *Flotilla Del Mare Rosso*, presented a threat to British communications which Wavell could not afford to ignore. The Italian submarine *Guglielmo* sank the tanker *Atlas* off the Farisan Islands on 6 October 1940 for example, and the destroyers *Pantera, Leone* and *Francesco Nullo* attacked the British convoy BN7 en route to Suez from India on 21 November 1940. However inconvenient it may have been for O'Connor, the simple fact was that the removal of the bases for such attacks was more of a strategic imperative than operations in the Western Desert.

The surrender of the remnants of the 1° and 2° *Libica* and 4° MVSN Divisions east of Sidi Barrani on the morning of 11 December removed the need for a blocking force on the road

running west from the town, and scouting by the 11th Hussars indicated that the Italians were not preparing to make a stand at Buq
Buq as expected either. The 7th Armoured Brigade therefore began to
probe west toward Sollum and soon ran into the *Catanzaro* Division,
dug in north of the Buq Buq-Sollum road. The Italians had chosen
a good position flanked by poor going for vehicles, as the 3rd Hussars
discovered when several Light Tanks became mired in a salt marsh
during in an impetuous charge. The 8th Hussars had better luck with
their Cruiser Tanks on the landward flank and while the Italian artillerymen once again stood their ground, their infantry compatriots
broke and abandoned their positions. By nightfall the British had
captured sixty-eight guns, 14,000 prisoners, numerous trucks and
large quantities of supplies.[2] The Italian POWs proved extremely co-
operative if not downright helpful to their captors; the 7th Armoured
Brigade's deputy commander noted that they assembled, refuelled
and drove their own vehicles full of men back to Maktila with no
escort whatsoever.[3]

By nightfall on 12 December 1940 the only Italian forces remaining on Egyptian soil were the garrisons drawn from 1° MVSN
Division just inside the border at Sidi Omar, and the 2° MVSN hold-
ing Sollum. O'Connor therefore adjusted his plans once again, from
exploitation west of Sidi Barrani to an outright incursion into Italian
territory aimed at the port of Bardia, roughly ten miles inside Libya.
The incursion was to be a pincer movement with the 4th Armoured
Brigade reinforced with two Squadrons from the 11th Hussars and
Combe Force, named after the 11th Hussars commander Lieutenant-
Colonel John Combe and made up of the rest of the 11th Hussars, the
Light Tank-equipped 2nd RTR and two batteries of artillery, looping
west and north into Libya to cut the Bardia–Tobruk road. The other
pincer was provided by the 7th Armoured Brigade augmented with
infantry companies drawn from the 2nd Battalion The Rifle Brigade,
which was to advance along the coast road, clearing Sollum and
securing Bardia.

The 4th Armoured Brigade, temporarily commanded by
Lieutenant-Colonel Horace Birks, crossed the border from its

concentration area twelve miles south of Halfaya just after midnight on the night of 13–14 December 1940, and by 07:00 had reached a point on the coastal escarpment twenty miles west of Bardia. There Combe Force moved forward to find a route down onto the coastal plain, screened by the 11th Hussar Squadrons. The Italian reaction to this incursion came mainly from the air, and the Hussars bore the brunt of it undergoing over twenty separate bombing and strafing attacks over the course of the day; the first alone cost one dead and six wounded along with five armoured cars, a fitter's vehicle and a truck destroyed. Despite all this by nightfall on 14 December the 2nd RTR's Light Tanks had also descended the escarpment and were blocking the stretch of the *Via Balbia* linking Bardia to Tobruk.[4]

However, events did not proceed as anticipated on the coast road axis and once Brigadier Caunter had resumed command of the Brigade O'Connor despatched it twenty-five miles to the south to deal with the camp at Sidi Omar held by the 1st MVSN Division, which was laid out around a white-painted French Foreign Legion style fort in the same manner as those to the east, with minefields, barbed wire and trenches. The 4th Armoured Brigade arrived west of Sidi Omar on 16 December and Caunter launched the 2nd RTR and 7th Hussars in a charge into the dust cloud thrown up by the RHA's preparatory bombardment that carried the tanks though the camp perimeter. The commander of C Squadron 2nd RTR, Captain Patrick Hobart, used his tank to breach the fort wall but damaged the rear idler in the process, immobilising the vehicle in the courtyard. Hobart was thus reduced to firing his pistol from his commander's cupola until his second in command, Lieutenant David Wilkie, manoeuvred his tank through the gap. The arrival of a second British tank inside the fort was too much for the defenders, who promptly began to surrender ending a battle that had lasted around ten minutes. The brevity of the action was due in part to the Italian deployment, subsequent investigation revealing that all the garrison's guns were emplaced facing east toward the Egyptian border and were thus unable to bear upon the advancing British armour.[5]

O'Connor had given explicit instructions that the Italian forces in the coast road area were not to be allowed to escape, but the 7th Armoured Brigade's advance failed to prevent the 2° MVSN Division withdrawing intact from Sollum to Fort Capuzzo, and thence north to Bardia, even though a squadron from the 1st RTR pursued its quarry right up to the Bardia perimeter before being driven back by Italian artillery fire that knocked out the squadron commander's tank. O'Connor laid the blame for this squarely on the 7th Armoured Brigade's inflexibility, specifically centralised maintenance and messing arrangements and a reluctance to operate at night.[6] If true, the latter was an early manifestation of operational habits that were to dog British armoured operations later in North-West Europe, perhaps most notably during Operation GARDEN, the abortive ground advance to relieve the British 1st Airborne Division at Arnhem. Be that as it may, such by-the-book operating procedures sat especially badly with O'Connor, who routinely modified or simply ignored Field Service Regulations and set great store on operational initiative and flexibility. He arranged conference discussions to ensure that his intentions were clear to subordinates, after which they were allowed plenty of latitude to perform their individual tasks within the larger scheme while O'Connor maintained control with a combination of succinct and concise verbal orders and contact in person or via liaison officers. His HQ arrangements were optimised for this mode of command; O'Connor himself ranged freely between subordinate unit HQs accompanied by only two staff officers and a mobile wireless from an Advanced HQ made up of his senior staff officers, while the rest of the staff and administrative machinery were located further back at a Rear HQ.[7] Although the 7th Armoured Brigade does not appear to have followed this example, its running mate 4th Armoured Brigade did; Lieutenant-Colonel Birks commanded the latter from a Tactical HQ made up of just two tanks in the move to cut the Bardia-Tobruk road on 13-14 December.[8]

With Egypt and the border region south of Sollum clear of Italian forces by 16 December, there were two obstacles preventing O'Connor moving immediately on Bardia. The first and more difficult obstacle was a lack of supplies. Moving beyond Sidi Barrani had imposed severe strain on the British supply system, for at that time the railway only ran as far as Mersa Matruh and the painstakingly stocked Forward Supply Depots established to service Operation COMPASS had only been intended to support a five day operation in the first place. The advance beyond Sollum into Libya pushed the front a hundred miles from those Depots and thus stretched the supply system to breaking point; according to a contemporary source the British armoured formations were consuming between 20,000 and 25,000 gallons of fuel per day.[9] While the logistics chain was subsequently extended with additional depots at or near Rabia, Sofafi, Sidi Barrani, Sollum and Fort Capuzzo, these took time to stock and the process was slowed by a critical shortage of drivers and transport vehicles; by the end of December 1940 the vehicle wastage rate was running at forty per cent, due to a combination of the harsh operating conditions, insufficient time for routine maintenance and a lack of workshop facilities. Measures to alleviate the situation included co-opting motor transport companies from units in the rear, issuing an unequipped Reserve Motor Transport Company with eighty captured Italian vehicles on 12 December, and drafting in fifty heavy trucks and drivers from Palestine two days later.

Supplies were also moved by sea, using pre-existing arrangements to supply Mersa Matruh. The Naval Officer in Charge there had prepared docking facilities, gathered supplies and arranged weekly 700 ton deliveries of water for onward by the water carrier *Petrella* for onward despatch; two large X-Type lighters had been pre-loaded with petrol and supplies for COMPASS ready for offloading at Sidi Barrani as soon as the port was secured. Efforts to extend the practice west following the capture of Sollum on 16 December were hindered by the lack of facilities at the latter, which consisted of two small piers with no docks or heavy lifting equipment. Troops from the 16th Brigade and The Cyprus Regiment were pressed into service as stevedores, with the supplies being carried forward by No.4 New Zealand Motor Transport Company. A lack of bulk storage facilities made offloading petrol especially difficult, for the standard four gallon cans were both awkward to handle and extremely flimsy. The work at Sollum was not only arduous but dangerous, for the port was within range of a heavy gun at Bardia, possibly a 210mm *Obice da 210/22 Modello 35*. More importantly, the port was vulnerable to air attack as only a single battery of 3.7-inch anti-aircraft guns could be spared to protect it, and there was no early warning system to guide RAF fighters. Bombing was therefore a regular occurrence, and one raid on 24 December killed and wounded sixty men. The most pressing shortage was of fresh water, and 12,000 gallons had to be brought by road from Mersa Matruh when storage tanks at Fort Capuzzo were found to be too salty for drinking. The problem was eventually alleviated by pumping water to Sollum from sources at Sidi Barrani and Buq Buq, and in the meantime vessels including the gunboats *Aphis* and *Ladybird* and the monitor *Terror* assisted the water carrier *Myriel* in delivering water direct to wheeled bowsers on the beach at Sollum.[10] Overall the British logistic effort thus relied heavily on captured Italian materiel; the orders for the move into Libya acknowledged that food and water would have to come from captured Italian stocks. The attack on Bardia was reliant on captured wire-cutters salvaged from abandoned Italian camps, for example.[11]

The second obstacle was a dearth of infantry, which was rectified by the arrival of the 6th Australian Division. Raised on 28 September 1939 under then Lieutenant-General Thomas Blamey DSO, the 6th Australian Division was a mixture of long-service Regular soldiers and civilian volunteers, and made up the 1st Australian Corps with the 7th Australian Division raised in March 1940. This was in turn part of the 2nd Australian Imperial Force (AIF) which, like the 1st AIF in the First World War, was intended for overseas service from the outset; in recognition of this the 2nd AIF's component units carried the prefix '2' in their titles, indicating that this was the second time the unit had been raised for such service. The 6th Division's infantry strength was all-volunteer, consisting of the 16th Australian Brigade raised in New South Wales, the 17th Australian Brigade raised in Victoria, and the 18th Brigade with battalions raised in Queensland, South Australia, Western Australia and Tasmania, and deployed to Palestine via

Egypt in three increments in the first half of 1940. The 16th Brigade disembarked in mid-February and the 17th Brigade in mid-May, but the 18th Brigade was redirected to the UK three days after sailing from Fremantle on 12 May 1940. It was replaced by the 19th Australian Brigade, formed in Palestine in April 1940 using surplus infantry battalions created by a reorganisation of the four-battalion Australian infantry brigades to conform to the standard British triangular structure.

The 6th Australian Division returned to Egypt in August 1940 after undergoing a rigorous training programme at Julis near Gaza. While the formation had its full infantry complement, it was still lacking its machine-gun battalion, anti-tank regiment and a field artillery regiment along with much of its equipment; one of the existing field artillery regiments was equipped with obsolete guns, there were only a dozen anti-tank guns scattered across the three infantry brigades, and there was a general shortage of mortars, Universal Carriers and motor transport. Nonetheless Brigadier A.S. Allen's 16th Australian Brigade was brought forward to act as the reserve for Operation COMPASS at Mersa Matruh, while the remainder of the division continued training. The 4th New Zealand Brigade, part of the New Zealand Division that had arrived in Egypt in February and September 1940, was also in the region of Mersa Matruh. However Major-General Bernard Freyberg VC, commanding the New Zealand Division, refused to permit his men to be committed to battle except as a complete formation, with the full support of the New Zealand Government; this presumably resulted from the perception that Dominion troops had been unfairly employed by British senior commanders during the First World War. Whether or not, the 6th Australian Division's commander, Major-General Iven Mackay, laboured under no such constraints and Wavell's removal of the 4th Indian Division to Sudan soon placed his formation in the forefront of the action. The 16th Australian Brigade had already followed the action as far west as Sollum by 17 December, while the 17th Australian Brigade awaited transport to join them and the men of the 19th Australian Brigade threatened dire consequences should they be excluded from the action like their unfortunate compatriots from New Zealand.[12]

The 16th Australian Brigade moved up to the front line facing Bardia on the night of 19–20 December 1940, and the 2/2nd Battalion took over positions from the 1st KRRC straddling the road running west from Bardia to Tobruk just before dawn. It was joined by the 2/3rd Battalion the following night, and Major-General Mackay officially assumed responsibility for the Sollum area and operations to reduce Bardia on 21 December. The 17th Australian Brigade under Brigadier S. G. Savige arrived to relieve the 16th (British) Brigade covering the southern half of the Bardia perimeter on 27 December. The Australians immediately began a programme of night patrolling despite the freezing weather – the winter was widely acknowledged as the worst in living memory – intended to harass the Italian defenders and to familiarise themselves with their positions. To this end patrols after 22 December were accompanied by engineers who surveyed the wire, anti-tank obstacles and minefields; their work was presumably eased by the detailed plans of the Bardia defences captured by the 11th Hussars back in June. The Australian patrolling complemented ongoing harassment of Bardia from air and sea. The RAF had carried out 150 sorties against Bardia between 14 and 19 December, including an attack by thirty-six aircraft on the night of 15–16 December, while other aircraft including Wellingtons operating from Malta hit airfields at Castel Benito, Benina and Berka destroying forty-four Italian aircraft between 18 and 22 December. The monitor *Terror* had systematically bombarded targets within the Bardia perimeter for three days beginning on 14 December, avoiding damage at the hands of Italian aircraft and a surface vessel, possibly a *Spica* class torpedo boat, in the process. At dawn on 17 December the gunboat *Aphis* took things a stage further by boldly sailing into Bardia harbour and engaging a variety of targets at point-blank range before withdrawing unscathed; an attempt to repeat the audacious feat the following day was less successful and the gunboat was driven off by Italian artillery fire.[13]

On the Italian side *Maresciallo* Graziani had originally ordered that Bardia and Tobruk be held at all costs, but was having second thoughts by 17 December and suggested to Mussolini that concentrating on the defence of Tobruk might be a better option. *Il Duce* disagreed, pointing out that a prolonged defence at Bardia would be beneficial for future operations. The man charged with carrying out that prolonged defence was fifty-six year old *Generale di Corpo d'Armata* Annibale Bergonzoli, a Spanish Civil War veteran nicknamed *Barba Elettrica* (roughly 'electric beard') due to his rather spectacular facial hair. It is unclear whether Bergonzoli was aware of Graziani's wavering, but he was privy to the latter's original intent, having persuaded him to permit the withdrawal of the Italian forces at Sollum and Fort Capuzzo to reinforce Bardia on 15 December. By the following day the garrison of Bardia thus numbered between 40,000 and 45,000 men, made up of the almost intact 1° and 2° MVSN Divisions and *Marmarica* Divisions, and the remnants of the *Cirene* and *Catanzaro* Divisions. This force was augmented with around a 100 CV33 light tanks, a dozen M11/39 medium tanks, 100 light and 300 medium and heavy artillery pieces. This force was ensconced behind an eighteen mile belt of fixed defences, anchored at both ends on the sea and protected by six separate minefields, a continuous double apron of barbed wire and a vertically cut anti-tank ditch four feet deep and twelve feet wide. Inside this was a line of strongpoints with concrete trenches, bunkers and gun emplacements spaced at 500 to 800 yard intervals and protected by more wire, mines and defensive ditches; the latter were camouflaged with thin wooden boards covered with dust and sand designed to collapse under weights greater than that of a man.[14] Some sections were reinforced with a second line of strongpoints, with others built around vulnerable points behind that.[15] Bardia was thus a formidable obstacle by any standard, even allowing for the detailed plans held by the British.

Major-General Mackay decided to attack from the west, at a point just south of the Tobruk road where a rise offered clear observation over the Italian defences and was almost directly opposite Bardia, four miles from the perimeter. The attack was to be spearheaded by the 16th Australian Brigade, with the 17th Australian Brigade taking over when the advance reached the Bardia–Fort Capuzzo road, roughly half way to the port; the 19th Australian Brigade was held back at O'Connor's request in readiness for a swift advance on Tobruk. The attack was supported by a machine-gun battalion (the 1st Northumberland Fusiliers) and the twenty or so Matilda II tanks the 7th RTR had been able to repair in spite of a severe lack of spares. As the Italian anti-tank ditch presented a serious obstacle to the latter, the 2/1st and 2/3rd Battalions dug an exact replica based on information from patrols and spent much time and effort working out the fastest and most effective method of getting the twenty-six ton tanks across it. A total of 160 guns were gathered for the attack, ninety-six of which were assigned to the main axis of attack giving a density of almost one gun per seven yards of frontage, the same as at the Battle of Messines in June 1917. Twenty-four of the remainder were tasked to support a feint attack against the southern section of the perimeter, where patrolling was also stepped up as a disinformation measure. The RAF also stepped up their efforts, carrying out 100 bombing sorties against Bardia between 31 December and 2 January with an especially heavy attack by Wellingtons and Bombays from Nos. 70 and 219 Squadrons on the night of 2–3 January.

After a twenty-four hour delay due to ammunition supply difficulties, Zero Hour was finally set for 05:30 on Friday 3 January 1941. The lead elements of the 2/1st Battalion began moving up to the start line at 04:30, muffled in greatcoats against the cold and carrying respirators, 150 rounds of .303 ammunition and three days' canned rations in addition to personal weapons, digging tools and engineer stores. The attack opened on time with a 500 yard deep box barrage on a 2,500 yard frontage, under cover of which assault parties cleared mines, placed Bangalore Torpedoes in the barbed wire entanglements at sixty yard intervals and prepared six crossing points for the Matildas.[16] While this was going on patrols from the 7th Armoured Division Support Group acted as a distraction on the northern sector of the perimeter, and the 17th Australian Brigade launched a feint attack against strongpoints at the southern end of the perimeter. On the main attack axis the 2/1st Battalion passed through the gaps blown in the Italian wire, some incongruously belting forth the popular song 'South of the Border' and attacked the battered

Italian strongpoints and artillery emplacements facing the breaches. Within twenty minutes these had been cleared and over 400 POWs had been despatched to the rear. At 07:00 the 5th RTR's Matilda IIs moved over the six crossing points with the 2/2nd Battalion and swung south-east, followed by the 6th Australian Cavalry Regiment and the 2/3rd Battalion which advanced east toward Bardia.[17] Within two hours the attack had achieved its primary objective of establishing a two mile deep penetration into the Italian perimeter, with its left flank overlooking the Tobruk road to the north and the right flank resting on the Bardia-Fort Capuzzo road to the south. To keep the Italians off balance the battleships *Barham*, *Valiant*, *Warspite* and their destroyer escort unleashed a concentrated forty-five minute bombardment on the area north of the Tobruk road at 08:10.

The second phase of the attack began just over two hours later, at 11:30 with an attack by the 17th Australian Brigade against the perimeter south of the Fort Capuzzo road, supported by six tanks. The latter were late in arriving at the start line, and the attack did not progress as smoothly as further north. The 2/6th Battalion on the left was pinned down and the 2/5th Battalion's commander was killed by Italian artillery fire, but by the afternoon the attackers penetrated a subsidiary set of Italian defences known as the Switch Line from the rear, where they remained embroiled for most of the battle. Sporadic fighting went on through the night and the 16th Australian Brigade renewed the attack at 11:00 on 4 January. The 2/3rd Battalion, accompanied by three Matilda IIs, pushed north across the Tobruk road, while the 2/2nd Battalion and another six tanks moved east and overran Bardia before the defenders could sabotage the dock facilities and water plant; by nightfall the 2/5th Battalion had finally overcome the Switch Line, and the remnants of the Italian garrison were penned into the northern and southern extremities of the perimeter. Despite O'Connor's request, Mackay had found it necessary to bring the 19th Australian Brigade into the fight: the 2/8th Battalion thus covered the flank of the advance into Bardia, and the 2/11th Battalion was involved in reducing the last pockets of resistance when the Italians finally surrendered at 13:00 on Sunday 5 January 1941. The three day battle cost the 6th Australian Division 130 dead and 326 wounded, and reduced the 7th RTR to six serviceable Matilda IIs.[18] While the Italians were unable to penetrate the latter's thick armour, the tank's poorly designed turret ring was easily jammed by enemy fire and weak steering clutches were a frequent source of mechanical breakdown.[19]

Italian resistance once again varied between passivity and dogged courage. Some strongpoints surrendered on demand but others resisted until reduced with close range tank fire, grenades and bayonets. In the early stages of the attack on 3 January six M13/40 medium tanks approached to within thirty yards of the 2/3rd Battalion's left flank and were only recognised as enemy on opening fire. They moved stolidly through an Australian company despite a platoon commander climbing aboard one vehicle and emptying his pistol into the turret, before temporarily freeing a group of 500 Italian POWs and demanding the surrender of a group of Australians occupying a nearby strongpoint. When the latter replied with a fusillade of small-arms fire the tanks moved on, and the crews of two Matilda IIs lurking behind a nearby rise ignored word of the interlopers on the assumption it was a case of poor vehicle identification. The Italians were only prevented from penetrating into the Australian rear by the arrival of three 2-Pounder Portees, commanded by a Corporal Pickett. All six tanks were knocked out in a brisk exchange of fire that also disabled Pickett's vehicle.[20] The bulk of the Italians were content to surrender however, and by midday on 3 January the prisoner count had reached 30,000. This came as a considerable surprise to O'Connor's staff, which was working on the assumption that there were only a maximum of 25,000 Italian troops in Bardia. The final bag was 40,000, along with several hundred motor vehicles, around 400 assorted artillery pieces and over a hundred tanks of various types. The POW tally did not include *Barba Elettrica* Bergonzoli, however; the Italian commander slipped out of the perimeter on the morning of 5 January with some of his staff and made his way to Tobruk on foot.

The fall of Bardia meant that the Western Desert Force, which had been officially rechristened 13th Corps on 1 January 1941, had totally destroyed eight Italian divisions in just twenty-seven days, capturing around 100,000 POWs and hundreds of guns and vehicles in the process. This was a highly impressive feat by any standard, and one rendered all the more laudable for being achieved on a personnel, equipment and logistic shoestring. The next target was the port of Tobruk, seventy-five miles farther up the coast, and O'Connor launched his move on the port town while the mopping up was still going on at Bardia. On the morning of 5 January the 7th Armoured Brigade was ordered to advance on the major Italian airfield and aircraft repair depot El Adem, sixty miles west of Bardia, where it would be ideally placed to both protect the advance on Tobruk and cut the port's lines of communication. The 19th Australian Brigade moved directly on Tobruk as soon as it had finished its post-battle reorganisation on the evening of 6 January, and arrived unopposed the next day. By 9 January it had been joined by the 4th Armoured Brigade and the 16th Australian Brigade and Tobruk was effectively surrounded.

The port of Tobruk dated back to at least the Classical period, with the establishment of a Greek agricultural settlement of Antipyrgos on the site in the 7th Century BC. The Greeks were followed by the Romans, who established a border fort for their province of Cyrenaica on the site in the 2nd Century BC, which subsequently became a way station on the coastal caravan route. It was used as a base by Barbary pirates, provided water for elements of Napoleon's fleet en route to Egypt in 1798 and the Italians were careful to maintain control of the port after occupying it in 1911 during their first foray into what was then Ottoman Turkish territory, and for good reason. Tobruk was the best deep water anchorage between the Egyptian port of Alexandria over 400 miles to the east, and Sfax in Tunisia over a thousand miles to the west. More importantly from a 1940 perspective, Tobruk offered the best port facilities along the 300 miles of coast between Benghazi on the Gulf of Sirte and the Egyptian frontier. This fact was highlighted by Churchill in a Directive to the CIGS on 6 January 1940, which pointed out that possession of Tobruk's port facilities would significantly reduce the strain and necessity for road transportation from Alexandria.[21]

Both port and town were and remain located on the eastern face of a bluff, where the Libyan coast begins to bulge upward into the Mediterranean toward Crete 200 miles to the north. The anchorage, a U-shaped inlet roughly two and a half miles deep, is protected by a headland to the north, with the town extending for a mile or so along the northern shore, and was overlooked from the east, south and west by a plateau of high ground that sloped away from the coast. The landward approaches to Tobruk were restricted to the east and west by a series of steep and relatively deep valleys that channelled winter rainwater down to the sea, with the Wadis Zeitun and Belgassem to the east and Wadi Sehel to the west. Access was improved by the completion of the *Via Balbia*, which ran almost all the way to Tobruk from Acroma to the west before dog-legging south and then west just short of the port, which was linked via a short spur running the last mile or two into the port.

By 1940 Tobruk had developed into a fairly large garrison town and naval port with a floating crane capable of handling several cargo vessels simultaneously, and a large naval fuel storage plant. Barrack accommodation was provided for 10,000 men and a number of pro-tected shelters and store rooms for ammunition, fuel and supplies for the garrison had been burrowed into the solid rock of the northern headland. The non-military part of the town was grouped around the *Piazza Vittorio Emmanuele*, and boasted a town hall, a bank, three hotels and a combined restaurant and cabaret. The Italian inhabitants' spiritual needs were catered for by the Catholic Church of St. Francis, a mosque ministered to the needs of the indigenous 'Moslem Italian' population, and secular education was provided by the *Scuola Benito Mussolini*. The town infrastructure included a hospital, a coal-fired power station and a refrigeration plant. Water came from a number of sub-artesian wells and a water distillation plant, augmented with large amounts of *Rocoaro* brand mineral water imported from Italy as an alternative to the brackish liquid from the wells. Finally, an imposing three-storey structure, variously described as either a Fascist Party or naval headquarters, was under construction on the headland overlooking the town.[22]

The Italians had also put a great deal of effort into constructing an extensive belt of fixed defences to protect Tobruk. Starting from an anchor point nine miles west of the port, the defences ran roughly south for nine miles or so and across the Ras El Medauar, the only major piece of high ground in the area, west for thirteen miles and then another seven miles north back to the sea. The defence line thus totalled around thirty miles in length, enclosing an area of approximately 135 square miles that sloped upward via three escarpments toward the coast, each between fifty and a hundred feet high. The perimeter included a large airfield at El Gubbi alongside the *Via Balbia* three miles or so south of the port, and two forts in the western half of the perimeter. Fort Solaro lay on the third escarpment five miles west of the port and a mile or so south of the *Via Balbia*, while Fort Pilastrino lay three miles to the south-west of Solaro on the second escarpment; the latter was also the hub of a network of unsurfaced tracks linking various points within the perimeter. In addition to the *Via Balbia* running west to Acroma and Benghazi and east to Bardia and Sollum, another road ran south to El Adem from a junction five miles south of Tobruk.

The defences themselves were similar in construction to those at Bardia. The outer boundary was marked by an anti-tank ditch measuring twenty feet wide and twelve feet deep protected by a line of booby-traps extending up to a hundred metres beyond the ditch in places; the latter were a new development, consisting of canisters filled with explosive and ball-bearings or other shrapnel detonated by trip-wire. Constructing the ditch was a considerable feat in its own right given the rocky nature of the terrain, and a four-mile section running east from the El Adem road was still unfinished when the Australians arrived at the perimeter, as was a longer section further west. Convenient wadis were co-opted in the northern stretches of the perimeter, the Wadi Sehel in the west and Wadi Zeitun in the east, and minefields were laid to cover areas where the nature of the ground made digging impractical or there were no natural features to obstruct an attacker. The mines were backed by a double apron of barbed wire, laid out in a zigzag pattern standing five feet high and laced with more booby-traps.

Behind this came the outer line of seventy-seven concrete defence posts which butted up to the wire and consisted of three circular weapon pits linked by communication trenches, covering an area approximately ninety metres in diameter. Each post had its own protective ditch and barbed wire entanglement, and was sited to cover the outer anti-tank ditch and provide mutual support for neighbouring posts. A second line of fifty-one posts lay roughly 500 metres to the rear of the first line, most staggered to cover the gaps in the first line and again sited to provide mutual support. The posts were numbered sequentially, divided into groups of around sixteen for administrative purposes, and were linked to one another and to rear HQs by field telephone. They were manned by the *Sirte* Division, reinforced with two infantry battalions, some tanks and around 200 artillery pieces, all commanded by *Generale di Corpo d'Armata* Enrico Petassi Manella.[23] Furthermore the Tobruk garrison was alert and willing to fight. The lead elements of the 19th Australian Brigade were greeted with brisk and accurate fire on reaching the Tobruk perimeter on 6 January, and the Italians also proved willing to sally forth from the security of their posts against Allied patrols detected probing their defences.

The 6th Australian Division was given responsibility for capturing Tobruk while the remainder of 13th Corps pressed further west into Cyrenaica, and Major-General Mackay took twelve days to plan and prepare his assault on the defences protecting the port. The shape of the Italian positions and their protective barbed wire were carefully pieced together from information gathered by the patrols that probed the perimeter after dark. Engineers accompanying such patrols surveyed the Italian minefields and determined the type of mines employed and the best method of disarming them. These techniques were then disseminated to the infantry formations slated to spearhead the attack, along with information on neutralising the equally deadly booby-traps the Italians had scattered in front of the anti-tank ditch and among the barbed wire entanglements. Full-scale mock-ups of the defences were constructed to allow the attackers to ascertain the best way of tackling the defences and what equipment was necessary, such as Bangalore Torpedoes improvised from lengths of three-inch steel water pipe.[24] The mock-ups were also used by the assault units to work out and practice their attack drills. Information on the nature of Italian deployment behind the outer perimeter defences was provided by the Westland Lysanders of RAF Nos. 6 and 208 Army Co-Operation Squadrons, flying at low level for extended periods in the face of stiff anti-aircraft fire. Particular attention was paid to Italian gun emplacements and distinguishing between the genuine article and pre-prepared dummy battery positions. By the time of the attack the location of every Italian gun had been plotted and passed on to the British artillery, with particular attention being paid to those capable of firing on the attack point. In addition, the Lysanders also photographed virtually every square yard of the Italian defences for conversion into maps for the attacking ground troops. However, assembling the photographic prints into maps was only completed two days before the attack was scheduled to begin, which then had to be rushed back to Cairo for printing; the finished items arrived back at the Tobruk perimeter barely in the nick of time.[25]

After assessing the reconnaissance information Mackay elected to attack at a point three miles east of the El Adem road, where the anti-tank ditch was only two feet deep and thus easily prepared for vehicle crossing. The Italians were to be distracted by the 17th Australian Brigade making demonstrations against the perimeter to the east, while the 7th Armoured Brigade's Support Group did the same farther west. The diversionary effort was to be augmented by RAF bombers and the RN's Inshore Squadron, as the group of vessels operating in support of O'Connor's force had been designated on 5 January. The new unit's commander, Captain H. Hickling RN was also tasked to act as naval liaison with senior army and RAF commanders, and maintained a mobile HQ for that purpose. Arrangements for the Inshore Squadron's involvement, which included a covering bombardment and clearing and restoring Tobruk's port facilities, were agreed at a planning meeting at 13th Corps HQ on 16 January and approved by Admiral Cunningham's HQ in Alexandria the following day.[26] The first stage of the attack was to be carried out by the 16th Australian Brigade, supported by eighteen Matilda IIs from the 7th RTR. The brigade's task was to penetrate the defensive perimeter, prepare the way for the tanks and then advance as far as the field artillery positions behind the second line of defensive posts before peeling off to the left and right and clearing the defences to open a gap in the defences eight miles in width. The 19th Australian Brigade would then move through the gap, aiming for the junction of the El Adem road and the *Via Balbia* running east to Bardia, five miles from the perimeter and midway to Tobruk proper. The 17th Australian Brigade could then be called upon to reinforce if necessary. The attack was scheduled to begin at dawn on Monday 20 January, 1940.

In the event, the attack was postponed for twenty-four hours because preparations were hampered by sandstorms and gale force winds. The Inshore Squadron was particularly badly affected by the latter. The Squadron's commander, Captain Hickling, was flying to his shore HQ at Sollum when his aircraft force landed in the desert, obliging Hickling and his companions to walk the twenty-five miles back to Mersa Matruh. The bombardment force, consisting of HM Monitor *Terror*, the destroyer *Voyager*, the gunboats *Aphis*, *Gnat* and *Ladybird* and the minesweeper HMS *Bagshot* were also delayed by weather that seriously damaged the *Aphis*, to the extent that the gunboat had to return to Port Said for repair. The remaining vessels successfully assembled off Bardia on 20 January and departed for their attack positions at sunset, with the *Bagshot* sweeping ahead of the *Terror*. A navigation light had been set up as a gunnery reference aid at Ras el Mehta, with another located with the 17th Australian Brigade troops to the Tobruk perimeter. Using these navigation lights as a substitute for ranging shots the *Terror* opened fire from a point fifteen miles north-west of Tobruk at 23:25 on 20 January. The monitor fired approximately 100 rounds of 15-inch ammunition at an Italian troop concentration in the area of Wadi Sehel, prompting a noisy but ineffective response from the Italian defensive guns. The *Bagshot* continued to sweep up to 5,000 yards from the shore, pulling back only when illuminated by Italian searchlights, and *Gnat* and *Ladybird* moved in and fired a twenty-two minute close range bombardment of their own an hour and thirty-five minutes after *Terror*.[27]

The Australian infantrymen who were to carry out the ground assault were ensconced in their forming up positions by the evening of 20 January. The greatcoats and respirators they had carried at Bardia had been discarded in the interests of mobility and the troops were arrayed in battle-order, carrying just weapons, ammunition and iron rations apart from assault stores and equipment. Blanket-lined sleeveless leather jerkins of First World War vintage had been issued in lieu of greatcoats, worn inside out to minimise reflection; a special batch of 11,500 jerkins had been rushed forward from Cairo at the beginning of the month.[28] Unit cooks provided a hot meal at dusk, augmented with a ration of GS rum in recognition of the bitter cold. The engineers were the first to move, creeping forward in the gloaming to carry out the hazardous task of disarming the Italian booby-traps along the attack frontage in the pre-moon darkness. The assault troops were served another hot meal at 02:30 on Tuesday 21 January and began to move up to the start line an hour later. Their movement was masked by Vickers Wellingtons from Nos. 37 and 38 Squadrons, which began bombing targets within the Tobruk perimeter at 03:00 and maintained a presence overhead until 06:00. Other bombers hit the bases used by their Italian opposite numbers at Benina and Berka to the west, to prevent them interfering with the attack. The bombing at Tobruk ceased at 05:30 and after ten minutes of silence the pre-attack barrage began dead on 05:40, pounding a section of the Italian perimeter 2,500 yards wide and 800 yards deep and paying particular attention to Italian gun positions. At the same time another barrage fell on the Italian positions either side of the point where the *Via Balbia* passed through the perimeter east to Bardia, where the 2/5th Battalion from the 17th Australian Brigade were to put in a diversionary attack.

The main attack was spearheaded by the 2/3rd Battalion, which left the start line as the barrage commenced accompanied by assault engineers carrying the improvised Bangalore Torpedoes to breach the Italian wire. At the same time the engineers who had been dealing with the Italian booby-traps turned their attention to clearing paths through the minefields for the attackers. The 2/3rd Battalion reached the anti-tank ditch at 05:55, losing several casualties to a booby-trap when a flanking platoon strayed beyond the cleared zone in the darkness. The infantry paused there while the barrage shifted to concentrate on the Italian positions facing the main attack point, posts Nos. 55, 56 and 57. The engineers used the time to finish lifting mines in the cleared lanes through the minefields and constructing crossing points over the two foot deep ditch by breaking down the soft sides and making ramps with the spoil. The barrage lifted at 06:05 and the engineers accompanying the 2/3rd Battalion pushed five Bangalore Torpedoes into the wire; four of the five detonated on cue from a red flare and the infantry swept forward through the resulting gaps in the pre-dawn darkness. By 06:40 they had overrun the three forward posts and two in the support line, opening a gap a thousand yards wide and deep in the Italian defensive line. Within five minutes the 16th Australian Brigade's other two battalions and the 7th RTR's eighteen Matilda IIs were moving through it in the grey dawn light, passing the first parties of Italian POWs moving in the opposite direction.

The 2/2nd Battalion, accompanied by nine Matildas, pushed straight on north through the 2/3rd Battalion lines, overrunning the three Italian artillery positions that were its primary objective and reaching its own stop line on the *Via Balbia* by 09:10. The Italian artillerymen were uncharacteristically passive, apparently due to the shock of the pre-attack bombardment and poor visibility due to the smoke and dust. The 2/3rd Battalion moved west along the defence line toward the El Adem road after linking up with a troop of three Matildas, clearing the Italian defensive posts as it went. The Battalion's advance finally came to a stop near post 45, on a ridge of high ground overlooking the road. With all three Matildas out of action due to battle damage or mechanical breakdown, the infantry contented themselves with sniping at Italian positions on the other side of the road, while the Battalion's right flank was secured by a mixed force made up of two companies from the 1st Northumberland Fusiliers, a troop of anti-tank guns from the 3rd RHA and three troops from the 6th Australian Cavalry Regiment mounted in Universal Carriers. The most spectacular progress was made by the east-moving 2/1st Battalion. Also accompanied by a troop of three Matildas, the Battalion had cleared or captured twenty-one Italian posts by 09:00, when it reached the *Via Balbia* just west of the point where it passed through the perimeter toward Bardia. However, this also involved by-passing an especially stubbornly defended position to be dealt with by the supporting 2/6th Battalion. post 26 also contained an Italian sector HQ, and its forty-six strong garrison held out against determined attacks for over three hours. They only surrendered after losing eleven dead and following a demonstration by the 2/6th Battalion's Pioneer Platoon that involved igniting a mixture of kerosene and crude oil that had been poured into a section of the post's communication trench.

All this was done to a backdrop of artillery concentrations on Italian gun positions and bombing by Blenheims from RAF Nos. 45, 55 and 113 Squadrons, while Gladiator and Hurricane fighters from RAAF No. 3 Squadron and RAF Nos. 73 and 274 Squadrons respectively protected the battlefield from interference by the *Regia Aeronautica*. The second phase of the attack began at 08:40, when Brigadier H.C.H Robertson's 19th Australian Brigade moved off from its start line to continue the advance north. The brigade moved through the 16th Brigade's lines in extended order behind a creeping barrage from seventy-eight guns that lifted 200 yards every two minutes with the 2/8th Battalion on the left, the 2/4th Battalion in the centre and the 2/11th Battalion on the right, supported by elements of the 6th Australian Cavalry Regiment. The latter were mounted in Universal Carriers and a number of Italian M13/40 tanks captured at Bardia; the ex-Italian vehicles were painted with large white kangaroos as a recognition measure, and their deployment marked the first use of tanks by Australian troops in the Second World War. The

2/11ᵗʰ Battalion reached its objective, one of the stepped escarpments just over a mile north of the east running section of the *Via Balbia*, without problems and without suffering a single casualty and on arrival tied in with the 16ᵗʰ Australian Brigades flank. The 2/4ᵗʰ Battalion in the centre made similarly good progress until its lead company was hit by flanking machine-gun fire near the junction between the *Via Balbia* and El Adem road that caused a number of casualties including the company commander.

The fire came from a complex of Italian positions in the path of the adjacent 2/8ᵗʰ Battalion, made up of bunkers and artillery emplacements protected with the usual minefields and booby-trapped barbed wire entanglements. It also boasted a new twist in the shape of a number of tanks, possibly CV33s, dug in as makeshift machine-gun posts complemented with fully mobile vehicles. The Battalion's advance thus degenerated into a jumble of small scale fights as its constituent companies broke down into platoons and tackled the nearest enemy strongpoint with rifles, bayonets and grenades. One stretch of seemingly unoccupied concrete trench proved to be the entrance to a deep concrete bunker, and the investigating Australians promptly captured *Generale di Divisione* Umberto Berberis, the garrison's senior artillery officer with all his HQ staff. The Italian positions were oriented to face an attack from the south rather than the east and were therefore unable to provide mutual support. This was especially fortunate as all but one of the 6ᵗʰ Australian Cavalry Regiment's M13/40s rapidly succumbed to mechanical breakdown, leaving the infantry reliant on the single exception and machine-gun and Boys anti-tank rifle armed Universal Carriers for fire support. This made dealing with the dug-in Italian tanks especially difficult, and many were cleared at close quarters with hand grenades or by firing Bren guns into vision slits. Even so, the Italians put up a dogged resistance that cost the attackers an unprecedented number of casualties and one company was down to only twenty-one men when the complex was finally cleared at around midday on 21 January.

Determined to keep up the momentum of the attack, Brigadier Robertson quickly assigned his battalions fresh objectives, utilising the fact that the morning's action had drawn the Brigade off its northerly axis to the west. The 2/8th Battalion was thus ordered to continue moving west along the escarpment to Fort Pilastrino, where the Italians were regrouping according to RAF reconnaissance. The 2/4th Battalion was to advance north-west and secure Fort Solaro, which Robertson was convinced housed the Tobruk garrison HQ, while the 2/11th Battalion was to protect the right flank of the advance by moving north and securing the ridge of high ground overlooking the south side of Tobruk harbour. The advance was resumed at 14:00 and once again the 2/8th Battalion bore the brunt of the action, almost immediately running into an Italian counter-attack involving several hundred infantry supported by around a dozen M13/40 tanks, seven of which got in amongst the Battalion's left hand company and overran its leading platoon. Initially the Australians had nothing to counter the tanks except a few marginally effective Boys anti-tank rifles but nonetheless succeeded in disabling some vehicles in a deadly game of hide and seek among the abandoned Italian trenches and fighting positions. The situation was saved by two Australian sergeants manhandling a captured Italian anti-tank gun into action and the arrival of two 2-Pounder Portees from the 3rd RHA. The surviving Italian tanks finally withdrew with the appearance of two of the 7th RTR's Matilda IIs from the south. The 2/8th Battalion then came under accurate Italian artillery fire, including airbursts from anti-aircraft guns, mortar and machine gun fire from Fort Pilastrino itself. Despite having been on the move since 04:30 and covering twenty miles in the process the Australians attacked the outlying defences and by dusk were within reach of the Fort proper. This proved to be little more than an abandoned barracks, which was secured by 21:30.

Because the 2/8th Battalion had soaked up the Italian counter-attack, Robertson's other two battalions made swifter progress. The 2/4th Battalion moved quickly across Tobruk airfield in spite of fire from its anti-aircraft defences, the accompanying 2-Pounder Portees belonging to the 3rd RHA driving off some Italian tanks that appeared briefly on the Battalion's left flank; these may have been survivors from the ill-fated counter-attack against the

2/8th Battalion. Be that as it may, the 2/4th Battalion reached Fort Solaro at dusk, in time to see six Italian trucks departing in the direction of Tobruk. The Fort was secured after a skirmish with a machine-gun post, and also proved to be a collection of abandoned barrack buildings with no sign of *Generale* Petassi Manella's garrison HQ. In the process of clearing the barracks the Battalion's lead company came under fire from four machine-gun posts covering the track running up the final escarpment to Tobruk. After eliminating the posts the Australians noticed they were also protecting some hitherto unnoticed cave entrances, which proved to be occupied by a large number of Italian troops who perhaps fortunately were inclined to surrender rather than fight. While his men were chivvying their prisoners out into the open, one of the Australian subalterns, a Lieutenant Copland, was approached by a well dressed Italian major. The major proved to be a member of the garrison HQ staff, and he led Lieutenant Copland to a deep chamber where the aged and tearful *Generale* Petassi Manella formally surrendered his sidearm after a stilted conversation in schoolboy French.

While all this was going on the 2/11th Battalion reached the ridge overlooking Tobruk harbour at 16:00, from where they could see demolitions being carried out in the town and harbour area. The water distillation plant located on the south side of the harbour was a priority objective, and as it lay only half a mile in front of the Battalion position, a platoon was despatched to prevent the Italians from sabotaging or destroying it. On finding the plant's defenders enjoying a meal the platoon made them prisoner and despatched them to the rear before finishing off the food themselves. By nightfall on 21 January the 6th Australian Division was in possession of almost half the area inside the Tobruk perimeter, and had taken around 8,000 POWs; the 2/8th Battalion alone had taken 1,600 prisoners in the final hour of fighting. For some unfortunates this proved to be literally a case of exchanging the frying pan for the fire; Italian aircraft mistakenly bombed the fires lit by a large concentration of POWs for warmth, killing between fifty and wounded 300.[29] On the line the night passed relatively quietly. Apart from one battalion taking advantage of the darkness to deal with two strongpoints, the Australians restricted their activity to routine patrolling and the sentries watching over the resting men were treated to a sound and light show as the Italians burned and blew up stores and installations. Out at sea the Australian destroyers *Stuart*, *Vampire* and *Voyager* were patrolling west of Tobruk in case the Italian cruiser *San Giorgio* attempted to break out of the port. They were recalled after reports that their quarry was aground and on fire in Tobruk harbour, and in the process ran into the Italian schooner *Diego* which was promptly sunk after the ten man crew had been taken off.[30] The 6th Australian Division staff spent the night gathering the information to permit Major-General Mackay to issue orders for finishing the job on 22 January. The 19th Australian Brigade was tasked to secure Tobruk town and harbour, the 17th Australian Brigade to mop up the remaining Italian outposts to the east, and the 16th Australian Brigade was ordered to regroup along the El Adem road before clearing the western side of the Tobruk perimeter and linking up with the 7th Armoured Division's Support Group which was blocking the road west to Gazala and Derna.

The advance was resumed at dawn on Wednesday 22 January, supported by Hurricanes and Lysanders from RAF No. 208 Army Co-operation Squadron, and it quickly became apparent that the fight had gone out of the Italian defenders. The commander of the *Sirte* Division, *Generale* Vincenzo Della Mura, surrendered to the 2/8th Battalion near Fort Pilastrino after sending forward an emissary just after first light under a makeshift white flag. The *Generale* initially refused to hand himself over to a Lieutenant Phelan on the grounds that he was insufficiently senior, but honour was satisfied by the arrival of a somewhat brusque Major Key, Phelan's company commander.[31] Elsewhere an Italian officer was persuaded to order other positions under his command to surrender via field telephone, and the commander of the 2/1st Battalion, Lieutenant-Colonel Kenneth Eather DSO, came upon an a 3,000 strong Italian unit waiting to surrender in parade order complete with packed baggage. The first Australians into Tobruk proper were two Universal Carriers from the

6th Australian Cavalry Regiment, commanded by Lieutenant E.C. Hennessy and Sergeant G.M. Mills, despatched to reconnoitre ahead of the 2/4th Battalion. Hennessy cleared a makeshift roadblock on the outskirts of the town with the enthusiastic assistance of some nearby Italians and reached the centre of the ton before being accosted by an immaculately turned out naval officer who informed him that the senior Italian naval commander, *Ammiraglio* Massimiliano Vietina, was waiting to surrender his command at his nearby HQ. Hennessy ascertained that this was indeed the case, informed Vietina that he could not accept his surrender or accompanying dress sword, and despatched Sergeant Mills to fetch Brigadier Robertson, who arrived accompanied by a small staff and a number of War Correspondents. The *Ammiraglio's* surrender was accepted after a brief negotiation regarding booby-traps and demolitions and six red flares fired from the roof of the naval HQ signalled the end of resistance in the town. An anonymous Australian reinforced the point by hoisting a slouch hat on the HQ's flagpole, and the last post on the perimeter surrendered to the 16th Australian Brigade at 15:45.[32]

The fight for Tobruk cost the 6th Australian Division forty-nine dead and 306 wounded, and units attached to the division suffered an additional forty-five casualties. Italian casualty figures are unclear, but the Australians captured 87 tanks, 208 assorted artillery pieces, approximately 200 motor vehicles and between 25,000 and 27,000 POWs; the difference may be the inclusion or otherwise of *Ammiraglio* Vietina's naval contingent, which numbered in the region of 2,000 men.[33] The sheer number of Italians was problematic in itself for the vastly outnumbered Australians, who could do little to prevent those inclined from slipping away to join their compatriots to the west. Among these hardier souls was *Generale* 'Electric Beard' Bergonzoli, the erstwhile commander of the Bardia garrison who had walked to Tobruk on 5 January. Supplies for the POWs were not a pressing problem, given that dumps and warehouses in and around Tobruk contained sufficient food to feed 25,000 men for two months. The problem was getting the food and water to the POWs – it took the 2/7th Battalion seven hours to issue all its captives with a basic ration, for example – and providing them with accommodation. Initially the Australians could do little apart from herd their charges into open wire compounds where messing and sanitary arrangements were minimal to non-existent. Discipline swiftly evaporated into mob rule exacerbated by a general abrogation of responsibility by Italian officers, and initial attempt to distribute water sparked a near riot. Order was restored with difficulty and open concrete water tanks were installed but it took the 2/2nd Battalion several days to provide every prisoner with a drinking vessel of some description, many of which were unofficially liberated from houses in Tobruk by the sympathetic Australians. One official observer rated the POW's sanitary arrangements as indescribable and was amazed that they did not result in a serious epidemic.[34] Reducing the scale of the problem by shipping prisoners east to Egypt took time, and by the end of February they were being replaced by a fresh influx from the fighting further west.

Returning Tobruk harbour to service was the key priority, and the necessary arrangements had been made following the planning meeting held at 13th Corps HQ five days before the attack on the port commenced. Commander W.P. Carne RN was appointed Clearance Officer Tobruk and placed in charge of a temporary naval clearance party tasked to survey and sweep the harbour and immediate approaches for mines, organise salvage and undertake immediate repairs to the piers. Once this was done the harbour was to be handed over to a permanent Naval Base Party commanded by Commander F.M. Smith RNR, who rejoiced in the title of Naval Officer in Charge, Tobruk. Smith was to be responsible for maintaining the harbour boom defence and swept access channel, berthing and refuelling arrangement and the establishment of a Port War Signal Station, a wireless telegraph station and defence arrangements. The aim was get the port open and operational as quickly as possible and handling a weekly throughput of 9,000 tons of stores, 2,500 tons of cased petrol, 1,500 tons of water, 500 personnel and 350 casualties for evacuation. The necessary sea transport stores, tugs and lighters were to be provided by the Principal Sea Transport Officer, Egypt at Alexandria once the state of existing facilities and equipment at Tobruk had been assessed.

Commander Carne arrived at Tobruk aboard the minesweeping trawler *May* at first light on Friday 24 January, accompanied by a small fleet of vessels assigned to clearing the harbour. These were the minesweeper *Bagshot*, the anti-submarine trawler *Southern Maid*, the long-line minesweepers *Arthur Cavanagh* and *Milford Countess*, and the Boom Defence Vessel *Magnet*. In addition the *Southern Maid* was carrying the commander of the Inshore Squadron, Captain H. Hickling RN, who was apparently still trying to reach his land HQ at Sollum after his aircraft had forced landed near Mersa Matruh on 19 January. Carne entered the harbour via the open boom and initially the signs were not promising. The naval fuel storage depot had been destroyed, the port's floating crane had been sunk and the 15,000 ton liner *Marco Polo* and freighter *Liguria* had been beached and burned on the southern shore of the harbour. The cruiser *San Giorgio* was awash and burning inside its anti-torpedo netting off the north side of the harbour. Damaged by RAF bombers on 11 June 1940, the cruiser had been fitted with additional automatic weapons and a protective layer of sandbags and became a key part of Tobruk's anti-aircraft defences; her crew had blown out the vessel's bottom with scuttling charges thirty minutes after the last perimeter strong-point surrendered on 22 January.

However, closer inspection showed that the damage was not as severe as it appeared, for apart from the sunken floating crane and fuel storage plant there had been no concerted attempt at sabotage, and there were no mines or booby-traps in the harbour or its infrastructure. The harbour boom was almost completely intact, there were numerous small vessels in serviceable condition and the piers were unharmed apart from some minor damage. The harbour side water distillation plant had already been secured by the 2/11ᵗʰ Battalion, but the port's sub-artesian well system was also functioning and intact, with a large quantity of water stored in cisterns, and a further 10,000 tons of *Rocoaro* brand mineral water was stored in a harbour side warehouse. The port's bulk petrol storage facility was undamaged, as was the coal-fired power station; 4,000 tons of coal for the latter was stockpiled next to an unloading pier linked to the power station by a light railway. A task that had been expected to take at least two weeks was thus completed in under six hours, and Commander Carne was able to declare Tobruk harbour safe for shipping at midday on 24 January. The first supply ship commenced unloading three days later, the port was capable of handling four vessels simultaneously by 29 January, and the monitor *Terror* arrived the following day to provide temporary air and sea defence.[35] In less than a week Tobruk was thus been transformed back into a fully functioning port, ready to play its part in supporting the ground forces pursuing the Italians westward.

5
COMPASS Concluded: The Conquest of Cyrenaica and the Battle of Beda Fomm 22 January 1941 – 9 February 1941

The capture of Tobruk by the 6th Australian Division on 22 January 1941 came after forty-five days of continuous operations by the recently renamed British 13th Corps. This had pushed the fighting front well over a hundred miles to the west, capturing Sidi Barrani, Sollum and Bardia and approximately Italian 100,000 POWs. There was to be no rest for the tired men and their equally tired machines of the former Western Desert Force however, as their success had attracted the attention of a Prime Minister and Whitehall hungry for good news to boost the morale of a British public suffering the depredations of the Blitz. Thus on Tuesday 21 January the Chiefs of Staff informed Lieutenant-General Wavell, Commander-in-Chief Middle East that the major port of Benghazi was to be secured forthwith, and Wavell duly passed the order on to Major-General O'Connor at 13th Corps HQ. On the surface this was a tall order, given that Benghazi lay over 200 miles deeper inside Libya, but in fact O'Connor was already organising what would prove to be the first stage of such an additional advance. The simple fact was that O'Connor could not afford to halt his advance, for to do so would hand the initiative to the Italians and risk the British force being pinned down and wiped out; paradoxically therefore, the safest course was to keep pushing forward to ensure the Italians remained off balance. To that end and before the assault on Tobruk had actually commenced, the 7th Armoured Brigade had been ordered to advance north-west along the hundred miles or so of coast road toward the port of Derna, and the 4th Armoured Brigade had been ordered to move west to Mechili, the hub of a network of camel tracks that crisscrossed the area.

Thus by the time the Tobruk garrison surrendered to the 6th Australian Division twenty-four hours later, the 7th Armoured Brigade was in contact with Italian forces at Martuba, eighty miles or so west of Tobruk and twenty miles short of Derna, and the 4th Armoured Brigade was approaching Mechili to the south. More importantly the ever-present eyes of the 11th Hussars, once again ranging far ahead of the fighting front, in conjunction with photo reconnaissance by RAF Nos. 6 and 208 Army Co-Operation Squadrons had provided O'Connor's HQ with a fairly complete picture of Italian strength and dispositions. Their reports showed that the once mighty 10° Armata that had invaded Egypt back in September 1940 had in practical terms been reduced to Generale di Corpo d'Armata Ferdinando Cona's 20° Corpo of three infantry divisions and an armoured brigade. The Pavia and Brescia Divisions were located at Cirene and Slonta respectively, well behind the fighting line. At the front Generale di Divisione Guido Della Bona's Sabratha Division, minus one of its two infantry regiments, was deployed in the north around Derna. The missing regiment was at Mechili, forty miles or so to the south, attached to the sole remaining Italian armoured unit in Libya, the Brigata Corazzata Speciale (Special Armoured Brigade) commanded by Generale di Divisione Valentino Babini. The latter was an all-arms formation established in November 1940 and consisted of the 3° and 5° Battaglione del Carro Armato equipped with fifty-seven M13/40 medium tanks, three battalions of Bersaglieri light infantry, a motorcycle battalion and an artillery regiment; another eighty-two M13/40s were being modified for desert service after unloading at Benghazi.[1] Both formations were spread along terrain features toward one another in a semblance of a coherent line, but with a twenty-five mile gap that precluded mutual support.

O'Connor decided to take advantage of their relative isolation and deal with them individually, concentrating initially on the *Brigata Corazzata Speciale* at Mechili. *Generale* Babini's formation was clearly the more dangerous foe, for an aggressive and well-handled armoured force of that size was capable of inflicting the same kind of damage on 13th Corps as the latter had meted out between Sidi Barrani and Tobruk. O'Connor's chosen focus required some reshuffling of forces however, and as was his custom he summoned Major-General Iven Mackay of the 6th Australian Division and the 7th Armoured Division's commander, Major-General Michael O'Moore Creagh, to a conference at 13th Corps HQ. Mackay agreed to release one of his formations to relieve the 7th Armoured Brigade as swiftly as possible, and by 24 January Brigadier H.C.H. Robertson's 19th Australian Brigade was pushing against the *Sabratha* Division's positions covering Derna. Creagh was assigned to carry out the attack on the Italian force at Mechili with a pincer movement involving the 4th and 7th Armoured Brigades. The former was to loop south around Mechili and seal off its avenues of retreat, while the latter attacked from the north straight off the march from Martuba. O'Connor also stressed the vital necessity of trapping and destroying the *Brigata Corazzata Speciale* and gave Creagh explicit orders to that effect.[2]

The 4th Armoured Brigade reached the vicinity of Mechili via a moonlight march on the night of 22–23 January, with ninety-five Light Tanks and around fifty A13 Cruiser Tanks. Brigadier Caunter's men arrived in some disarray due to a combination of inadequate maps and a dust storm. They also appear to have been ignorant of the presence of the *Brigata Corazzata Speciale*, and it took around twenty-four hours for them to reorganise, become aware of the Italians and attack them. By that time Babini had also been ordered to attack, in order to relieve the pressure on the *Sabratha* Division to the north.[3] As a result when the British began probing forward with Light Tanks on the morning of Friday 24 January they ran into a dozen M13/40 medium tanks, which knocked out several and drove the remainder back. By mid-morning the Italian score had risen to six Light Tanks and two A13 Cruisers for two M13/40s, but British reinforcements then caught the Italians on a skyline and knocked out seven M13/40s in quick succession. This prompted an Italian withdrawal toward Mechili at 13:30.

Despite O'Connor's explicit instructions to prevent Babini's force from escaping, which were reiterated when word of the clash reached 13th Corps HQ that night, the 4th Armoured Brigade did not respond with any special urgency. As one source succinctly puts it, the 4th Armoured '…spent those parts of the night when they had not been on guard soundly asleep.'[4] As a result the formation failed to occupy its blocking positions as ordered, and on the night of 26–27 January a patrol from A Squadron, 11th Hussars operating over twenty miles from Mechili reported a large column of Italian vehicles moving north-west. This was the *Brigata Corazzata Speciale*, as patrols from the 7th Armoured Brigade discovered on entering an abandoned Mechili on the morning of 27 January. A belated pursuit by the 4th Armoured Brigade was stymied by Italian rearguards, fuel shortage and heavy rain that turned the camel tracks into glutinous mud, and was abandoned on 29 January; RAF attacks on the Italians in the region of Slonta do not appear to have made much impression either. Although a variety of excuses were offered for the 4th Armoured Brigade's failure, the root of the problem appears to have once again been the reluctance of British armoured formations to operate at night, the same fault that had permitted the 2° MVSN Division to evade the 7th Armoured Brigade and withdraw intact from Sollum to Bardia in December 1940. This was certainly O'Connor's view; his report referred to the '…disinclination of [British] armoured forces to take any action at night', and pointed out that if '…the Italians were able to move their tanks away at night, I see no reason why we should not have been able to operate ours.'[5] Eye-witnesses noted that O'Connor was extremely angry over the 7th Armoured Division's collective failure, as well he might have been given the potentially dire consequences had Babini driven aggressively east instead of retiring to the north-east. Indeed, the he appears to have only been deterred from doing exactly that by *Maresciallo* Rodolfo Graziani's failure to provide the necessary reinforcements.

Be that as it may, events unfolded in a more satisfactory manner farther north, where the 19th Australian Brigade found itself fighting in rather different circumstances. Forty miles west of Tobruk the Libyan coast veers north-west and bulges sixty miles or so into the Mediterranean before curving back down into the Gulf of Sirte at Benghazi. The bulge contains not only a small mountain range rising to 2,500 feet and the town of Cyrene that gave the Italian province of Cyrenaica its name, but also the most fertile land in the area that led to the region being dubbed the Jebel Akhdar, or Green Mountains. The region was the focus of the effort to turn Libya into Italy's colonial 'Fourth Shore' and a receptacle for her surplus peasant population in the late 1930s. The first 20,000 settlers, dubbed the *ventimilli*, had arrived in October 1938 and by 1940 there were 110,000 Italian colonists in Libya. Around 90,000 were ensconced in the Jebel Akhdar, and a large portion of the remainder lived in the port city of Benghazi. In contrast to the barren, dusty and largely empty terrain to the west and south therefore, the Jebel Akhdar was verdant, cultivated with crops including cauliflowers, onions and radishes, boasted an additional major metalled road paralleling the *Via Balbia*, and was occupied by large numbers of Italian and indigenous civilians.

The verdant and cultivated aspects of the scenery were less apparent than they might have been to the Australians, for driving winter rain had turned the fields and unsurfaced roads into muddy quagmires. Despite this, the 19th Australian Brigade succeeded in pushing the forward elements of the 60th *Sabratha* Division back to its main defensive positions at Derna proper. The port sat at the sea end of the steeply sided, south running Wadi Derna which was 700 feet deep and up to a mile wide in places, and rose into a 400 foot high escarpment that dropped sharply to the sea at the north-eastern end. The

southern end of the Wadi was protected by well sited and camouflaged defensive positions and minefields, as the 6th Australian Cavalry
Regiment discovered when they tried to outflank the main Italian
position; Sergeant G. M. Mills, whose Universal Carrier was one of
the first two into Tobruk and who had chauffeured the commander
of the 19th Australian Brigade in to accept *Ammiraglio* Vietina's surrender on 22 January, was among the dead.[6] The Australians thus
spent several days locked in a slogging match along the line of the
Wadi Derna, in the course of which the 2/11th Battalion succeeded
in securing the escarpment overlooking Derna. The task was complicated yet further by a competent and spirited Italian defence,
with their artillery proving especially effective. On the evening of 29
January the Italians began a sustained bombardment of the Australian
forward positions that went on until daylight on 30 January. At first
the Australians assumed it was in preparation for an Italian counter-
attack, but none materialised and the shelling was too heavy to put
out reconnaissance patrols. When the bombardment finally ceased
after dawn a group of local Arabs approached the 2/11th Battalion's
positions overlooking Derna and informed the Australians that the
Italians had withdrawn during the night; hasty probes confirmed
this and found Derna empty apart from a rapidly increasing mob of
Arabs intent on looting anything that was not firmly nailed down.

Anxious to avoid giving the Italians an opportunity to reorganise,
the Australians pressed west from Derna on Friday 31 January, with
the 19th Australian Brigade following the line of the *Via Balbia* and
the 17th Australian Brigade on the left following the parallel metalled
road fifteen miles further inland; the advance was screened by the
11th Hussars ranging as far south as Chaulan, thirty miles from the
coast. While the Australians were regaining contact with the *Sabratha*
Division just six miles west of Derna, O'Connor was plotting his
next move with his Senior Staff Officer, Brigadier John Harding,
Major-General Creagh and Brigadier Eric Dorman-Smith, HQ
Middle East's adviser with 13th Corps. O'Connor was still looking
to destroy the Italian forces in Cyrenaica. The 6th Australian Division
was to provide the northern pincer of the attack, pushing the Italians

back through the defensible Jebel Akhdar toward Benghazi, while the southern pincer was provided by the 7th Armoured Division. Sending the latter directly west from Mechili toward Benghazi via El Abiar would involve routing the armoured formation through the southern edge of the Jebel Akhdar range, where it could easily be blocked. A better option was to move south-west to Msus and then west through Soluch to cut the *Via Balbia* near Ghemines on the coast, thirty miles south of Benghazi, and this was duly selected with a tentative start date of 10–12 February 1941.

There were two major obstacles to implementing this plan immediately. The British supply chain had been extended as far as Tmimi, over sixty miles west of Tobruk with supplies channelled through that port, and No. 14 Field Supply Depot was in the process of being established near Mechili. However it would still take an estimated twelve days to amass the ten day minimum supply of rations, fuel and water considered necessary. This enforced delay could be used to address the second problem, which was the state of the 7th Armoured Division's vehicles. All were suffering the effects of operating virtually non-stop for the better part of two months, and while most could be kept serviceable with field maintenance and repair the formation's surviving A13 Cruiser Tanks were overdue for major mechanical overhaul that could only be carried out at the Base Workshops at Abbassia in Egypt; by 27 January only fifty were in running condition. It was therefore decided to bolster the 4th Armoured Brigade by transferring the best Light and Cruiser Tanks from the 7th Armoured Brigade, and by giving O'Connor two Cruiser-equipped Regiments from the 2nd Armoured Division which had recently arrived in Egypt from the UK. The latter were slated to arrive at Mechili between 7 and 9 February 1940, giving a couple of days' grace before the move on Msus was scheduled to commence. Brigadier Dorman-Smith was despatched to Cairo to obtain Wavell's permission for the attack which was immediately forthcoming, not least because it allowed Wavell to reply to a 30 January enquiry from the Chiefs of Staff regarding progress toward seizing Benghazi; O'Connor's scheme permitted him to inform his superiors that the port would be in British hands by the end of February.

Dorman-Smith returned to Mechili bearing Wavell's blessing on 2 February, but once again plans had been overtaken by events. The previous day RAF reconnaissance had noted Italian activity moving west between Barce and Giovanni Berta; the 19th Australian Brigade occupied the latter, just over twenty miles west of Derna, later the same day while a patrol from the 11th Hussars found the Italians had also abandoned Chaulan. On 2 February the Australians found that the Italians had broken contact along their entire front, and O'Connor's growing suspicion that the Italian activity the previous day was the start of a general Italian withdrawal was confirmed. Graziani had been closely monitoring British activity from Benghazi and initially pinned his hopes on them emulating his own partial advance into Egypt in September 1940, and being satisfied with simply securing Tobruk. When it became clear that the British were intent on occupying Cyrenaica in its entirety, Graziani swiftly reached the conclusion that extended resistance in the Jebel Akhdar region would merely result in the remainder of the 10° *Armata* being cut off and destroyed for no practical gain. He therefore informed Mussolini of his intention to withdraw from Cyrenaica on 1 February and ordered *Generale d'Armata* Italo Gariboldi, commanding the 5° *Armata* from Tripoli, to organise a defence on the Gulf of Sirte. The commander of the 10° *Armata*, *Generale d'Armata* Guiseppe Tellera, was ordered to take command of all Italian forces in Cyrenaica with effect from 3 February and organise their withdrawal into Tripolitania to regroup. The latter order appears to have been delivered in person, given that Graziani left Benghazi by car the same day.

It rapidly became apparent that there was more to the Italian activity facing the Australians than tactical manoeuvring. Reconnaissance aircraft reported numerous large columns of Italian vehicles moving west in the Jebel Akhdar and south from Benghazi, sixty tanks were seen being loaded onto railway wagons at Barce and the lack of air activity indicated that the *Regia Aeronautica* was abandoning its forward airfields as well. The RAF attempted to interfere by bombing Barce with Blenheims, calling in Wellingtons from the Suez Canal region and Malta to hit targets near Tripoli, and allowing fighters to strafe the roads. Graziani himself commented on the damage inflicted by the latter, but the effort was handicapped by a severe shortage of serviceable aero engines that virtually grounded the RAF fighter component; by 3 January there were no spare Rolls Royce Merlin engines anywhere in Egypt while thirty-two awaited over-haul at RAF maintenance depots. Like the 7ᵗʰ Armoured Division, Air Commodore Collishaw's No.202 Group was also coming to the end of its maintenance tether, and could only provide O'Connor with a single mixed flight of Lysanders and Hurricanes from No. 208 Army Co-operation Squadron to support the armoured formation's impending advance to the coast via Msus.[7]

By 2 February it was clear that the twelve day period for 13ᵗʰ Corps to reinforce and build up supplies was fast evaporating, and that most if not all of the 10° *Armato* would be long gone if the 7ᵗʰ Armoured Division stuck to its scheduled start date of 10 or 12 February. A swift review of the supply situation showed that by 4 February there would be sufficient materiel in the system to permit the 7ᵗʰ Armoured Division a complete fill-up and resupply for all its vehicles, and to put together a convoy carrying two full resupplies of ammunition and sufficient rations, petrol and water to sustain the division's units for two days. O'Connor therefore gave the 7ᵗʰ Armoured Division a warning order on the evening of 2 February, followed on the morn-ing of 3 February by an order for Creagh to start the move to Msus no later than dawn on 4 February, while the 6ᵗʰ Australian Division was ordered to continue its advance on Benghazi from the north with all possible speed. This was a risky gambit, for it would virtually denude the supply system west of Tmimi, if not Tobruk, thus leav-ing little latitude for unforeseen circumstances. However, while the decision must have taken a good deal of nerve, the blunt fact was that O'Connor had little choice because he simply could not afford to allow a force the size of the 10° *Armato* to escape to fight another day intact, and especially while it included such a potentially potent force as the *Brigata Corazzata Speciale*. The soundness of O'Connor's reasoning and decision was confirmed by Wavell, who endorsed it when he flew out to Tmimi to check on progress on the effort to secure Benghazi on 4 February.

In the Jebel Akhdar the Australians were only too happy to comply with O'Connor's urging to maintain the pressure on the faltering Italians. Brigadier Robertson's 19th Australian Brigade had occupied the town of Cyrene on the *Via Balbia* by the evening of 3 February, while to the south the 17th Australian Brigade pushed on to Slonta, both formations pushing ahead in the face of mines, booby-traps, Italian rearguards, rain and mud. While the latter was moving largely on foot, the former had been fortunate enough to commandeer a number of Italian vehicles and the Italian fuel to run them. Thus elements of the 6th Australian Cavalry Regiment were being closely tailed by the 2/8th Battalion when they entered Barce on the afternoon 5 February. There was no resistance as the Italians had withdrawn but the officer in charge of the cavalry detachment narrowly escaped death when a large ammunition dump in the town centre exploded shortly after he had inspected it. The 19th Brigade's infantry entered the town at dusk and were initially employed in bringing the Arab looters under control, while Brigadier Robertson ordered the advance on Benghazi, by now only fifty miles or so to the south west, to recommence at first light on 6 February.

The 7th Armoured Division's advance began as ordered just after dawn on 4 February when A and C Squadrons of Lieutenant-Colonel John Combe's ubiquitous 11th Hussars and B Squadron, 1st King's Dragoon Guards (1st KDG) left Mechili for Msus. The 1st KDG were new to the Middle East, having only disembarked at Port Said on 30 December 1940, and were in the process of trading Light Tanks for South African-built Marmon-Herrington Armoured Cars at Tahag Camp in the Canal Zone when the order to detach a Squadron to the 11th Hussars was received; it arrived at Mechili on 2 February. The Hussars and Dragoons were moving into the unknown both figuratively and literally, for O'Connor had forbidden any ground reconnaissance of the approaches to Msus to avoid any possibility of alerting the Italians of his intentions. The route was cut by numerous wadis and littered with large rocks and the first fifty miles presented some of the worst going the 11ᵗʰ Hussars had experienced to that date, which was compounded by a sandstorm. The armoured cars had nonetheless covered the ninety-four miles to Msus by 15:00 and after scattering a small Italian garrison Lieutenant-Colonel Combe sent the two 11ᵗʰ Hussar Squadrons to scout a further thirty miles south-west to Antelat, a task that took them all night.

Behind Combe came the 4ᵗʰ Armoured Brigade with ninety-five Light Tanks and fifty assorted Cruiser Tanks, travelling at night on this occasion, followed by the portion of the 7ᵗʰ Armoured Support Group that had been able to move at short notice; when the movement order arrived the Support Group was stood-down for routine maintenance and Brigadier Gott had handed temporary command to Lieutenant-Colonel Callum Renton, CO of the 2ⁿᵈ Rifle Brigade, in readiness to depart on leave. This consisted of the 2ⁿᵈ Rifle Brigade, C Battery 4ᵗʰ RHA with their 25-Pounders and some 2-Pounder Portees drawn from either the 3ʳᵈ or 106ᵗʰ RHA. The remainder of the Support Group were to follow at best speed. By dawn on 5 February all of these units were concentrated just east of Msus with 7ᵗʰ Armoured Division HQ. Acutely aware of O'Connor's exhortations for speed at all costs and the time the difficult going had cost, Major-General Creagh then divided his force. As wheeled vehicles were still capable of moving faster than tracks despite the poor going, he placed the 1ˢᵗ KDG Squadron and the Support Group's lead element under Lieutenant-Colonel Combe, ordering him to pick up the 11ᵗʰ Hussars at Antelat and then move with all possible speed directly west via Sidi Saleh and block the *Via Balbia*. The 4ᵗʰ Armoured Brigade would follow at best speed, and the remainder of the Support Group were despatched to attack the Italian fort at Sceleidima, twenty-five miles west of Mechili.

Patrols from the 11ᵗʰ Hussars reached the *Via Balbia* at a point eight miles due west of Sidi Saleh at 12:40 and reported light two-way traffic, indicating that the Italian withdrawal was not yet underway. By just after 14:00 the rest of Combeforce had arrived and set up its blocking position with A Company, 2ⁿᵈ Rifle Brigade straddling the road facing north, with the 1ˢᵗ KDG deployed just to the east to protect the inland flank. The left flank, running down to the sea was left open at this point, possibly due to time constraints. The 4th RHA set up its 25-Pounders to the rear, protected by the rest of the 2nd Rifle Brigade. According to one account an observation post was also established on a small hillock overlooking the east side of the road nicknamed 'The Pimple', seven miles farther north, presumably by the 11th Hussars.[8] The blocking force was barely in position when an Italian convoy carrying the 10° *Bersaglieri* Regiment approached from the north, and the thirty-six hour Battle of Beda Fomm was underway. The crews of some escorting tanks abandoned their vehicles on coming under fire from the RHA anti-tank guns and 1st KDG armoured cars, and the convoy degenerated into chaos as the Rifle Brigade company shot up the stalled vehicles. Nonetheless some *Bersaglieri* did attempt to attack the Rifle Brigade position, but were cut down by the riflemen's well directed small-arms fire. Another convoy of thirty vehicles carrying around 200 troops rolled into the ambush ten minutes later and the newcomers, apparently overawed by the destruction meted out to their predecessors, swiftly surrendered bringing the first clash to an end. The POWs were gathered temporarily near the 4th RHA's gun positions, but as the gunners lacked the necessary facilities or indeed the manpower to guard them they were shooed off in the general direction of Antelat.

The 2nd Rifle Brigade's commander appears to have used the lull to address the open left flank by redeploying his A and Support Companies across the two mile gap between A Company and the sea. This may have been instructions from Lieutenant-Colonel Combe, given that the latter contacted 4th Armoured Brigade by radio at around 16:30 and requested another force be despatched to cut the *Via Balbia* further north; Brigadier Caunter responded by promptly despatching a force of Light Tanks from the 7th Hussars with six A13 Cruiser Tanks from the 2nd RTR. The redeployment and request again proved to be in the nick of time, for at around 17:00 another Italian convoy arrived in Combeforce's kill zone, and according to a contemporary account this one was approximately ten miles long.[9] The 4th RHA immediately brought down fire on the head of the column but this the Italian infantry debussed and formed up to attack the roadblock while their artillery began deploying either side of the road to provide support. Before long the pressure was starting to build against the badly outnumbered 2nd Rifle Brigade, but the situation was reversed by the arrival of the force despatched by Caunter near the rear end of the Italian column at around 18:00, after a breakneck, cross-country dash from Antelat. The Light Tanks and A13 Cruisers shot up and burned a number of Italian vehicles before moving south along the column and falling on the deployed Italian guns from the rear. The sudden and unexpected appearance of rampaging British tanks from what the Italians considered their rear caused some understandable consternation, and prompted a large number of surrenders; before long the 4th RHA and C Company 2nd Rifle Brigade were again responsible for around 5,000 POWs gathered near the formers gun line.[10]

When yet another Italian column appeared in the gathering dusk, the British went over to the attack. A patrol from the 2nd Rifle Brigade worked its way up the west side of the road, supported by two of the RHA 2-Pounder Portees, while the 7th Hussars' and 2nd RTR's tanks cruised up the east side, crushing guns and equipment with their tracks and machine-gunning trucks and infantry with impunity. The fighting went on into the night, with the inevitable confusion of fighting in the darkness being compounded by heavy rain. At one point an A13 Cruiser was despatched to spike some abandoned Italian guns and came upon the black shapes of two M13/40 medium tanks at the end of a row of trucks. After cautiously approaching to within fifty feet with no reaction, the officer commanding the Cruiser sent his radio operator forward to 'get the crews out' after refusing to let his eager gunner perforate the enemy vehicles with his 2-Pounder, on the grounds that the muzzle flash would give away the tank's position. The operator rounded up seven Italian crewmen by the simple expedient of tapping on the M13/40s side hatches with his pistol, and began to escort them back down the side of the convoy trailed by his comrades in their Cruiser tank. Part-way back a truck suddenly turned on its headlights, bathing the POWs, the pistol wielding radio operator and the Cruiser tank in white light, and the gunner took the opportunity to extinguish the lights by shooting the truck's cab to pieces with his co-axial Besa machine-gun. The party reached the safety of the Combeforce perimeter without further incident, and the radio operator was subsequently awarded the Distinguished Conduct Medal.[11]

Meanwhile Brigadier Caunter and the 4th Armoured Brigade had reached Antelat at 16:30. After sending off the detachment from the 7th Hussars and 2nd RTR to Lieutenant-Colonel Combe, Caunter moved on the latter's advice north-west through the night, reaching the *Via Balbia* via Beda Fomm before dawn with forty-five Light Tanks and between twenty-two and twenty-nine Cruisers. The move and remaining mobile thereafter was only possible because the 4th Armoured Brigade's tanks had commandeered all the fuel for Brigade's accompanying artillery as well as fuel supplies intended for Combeforce, leaving the latter virtually immobile; even then Caunter was obliged to siphon the petrol from every Italian vehicle they came across. Thanks to all this by first light on 6 February the 2nd RTR had nineteen Cruisers deployed behind a ridge a mile or so east of the road and seven miles north of Combe's roadblock; the sheltering feature was nicknamed 'the Mosque', after a white stone tomb constructed on it crest. Caunter had despatched the 3rd and 7th Hussars north, reinforced with a few of the 2nd RTR's Cruisers to give them a chance of tackling any Italian M13/40s they might run across, to seek out the tail-end of the Italian column. Daylight exposed the futility of this mission however, for the road was jammed three abreast with more vehicles spread out along both sides for as far north as the British tank crewmen's eyes could see. It was thus immediately clear to Caunter that he had to attack the Italian horde stretched out along the road immediately, in order to prevent it sweeping away Combeforce by sheer weight of numbers, and he chose to turn the Pimple into a makeshift choke-point.

Italian attempts to break through the roadblock began at first light on 6 February, with *Bersaglieri* light infantry attacking in the grey rain supported by a handful of CV33 Light Tanks and fire from a number of guns deployed straight out of the column. Combe's men responded by calling down fire from the 4th RHA's 25-Pounders. The first shells fell squarely on the phalanx of trucks jockeying forward just behind the attackers, subsequent salvos effectively suppressed the sparse Italian artillery support by destroying a gun with a direct hit, and the Bersaglieri were cut down or driven to ground by accurate small-arms fire from the Rifle Brigade. When a second attempt met with the same response, the Italians drew back to regroup. Responsibility for breaking through what the Italians erroneously imagined to be a formidable British roadblock was devolved during the night of 5–6 February to serial escapee *Generale* Bergonzoli. The most appropriate tool for the job would have been the *Brigata Corazzata Speciale*, but Babini's force was fully occupied acting as a mobile rearguard to the north, protecting the tail end of the retreat from the advancing 6th Australian Division. Bergonzoli was therefore obliged to issue a typically convoluted Italian order for tanks caught up in the traffic jam to make their way to the head of the column while remaining prepared to concentrate if necessary, and to investigate the possibility of bypassing the roadblock to the east in the process.[12]

The first response to Bergonzoli's order came from a group of ten M13/40s that eased out of the traffic jam two miles north of the Pimple and advanced on the feature at around 07:30. When they closed to within 600 yards a group of the 2nd RTR's Cruisers on the reverse slope reduced eight of the Italian vehicles to burning wrecks with a volley of 2-Pounder armour piercing shot, and disabled the two survivors with flanking shots as they turned away. The RTR tanks then pulled back quickly to Mosque Ridge and repeated the trick against another group of seven M13/40s that had swung out further east of the road before turning their attention to a portion of the Italian column that had succeeded in moving past the Pimple during the tank fight. Another group of Cruisers ambushed an unwary group of M13/40s motoring parallel with the ridge further north before reoccupying the Pimple, where they came under uncomfortably accurate Italian artillery fire that hit two of their number. By mid-morning the strain was mounting on the tanks holding the Pimple, and Brigadier Caunter ordered the 3rd and 7th Hussars to intensify their attacks to the north in an attempt to relieve the pressure. While so engaged the Hussars were approached by yet another large convoy from the north led by an ex-11th Hussars Rolls Royce armoured car. The Hussars turned their attention to the newcomers, ramming the Rolls Royce out of action in the process, but were soon obliged to retire by the arrival of over twenty M13/40 tanks from the north-east. These were the vanguard of the garrison Sceleidima, which had been ordered to join the main Italian force on the coast road by Bergonzoli following an attack on their fort; the attack was carried out by the main body of the Support Group, which had been despatched there as the 4th Armoured Brigade commenced its march to Beda Fomm in the evening of the previous day.

By midday on 6 February the 4th Armoured Brigade's situation was critical, in part because the relentless Italian pressure had reduced the 2nd RTR to just fifteen running Cruiser tanks.[13] More seriously, the latter's stock of 2-Pounder ammunition was reaching exhaustion; the gunner who had shot up the Italian truck some hours earlier had 'a good fall out' with his loader when the latter informed him that they were down to the last two of their 112 rounds in the midst of a duel with an oncoming M13/40.[14] The hurried transfer of ammunition from unit HQ tanks to vehicles on the line provided only momentary relief, and with an estimated fifty M13/40s manoeuvring east of the road to attack on the Pimple the 2nd RTR had little option but to withdraw to Mosque Ridge. A resupply column carrying ammunition and fuel arrived at 13:00 but accessing it was problematic in itself; the 3rd and 7th Hussars' Light Tanks were obliged to keep the Italians occupied by mounting spoiling attacks against threatening Italian concentrations to conceal the removal of the Cruisers to replenish, in conjunction with artillery fire from the RHA. These forays were extremely hazardous in their own right. On one occasion a group of the 7th Hussars' Light Tanks accompanied by a single Cruiser sallied forth to attack part of the Italian column but pulled up short on spotting a number of previously unnoticed M13/40s on the far side of the road. At that point the Cruiser snapped a track, and all concerned spent the twenty-five minutes it took the crew to make running repairs maintaining a delicate balance between kicking up enough movement dust to conceal the Cruiser's plight without attracting unwelcome attention. The ploy worked and the party was able to retire to safety. Neither was the replenishment carried out without mishap; three Cruisers suffered mechanical breakdowns while moving to the resupply vehicles, one with a seized engine. This reduced the 2nd RTR's crucial Cruiser strength to twelve.

The 4th Armoured Brigade's situation at Pimple may have been critical, but it had at least succeeded in relieving the pressure on Combeforce at their roadblock. Italian activity had tailed off markedly after the two attacks just after dawn, and for a brief period the tired riflemen and gunners were left awaiting a renewal of the Italian onslaught. In a gesture that begged comparison with Noël Coward's 1932 ditty 'Mad Dogs and Englishmen' the OC of the 2nd Rifle Brigade's HQ Company decided it would be a good idea to erect the Battalion Officer's Mess tent, which then became an aiming mark for Italian artillery; the opinion of the riflemen tasked to carry this piece of military eccentricity is unknown. By early afternoon Italian activity began to increase, with the defenders being engaged from the expanding field of wreckage to their front and increasing numbers of Italian fugitives were filtering past the roadblock via the dunes lining the seashore. The pressure mounted inexorably as time went on, again raising the very real possibility of the road block simply being swept away by the sheer weight pressing forward against it. The catalyst for this lay to the north around the Pimple, now serving as an Italian artillery position, where by 15:00 the battle was reaching its tipping point. While the 7th Hussars had finally located and attacked the tail of the vast Italian column, the 3rd Hussars' Light Tanks had run into a large group of the superior M13/40s advancing roughly mid-way along the column and Brigadier Caunter had no option but to tell them to prevent the Italian vehicles from breaking out to the east at all costs. The 2nd RTR had been rebuffed in an attempt to retake the Pimple by crossing the choked *Via Balbia* and attacking it from the west. With Italian guns emplaced on the Pimple, every British movement beyond Mosque Ridge was exposed to increasingly effective artillery fire, and the Italian tanks were slowly but surely forcing the 3rd Hussars.

Two developments prevented the situation slipping beyond British control. First, the 4th RHA battery supporting the 4th Armoured Brigade managed to establish clear communications with a replacement forward observer element, the original having been knocked out earlier in the battle. This permitted the gunners to smother the Pimple with an accurate concentration of 25-Pounder fire that totally destroyed the Italian guns set up on the hillock, and permitted four nearby Cruiser Tanks from the 2nd RTR to hastily reoccupy it. The second was the arrival of eleven more Cruiser Tanks from the 1st RTR, the lead element of the 7th Armoured Brigade. The brigade was the 7th Armoured Division's last armoured reserve, and Brigadier Caunter had repeatedly requested its deployment over the past few hours. Major-General Creagh had released the Brigade to move on 5 February but its night march from Msus to Antelat was delayed by a shortage of petrol, likely resulting from the stripping of the supply system to allow the initial move to the coast by Combeforce and the 4th Armoured Brigade. Matters were complicated yet further by communication difficulties; Caunter had been unable to get acknowledgement for his requests and the 7th Armoured Brigade's commander, Brigadier Hugh Russell, was out of contact with his command when he arrived at Caunter's HQ on the afternoon of 6 February. In the event the 7th Armoured Brigade was able to refuel at Antelat and then made a frenetic cross-country march toward the sound of the guns, arriving just north of the Pimple just in time for the 1st RTR's Cruisers to fall upon the M13/40s threatening to overrun the 3rd Hussars and drive them back through the traffic jam to the west side of the road.

The arrival of the 7th Armoured Brigade provided a respite but the overall situation remained perilous, for the Italians still outnumbered their attackers manifold and more importantly, they were still determined to escape from the trap. Thus the M13/40s driven back by the 1st RTR regrouped before moving south along the western side of the road and attacked the Pimple from there, destroying one of the 2nd RTR's Cruisers in place and driving the other three off the hillock and back to Mosque Ridge, covered by fire from the 4th RHA. By this time the British tanks were once again running low on ammunition and fuel, and were unable to prevent a number of Italian vehicles including tanks pushing south past the Pimple. With the onset of darkness and arrival of another supply column Brigadier Caunter pulled the 4th Armoured Brigade and its attached units back into a night laager near the mosque, where the tired crews started the night by replenishing their vehicles' ammunition racks and fuel tanks. Next came repairs and routine maintenance, and only then was there time for a hurried meal and sleep. The day's fighting had cost Caunter's units a total of nine tanks destroyed by enemy action, with a further eight put out of action by other causes and forty-eight tanks had sustained varying degrees of damage but were still serviceable. By nightfall on 6 January the 4th Armoured Brigade's undamaged strength amounted to thirty-nine tanks, including the newly arrived 1st RTR's eleven Cruiser Tanks.

While all this was going on the 6th Australian Division had been pushing hard to close the trap behind the retreating Italians. The advance was resumed from Barce at first light on 6 February, and while there was resistance from the occasional Italian rearguard the most serious delay came from the incessant heavy rain and demolitions on the route; as a war correspondent accompanying the Australians put it, the advance 'developed into a contest between the [Australian] engineers and the squads of Italian minelayers and dynamiters.'[15] The town of El Abiar, midway between Barce and Benghazi, was occupied without a fight, and a forward patrol from the 6th Australian Cavalry Regiment entered Benghazi in the evening to an enthusiastic welcome from the Arab, Greek and Jewish residents of the city, augmented by a large number of Italian deserters in civilian clothes. The 19th Australian Brigade were still in the forefront of the 6th Division's advance, and Brigadier Robertson issued two orders after arriving at the outskirts of Benghazi. The first, presumably prompted by the widespread looting witnessed in the advance across the Jebel Akhdar, was addressed to the mayor of Benghazi and informed him that the Australians would be formally entering the city in the morning and that the Italian authorities were fully responsible for the maintenance of order until then. The second was to the commander of the 2/8th Battalion, Lieutenant-Colonel John Mitchell DSO & Bar. Mitchell was ordered to gather a Squadron from the 6th Australian Cavalry Regiment and detachments of armoured cars, artillery and anti-tank guns to his battalion and push on toward Ghemines as quickly as possible.

While the 2/8th Battalion were gathering their attachments just north of Benghazi and the 4th Armoured Brigade were replenishing behind Mosque Ridge, Combeforce was beating off a series of attacks that went on throughout the night. The first, by the Italians who had slipped past the Pimple at dusk, began at around 21:00 with a three-pronged assault on the 2nd Rifle Brigade's positions supported by several M13/40 tanks. The attackers ran into a hastily laid minefield and lost four tanks to mines and fire from the covering 2-Pounder Portees, but the latter were put out of action in the subsequent fighting; while the portee was an effective method of providing guns with mobility, it provided little to no protection for the gun crew against small-arms fire or shrapnel. Four more M13/40s and a number of trucks succeeded in breaking through the Rifle Brigade's line and disappeared into the darkness, leaving 500 of their compatriots to surrender. The defenders swiftly repaired and extended their minefield by 22:00, when more RHA anti-tank guns arrived to bolster the line, and the next attack netted 150 prisoners after the attacker's lead vehicle ran onto the newly laid mines. At midnight another Italian column that made the mistake of moving across the 2nd Rifle Brigade's frontage was badly shot up, and two M13/40s that tried to sneak past the roadblock by moving along the waterline at 04:00 were stopped by a senior NCO and a Rifleman who closed up to the vehicles and fired their rifles through the vision slits; the tank crews promptly bailed out and were captured.

The Italians launched their final attempt to break through the roadblock early on the morning of 7 February. It began at 06:30 with a heavy artillery barrage on the roadblock, followed by thirty M13/40 tanks and two tightly packed columns of trucks barrelling straight down the *Via Balbia*. The tanks passed straight through the perimeter despite the efforts of the RHA 2-Pounders, and when the 2nd Rifle Brigade's concentrated small-arms fire brought the transport columns to a stop the defence degenerated into a myriad of individual fights for platoon locations or even single slit trenches in a swirling, barely penetrable cloud of dust and smoke; the confusion was such that the commander of the supporting battery from the 4th RHA Gunners requested and received permission to engage targets inside the Rifle Brigade positions. The most serious threat came from the tanks, which continued to push deeper into the Combeforce perimeter despite the best efforts of the eleven RHA anti-tank guns, which dropped out of action as the unprotected portee crews again fell victim to Italian fire. After witnessing the demise of his last portee crew the RHA commander, a Major Burton, put together a scratch crew that included his batman and a cook and re-manned the vehicle. After driving the portee into cover to check that the 2-Pounder was undamaged, Burton sallied forth in the gunner's seat and engaged five M13/40s that were still advancing into the very heart of the British position. In an exemplary demonstration of gunnery skill he knocked out all five in quick succession, the last coming to a halt only yards from the Rifle Brigade Officer's Mess tent.

The destruction of the armour effectively broke the Italian assault, and the Rifle Brigade began to gain the upper hand in the infantry fight and force the attackers back out of their positions. Large numbers of Italians took the option to surrender rather than retire, and it soon became apparent that the fight had gone out of the Italians overall. The 4th Armoured Brigade's tanks rolled forward over Mosque Ridge near the Pimple to renew their attack on the stalled column while the fight at the roadblock was still underway. At first the tank crewmen were suspicious of the lack of reaction to their appearance, but as they drew closer the stalled column became a mass of white flags and hundreds of Italians came forward to surrender. Lieutenant-Colonel Mitchell's 2/8th Battalion received the same reception as it closed on the tail of the Italian column after an all night march via Ghemines and El Magrun, fifteen miles north of the Pimple. His battalion was only two hours ahead of the remainder of the 19th Australian Brigade, Brigadier Robertson having been ordered to move south as quickly as possible by O'Connor during the night; the mayor of Benghazi would have to wait until 9 February for the official Australian move into his city. That this was an official surrender rather than individuals and groups taking matters into their own hands became apparent when the 10° *Armata* Chief of Staff was escorted to Brigadier Caunter's HQ to discuss terms; *Generale* Tellera had been wounded commanding a tank in the final attack on the Combeforce roadblock, and died later that day.[16]

The Italian surrender at what became known as the Battle of Beda Fomm cost the Italians 112 assorted tanks, many knocked out or burned but some abandoned or surrendered in full working order, along with 1,500 serviceable wheeled vehicles, 216 assorted artillery pieces and an immense amount of kit and equipment ranging from wine and chocolate to clothing, motorcycles, fitters tools and medical equipment.[17] The wreckage and detritus of battle stretched for fifteen tightly packed miles along the *Via Balbia*, made up of burned or abandoned vehicles, spiked guns, abandoned uniforms and weapons and countless unburied bodies. Much of the usable equipment was swiftly earmarked for reuse by the resource-starved 13th Corps, and according to one account O'Connor ordered Brigadier Gott to set up a block with his Support Group to prevent the 19th Australian Brigade from looting its way along the whole length of the column.[18] It also yielded 25,000 prisoners, which took their British and Australian captors three days to round up and organise, among them at least seven general officers of various ranks including *Generale* Bergonzoli; *Barba Elettrica's* luck had finally run out in more ways that one. Reporting himself unwell at the time of his surrender, he was subsequently found to be suffering from appendicitis and was flown to hospital in Cairo for treatment.

Once again the Italian performance in the battle had been marked by their characteristic and peculiar mixture of reckless courage and military ineptitude, with the latter effectively nullifying the former. With the exception of the final attack that began at 06:30 on 7 February, all the attacks on the Combeforce roadblock were made without any attempt to ascertain the shape, extent or strength of the British position. In the circumstances a modicum of reconnaissance might well have allowed the Italians to organise and co-ordinate their efforts, overcome the roadblock and permitted the 10° *Armata* to escape from the flimsy trap the British had erected to contain it. As it was, the attackers preferred to repeatedly hurl themselves blindly at an undefined enemy with predictable results, and the Italians surrendered with the firm conviction that they had been grossly outnumbered whereas the precise opposite was actually the case. It is therefore difficult to escape the suspicion that Italian actions were prompted more by the dictates of face-saving machismo than military good sense. This is supported by a remark *Generale* Bergonzoli made to the war correspondent Alan Moorehead at the farmhouse near Soluch where the senior Italian officers were held after their surrender: 'You were here too soon, that is all. But we gave battle at once...'[19]

Be that as it may, the British victory at Beda Fomm marked the end of Operation COMPASS, and Major-General O'Connor marked the fact with a signal to Lieutenant-General Wavell at HQ Middle East on the morning of 7 February 1940 that began with the hunting term 'fox killed in the open'. The Operation had lasted for sixty-one days, during which the Western Desert Force/13th Corps had advanced approximately 500 miles from Mersa Matruh to Beda Fomm, successfully conducted two major sieges and totally destroyed the Italian 10° *Armata*, capturing 180 medium and 300 light tanks, 1,300 artillery pieces, countless wheeled vehicles and up to 133,295 prisoners.[20] In addition, the *Regia Aeronautica* had lost fifty-eight aircraft in combat, while 1,100 damaged machines were captured on overrun airfields along with ninety-one undamaged aircraft. RAF aircraft losses from all causes during the operation totalled eleven fighters, fifteen bombers, and under sixty-eight casualties.[21] It cost O'Connor's men 500 dead, 1,373 wounded and fifty-five missing believed killed;[22] the material cost was equally heavy. Only twenty per cent of the vehicles with which the Western Desert Force had begun Operation COMPASS remained serviceable to any degree, almost all of those were subsequently written off by base workshops, and the only vehicles that had not exceeded their projected service mileage were the newly arrived 1st KDG's Marmon Herrington armoured cars. The remaining eighty per cent of the vehicles had been destroyed by enemy action, the terrain or were simply worn-out and abandoned; the same applied to weapons, equipment and uniforms. The 13th Corps was thus in need of not just reinforcement, rest and recuperation, but replacement of just about everything from what the troops stood up in onward.

Whatever their physical and material condition, the men of the Western Desert Force had nonetheless won a remarkable victory by any standard, and especially so considering the disparity between the two forces involved from start to finish. They were not to be allowed to rest on their laurels however, for forces were shifting in the background that would shortly alter the situation out of all recognition.

6

Tobruk Menaced: The Arrival of the *Deutsches Afrikakorps* in Libya and the British Retreat from Cyrenaica
7 February 1941 – 8 April 1941

Decisive as it was, the destruction of the Italian 10° *Armata* did not mark the end of hostilities in Cyrenaica, and Major-General O'Connor ordered Lieutenant-Colonel Combe's 11th Hussars to scout to the south for signs of the Italians regrouping almost before the fighting at Beda Fomm was over. They were reinforced shortly afterwards by the 7th Armoured Division's Support Group, while the remainder of Major-General Creagh's 7th Armoured Division set about clearing the battlefield and sorting the booty. Major-General Mackay's 6th Australian Division, meanwhile, were sent back north to oversee putting the port of Benghazi back into operation as quickly as possible. The 11th Hussars soon made contact with the garrison at Agedabia thirty miles south of Beda Fomm in the afternoon of 7 February, but the Italians, who included personnel from a light tank unit that had evaded the Combeforce roadblock only to become bogged in a salt marsh, surrendered without a fight. After regrouping the Hussars continued south-west along the Gulf of Sirte in

freezing rain, and by nightfall on 8 February 1940 they had covered the eighty miles to the Italian fort at El Agheila, on the border
between the Cyrenaica and Tripolitania. Patrols despatched a further
ten miles or so into the latter failed to locate any enemy activity,
organised or otherwise.

A few incidents lightened the atmosphere at this time. The *Colonello*
commanding the bogged Italian light tank unit not only spoke flu-
ent English, but enquired of his captors regarding pre-war friends
serving with the 12th Lancers. On arrival at El Agheila in the pour-
ing rain, the Hussars enthusiastically took advantage of the deserted
Italian barracks to spend an unaccustomed night under a solid roof.
Their plans were interrupted by the arrival of a Libyan senior NCO
and his orderly on horseback, who informed Lieutenant-Colonel
Combe that a further 400 fully-armed cavalry were lurking nearby
and requested that the English please take them all prisoner. Rather
than turf his men out from their dry billets into the rainy darkness,
Combe sternly ordered the NCO to parade his men at 10:00 the
following morning on pain of being shot if they failed to comply.
All 400 duly turned up as instructed, accompanied by twenty Italian
soldiers, some sailors, and an Arab woman. The Hussars were less
amused on discovering an abandoned Italian remount depot. The
horses therein, some of which were wounded or carried other inju-
ries, had been left unfed and without water for a considerable period,
and one troop spent the afternoon of 9 February leading the animals
individually to a watering point and making up feed while their
compatriots probed into Tripolitania.[1]

The men of 13th Corps were by all accounts ready and willing to
press on to Tripolitania and finish the job of ejecting the Italians from
North Africa altogether. Their sentiment was shared by O'Connor
who, determined not to lose the initiative, put together a case for
continuing the advance all the way to Tripoli with HQ Middle
East's representative at 13th Corps, Brigadier Eric Dorman-Smith.
As Wavell had reorganised command arrangements, Dorman-
Smith's first call was to the newly appointed Military Governor
and General Officer Commanding-in-Chief Cyrenaica Command,

Lieutenant-General Henry Maitland Wilson, who had set up his HQ at Barce on 9 February. With Wilson persuaded, Dorman-Smith travelled to Cairo via Tobruk on 11 February to argue the case with Wavell in person, and there the idea came to a stop at a 10:00 meeting the following day. Dorman-Smith was about a month too late, for Churchill had already restricted operations in Cyrenaica to securing the 'most delectable prizes on the Libyan shore', which the Chiefs of Staff transmitted as an directive decreeing that there were to be 'no serious operations beyond Benghazi'.[2] British posture in Cyrenaica was therefore to revert to the defensive once the port had been secured.

While this was doubtless a disappointment for O'Connor and his men, it is difficult to disagree with it in the circumstances. Victory in Cyrenaica had not only been achieved on a personnel, equipment and logistic shoestring but also with an extremely large helping of pure luck. It would have taken very little to reverse the situation at any point during Operation COMPASS, and it is interesting to speculate on the outcome had *Maresciallo* Balbo not been killed in the friendly-fire incident at the end of June 1940, or if his replacement had been of a similar calibre. Be that as it may, total reliance on continuing Italian ineptitude and favours from Lady Luck were not a sound foundation for further operations even if 13th Corps had been in a fit state, and as we have seen that was far from the case; the 7th Armoured Division required replacement of its entire vehicle fleet, for example, and all the personnel involved in the Operation were in need of rest after over sixty-one days of continuous operations.

There was also the matter of supply. Tobruk harbour was capable of handling multiple vessels by 29 January 1941 but remained vulnerable to bad weather and air attack, with regular Italian air raids being augmented by newly arrived *Luftwaffe* minelaying aircraft from 4 February. The latter was especially problematic, for Tobruk's two minesweeping vessels were under repair. As a result a petrol tanker was damaged by an undetected German mine on 5 February and an ammunition ship was also damaged in the subsequent fire. Benghazi did not prove to be the solution to British logistical problems as O'Connor had assumed either. The RN party assigned to clear the harbour there was stranded at Tobruk by bad weather until 12 February, and came under repeated air attack when it finally did arrive; there was little to deter these attacks, for the few army anti-aircraft guns available had been deployed at Tobruk. In addition, a shortage of coastal craft meant only small convoys could assembled and at only fortnightly intervals. The first, consisting of four ships, arrived at Benghazi on 17 February but concentrated air attacks obliged it to withdraw to Tobruk without unloading. As a result, the forces in Cyrenaica remained reliant upon supplies carried forward the 450 miles from Tobruk by road, which were also liable to attack from roving *Luftwaffe* aircraft.[3]

All this ruled out further advance into Tripolitania, and in any event Wavell had wider considerations to deal with. In Italian East Africa, the Duke of Aosta's 280,000 strong army still presented a serious threat to Egypt and the southern end of the Suez Canal, which was underscored by an incursion of 1,000 Italian irregular troops into Sudan on 15 October 1940.[4] In addition, the Italian occupation of British Somaliland the preceding August was having a more direct detrimental effect on the British sea supply position. Before the passing of the Lend-Lease Act on 11 March 1941, the demands of neutrality forbade US merchant shipping from sailing into 'combatant zones'. Italian possession of the southern coast of the Gulf of Aden led to the entire area being so designated, and US shipping was thus forbidden from accessing the southern end of the Canal. This in turn increased the burden on the already overstretched British merchant shipping, which had to trans-ship US carried supplies in from ports outside the Gulf of Aden combatant zone.[5]

Measures to alleviate the situation were underway before Operation COMPASS was launched. On 6 November 1940 Brigadier William Slim's 10th Indian Brigade, reinforced with six tanks from the 6th RTR attacked the Italians' foothold in Sudan at Gallabat and Metemma, supported by ten Gladiator fighters drawn from No. 1 Squadron SAAF and RAF No. 112 Squadron, six Vickers Wellesley bombers from No. 47 Squadron, four Hawker Hardy biplanes from No. 237 (Rhodesian) Squadron and six aircraft from No. 430 Army Co-operation Flight.[6] Gallabat was secured quickly but two Gladiators were shot down and a third damaged and forced down by Italian CR42 fighters, and all but one of the tanks suffered damage to their running gear from mines and the rough terrain. The advance on Metemma thus had to be postponed while the tanks were repaired, and the Italians quickly seized the initiative to unleash their Caproni Ca.133 bombers on the stalled and exposed enemy while their fighters dealt with the remaining Gladiators. The Italian bombing destroyed the truck bringing up spare parts for the damaged tanks and prompted something akin to panic among the British infantry; Slim himself recorded being shocked to see truck-loads of his men beating an unceremonious retreat.[7] Gallabat was held through the night but the bombing resumed in the morning of 7 November and in the afternoon Slim ordered a withdrawal to less exposed ground. The fighting cost Slim's force 42 dead, 125 wounded and 6 Gladiators, although the RAF exacted some retribution when they destroyed several Italian vehicles, supply dumps and inflicted a number of casualties on MVSN and colonial troops north of Kassala on 6 December.[8]

Subsequent British operations were more carefully prepared, with a concentrated effort to mobilise the native Abyssinian population against the Italian occupiers by Brigadier Daniel Sandford's Mission 101, which also organised the covert return of Emperor Haile Selassie from exile on 20 January 1940. Sandford's efforts were supplemented by Gideon Force commanded by Lieutenant-Colonel Charles Orde Wingate, who had gained a mixed reputation after organising irregular units made up of British soldiers and Jewish volunteers to combat Arab terrorist attacks in Palestine during the Arab Revolt of 1936–1939. The conventional end of the matter was a two-pronged invasion of Italian East Africa from Kenya by Lieutenant-General Alan Cunningham with the 1st South African Division and the 11th and 12th African Divisions, and from the Sudan by a larger force commanded by Lieutenant-General William Platt. This consisted of the 4th and 5th Indian Divisions, a temporary unit commanded by

Brigadier Harold Rawdon Briggs dubbed Brigg's Force consisting of two infantry battalions with attached artillery and engineer units, and the exotically named Free French *Brigade d'Orient* commanded by Colonel Raoul Magrin-Verneret said Monclar and built around the 1ere *Bataillon de la Légion Etrangère* and the 3me *Bataillon de Marche* (*Tchad*).

The offensive began early after the British decrypted signals ordering an Italian withdrawal from the border lowlands on 19 January. Platt's men quickly retook Kassala, captured by the Italians in July 1940, and pressed on toward Agordat, a major road junction a hundred miles to the east. On the way Colonel Messervy's Gazelle Force decimated an attack by Italian colonial cavalry while Brigadier Slim's 10th Indian Brigade overran a withdrawing Italian brigade and captured 700 men including the brigade commander. The Italians had prepared a major defensive line at Agordat stretching across fifteen miles of defensible terrain, held by three Colonial and three MVSN brigades and a number of M11/39 medium tanks CV33 tankettes. The position was taken after a two day battle that began on 28 January and cost the Italians 15,260 killed wounded and captured, along with twenty-four tanks, ninety-six guns and twenty aircraft.[9] The next objective was the town of Keren, which fell on 27 March after three separate attacks to clear the Dongolaas Gorge that cost the Italians a further 3,000 dead and the attacking 4th Indian Division 4,000 killed wounded and missing.

The fall of Keren broke the Italian defence in northern East Africa. Bera Bera on the Red Sea had been retaken on 16 March, and the major port of Massawa was captured on 8 April, but only after the Italian naval garrison had comprehensively wrecked the facilities. Mogadishu was captured in 26 February, followed by the Abyssinian capital Addis Ababa on 6 April; Emperor Haile Selassie re-entered the latter with some ceremony on 5 May, five years to the day after he had been driven out by the Italian invaders. The Duke of Aosta surrendered at Amba Alagi on 18 May, but *Generale di Corpo d'Armata* Guglielmo Nasi, who had conquered British Somaliland in August 1940, held out in the Gondar region west of Amba Alagi for another seven months, finally surrendering with full military honours on 27 November 1941. Even then, an estimated 7,000 Italians continued to carry out a low-level guerrilla campaign until 9 September 1943, when the Italian government formally surrendered to the Allies. Although overshadowed by events elsewhere, the East African campaign included some of the severest fighting on any front during the entire war. As the semi-official historian of the Indian Army put it, 'The unfortunate license of wartime propaganda allowed the British Press to represent the Italians almost as comic warriors; but except for the German parachute division in Italy and the Japanese in Burma no enemy with whom the British and Indian troops were matched put up a finer fight than those *Savoia* battalions at Keren.'[10] This opinion is supported by the fact that there were three awards of the Victoria Cross during the campaign, two of them posthumous.[11]

Be that as it may, unfolding events in Greece exerted a far more direct and detrimental impact on developments in Cyrenaica. British links to Greece went back to the Anglo-French guarantee of territorial integrity issued on 13 April 1939 in the wake of the Italian invasion of Albania, and the latter's unsuccessful invasion of Greece on 28 October 1940 thus prompted a British naval sweep of the eastern Mediterranean and the establishment of a brigade HQ and supply dump on Crete.[12] This was followed by an RAF contingent of three Blenheim units (Nos. 30, 84 and 211 Squadrons) and the Gladiator-equipped Nos. 80 and 112 Squadrons between October and December 1940. By March 1941 it had grown to the equivalent of eight squadrons with 200 aircraft commanded by Air Vice-Marshal J.H.D. D'Albiac, even though there was not a single all-weather airfield in Greece.[13] British interest in Greece was heightened by an increase in German activity focussed on the Balkans and the Mediterranean in January 1941. ULTRA decrypts revealed the movement of the *Luftwaffe*'s *Fliegerkorps* X from Norway to Sicily on 4 January,[14] and other reports indicated a build-up of German ground forces in Bulgaria for an attack on Greece. This prompted a series of meetings between Wavell with his Service heads and the Greek Prime Minister General Ioannis Metaxas beginning on 13

January; after some negotiation large-scale British assistance was secured following a further Anglo-Greek Agreement signed on 4 March.[15] Named W Force after its commander, Lieutenant-General Henry Maitland Wilson, the expeditionary force consisted of the 1st Armoured Brigade, the 2nd New Zealand Division and 6th Australian Division, with support troops from Palestine and Cyprus; Wilson was re-assigned from Cyrenaica in order to convince the Greeks of British commitment.

W Force began its move to Greece on 6 March via a series of convoys codenamed Operation LUSTRE, and was deployed covering the Metaxas Line along the Bulgarian border. It was therefore in the wrong place when the Germans invaded via Yugoslavia, outflanking the Metaxas Line and threatening W Force with encirclement. The British withdrawal began on 13 April and within seven days had been driven back over 150 miles to Thermopylae, by which time some troops had already been lifted from the ports of Piraeus and Volos. The official decision to evacuate W Force was made at a meeting between Wavell and King George II of Greece on 21 April, and W Force was obliged to continue its fighting retreat south-west to the Peleponnese isthmus, which was separated from the mainland by the Corinth Canal. A combined parachute and glider assault by two battalions from *Fallschirmjäger* Regiment 2 narrowly failed to secure the single bridge across the Canal at around 07:00 on 26 April and also just missed capturing Lieutenant-General Maitland Wilson who had crossed the bridge shortly before dawn. The evacuation commenced on 24 April and a total of 50,732 men had been lifted to safety when the operation ceased on 1 May. A further 7,000 men did not make it and surrendered at the port of Kalamata at 05:30 on 29 April.[16] A large number of W Force were evacuated to Crete, which fell to a German airborne assault on 1 June after a ten day battle that cost the attackers 6,000 killed, wounded or missing and the British and Empire forces another 1,800 dead, 1,679 wounded and 12,000 taken prisoner.[17]

The ill-fated Greek expedition was only achieved at the expense of 'stripping Cyrenaica to the bone',[18] although it might be more accurate to say that it maintained the status quo given COMPASS was conducted on a stripped-to-the-bone basis throughout. Semantics aside, the demands of W Force undoubtedly exacerbated the situation. The transfer of the 6th Australian Division halved the available combat-tested strength, the withdrawal of the 7th Armoured Division to Abbassia in the Suez Canal Zone to rest and re-equip reduced it to nil, and the removal of the 1st Armoured Brigade from the 2nd Armoured Division made an equally serious dent in what was left. This was accompanied by high-level reorganisation in Egypt and Cyrenaica. Major-General O'Connor took up the post of Commander British Troops in Egypt on his return from sick leave in Palestine to recover from stomach problems that manifested themselves in the closing stage of COMPASS and were thus likely stress-induced. He was replaced as commander of 13th Corps by Lieutenant-General Sir Noel Beresford-Peirse, fresh from commanding the 4th Indian Division in East Africa. However, the Corps HQ staff that had worked so successfully for O'Connor during COMPASS had been dispersed to other posts. Their function was supposed to have been assumed by a new 1st Australian Corps HQ under Lieutenant-General Thomas Blamey, but this had been forestalled by the despatch of the latter to Greece with the 6th Australian Division. Beresford-Peirse was thus obliged to form and train his staff from scratch and as a result, there was no functioning, intermediate level of command between the division and the newly formed Cyrenaica Command.

The man selected to take responsibility for this ad hoc and less than satisfactory arrangement was Lieutenant-General Philip Neame VC, who replaced Maitland Wilson as head of Cyrenaica Command at Barce. Commissioned into the Royal Engineers in 1908, Neame had been awarded the VC for a single-handed attack on German trenches and rescuing a number of wounded at Neuve Chappelle on 19 December 1914, and had won a Gold Medal at the Paris Olympics in 1924. He occupied a number of Staff positions in India in the interwar period, and was Commandant of the Royal Military Academy, Woolwich in 1938–39 before serving as a Deputy Chief-of-Staff with the British Expeditionary Force in

France. After that he briefly commanded the 4th Indian Division in late 1940, followed by stints as GOC Palestine and Trans-Jordan and GOC Cyprus. Neame was therefore a courageous, competent and experienced officer, qualities which his new post would require in some measure. The two formations that comprised his Command, the 2nd Armoured and 9th Australian Divisions, were both inexperienced and understrength, and the same strictures applied to his naval and air support. The monitor *Terror* was sunk off Derna by *Luftwaffe* Junkers 88 bombers operating from Sicily on 24 February 1941, and at around the same time Air-Chief Marshal Longmore withdrew No. 202 Group HQ and a number of RAF units from Cyrenaica to form a reserve for the planned operations in Greece. It was replaced by HQ RAF Cyrenaica located at Barce, commanded by Group-Captain L.O. Brown and consisting of the Hurricane-equipped RAAF No. 3 Squadron and RAF No. 73 Squadron, No. 55 Squadron equipped with Blenheim bombers and the Lysanders of No. 6 Army Co-operation Squadron.

Neame was therefore in the position of having to hold Cyrenaica with significantly less, numerically and qualitatively, than O'Connor had had available to capture it, and he was also facing virtually the same geographic and logistical limitations that had played a major role in the destruction of *Generale* Tellera's 10° *Armata* just a short time earlier.[19] Furthermore, Neame's superiors made it clear that the situation was not about to change in the near future. In mid-March 1941 Wavell and CIGS Dill visited Cyrenaica and warned Neame to conserve his forces as no significant reinforcements would be available until at least May, and as a stop-gap measure ordered him to deploy the 2nd Armoured Division in the forward zone in exchange for the 6th Australian Division, on the not unreasonable grounds that the terrain south of Benghazi was too open for an immobile infantry formation. Unavoidable as it was, the British situation would have been precarious had their only opposition been the courageous but inept and timid Italians. The problem was that they were shortly to be faced with a new foe, and one that was anything but inept or timid.

The Germans had followed Italian activities in Cyrenaica via *Generalmajor* Enno von Rintelen, their Military Attaché in Rome who, after monitoring preparations for the invasion of Egypt, had informed Berlin on 11 September 1940 of the tactical nature of the planned operation and that it was unlikely to reach Alexandria or provide a link to Italian East Africa.[20] September 1940 also saw the despatch of *Generalmajor* Wilhelm Ritter von Thoma to Libya by *Oberkommando der Wehrmacht* (OKW), to investigate the possibility of deploying an armoured force to assist the Italians, and 3 Panzer Division was warned off for possible North African service. Von Thoma's mission was prompted in part by OKW looking for another theatre to combat the British following the cancellation of Operation *Seelöwe* on 17 October 1940, and was also supported by *Grossadmiral* Erich Raeder at *Oberkommando der Kriegsmarine* (OKM), who was seeking a means of securing the Suez Canal. Interest subsided when Mussolini proved lukewarm to Hitler's offer of assistance at their meeting at the Brenner Pass on 4 October 1940, and more especially after von Thoma counselled against any German involvement in the region before the Italians had secured Mersa Matruh, because the road net was incapable of handling the logistical demands of a mechanised force.[21] Hitler appears to have concurred with Von Thoma's view, given that he rebuffed Mussolini's attempts to obtain material support for operations in North Africa at the end of December 1940 and advised *Il Duce* to concentrate on tackling the British at sea.

However, Hitler's view shifted with the ejection of the Italians from Egypt and the fall of Bardia on 5 January 1941; he also appears to have been influenced by a further report by von Rintelen that placed much of the blame for the poor Italian showing on substandard senior leadership and recommended that any German forces deployed to North Africa should do so under German command. Correctly reading the course of future events, Hitler therefore issued a directive on 11 January declaring that Tripolitania had to be held 'for strategic, political and psychological reasons' and ordering OKW to organise and despatch a *Sperrverband* (roughly special blocking detachment) to Tripoli as quickly as possible. It took OKW twenty-five days to work out the details, and the order to launch the aptly named Operation *Sonnenblume* (Sunflower) went out to the individual service high commands, the *Oberkommando des Heeres* (OKH) and *Oberkommando der Luftwaffe* (OKL) on 10 February.

The ground component of the *Sperrverband* was to consist of two divisions. The first to arrive in Libya was built around Panzer Regiment 5, which had been detached from 3 Panzer Division when the latter was re-assigned to participate in the upcoming invasion of the Soviet Union. Panzer Regiment 5 was equipped with twenty-five Panzer Is, forty-five Panzer IIs, seventy-five Panzer IIIs and twenty Panzer IVs; 130 of these were standard gun tanks, the remaining thirty-five being command or specialist observer vehicles. Other units assigned to the *Sperrverband* included *Infanterie* Regiment *zbV* 200, *Aufklärungs Abteilung* 3, *Panzerjäger Abteilung* 39, two machine-gun and two anti-aircraft battalions and a large number of support units including five transport battalions, along with five water transportation and two water filtration units. The first elements left Naples on 8 February and began to disembark at Tripoli on 14 February, although the last of the Panzer units did not arrive for almost another month.

On 7 February 1941 this motley accretion of units came under command of *Generalmajor* Johannes Streich, and on 18 February it was formally named 5 *Leichte* Division, sometimes rendered as 5 *Leichte Afrika* Division. By that time the *Sperrverband* proper had been labelled *Aufklärungsstab* Rommel in honour of its first commander, and on 19 February it too was renamed when Hitler dubbed the German expeditionary force to North Africa the *Deutsches Afrikakorps*. The second formation, 15 Panzer Division, was not scheduled to arrive in Libya until May 1941. The *Luftwaffe* contribution to the *Sperrverband* was drawn from *Generalleutnant der Flieger* Hans Geissler's X *Fliegerkorps*, a mixed force of fighters, dive and medium bombers that had arrived at bases in Sicily in late December 1940 and early January 1941. The detachment was commanded by *Generalmajor* Stefan Fröhlich, who also rejoiced in the title of *Fliegerführer Afrika*, and consisted of approximately twenty

Messerschmitt 110 twin-engine fighters from *Zestörergeschwader* (ZG) 26, fifty Junkers 87 dive-bombers from *Sturtzkampfgeschwader* (StG) 3 and a *Staffel* of light reconnaissance aircraft; this was augmented in April 1941 with elements from *Jagdgeschwader* (JG) 27 commanded by Major Eduard Neumann, equipped with Messerschmitt 109 fighters. Fröhlich could also call on longer ranged Heinkel 111 and Junkers 88 medium bombers from *Kampfgeschwader* 4 and 26 and *Lehrgeschwader* 1 respectively, based at Catania and Comiso in Sicily.

The man appointed to command the *Deutsches Afrikakorps* was *Generalleutnant* Erwin Johannes Eugen Rommel. Born on 15 November 1891 at Heidenheim in Württemberg and the second son of a schoolmaster, Rommel enlisted as a cadet in *Infanterie* Regiment 124 at Stuttgart on 19 July 1910, and was commissioned as a *Leutnant* on 27 January 1912. Wounded in France in the early stages of the First World War, Rommel returned to duty in January 1915 after three months of convalescence and was subsequently awarded the Iron Cross 1st Class and promoted to *Oberleutnant*. In September 1915 he was posted to a mountain battalion with which he served on the Carpathian Front in Rumania and then on the Isonzo Front in the Italian Alps; at some point during the latter he was captured by the Italians but escaped. While commanding the unit in October 1917 Rommel led a successful operation to secure the peak of Mount Matajur after almost fifty hours of continuous combat, capturing 9,000 Italians and a large number of guns in the process, a feat that won him promotion to *Hauptmann* and the *Pour le Mérite*. He saw the remainder of the war out in a variety of staff positions before being posted back to *Infanterie* Regiment 124 in December 1918. Apart from a brief spell commanding an internal security company at Friedrichshafen in mid-1919, Rommel remained on routine garrison duties at Stuttgart until October 1929, when he took up a four year posting to the *Infanterie Schulen* at Dresden, during which he was promoted to Major. This was followed by promotion to *Oberstleutnant* and command of an *Alpenjäger* unit, and then a post on the staff of the *Krieg Akademie* (War Academy) at Potsdam, during which he published *Infanterie Greift an* (Infantry on the Attack) based on his experiences during the First World War; the book proved to be a best seller. In 1938 Rommel was promoted to *Oberst* and appointed commandant of the *Krieg Akademie* at Wiener Neustadt, but shortly afterward was posted to command the *Führerbegleitbataillon*, a *Heer* unit that provided security for Hitler, and was promoted to *Generalmajor* in August 1939.

On 5 February 1940 Rommel took command of 7 Panzer Division, which had been converted from 2 *Leichte* Division on 18 October 1939 and had fought with *Armee Gruppe Süd* in Poland; the transformation was achieved by making extensive use of ex-Czech equipment, with the Panzer 38(t) tanks making up almost half of the formation's 225 tanks. As part of 15 *Panzerkorps* assigned to carry out the armoured thrust through the Ardennes in May 1940, Rommel's new command was in the very forefront of the action from the outset. After crossing the River Meuse near Dinant on 12 May, 7 Panzer pushed west through Philippeville and Avesnes, and crossed the River Sambre at Le Cateau before being held up by a British armoured counter-attack near Arras on 20 May. 7 Panzer then seized Lille on 28 May, blocking the evacuation route for the French 1st Armée to Dunkirk and after a brief rest continued to push west through Abbeville and across the River Seine near Rouen. Thereafter it overran a French motorised unit near Fécamp and captured Saint-Valéry on the Channel coast, and by 19 June had taken the surrender of the garrison at the port of Cherbourg, at the northern tip of the Cotentin Peninsula in Normandy. Rommel was then directed to advance south along the French Atlantic coast and was on the way to Bordeaux when the Armistice brought operations to a halt on 25 June 1940. In forty-five days of almost constant operations 7 Panzer Division had thus crossed the breadth of France, capturing 97,468 prisoners including twenty-two generals and five admirals, 458 armoured vehicles, 341 assorted guns, over 4,000 trucks and fifteen aircraft; a further fifty-two of the latter were claimed shot down.[22] The formation also gained the nickname of the *Gespensterdivision* (ghost or phantom division) because its location was frequently a mystery to the enemy and friendly high command alike.

All this supports the popular perception of Rommel as a master of tactics and operational art, capable of effortlessly running rings around less gifted opponents and peers alike. However, while Rommel's performance in the invasion of France was undoubtedly creditable closer inspection shows that there was a bit more to it, and that even at this early stage Rommel's reputation was not quite as flawless as it is often presented. However he performed thereafter, the fact remains that Rommel only gained command of 7 Panzer Division by shamelessly exploiting his personal relationship with Hitler. The latter had sought a meeting with then *Oberstleutnant* Rommel after reading *Infanterie Greift an* in 1936, a contact that appears to have led to Rommel's attachment to Hitler's military escort during the Nuremburg Rally the same year and subsequent selection to command the *Führerbegleitbataillon*. This brought Rommel into extended personal contact with Hitler and other members of the Nazi elite and particularly *Reich Minster für Volksaufklärung und Propaganda* Joseph Goebbels. There appears to have been a good deal of mutual admiration in this relationship, and it is therefore unsurprising that Goebbels subsequently played the major role in fabricating the Rommel legend as a propaganda tool. Having seen the importance and capabilities of armoured forces first-hand in Poland, Rommel requested a Panzer command when his stint with the *Führerbegleitbataillon* finished at the end of the Polish campaign. When the *Heer* personnel department refused his request on the not unreasonable grounds that Rommel had no relevant expertise or experience, he approached Hitler directly with a point-blank request for command of a Panzer division that led directly to his 5 February appointment to command 7 Panzer Division.

Rommel himself subsequently admitted that his action had been 'immoderate',[23] and the fact that such commands were at a premium even for more senior and properly qualified officers did little to enhance his popularity with his peers. This was exacerbated by his behaviour in France, where Rommel was criticised on a number of counts by both superiors and peers, principally for his arrogant and abrasive manner and excessive risk-taking. *Generaloberst* Hermann

Hoth, Rommel's immediate superior in France, confidentially recommended that Rommel be denied further promotion until he had
gained more experience and better judgement, for example. Hoth's
comment was doubtless prompted at least in part by Rommel's
habit of simply severing communications with his superiors and rear
echelon when it suited him. The latter tendency led to 7 Panzer
Division acquiring its *Gespensterdivision* nickname but drew criticism
from Rommel's own chief-of-staff for not keeping him sufficiently
well informed; at one point the latter held back fuel supplies when
the division reached Cambrai on 18 May, on the assumption that
silence from Rommel and the divisional spearhead indicated they
had been lost. Hoth also referred to Rommel downplaying the role
of others in his triumphs, a charge levelled more bluntly by the commander of 4 *Armee*, *Generaloberst* Hans von Kluge. Von Kluge bluntly
accused Rommel of falsely claiming credit due to others and of
deliberately misrepresenting and belittling their activities to enhance
his own achievements. He also cited two instances of Rommel com-
mandeering bridging equipment belonging to *Generalleutnant* Max
von Hartlieb-Walsporn's 5 Panzer Division, 7 Panzer Division's running mate in 15 *Panzerkorps*, during crossings of the Rivers Meuse
and River Scarpe on 14 and 28 May respectively; 5 Panzer Division's
advance was delayed by several hours on each occasion.

Similarly, there was also more to Rommel's operational performance than the bare, praiseworthy bones of 7 Panzer Division's
activities would suggest. Although it is not apparent from most
accounts, Rommel's command was not part of *Panzergruppe* Kleist,
the armoured force tasked to carry out the main armoured thrust
through the Ardennes into France. Hoth's 15 *Panzerkorps* was tasked
to protect *Panzergruppe* Kleist's right flank as part of Kluge's 4 *Armee*,
and Rommel's haring off on his own initiative could very easily
have had serious repercussions for the operation as a whole, by pre-
maturely alerting the enemy to the location of the German attack
and by leaving the northern flank of the main attack exposed. This
point devalues the kudos Rommel is routinely afforded for 7 Panzer
Division being the first across the River Meuse near Dinant as

does the fact that it was done at the expense of the remainder of 15 *Panzerkorps* and, unlike the later and larger crossing by *Panzergruppe* Kleist at Sedan, largely unopposed. The nearest elements of the French 18th *Division d'Infanterie*, the unit responsible for defending the Dinant area, were over fifty miles from their allotted positions when the German attack began on 10 May, and were still en route when 7 Panzer crossed the Meuse in the early hours of 13 May.[24] Furthermore, Rommel's reliance on the shock effect of hasty attacks when faced by opposition was a risky practise which only succeeded due to the poor training, disorganisation and demoralisation of the enemy, and the consequences of assuming that the enemy would always crumble was to be ruthlessly exposed at Tobruk. There was also the human price Rommel's aggression and constant pushing extracted from his own men. Although it was in combat for no longer than many of its contemporaries and spent a significant portion of that time facing negligible to non-existent opposition, 7 Panzer Division's casualties, at 682 dead and 1,912 wounded and missing, appear to be the highest casualty rate for any division in the invasion of France.[25] All in all therefore, an objective evaluation of the actions that launched Rommel's reputation strongly suggest that his primary motivation was always the greater glory and personal gratification of Erwin Rommel over and above anything else.

Be that as it may, Rommel's self-promotion achieved the desired effect for his performance in France not only earned him the Knight's Cross of the Iron Cross at Hitler's request, but also promotion to *Generalleutnant* and a corps-level command when Hitler personally asked him to command the North African *Sperrverband* on the afternoon of 6 February 1941. Thereafter the substance behind the criticisms levelled at Rommel by Hoth and Kluge after the French campaign soon became apparent. Rommel was issued with his detailed orders in person by *Generalfeldmarschall* Walter von Brauchitsch and *Generaloberst* Franz Halder, the *Heer* commander-in-chief and head of OKH respectively. With regard to command arrangements, Rommel was to be technically subordinate to the senior Italian commander in Libya, but this extended only to

tactical matters. Under no circumstances were the German formations to be broken up and employed piecemeal under Italian
command, and Rommel was given a direct line of communication to OKW to query any Italian orders that ran contrary to these
instructions.

However, Rommel was not given a *carte blanche* either. His orders
not only stressed the defensive nature of the German deployment,
but expressly forbade Rommel from undertaking any offensive
action apart from reconnaissance before his new command was fully
up to strength, and 15 Panzer Division was not scheduled to join
5 *Leichte* Division in Libya until May 1941; as we shall see, OKH
also intended to keep a close watch his activities once in theatre.[26]
On 11 February Rommel flew to Rome to receive the Italian view
on the situation in Libya from the deputy chief of staff at *Comando
Supremo*, *Generale* Alfredo Guzzoni. This was followed by a meeting
with military attaché *Generalmajor* von Rintelen, where Rommel
commented on the indolence of the Italian command and bluntly
announced that he intended to disregard his orders to refrain from
offensive action and 'take the command at the front into my own
hands as soon as possible.'[27]

Rommel began the process of taking the situation into his
own hands almost immediately, by flying to X *Fliegerkorps* HQ at
Catania and requesting that *Generalleutnant* Geissler begin bombing
Benghazi and the roads to the south immediately. Perhaps unsurprisingly Geissler demurred, pointing out that he had been specifically
requested to avoid bombing Benghazi by the Italians; Rommel
responded by resorting to his direct channel to the top, and the first
German bombing raid on Benghazi went in that same night. He
continued in the same vein on arrival in Tripoli on 12 February.
Generale d'Armata Italo Gariboldi, who had just been installed as
senior Italian commander in Libya following the resignation of
Maresciallo Graziani, had his own ideas for a defence line swept aside
by Rommel, who informed his nominal superior that the defence
line would be at Sirte, 200 miles further forward than Gariboldi had
envisaged before departing on a solo aerial reconnaissance of his new

area of operations in a Heinkel III. On his return a despatch from Mussolini authorising Rommel to take command of Italian motor-ised units in the vicinity of Tripoli prompted the westward despatch of not just the *Ariete* Armoured Division, which had arrived in Tripoli on 24 January, but also the *Pavia* and *Brescia* Divisions which were neither armoured nor motorised. The Tripoli dock authori-ties were next to experience Rommel's ire. When the first convoy carrying 5 *Leichte* Division arrived in the afternoon of 14 February, Rommel insisted that unloading continue through the night under electric lighting despite the risk from RAF bombers, and the convoy was duly unloaded within twenty-four hours. Thus the first German troops to set foot in Libya were able to parade through Tripoli on the afternoon of 15 February before setting off for Sirte, to cries of '*Viva Italia!*' from some presumably bemused locals.[28]

As in France, Rommel's hectoring if not outright bullying had the desired effect. By 16 February *Aufklärungs Abteilung* 3 was in place at Sirte, 260 miles down the *Via Balbia* from Tripoli. The reconnaissance unit was joined shortly thereafter by *Panzerjäger Abteilung* 39, and their numbers were padded out by a number of light vehicles disguised to look like armoured vehicles to prying RAF reconnaissance aircraft. They were covered from the air by *Generalmajor* Fröhlich's *Luftwaffe* detachment, which was by this time operating around seventy aircraft from Libyan airfields, which had already begun imparting a healthy respect on British troops operating around El Agheila. The Axis line did not remain at Sirte for long, for Rommel pushed *Aufklärungs Abteilung* 3 forward a further eighty miles to a point west of Nofilia after a cou-ple of days. These movements were not straightforward in themselves, for the Germans had no experience of desert conditions and had to make modifications, such as fitting vehicle engines with additional air filters and adjusting carburettor settings, as they went along. Matters were complicated by a shortage of transport vehicles and fuel; German supplies of the latter did not start to arrive in Libya until March, and there were complaints about the quality of Italian fuel sourced as a stopgap. There was also some friction between Rommel's staff and that of 5 *Leichte* Division over the placement of supply stocks.

However, the difficulties were tackled with the customary German efficiency and thoroughness. Supplies of fresh vegetables were located and procured to address an unforeseen deficiency in ration provision, and Rommel's quartermaster staff quickly assembled a fleet of small vessels to ferry supplies of fuel and ammunition from Tripoli to Buerat and Sirte as a means of circumventing the shortage of trucks. All this did not go unnoticed by the British. An RAF reconnaissance aircraft reported a possible sighting of a German *Sdkfz* 231 8-*rad* armoured car west of El Agheila on 21 February, German troops were positively identified in the same area three days later along with an increase in road traffic in and around Nofilia, and the flow of sea traffic into Buerat was also noted. All this, along with the suspicion that the Germans had set up a forward HQ in the region was duly relayed to the War Office by Wavell on 2 March.[29] Confirmation that German troops were indeed on the ground in Libya came from the first contact between the newcomers and the forward elements of Cyrenaica Command. On 20 February a patrol from the 1ˢᵗ King's Dragoon Guards (1ˢᵗ KDG) moving west along the *Via Balbia* beyond El Agheila met a similar patrol from *Aufklärungs Abteilung* 3 motoring in the opposite direction. The encounter appears to have come as a mutual surprise, as the patrols had passed each other before realising one another's identity, and after a brief exchange of fire the Dragoons evaded a German attempt to block the road by circling to the south. The German patrol was part of a deliberate tactic by Rommel to dominate the no-man's land between El Agheila and Nofilia, and hopefully discourage further British movement west.

Aufklärungs Abteilung 3 secured a better result on 24 February, assisted by their opponent's complacency. Noting that the British despatched their early morning patrols into Tripolitania at roughly the same time each day, a strong fighting patrol made up of three armoured cars, seven Panzers and a section of motorcycle troops was despatched to set up an ambush. The site selected was near the abandoned fort at El Agheila, where the 11ᵗʰ Hussars had taken shelter just sixteen days earlier. The Germans shot up a pair of 1ˢᵗ KDG Marmon-Herrington armoured cars that triggered the ambush, setting one vehicle ablaze, damaging the other and taking three crewmen prisoner, one of them wounded. While the Germans were seeing to their prisoners and organising a tow for the damaged Marmon-Herrington they were joined by an anti-tank unit from the 6th Australian Division which, misreading the situation, stopped to assist and unwittingly sparked the first clash of the war between the 2nd AIF and German troops. The Germans came out on top by shooting up the Australian vehicles, destroying a truck and the officer's command car before withdrawing at speed with their prisoners and booty.[10] On 4 March 5 *Leichte* Division completed its move up to Nofilia, and *Generalleutnant* Streich formally assumed responsibility for the front. Rommel immediately prompted him to set up a forward blocking position at Mugtaa, 100 miles east of Nofilia and just inside the Cyrenaica–Tripolitania border, where manoeuvre was restricted by salt marshes that stretched twenty miles inland from the coast. This fulfilled the primary objective of despatching *Aufklärungsstab* Rommel to Libya, and the defensive line was strengthened by the arrival of the *Ariete* Division near Nofilia, and the unchallenged occupation of the oasis at Marada, sixty miles to the south.

By the beginning of March 1941 Rommel was satisfied that the British did not intend to continue their advance west into Tripolitania. He had also decided that there were scant forces facing him in Cyrenaica and, erroneously concluding that heavy road traffic reported in the area of Tobruk connected to the despatch of W Force to Greece was running in the opposite direction, assumed that the favourable situation was unlikely to last much longer. Rommel therefore observed the legal nicety of securing Gariboldi's agreement to a plan for an attack into Cyrenaica before forwarding the plan to OKH for approval and issued *Generalmajor* Streich with a warning order for an attack on British positions near El Agheila on 24 March. He then departed for Berlin on 18 or 19 March, to receive the Oakleaves to his Knight's Cross from Hitler in person, and to sell his plan to OKH and obtain the requisite reinforcements in person. Unfortunately *Generalfeldmarschall* von Brauchitsch and *Generaloberst*

Halder were unimpressed and their response clearly shows that Rommel's maverick reputation was foremost in their minds. They therefore reiterated the defensive nature of the *Sperrverband* mission along with the facts that no reinforcements would be forthcoming apart from 15 Panzer Division in May and that no offensive action was permitted before that time, and attached two additional strictures. Rommel was explicitly forbidden from advancing beyond Agedabia without specific permission, and he was required to return to Berlin to brief his superiors in person before launching any attack after the arrival of 15 Panzer Division. Rommel's bid to loosen his operational constraints thus resulted in a further loss of autonomy, and his modified orders were confirmed in writing to avoid any misunderstanding on 21 March.[31] Rommel's immediate response to all this is unclear, but his overall reaction is clear from subsequent actions. He simply ignored everything von Brauchitsch and Halder had said and their written orders, and went ahead with his own plans regardless.

By the time Rommel arrived back in Libya on 23 March 5 *Leichte* Division had been brought up to full strength by the arrival of Panzer Regiment 5 at Nofilia via a road march from Tripoli, thereby disproving concerns that the unit's tanks might not be able to cope with the conditions,[32] and signal intelligence indicated that the British were withdrawing units from the region of Agedabia. The latter was probably connected to the 6th Australian Division handing over its forward locations to the 2nd Armoured Division as ordered by Wavell during his inspection, but the picture of general British weakness was reinforced by reconnaissance showing that the fort and landing strip at El Agheila was only lightly held. *Generalmajor* Streich had therefore not only completed his planning to secure the latter as ordered, but had also put together a scheme for a reconnaissance in force toward Mersa Brega twenty-five miles to the east.[33] *Aufklärungs Abteilung* 3 seized El Agheila on 24 March, almost capturing the commander of the 1st KDG Troop screening the place, and after again securing *Generale* Gariboldi's permission Rommel ordered *Generalmajor* Streich to prepare for a further advance to Mersa Brega beginning on 31 March.

As we shall see, within three weeks of Rommel setting foot back in Libya the *Deutsches Afrikakorps* had not only secured Mersa Brega but had pushed clear across Cyrenaica to the Egyptian border, bottling up the 9th Australian Division in Tobruk in the process. This was undoubtedly a highly laudable achievement for which Rommel is invariably given most if not all the credit, and which is usually presented as a text-book example of his operational genius and superiority over his staid and plodding British opponents. However, while Rommel certainly gave the orders and hectored if not simply bullied his subordinates into compliance, he had little to do with the latter's high standard of tactical and operational competence and professionalism, without which his badgering would have availed little. That was down largely to *Generalmajor* Streich, who planned and implemented the scheme that gave Rommel his opportunity for exploitation, and had welded a motley collection of units into an efficient and smoothly functioning combat formation in trying and unfamiliar circumstances. In addition Streich in turn owed something to those who had commanded and trained his units hitherto. Over and above all this however, were the facts that there was not really much to stop the German advance in Cyrenaica, militarily or geographically, and that British were beset by a variety of problems and difficulties at all levels, some unavoidable and some self-inflicted.

The problems began with condition of the formations facing Rommel's force on the front line, especially the 2nd Armoured Division. This unit had been raised in the UK on 15 December 1939 and arrived in Egypt between late December and early January 1941, commanded by Major-General J.C. Tilly. Originally made up of the 1st and 3rd Armoured Brigades, the 2nd Support Group plus divisional units the division was initially employed on line of communication duties, but matters soon took a turn for the worse. Major-General Tilly died at the beginning of January 1941, apparently from natural causes, and was replaced by Major-General Michael Gambier-Parry on 12 February 1941. The 1st Armoured Brigade was stripped away to join W Force toward the end of February along with some units from the 2nd Support Group, all of which effectively halved the division's strength and reduced it to a weak armoured brigade in real terms; the situation was exacerbated yet further by the state of the formation's equipment. The 3rd Armoured Brigade's tanks had already suffered a degree of wear and tear before leaving the UK, and training in desert conditions rapidly wore them out. Tracks were especially problematic because replacements were in short supply, and items sourced from manufacturers in Australia proved insufficiently durable. Thus by the time the 2nd Armoured Division was sent forward into Cyrenaica to relieve the 7th Armoured Division all its vehicles had exceeded their recommended engine mileage, making them prone to regular mechanical breakdown, as illustrated by the large number of vehicles that dropped out of a road march from El Adem to Mechili in late March. In addition, the 3rd Armoured Brigade was understrength, having only eighty-six of its official complement of 156 tanks, and the 6th RTR had to be issued with reconditioned Italian M13/40 tanks.[34] By the end of March the number of Cruisers had fallen to fifty-two, approximately half of which were undergoing workshop-level repair.[35]

The other formation immediately available to Cyrenaica Command was the 9th Australian Division, which began to relieve the 6th Australian Division around Mersa Brega from 8 March.[36] Its stay was short-lived. Concerned by the vulnerability of a static unit in such relatively open terrain during his visit to Cyrenaica with CIGS Dill in mid-March, Wavell ordered the 2nd Armoured Division to take responsibility for the Mersa Brega positions while the Australians withdrew north to more defensible terrain near Benghazi with effect from 20 March.[37] This interference with Neame's deployments highlights the flaws and frictions in the higher levels of the British command structure. According to his biography, Wavell left Cyrenaica in mid-March feeling anxious, depressed, full of foreboding and with his confidence in Neame shaken by the latter's pessimism, requests for reinforcements and 'crazy' tactical dispositions.[38] This was unfair to Neame, for his dispositions were dictated largely by the situation he had inherited and the overall lack of transport, which was insufficient to permit him to provide even a modicum of mobility for the unmechanised portion of his force whilst simultaneously maintaining the 300 mile supply line from Tobruk.

More particularly, the one area where Wavell was justified in his dissatisfaction was actually down to Neame's predecessor, Maitland Wilson. The latter had led Wavell to believe that the ridge of high ground running south from Benghazi was impassable to vehicles apart from at some isolated passes and therefore defensible. Wavell was less than impressed to discover on inspection that the impassable ridge was in reality a very passable line of low hills, leading Dill to report to the War Office on 18 March that there were no readily defensible locations between El Agheila and Benghazi. This reality was apparent in the orders Wavell issued subsequently. In the event of an enemy incursion into Cyrenaica Neame was instructed to fight a delaying action while preserving his force and particularly his armour, and was authorised to abandon Benghazi if necessary although the high ground overlooking the port from the north and west was to be held for as long as possible. Quite how Neame was supposed to carry out a delaying action in such indefensible terrain against a mechanised enemy with a weak armoured brigade mounted in worn-out and mechanically unreliable vehicles and an immobile, untried, partially trained infantry division lacking much of its most basic equipment was not explained. Given all this Neame's badgering for reinforcements and alleged pessimism was hardly surprising and excusable, and Wavell's biographical comments look suspiciously like special pleading if not outright buck passing.

Be that as it may, Gariboldi gave Rommel permission to take Mersa Brega on the understanding that he would not advance further without additional explicit permission and the attack began early in the morning of 31 March after seven days of preparation. The 2nd Support Group, commanded by Brigadier H.B. Latham, was occupying a frontage of roughly eight miles at Mersa Brega, overlooked to the front by a feature nicknamed Cemetery Hill with its right flank resting on the Mediterranean seashore. The 3rd Armoured Brigade was deployed in support approximately five miles to the north-east. The force Rommel sent against them consisted of Panzer Regiment 5, *Aufklärungs Abteilung* 3, *Maschinengewehr Bataillon* 2, *Maschinengewehr Bataillon* 8 and anti-tank and artillery elements, divided into two columns. *Aufklärungs Abteilung* 3 began feeling out the outlying British positions at around 08:00 and by 10:15 had pushed them back to the main position occupied by the 1st Battalion, The Tower Hamlets Rifles. The main position was then dive-bombed by *StG* 3 before being probed by tanks from Panzer Regiment 5. The dive-bombers were called in again at 14:00 after direct fire from the 104th RHA's 25-Pounders obliged the Panzers to take shelter behind Cemetery Hill, which had by that time been occupied by German infantry and provided perfect observation over the British positions.

Generalmajor Streich then spent two hours preparing an attack against the British seaward flank which went at 16:30. This swiftly threatened to outflank the entire British position, and was followed by a second attack spearheaded by *Oberstleutnant* Dr. Friedrich Olbrich's Panzer Regiment 5 from Cemetery Hill. Appeals for assistance from the 3rd Armoured Brigade were refused by Major-General Gambier-Parry because it was too late in the day for tanks to operate in daylight. This may have been in accordance with Wavell's directive to conserve armoured strength, another manifestation of the reluctance of British armoured units to operate at night, or merely inexperience on the part of Gambier-Parry and/or his staff; Wavell noted that the latter had brought forward his entire divisional HQ to gain experience, which he (Wavell) considered a 'dangerous encumbrance' in the event of an attack.[39] Whatever the reason, it was cold comfort for the 1st Tower Hamlets Rifles who were overrun by Panzers that destroyed several vehicles and forced a retreat north up the *Via Balbia* in the gathering darkness. The rest of the 2nd Support Group and the 3rd Armoured Brigade also withdrew sixty miles to a new position south-west of Agedabia.

Predictably, Rommel had been in the forefront of the action, monitoring the performance of 5 *Leichte* Division's constituent units and according to one source, personally conducting the reconnaissance for the 16:30 attack through the dunes that unseated the British position.[40] The next day, 1 April 1941, was spent in mutual reconnaissance, with RAF aircraft reporting large numbers of vehicles moving east in the area of El Agheila while Rommel's side informed him that there were no British forces between him and a point southwest of Agedabia. He therefore gave the order to resume the advance on 2 April in direct contravention of Gariboldi's instructions, and by 07:00 elements of *Aufklärungs Abteilung* 3 were again in contact with the 2nd Support Group. There followed another day-long fight that again ended with a British withdrawal, although this time the 1st Tower Hamlets Rifles paid a heavier price; the battalion lost over a company in the action and was only able to break contact under cover of a counter-attack. The 2nd Armoured Division's withdrawal was covered by the 5th RTR, and the first direct clash between British and German tanks cost the former between five and seven Cruiser Tanks and 5 Panzer Regiment three vehicles. By this time the British formation's tank strength had been reduced to twenty-five Light and twenty-two Cruiser Tanks, and Gambier-Parry reported an estimated breakdown rate of one tank every ten miles. By nightfall *Generalmajor* Streich's men had occupied Agedabia and the small port of Zuetina fifteen miles further up the coast.[41]

Understandably alarmed by the rapidly deteriorating situation, Wavell flew out to Neame's HQ at Barce in the afternoon of 2 April but was unable to prevent the 2nd Armoured Division withdrawing to Sceleidima while virtually disintegrating in the process; a report from 2nd Armoured Division HQ received at Barce at 06:00 on 3 April stated that the 2nd Support Group had lost half its infantry strength, while the 3rd Armoured Brigade was 'scattered, disorganised and short of petrol' and had abandoned more of its tanks to mechanical breakdown as predicted earlier.[42] Gambier-Parry's failure to comply with Wavell's orders has been characterised as simple disobedience, and cited as an early manifestation of an alleged tendency among British division-level commanders to treat orders as a basis for discussion rather than instructions to be obeyed.[43] This verdict, however, conveniently overlooks the fact that Gambier-Parry had been saddled with a virtually impossible task given the circumstances

and tools at his disposal, that his long-standing orders had been literally reversed at a stroke while the battle was underway, and that the
new orders in practical terms amounted to an order to be destroyed
in place. Given all this it could just as easily be argued that any fault
belonged to Wavell, for knowingly issuing impracticable orders in
the first place, attempting to micromanage from a distance, inconsist-
ency if not outright vacillation after the event, and ambiguity. Be
that as it may, Wavell also failed in an attempt to replace Neame with
O'Connor. The latter was summoned to Barce with newly promoted Brigadier John Combe, the erstwhile commander of the 11th
Hussars and Combeforce, on the evening of 2 April, but O'Connor
unsurprisingly balked at assuming command in such circumstances.
Instead Wavell was persuaded to accept a compromise that attached
O'Connor to Neame's HQ as an adviser, a questionable decision
that did little to resolve matters and that was to have serious and far
reaching repercussions.

There was none of this on the other side of the hill – quite the
opposite. Rommel moved his HQ up to Agedabia on 3 April and
immediately ordered 5 *Leichte* Division to prepare to advance north-
east on Antelat and Msus. A detachment under *Oberst* Graf von
Schwerin was despatched toward Giof el Matar to ascertain if the
British were evacuating Cyrenaica via Mechili, while *Aufklärungs
Abteilung* 3 pushed on up the *Via Balbia* toward Soluch. Rommel personally disproved claims by the commander of the *Brescia* Division,
Generale de Divisione Bertolo Zamboni, that von Schwerin's route to
Mechili was impassable. He also gave *Generalmajor* Streich short shrift
when he expressed concerns over tank serviceability, pointed out
that fuel stocks would only stretch for another hundred miles and
that it would take at least four days to build up stocks for a move on
Msus; Rommel swept the maintenance query aside as a mere trifle
and ordered Streich to obtain the necessary fuel and supplies within
twenty-four hours by using every vehicle he possessed to shuttle
supplies forward. *Generale* Gariboldi received similar treatment when
he arrived at Agedabia in the evening to clarify why Rommel had
ignored his instructions not to proceed beyond Mersa Brega. His

objections and suggestions were simply rejected out of hand in the course of an extremely frank and forthright exchange of views, and Rommel's position became unassailable with the timely arrival of a signal from OKH relaying Hitler's personal congratulations and granting him full freedom of action.

With official permission to do what he probably intended to do anyway and air reconnaissance reports indicating a continuing British withdrawal, Rommel launched into a veritable frenzy of unit shuffling, harassment and personal aerial reconnaissance to increase the tempo of the advance over the next few days. *Oberstleutnant* Freiherr von Wechmar's *Aufklärungs Abteilung* 3 entered Benghazi without a fight in the early hours of 4 April, to the same enthusiastic welcome as the 6th Australian Cavalry Regiment had received almost exactly two months previously. Von Wechmar's men did not have long to enjoy their welcome, for they were relieved by the *Brescia* Division at around midday and immediately set off eastward toward Mechili, while the Italians prepared to continue their advance north and east up the *Via Balbia* toward Derna; Rommel had co-opted *Generalmajor* Heinrich Kirchheim, who was merely paying a courtesy visit to Libya, to ensure that Zamboni and his men gave their task due diligence.

Back at Agedabia, Rommel took the risky decision to break 5 *Leichte* and *Ariete* Divisions into several parts and despatch them in different directions. *Generalmajor* Streich was lead the more mobile elements after von Schwerin, accompanied by two Italian units: a *Colonna* (column) made up of a motorised infantry battalion and some artillery commanded by *Tenente Colonnello* Gino Fabris, and a mixed motorised group led by *Maggiore* Nicolini Santamaria. *Oberstleutnant* Friedrich Olbrich took the bulk of Panzer Regiment 5, *Maschinengewehr Bataillon* 2 and approximately forty tanks from the *Ariete* Division on a more northerly route to Msus. All these detachments were issued with multifaceted instructions intended to cover all eventualities, given tentative objectives as far east as El Adem, Tobruk and Tmimi, and left in no doubt that they were to push on relentlessly whatever happened. Rommel may have imposed his will on Streich's formation, but the latter did not comply meekly and forcefully pointed out that his units were still short of fuel, and were now also losing vehicles to mechanical breakdown due to insufficient maintenance time. The result was a mutual loss of temper. Rommel accused Streich of cowardice and latter responded by tearing off his own Knight's Cross and threatened to throw it at Rommel's feet unless he withdrew the slur. Rommel then grudgingly apologised, but unsurprisingly the meeting ended with mutual bad feeling.[44]

Nonetheless, by 7 April Rommel's force had covered an impressive amount of ground comparable to that of the British Western Desert Force/13th Corps during the second phase of Operation COMPASS. In the north *Generalmajor* Kirchheim and the *Brescia* Division had pushed getting on for 150 miles along the coast and were approaching Derna. The remainder had closed on Mechili, 160 miles from Agedabia as the crow flies and many more on the various routes that passed through Antelat, Charruba, Msus and Tengeder among others. Von Schwerin's force sealed off Mechili from the north, *Colonna* Fabris and another column commanded by *Colonello* Ugo Montemurro did the same from the east and south respectively, and the west was left to Streich and Olbrich coming up from Msus. Rommel also despatched *Oberstleutnant* Gustav Ponath and *Maschinengewehr Bataillon* 8 directly north to cut the *Via Balbia* east of Derna, in order to trap any tardy British forces in the Jebel Akhdar; Ponath's men were in position by the late morning of 7 April. All this was not achieved easily or without opposition, however. *Aufklärungs Abteilung* 3 suffered temporary rebuffs at Er Regima and Charruba on its move east from Benghazi, and *Maschinengewehr Bataillon* 8 ran into a force grouped around a handful of tanks from the 5th RTR commanded by Lieutenant-Colonel H.D. Drew south of Derna that held the Germans back long enough for other British troops in the area to escape eastward.[45] To the south von Schwerin, Olbrich and Fabris were all stranded for want of fuel at some point en route to Mechili, progress was disrupted by sandstorms and mirages, and the rough going also took a serious toll of their vehicles, as it had on those of the 11th Hussars and 4th Armoured Brigade at the beginning of February. In addition, the uncertain conditions almost did for Rommel himself. On 6 April his car almost drove into a British outpost after becoming lost, he was almost tricked into landing his personal Fieseler Fi156 *Storch* liaison aircraft alongside another British unit that helpfully laid out a cloth recognition signal later the same day, and on 8 April he came close to being shot down by a *Bersaglieri* unit from the *Ariete* Division near Mechili; Rommel was reportedly outraged by the fact that the Italians failed to score a single hit while being overflown at an altitude of just 300 feet.[46]

The bulk of the problems encountered by Rommel's force were thus connected to the terrain, climatic conditions and logistics because the only British unit remotely capable of putting up mean-ingful military resistance, the 2nd Armoured Division, had virtually ceased to exist. As we have seen the division had been unable to comply with Wavell's orders on 3 April, not least because the 3rd Armoured Brigade and 2nd Support Group had been reduced to around half their original strength, and the situation deteriorated rapidly thereafter as attempts to comply with late and contradic-tory orders burned precious fuel and track miles. The 3rd Armoured Brigade lost communications because the constant movement allowed no time for battery charging and became stranded at Msus without fuel because the garrison troops destroyed the fuel dump there after receiving erroneous reports of an approaching German force. An ordered move north to Charruba on the afternoon of 4 April could only be undertaken by pooling what fuel was available, as three fuel convoys despatched to Msus from Maraua on 4 and 5 April had been destroyed by the *Luftwaffe*. As a result it took half a day to cover fifteen miles, and when they finally reached Charruba the 5th RTR had been reduced to eight Cruiser and fourteen Light Tanks. The 6th RTR had only two of its ex-Italian M13/40s, the remainder having been destroyed after running out of fuel or suf-fering irreparable breakdown.[47] Thereafter the formation appears to have simply melted away, with some personnel moving east by whatever means possible while others somehow managed to keep their vehicles moving. The 5th RTR lost its last four tanks in the fight with Ponath's *Maschinengewehr Bataillon* 8 just south of Derna on the morning of 7 April.

2nd Armoured Division HQ and the remains of the 2nd Support Group finally fetched up at Mechili on 4 April, where Neame was trying to establish a defensive line running north to Derna. To that end Neame had also ordered Brigadier Edward Vaughan's 3rd Indian Motor Brigade to establish a blocking position at Mechili; as the latter was understrength and lacked any equipment apart from its vehicles and small-arms, it was reinforced with a battery from the 3rd Australian Anti-Tank Regiment and a number of other units, all of which came under Major-General Gambier-Parry's command as senior officer present. Neame ordered a further withdrawal to El Adem on the night of 6–7 April, but by that time Mechili was encircled although Rommel's force lacked the fuel and supplies to attack. While Blenheims from Nos. 45 and 55 Squadrons harassed and delayed the advance of Olbrich and Panzer Regiment 5 from the west, Gambier-Parry had his men probe the German and Italian positions in search of a weak spot. A gap was discovered to the south–east, on the boundary between *Colonna* Fabris and *Colonna* Montemurro, and the break out was launched at dawn on 8 April spearheaded by a Squadron from the 18th King Edward VII's Own Cavalry, usually rendered as the 18th Indian Cavalry Regiment. The would-be escapers came under heavy Italian artillery fire and *Colonello* Montemurro swiftly redeployed his *Bersaglieri* light infantrymen to block the initial breakthrough and Gambier-Parry was obliged to surrender along with Brigadier Vaughan and 1,200 of his men.[48] Some isolated units and groups did succeed in escaping the trap, among them a Squadron from the 2nd Royal Lancers (Gardner's Horse) commanded by Major Maharaj K.S. Rajendrasinhji, who became the first Indian soldier to be awarded the DSO, for leading his men back to friendly lines after dark with sixty prisoners taken in skirmishes along the way.[49] The victory must have been especially sweet for the men of the *Ariete* Division, partly as recompense for past humiliations at British hands, and partly because it was an all-Italian triumph; *Generalmajor* Streich, *Oberstleutnant* Dr. Olbrich and Panzer Regiment 5 arrived too late to take part in the action and Gambier-Parry actually surrendered to *Colonna* Montemurro.

The capitulation of the 2nd Armoured Division and the 3rd Indian Motor Brigade at Mechili eliminated half of Cyrenaica Command's strength at a stroke. All Rommel had to do to complete the reconquest of Cyrenaica was deal with the other half, in the shape of the 9th Australian Division.

7
Tobruk Invested:
8 April 1941 – 12 April 1941

With the occupation of Benghazi, Derna and Mechili, Rommel's *Deutsches Afrikakorps* had driven the British back out of almost half of Cyrenaica, and the surrender of the 2nd Armoured Division and the 3rd Indian Motor Brigade left the British with little to oppose any continuation of the German advance to the Egyptian border. However, such a move was not immediately feasible even for Rommel without a pause to allow the supply columns to catch up and permit the teeth units to regroup and carry out essential vehicle maintenance. There was also the matter of occupying the remainder of the Cyrenaican coastline, and as *Oberstleutnant* Ponath and *Maschinengewehr Bataillon* 8 had failed to cut the *Via Balbia* near Derna on 7 April, dealing with the British forces that had withdrawn north and east from the region of Benghazi in front of the *Brescia* Division. Essentially, this meant the 9th Australian Division.

Commanded by Major-General Henry Wynter, the 9th Australian Division was the fourth division raised as part of the 2nd Australian Imperial Force (AIF). However, unlike its predecessors, it was actually formed in the UK at the end of October 1940 around the 18th Australian Brigade, the 1st Australian Anti-tank Regiment and the 2/1st Machine Gun Battalion. These units had originally been part of the 6th Australian Division but were directed to the UK after the fall of France and were joined by the 25th Australian Brigade, formed around a cadre from the 18th Australian Brigade. When the threat of German invasion receded the division was despatched to Egypt in January 1941, where it was joined briefly by the partially trained 24th Australian Brigade direct from Australia; the latter then moved to Palestine for training. At the end of February the remainder of the division was ordered to Cyrenaica to relieve the 6th Australian Division for service with W Force, and exchanged the 18th and 25th Australian Brigades for the 20th and 26th Australian Brigades from the 7th Australian Division, which was also slated to join the Greek expeditionary force. This was a gain for the 9th Division, for the new-comers possessed more motor vehicles and had undergone more training than the units they replaced. The 9th Division also received a new commander at this time, in the shape of newly promoted Major-General Leslie Morshead, who had been present as an observer when Brigadier Horace Robertson had formally accepted the surrender of *Ammiraglio* Massimiliano Vietina at the Italian naval HQ at Tobruk on 22 January 1940.

Morshead took command of a formation that was only partially trained and lacked basic items like Bren Guns, signalling equipment and anti-tank guns. The most serious shortage was of transport, for only five of the division's eight infantry battalions had their full allocation of vehicles and more seriously, brigade level transport was deficient to a degree that rendered the formation virtually immobile. Nonetheless, the demands of W Force left Lieutenant-General Neame at Cyrenaica Command with little option but to deploy the division, and the move to relieve the 6th Australian Division began on 1 March. Brigadier John Murray's 20th Australian Brigade took over positions from the 16th Australian Brigade around Mersa Brega seven days later, and the entire Division was ensconced in that area by 12 March.[1] This all changed following a visit to Cyrenaica by Lieutenant-General Wavell and CIGS Sir John Dill. According to the official history, Wavell concurred with concerns expressed by Neame and Morshead regarding the largely immobile 9th Australian Division's vulnerability in such open terrain, whereas Wavell's biography criticises Neame's 'crazy' tactical dispositions and states that

he (Wavell) ordered remedial measures. To muddy the waters further, a contemporary account refers to Morshead unsuccessfully
urging Neame to withdraw the 20th Australian Brigade because
'…with little transport and supporting artillery, it would only be
an embarrassment to the British armoured forces when the attack
came.'[2] Whichever version was actually the case, the upshot was the
2nd Armoured Division taking over at Mersa Brega by 23 March
while the Australians redeployed further north to the heights east of
Benghazi.[3] The division's new home stretched for sixty-two miles
running north-east from Er Regima to Tocra on the coast, held by
the 20th Australian Brigade and part of the 26th, supported by the
sixteen-gun 51st Field Regiment RA; the divisions third brigade, the
24th, was completing its training further east in the Gazala/Tobruk
area.[4] The move did not totally remove the Australians from the firing line, for a good deal of German aerial reconnaissance was noted
along with the occasional *Luftwaffe* bombing attack.[5]

The 9th Australian Division HQ had no direct communication
with the 2nd Armoured Division, and the Australians were thus unaware of the German attack on Mersa Brega on 31 March or their
subsequent advance north. The first inkling came with the arrival of
Wavell and Neame at 9th Australian Division HQ on the morning
of 3 April. They informed Morshead of the gravity of the situation
unfolding to the south and that Major-General O'Connor had been
summoned back to Cyrenaica. This was alarming news given that the
division had not completed their defences, and the alarm was reinforced in the afternoon. Air reconnaissance reported German troops
in the area of Msus, only forty miles or so south-east of Er Regima,
and Morshead was issued with a warning order to prepare to send the
2/13th and 2/24th Battalions north to Barce to prepare defences for a
subsequent withdrawal. This was part of Neame's plan to establish a
defensive line running south from Derna to Mechili, but events were
acclerated in light of the unexpectedly rapid German advance. On
the morning of Friday 4 April O'Connor, acting in Neame's stead
while the latter was absent from his forward HQ at El Abiar, ordered
the 9th Australian Division to hold at Er Regima until nightfall or

until forced to withdraw, and then pull back to the escarpment east of Barce.[6] The Australians' left flank was to be covered by the 2nd Armoured Division, which had also been ordered to withdraw to Charruba.

In the event, the left flank cover did not materialise because the 2nd Armoured Division was well on the way to disintegration, and the withdrawal order came in the nick of time. Lieutenant-Colonel F.A. Burrows' 2/13th Battalion, minus one company but reinforced with four 4.5-inch howitzers and two captured Italian anti-tank guns, was occupying positions blocking a pass on the road to El Abiar and an adjacent *wadi* through the escarpment overlooking Benghazi; Burrows had been ordered to hold his position until 19:00, the earliest time that transport was expected to be available. At approximately 14:00 on 4 April a number of enemy vehicles were spotted near Benina airfield, six miles from the Battalion positions; the vehicles belonged to *Oberstleutnant* Freiherr von Wechmar's *Aufklärungs Abteilung* 3, fresh from liberating Benghazi.

By 15:30 the handful of vehicles had grown to sixteen tanks, a number of armoured cars and around 2,000 infantry. An hour later the German force came within howitzer and artillery range, and at 17:00 they launched a deliberate attack on the 2/13th Battalion's D Company with tanks and infantry, while four armoured cars tried to outflank the Australian positions with the aid of an Arab who guided them through a gap in the defensive minefield; fortunately these were stymied by an old Italian anti-tank ditch running along the top of the escarpment. Three German tanks penetrated the pass, shooting up a number of sangars in the process; one Panzer was destroyed when attached sappers detonated a road demolition charge beneath it and another was knocked out further up the pass in a duel with a troop of 18-Pounder guns from the 51st Field Regiment RA; the crew of the third tank surrendered to a Private S. Eland after their vehicle was disabled with a Boys anti-tank rifle. Back down the pass Captain E.A. Handley's D Company fought a dogged action against the German infantry, holding each position for as long as possible before giving ground. One platoon, commanded by Sergeant Roy

1 British convoy on the move in the desert near Bardia. The tell-tail dust trail illustrates the problem inherent in moving large numbers of vehicles unnoticed, and the crucial importance of aerial reconnaissance.

2 A British vehicle, possibly a Chevrolet 8 cwt truck, illustrates the difficulty of moving without creating dust, and the threat the latter posed to engines and mechanical parts.

3 Desert brew up: the crew of a British Vickers Light Tank prepare tea and a meal over a makeshift fire. The crewman on the right is using a 5-gallon can, dubbed 'flimsies' due to their fragility, as a seat; flimsies were the primary container for carrying fuel and water before the adoption of the German 'Jerry can'. The cooking vessel on the fire is also fashioned from a flimsy.

Middle: 4 Vickers Light Tanks moving across the type of rocky terrain that rapidly wore out tracks and running gear. They are painted in the so-called 'Caunter Scheme' formulated by the commander of the 4th Armoured Brigade, Brigadier John Caunter. Used in Egypt in 1940-41 the Scheme was intended to make vehicles blend with the desert horizon, utilising a near-horizontal splinter pattern in light stone, light grey-green and dark slate grey. Individual vehicle names beginning with the letter A show vehicles belong to A Squadron of their Regiment.

5 Logistic lifeline: 5-gallon flimsies full of water, as indicated by the 'W' markings, being unloaded for distribution.

6 Universal Carriers, possibly from the 6th Australian Division Cavalry Regiment, manoeuvring at speed. The latter unit was the first Australian unit to see action in the Second World War during Operation COMPASS and were involved in the capture of Bardia in January 1941.

7 A Morris CS9 Light Armoured Car crossing the border wire into Cyrenaica from Egypt, probably from the 11th Hussars, who deployed thirty in the Western Desert fitted with special sand tyres. Based on the Morris Commercial 15-cwt truck chassis, the CS9 weighed four and a half tons and was armed with a .55 Boys Anti-tank Rifle in the turret and a Bren gun for close and anti-aircraft defence on a pintle mount at the rear of the turret.

8 Universal Carriers mounting Boys Anti-tank Rifles and Bren Guns in the ruins of Fort Capuzzo after the latter's capture in December 1940.

9 Hawker Hurricane fighters taking off from a forward airstrip; the machines could belong to a number of units including No.3 Squadron RAAF and RAF No. 33 and 73 Squadrons.

10 A formation of Bristol Blenheim Mk. IV bombers *en route* to attack Italian targets during the initial stages of the fighting in the Western Desert.

11 Italian trucks, probably from the 1° *Libica* or *Cirene* Divisions escorted by a *Bersaglieri* motor cyclist passing through the Sollum Escarpment, possibly at the Halfaya Pass, during the Italian advance into Egypt in mid-September 1940. The tank is a British A10 Cruiser, probably lost during one of the delaying actions fought by the British at the time.

12 British artillery observers controlling artillery fire on the Italian advance into Egypt in September 1940.

13 Italian infantry advancing near Sidi Barrani during the Italian invasion of Egypt in September 1940. The men at the extreme left and right of the front file are carrying 6.5mm Breda *Modello* 30 light machine guns, which featured a permanently attached twenty-round box magazine with an integral cartridge oiler to ease extraction.

14 On the brink: British tanks, possibly from the 7th Royal Tank Regiment, move forward to the start line for Operation COMPASS on the night of 8–9 December 1940.

15 Italian troops seek cover from RAF bombing. The weapon on the anti-aircraft mounting is an 8mm Schwarzlose medium machine gun obtained from the Austro-Hungarians as reparations at the end of the First World War.

16 British warships bombarding Fort Capuzzo during Operation COMPASS.

17 Italian stone-built artillery sangar with abandoned gun; note the raised platform in the centre of the sangar to allow the gun to clear the sangar wall.

18 British 60-Pounder gun shelling Axis positions in Libya; the breech mechanism appears to have been blanked out by the censor.

Above: 19 Bombardment of Bardia in preparation for the assault on the port by the 6th Australian Division on Friday 3 January 1941.

Right: 20 Infantrymen from the 6th Australian Division move up to the start line for the attack on Bardia, 2 January 1941.

Below: 21 Aerial view of some of the 40,000 Italian troops captured at Bardia, corralled in a makeshift compound.

Upper left: 22 A partly burned *Regia Aeronautica* Fiat CR42 *Falco* fighter. Armed with two 12.7mm machine-guns and with a top speed of 268 mph (430 kph), the Falco was the most numerous Italian fighter in North Africa and continued in production until 1944, by which time 1,782 had been built.

Left: 23 Booty: captured Breda *Cannone-Mitragliera da 20/65 Modello 35* 20mm anti-aircraft guns.

Above right: 24 Hard living: a Royal Artillery gun crew snatch some sleep in front of their 25-Pounder gun, which is carefully covered to protect it from wind-blown sand and dust.

25 The *Regia Marina* cruiser *San Giorgio* burning in Tobruk harbour after an attack by RAF Blenheim bombers on 21 January 1941. Damaged by RAF bombing on 11 June 1940, the cruiser had been a key part of Tobruk's anti-aircraft defences and was scuttled by her crew.

26 The scuttled *San Giorgio* in Tobruk harbour; the British vessel in the foreground may be part of Commander W. P. Carne's naval clearance party, which was tasked to return the harbour to service as quickly as possible after the Italian surrender on 22 January 1941.

27 Destroyed Italian aircraft at El Adem airfield, twenty miles south of the Tobruk perimeter.

Left: 28 *Regia Marina* personnel march to captivity through the streets of Tobruk after the Italian surrender on 22 January 1941.

Left: 29 Booty: captured Italian motor transport gathered south of Tobruk harbour after the Italian surrender on 22 January 1941, with smoke from burning fuel and supply dumps nearer the town and harbour in the background.

Below: 30 British or Australian troops manning a .303 Vickers Medium Machine Gun in the fighting near Derna in January 1941.

31 Into the bag: some of the 27,000 Italian troops who surrendered at Tobruk on 22 January 1941 marching into captivity.

32 A Chevrolet 30-cwt truck of the Long Range Desert Group (LRDG) on patrol in Libya. The LRDG carried out patrols and raids over a thousand miles behind Axis lines. The vehicle is armed with a Boys anti-tank rifle in the truck bed and a .303 Lewis Gun mounted by the front passenger seat.

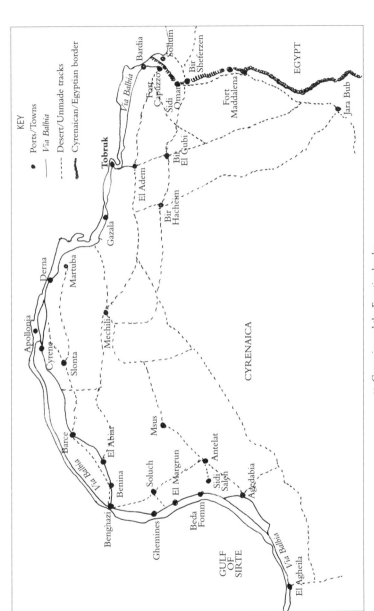

KEY

- Ports/Towns
- *Via Balbia*
- --- Desert/Unmade tracks
- ~~ Cyrenaican/Egyptian border

EGYPT

Bardia
Sollum
Fort Capuzzo
Sidi Omar
Bir Sheferzen
Fort Maddalena
Jara Bub
Bir El Gubi
El Adem
Bir Hacheim
Tobruk
Gazala
Derna
Apollonia
Cyrene
Martuba
Slonta
Mechili

CYRENAICA

Barce
El Abiar
Msus
Benina
Soluch
El Margrun
Antelat
Benghazi
Ghemines
Beda Fomm
Sidi Saleh
Agedabia

GULF OF SIRTE

El Agheila

Via Balbia

33 Cyrenaica and the Egyptian border.

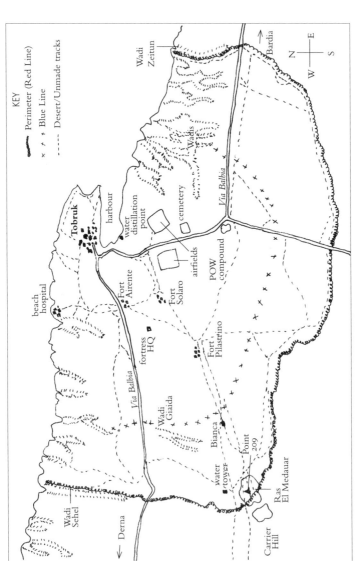

KEY

—— Perimeter (Red Line)
× × Blue Line
- - - Desert/Unmade tracks

N
W — E
S

Bardia →

Wadi Zeitun

harbour

Tobruk

water distillation point

cemetery

Via Balbia

beach hospital

Fort Airente

airfields

POW compound

Fort Solaro

Via Balbia

Wadis

fortress HQ

Fort Pilastrino

Via Balbia

Wadi Giaida

Bianca

Point 209

← Derna

Wadi Sehel

water tower

Ras El Meduaur

Carrier Hill

34 The Tobruk perimeter.

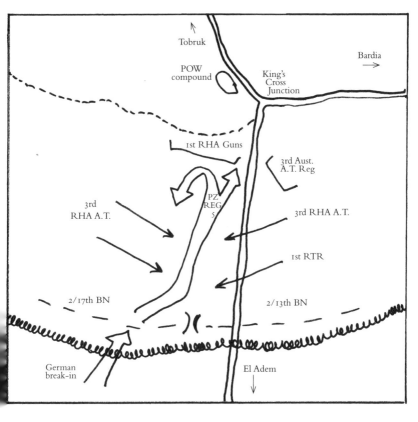

Tobruk

Bardia
→

POW
compound

King's
Cross
Junction

1st RHA Guns

3rd Aust.
A.T. Reg

3rd
RHA A.T.

PZ
REG
5

3rd RHA A.T.

1st RTR

2/17th BN

2/13th BN

German
break-in

El Adem
↓

35 El Adem Road Sector, scene of Rommel's first attempt to take Tobruk, 14 April 1941.

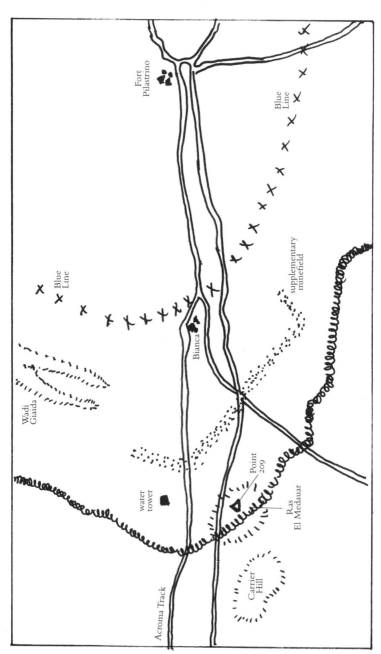

Fort
Pilastrino

Blue
Line

Blue
Line

supplementary
minefield

Wadi
Giaida

Bianca

water
tower

Point
209

Ras
El Medauar

Acroma Track

Carrier
Hill

36 Ras El Medavar Sector, scene of Rommel's second attempt to take Tobruk, 30 April – 2 May 1941.

Simmonds, waited too long and was overrun, with only five men escaping. Eventually Handley's men were forced up and across the anti-tank ditch on the crest of the escarpment, but the Germans did not push their advantage in the failing light and the 2/13th Battalion was able to break contact in the darkness and at 23:00 rendezvoused with the transport that carried them north to Barce. The stubborn defence put up by Burrows' men allowed the remainder of the division to withdraw unmolested, but at a cost of eighty-two killed and missing, with a further sixteen wounded.[7]

The 9th Australian Division remained unmolested at Barce on Saturday 5 April, although enemy activity was noted across the divisional frontage throughout the day. At 11:00 Morshead attended a meeting with Neame at a desert track junction between D'Annunzio and Slonta, where he was presumably given a situation report and learned that O'Connor had declined the offer of command in Cyrenaica. In the afternoon reports of a large column of vehicles moving east of El Abiar prompted Neame to order Morshead to withdraw after dark to the Wadi Derna, a hundred miles or more east of Barce.[8] The move started promptly as soon as it was fully dark and was well underway when the order was cancelled as the column had been identified as friendly; it may have been part of the 2nd Armoured Division making its way to Charruba. Despite the resulting confusion, all the division's units were back in their original positions by 23:00 on the night of 5 April. The views of the troops to all this can be well imagined, especially when the movement order was reinstated shortly thereafter. By 6 April the German advance had encircled Mechili, thus raising the very real possibility of the 9th Australian Division and every other British unit in north-western Cyrenaica being cut off to share the same fate as *Generale* Guiseppe Tellera's 10° *Armata* at Beda Fomm two months earlier.

Morshead was therefore ordered to withdraw as quickly as possible to the Wadi Derna, and then a further fifty miles to Gazala. The order underscored the gravity of the situation by stipulating that it was to be carried out in daylight, rather than waiting for darkness as per the previous withdrawal from Er Regima. This was potentially risky, for the demands of the Greek expedition had left only six RAF squadrons in Cyrenaica, only two of which were fighters units,[9] and they were handicapped by the wide ranging nature of Rommel's advance. The fighters therefore concentrated on covering the main routes running east from Benghazi and with some success, given that the vulnerable columns of slow moving vehicles remained unmolested throughout the retreat. Maintaining air cover was no easy task because the RAF ground elements were obliged to divide their attention between maintaining aircraft and keeping up with the eastward exodus; No. 3 Squadron RAAF moved location seven times in six days, for example.[10] This degree of ground mobility was only possible because the Air Officer Commanding, Cyrenaica Command, Group-Captain L. O. Brown, had presciently ordered his ground units to be ready to move at short notice as early as 22 March 1941. Perhaps fortunately for Neame and his men, the situation was the same for their *Luftwaffe* opponents. *Generalmajor* Fröhlich's detachment numbered only twenty to twenty-five Messerschmitt 110 twin-engine fighters and fifty Junkers 87 dive-bombers, and was no better connected to Rommel's intentions than the RAF. Air operations by both sides were thus hit-and-miss affairs. A force of thirteen *Stukas* thus destroyed two fuel convoys moving outside the RAF fighter envelope from Msus to Maraua to resupply the 2nd Armoured Division, while RAF Hurricanes carried out strafing attacks on the German and Italian troops around Mechili. The final loss tally was two Hurricanes, one Messerschmitt 110 and nine Junkers 87s, with one contemporary account claiming that all the *Luftwaffe* machines were lost in a single engagement with Hurricanes from No. 3 Squadron RAAF.[11]

In the event, the 9th Australian Division did not begin its withdrawal, dubbed the 'Benghazi-Tobruk Handicap' or the 'Tobruk Derby' by some of those involved, until 17:00 on Sunday 6 April. Whether this was a deliberate delay to minimise daylight movement is unclear, for it may have been due to the shortage of transport; moving the entire division en mass at such short notice obliged Morshead's men had to press every single vehicle the division possessed into carry troops. While the transport was being mustered the Australians set about destroying whatever could not be carried, covered by the 1st KRRC, newly arrived from rest and refitting in Egypt. The division moved off at 17:00 with the 2/13th Battalion, packed like sardines into captured Italian trucks, heading for Martuba to protect the division's flank by blocking the track running to Mechili. They arrived at the oasis just in time to rebuff a German patrol, and were left unmolested thereafter although a number of vehicles were seen moving north toward Derna at dusk; these belonged to Ponath's *Maschinengewehr Bataillon* 8, moving north too late to close the *Via Balbia* behind the Australians. The main body of the division was led by Brigadier Raymond Tovell's 26th Australian Brigade, and reached Tmimi, thirty-five miles south-east along the coast from Derna, at 04:30 on 7 April. There Tovell's men deployed in a defensive screen to protect the route east from pursuit or interference from the track running south-west to Mechili. They had been preceded by Cyrenaica Command's Advanced HQ from Maraua under command of Brigadier A. F. Harding, which had arrived at Tmimi in the early hours of 7 April. Despite being carried out largely in darkness the withdrawal appears to been carried out with a minimum of confusion. There was, however, one specific and extremely serious exception to this general rule.

Harding was expecting to find Neame and O'Connor at Tmimi, as the latter had left Maraua before the Advanced HQ. Prior to that Neame had spent most of Sunday 6 April searching unsuccessfully for Major-General Gambier-Parry and the 2nd Armoured Division east of Charruba before returning to Maraua in the early evening and ordering his Advanced HQ to join the withdrawal. Neame left before dark in his blue civilian sedan with O'Connor and Brigadier John Combe, as they lacked personal transport of their own. Initially Neame took the wheel to take the load from his worn-out driver, following a cross-country route to avoid congestion on the *Via Balbia*, and at some point he left the planned route east and began following another track leading north toward Derna. The error was realised before dark but as the track seemed secure the party continued, with

Neame in the front passenger seat and Combe and O'Connor asleep in the back. Unfortunately the track was not as secure as it seemed, and in the early hours of the morning of Monday 7 April they came upon two trucks stopped on the track. The officer and two men with the trucks were not Cypriot Service Corps personnel as Neame's driver initially assumed, but were from *Maschinengewehr Bataillon 8*, and thus the commander of Cyrenaica Command and his two high ranking advisers became prisoners of war. They were not the only high ranking British officers taken prisoner at this time; the commander of the 3rd Armoured Brigade, Brigadier Reginald Rimington, was captured near Derna after his car overturned while searching for fuel for his tanks. Neither were they alone in running into trouble on that track.[12] A German was killed after single-handedly holding up a convoy from 9th Australian Division HQ which made good its escape, forty-one members of the 2/8th Field Ambulance were taken prisoner after an ambush, and a total of 224 men from the 8th Light Anti-Aircraft Battery and the 2/15th Battalion were captured after being overrun by German tanks during a breakfast halt just after dawn. They included the commander of the 2/15th Battalion, Lieutenant-Colonel R.F. Marlan.[13]

This combination of miscalculation and ill luck at a stroke removed the most experienced and competent British commanders in North Africa, with the loss of O'Connor being especially grievous. Although his exploits have attracted far less popular acclaim than those of Rommel, he actually achieved as much if not more during Operation COMPASS, against greater odds, and with unassuming, efficient and technically competent leadership rather than bullying and bluster spurred by personal ambition and self-aggrandisement. It is interesting to speculate how the Desert War might have developed had Rommel been obliged to deal with O'Connor. Be that as it may, while the unfortunate O'Connor and his driving companions were beginning their journey to a prison camp, the 9th Australian Division continued to pass through the 26th Australian Brigade's protective screen at Tmimi throughout 7 April, along with anyone who had moved fast enough to avoid the developing German trap. Among the last appears to have been the 2/13th Battalion, which left Martuba at around midday with German tanks on their heels. Tovell's 26th Australian Brigade had now become the divisional rearguard, and beat off another German patrol that approached Tmimi at around the same time. The brigade held its position until nightfall and then retired to Gazala and Acroma on the morning of 8 April under cover of a sand storm. While all this was going on Morshead had set up his Divisional HQ in the Wadi Sehel, just outside the western face of the Tobruk defences, before motoring back to Gazala to sort out his units as they came in. By nightfall on 7 April he had deployed the 20th Australian Brigade in a blocking position across the *Via Balbia* 20 miles west of Tobruk, which the 26th Australian Brigade extended south to Acroma when it arrived the following morning, while the southern approach to Tobruk at El Adem was blocked by Brigadier Gott's newly arrived 7th Support Group, which had also provided the 1st KRRC to cover the initial stages of the withdrawal from Barce.

When he failed to find Neame awaiting him at Tmimi, Brigadier Harding established a small Forward Echelon HQ at Gazala and set the main body of Cyrenaica Command HQ back to Tobruk. When his commander had still failed to appear by 06:30 on 7 April, Harding reported his growing suspicion that some misfortune had befallen Neame's party to Wavell in Cairo. Fortuitously, Wavell had spent the previous afternoon discussing the situation in Cyrenaica with Secretary of State for War Anthony Eden, CIGS Sir John Dill, Air Chief Marshal Sir Arthur Longmore and Admiral Sir Andrew Cunningham. Mindful of the need to protect the naval base at Alexandria and military and civilian morale in Egypt, the conference decided that the best prospect was to make a stand as far west as possible. Tobruk was thus chosen as the site of the stand, in part to deny the port to the enemy, and because it was a ready water source and a large amount of stores had already been stockpiled there. After taking Harding's call Wavell therefore informed Churchill of the previous day's conference decision and then appears to have spent the remainder of the day making arrangements to support it. Some of the latter were already in hand. 107 Regiment (South Notts Hussars) RHA had been recalled from field firing at Tahag in the Canal Zone on 4 April, for example, and began the 700-mile road march to Tobruk at 07:30 on 5 April. Part of the 18th Australian Brigade was also en route to the port by sea after the 7th Australian Division's move to Greece had been cancelled, as were a number of tanks and crews from the 1st and 4th RTR that were to become the reconstituted 3rd Armoured Brigade; some elements of these units also travelled by road.[14] The 11th Hussars were despatched back to their old haunts on the Egyptian border to protect the southern flank of Gott's 7th Support Group at El Adem, and the 22nd Guards Brigade were sent forward to Bardia, where it was reinforced with a field artillery unit by sea.

With all this in hand Wavell flew out to Tobruk in an RAF Lockheed Lodestar on the morning of Tuesday 8 April, landing in the same severe sandstorm that had covered the 26th Australian Brigade's withdrawal to Acroma. He was accompanied by Major-General John Laverack, hitherto commander of the 7th Australian Division and now elevated to replace Neame as GOC Cyrenaica Command. There they met with Harding, Morshead and the latter's GSO1, Colonel Charles 'Gaffer' Lloyd, in a house on the outskirts of the port where Harding gave a situation report. The detail of what came next varies. According to a contemporary account, Harding then asked Wavell whether they were to hold Tobruk and the latter responded after studying the situation map by ordering Laverack to assume control of Cyrenaica Command and pointing out that there was nothing between Tobruk and Cairo.[15] A more recent account based on Wavell's biography refers to Morshead and Harding being asked for their opinion on whether Tobruk could be held and when they replied in the affirmative, Wavell told them to get on with it before appointing Laverack GOC Cyrenaica Command and suggesting Morshead be placed in charge of Tobruk.[16] Whatever the detail of the decision-making process, the upshot was Wavell writing out a clear and concise six point instruction for Laverack. This officially confirmed his command, instructed him to hold Tobruk, to maintain a mobile and aggressive defence to interfere with enemy operations against Egypt, and to allow time for a proper defence of the latter. Although he was authorised to prepare a withdrawal plan, Laverack was also forbidden to implement it without express authorisation from GHQ Cairo. The defence was expected to last for approximately two months. With that settled Wavell carried out an inspection of the Tobruk defences and paused for lunch before leaving for Cairo in the late afternoon.

Wavell's return flight to Cairo turned out to be far from straightforward. The sandstorm was still blowing, and takeoff was delayed for an hour by a malfunction in one of the Lodestar's brakes. Wavell spent the hour sheltering from the sandstorm in a hut with a group of Lysander pilots from No.6 Army Co-operation Squadron who, once the awe at the illustriousness of their visitor had receded, shared their supply of warm beer; the favour was returned a few days later when a case of champagne arrived at No. 6 Squadron's mess with Wavell's compliments. When the Lodestar finally took off the flight only lasted for fifteen minutes before an engine oil pressure failure obliged the pilot to put down at El Adem. The wait while the crew cleaned the oil filter was fraught, for the 7th Support Group had withdrawn from the former Italian airfield and the Germans were expected at any moment. The Lodestar took off again at sunset, but within twenty minutes the oil pressure failed again and the pilot's attempt to continue on one engine was thwarted when the surviving powerplant began to overheat. This time there was no handy airfield and while the pilot managed to put down on a flat spot, his efforts were undone by a reoccurrence of the Lodestar's brake problem after touchdown, which spun the aircraft so violently that one wing was torn off along with the twin-rudder tail plane. Fortunately no one was hurt and in time honoured British fashion passengers and crew set about brewing tea while taking stock of their situation. It was not promising, for the landing site was still some way inside Cyrenaica and there was thus a good chance that Wavell might also end up in German custody. Fortunately the first patrol to investigate the crash site was friendly and by 01:00 on 9 April Wavell was safe in Sollum to the great relief of his HQ in Cairo which, after six hours of silence, had begun to suspect the worst.[17]

Back at Tobruk Laverack finalised his command arrangements, confirming Morshead's responsibility for the defence of Tobruk while retaining personal control of the 18th Australian Brigade and the 7th Support Group; the latter was instructed to delay any German attempt to outflank Tobruk toward Bardia before falling back to join the 22nd Guards Brigade. On the morning of Wednesday 9 April he carried out a more detailed examination of the Tobruk defences with Morshead and Brigadiers Frederick Wooten, John Murray, Arthur Godfrey and Raymond Tovell, commanding the 18th, 20th, 24th and 26th Australian Brigades respectively. Wavell had suggested establishing a shorter defence line inside the original Italian perimeter around the post, in order to avoid the Italian error of spreading the available manpower too thinly. However, on personal inspection Laverack not only discovered that the Italian defences followed the only feasible line given the terrain, but that any contraction would put Tobruk proper within enemy field artillery range. He therefore authorised Morshead to utilise the existing defences and left him to get on with it as Wavell is alleged to have recommended.

Leslie James Morshead was born on 18 September 1889 at Ballerat, Victoria, the son of a gold-miner and the sixth of seven children. After graduating from Melbourne Teacher Training College in 1910, he held a number of teaching posts and obtained a commission in the Australian Army Cadets while teaching at the Armidale School in New South Wales. Enlisting as a private in the 2nd Infantry Battalion, 1st AIF on the outbreak of the First World War, Morshead was commissioned on 19 September 1914 and promoted to Captain on 8 January 1915. He landed at Anzac Cove on 25 April 1915 with the 2nd Battalion, was subsequently promoted to Major and distinguished himself in the Battle of Lone Tree on 6–10 August 1915 before being evacuated to the UK with dysentery in September 1915. On recovery he returned to Australia where he helped raise the 33rd Infantry Battalion, which he commanded after promotion to Lieutenant-Colonel on 19 April 1916. He then commanded the Battalion in France as part of the 3rd Australian Division, earning the DSO and five Mentions in Despatches for service at the Battles of Messines

Ridge, Passchendaele, Villers-Bretonneux and Amiens. After leaving the AIF in March 1920 Morshead tried his hand at farming before embarking on a career with the Orient Steam Navigation Company in 1924, but maintained links with the military via the Citizens Military Force and enlisted in the 2nd AIF in October 1939. Thereafter he was swiftly promoted Brigadier to raise and command the 18th Australian Brigade in the newly formed 6th Australian Division, and remained in command of the Brigade during its sojourn in the UK and redeployment to Egypt before being appointed to command the 9th Australian Division on 29 January 1941.[18] Morshead appears to have retained some of the air of a schoolmaster as a divisional commander, with one contemporary observer noting his precise and prim demeanour in comparison with rough and ready attitude of his men. However, the latter were in no doubt of his competence or the exacting standards he expected, as is clear from the nickname they gave him – Ming the Merciless.[19]

Apart from the damage inflicted by the 6th Australian Division's assault on the sector east of the Tobruk–El Adem road on 21 January, the Italian defences were essentially intact but suffering from the effects of neglect. The barbed wire aprons had fallen into disrepair in places while the anti-tank ditch and some of the communication trenches linking fighting positions and weapon pits had filled with wind-blown sand. Morshead put the troops occupying the Tobruk perimeter to work clearing, repairing and strengthening immediately, wearing gas goggles and face coverings for protection against the ongoing sandstorm. The engineers set about re-laying the Italian minefields and created more of their own, more often than not using captured Italian mines in lieu of British items, while the infantry repaired the barbed wire entanglement, a risky business as the Italians had sown them liberally with booby-traps. The infantry also set about renovating and modifying the 128 concrete defence posts that made up the Italian perimeter, which was dubbed the Red Line, adding extra gun pits and fighting positions, and digging additional posts to fill gaps or blind spots in the original layout and company-size reserve positions at roughly two mile intervals 500 yards to the rear.

Behind all this Morshead ordered the construction of a new inner perimeter two miles further back, possibly along a projected line traced out on some captured Italian maps.[20] Whatever its provenance, the inner perimeter was dubbed the Blue Line, and consisted of strongpoints containing anti-tank guns and automatic weapons spaced at roughly 500 yard intervals, protected by a continuous minefield and belt of barbed wire.[21] The troops deployed within it were also tasked to provide local protection for the artillery emplacements to their rear, and additional infantry positions were prepared among the emplacements for that purpose, along with additional protective minefields. Ultimately Morshead's intention was to expand the thin crust of the Italian defence line into an integrated system of self-contained defensive positions capable of providing all-round defence and mutual support, thus presenting defence in depth. The Red Line was thus intended to absorb the shock of any attack and channel and restrict the width of any enemy breakthrough, which would then be obliged to negotiate numerous minefields before coming up against the Blue Line; eventually there were so many minefields between the two Lines that the engineers lost track of their locations, and a number of vehicles were lost after inadvertently straying into them. The infantry positions dug among the artillery emplacements behind the Blue Line constituted a third line of defence augmented by the guns, the latter's crews being briefed to hold in place and operate in the direct fire role if necessary. Morshead appears to have taken inspiration from his First World War experience, as this defensive system was virtually identical to that developed by the British Expeditionary Force on the Western Front in the winter of 1917–1918. The latter consisted of a Forward Zone and Battle Zone, 2,000 to 3,000 yards apart, and interestingly the Cambrai sector also employed a primitive anti-tank minefield using adapted trench-mortar bombs.[22] Be that as it may, an important addition was a mobile reserve, tasked to seal off any enemy penetration of the Blue Line made up of three motorised infantry battalions, mobile anti-tank guns and an ad hoc armoured group.

The entire Tobruk system was thus an ambitious undertaking that would take a considerable time to complete, but in the immediate term the existing Italian works were sufficient and Morshead's most pressing problem was finding the personnel and means to man them. Only 18,000 of the 35,307 troops within the Tobruk perimeter were combat troops, and the former figure included only thirteen infantry battalions.[23] To stretch this force as far as possible, Morshead gambled by relying on eight captured Italian coastal guns and the Royal Navy to cover the twenty miles of coastline within the Tobruk perimeter, and concentrated his manpower on the thirty-odd miles of landward perimeter. This meant manning defence posts intended for twenty to fifty men with ten or fifteen, and the shortfall was partially rectified by substituting firepower for manpower. On occupying Tobruk the 9th Australian Division not only received many of the Bren Guns it had been missing, but also large numbers of captured Italian automatic weapons, including Breda, Fiat and water-cooled Schwarzlose medium machine guns of First World War vintage obtained as post-war reparations from Austria-Hungary.[24] These were distributed liberally among the defences; a contemporary account refers to a defence post manned by fourteen Australians being armed with a Thompson sub-machine gun, one British and two captured Italian machine guns, an anti-tank rifle and an Italian 47mm anti-tank gun, presumably in addition to their personal weapons.[25]

The situation was less favourable with regard to ant-tank weapons. Having detached a battery each to support the ill-fated defence of Mechili, the 3rd Australian Anti-Tank Regiment and 3rd RHA were understrength, although one source refers to at least some towed guns and Portees from these detached sub-units reaching Tobruk on 9 April.[26] In conjunction with the four infantry brigades' integral anti-tank companies, the Tobruk garrison could muster a total of 113 anti-tank guns. Approximately half of these were captured Italian 37mm and 47mm pieces, and in all only eighty-nine were available for employment in the defence posts as twenty-four of the 3rd RHA's 2-Pounder Portees were assigned to the mobile reserve. The total was later augmented with fourteen disabled tanks, which were dug in as anti-tank bunkers.[27] The position was a little better with regard to artillery. Approximately 250,000 rounds of assorted ammunition had been stockpiled at Tobruk for use by the 2/12th Field Regiment RAA, 1st and 104th Regiments RHA and 51st Field Regiment RA which appear to have arrived at Tobruk with the Australians, and they were shortly joined by 107 Regiment (South Notts Hussars) RHA. At around the same time the 14th Light and 235th Heavy Anti-Aircraft Brigades arrived to bolster Tobruk's air defences, although the former arrived by sea without its full complement of guns and had to be outfitted with captured 20mm Breda guns. By 11 April Tobruk's anti-aircraft defences boasted twenty-four 3.7-inch guns, four reconditioned Italian 102mm guns, seventeen 40mm Bofors, forty-two 20mm Breda automatics and ten searchlights, the bulk of which were deployed to protect Tobruk harbour.[28]

The bulk of Morshead's armoured reserve also arrived at Tobruk at this time aboard the freighter *Thurland Castle*. The latter brought in eleven Cruiser Tanks belonging to the 1st RTR, four Matilda II Infantry Tanks belonging to the 7th RTR and sixteen Light Tanks, some with crated and grease-packed guns and lacking radio sets; the crews worked on their vehicles non-stop during the voyage from Alexandria, having been warned that they might have to go into action immediately on disembarkation.. On arrival the 1st RTR contingent was augmented by another twelve assorted A9, A10 and A13 Cruisers rounded up from workshops in Tobruk, and an additional eight Matildas were subsequently shipped in from Egypt for the 7th RTR. In addition to the RTR units the 3rd Armoured Brigade had a composite Light Tank unit built on elements of the 3rd Hussars and the armoured cars of the 1st KDG.[29] The final element of Tobruk's defence force belonged to the RAF. No. 6 Army Co-operation Squadron, whose pilots had entertained Wavell during his enforced stop at El Adem, took up residence with its nine Hurricanes and four Lysanders at an airstrip in the western side of the perimeter, while No. 73 Squadron moved its twelve Hurricanes from Sidi Bouamoud to El Gubbi airfield just south of Tobruk proper.[30] They have a good claim to having been the first unit to fire a shot in defence of Tobruk, after a Pilot Officer Goodman shot down a Messerschmitt 110 from *Zestörergeschwader* 26 during a German raid on the port in the late morning of 9 April.[31]

The original plan had been for the 18th and understrength 24th Australian Brigades to man the Tobruk defences while the 20th and 26th Australian Brigades maintained blocking positions outside the perimeter until at least that date. However, reconnaissance flights by No. 6 Squadron's Lysanders the previous day (9 April) reported German armoured columns approaching Tobruk from Derna and Mechili. As the latter raised the possibility of the blocking position running north from Acroma being outflanked and cut off, the 20th and 26th Australian Brigades were withdrawn inside the Tobruk perimeter the same night. The accelerated withdrawal was a matter of some concern for the commander of 107 Regiment RHA who had arrived at Tobruk ahead of his unit making its four-day, 700 mile road march from the Canal Zone. In the event, concerns that the Regiment might be overwhelmed en route proved groundless as it came into Tobruk at 22:00.

With the arrival of 107 Regiment RHA and a variety of other stragglers and oddments the perimeter was closed, and Morshead deployed his relatively meagre force to its posts. The western sector of the perimeter facing Derna and Acroma was assigned to the newly arrived 26th Australian Brigade, the 20th Australian Brigade took over the southern sector facing El Adem and the two battalions from the 24th Australian occupied the eastern sector toward Bardia. The 18th Indian Cavalry Regiment, which had escaped the trap at Mechili, was deployed in the infantry role as a reserve in the west while a scratch battalion made up of Army Service Corps personnel fulfilled a similar role in the east.[32] Finally, the 18th Australian Infantry Brigade, which at that time was still under Laverack's direct command, was designated overall garrison reserve. This spread the garrison's infantry component thin, but Morshead had little alternative in the circumstances and the garrison settled into its fighting positions and set about making what preparations for whatever the future would bring. According to one account, the Australian infantrymen were 'grimly determined that no one would be able to call them the division which lost all that the 6th [Australian Division] had won',[33] and they were not kept in suspense for long. The sandstorm that had sheltered the final stage of the Tobruk Derby complicated the work of Morshead's engineers and almost did for Wavell finally abated at around midday on 10 April. As the dust settled, German activity could be seen along the west and south of the perimeter.

While all this was going on the *Deutsches Afrikakorps* were experiencing their own problems complying with Rommel's uncompromising demands. After almost being shot down by Italian troops from the *Ariete* Division east of Mechili on the morning of 8 April, Rommel was grounded there by a sandstorm, possibly the same one that had also delayed Wavell ninety miles or so to the east at Tobruk. He was therefore present when Major-General Gambier-Parry formally surrendered to *Colonello* Ugo Montemurro, along with the commander of 5 *Leichte* Division, *Generalmajor* Streich, and *Oberstleutnant* Olbrich of Panzer Regiment 5. Rommel did not permit the latter to tarry and ordered him to refuel his vehicles and follow *Oberst* Graf von Schwerin's detachment north toward Derna with all possible speed, and by 18:00 Rommel had flown to Derna himself. It is unclear whether the meeting took place that evening or the next day, but he met with *Oberstleutnant* Ponath of *Maschinengewehr Bataillon* 8 and *Oberstleutnant* Freiherr von Wechmar of *Aufklärungs Abteilung* 3. *Generalmajor* Kirchheim, who had been co-opted by Rommel to chivvy the *Brescia* Division around the Cyrenaican coast from Benghazi, had apparently been wounded in an RAF strafing attack while organising artillery to shell Tobruk harbour.[34]

Fortuitously for Rommel, Kirchheim's place was filled by *Generalmajor* Heinrich von Prittwitz und Gaffron, the commander of 15 Panzer Division. A cavalryman who had transferred to the *Panzerwaffe* in the late 1930s and had commanded tank formations in Poland and France, von Prittwitz had only recently arrived in Tripoli, although it is unclear whether he had flown ahead of his Division or travelled with its advance elements.[35] Whichever, Rommel confidently announced that the British were merely a beaten rabble and placed von Prittwitz in charge of *Aufklärungs Abteilung* 3, *Maschinengewehr Bataillon* 8 and *Panzerjäger Abteilung* 605. According to one source, Rommel made a comment to von Prittwitz along the lines that if a single battalion had been enough to secure Derna then his new command ought to be sufficient to deal with Tobruk.[36] With that Rommel went south again to browbeat *Generalmajor* Streich and especially Panzer Regiment 5, overriding the former's objections yet again and ordering *Oberstleutnant* Olbrich to have his tanks in position to attack Tobruk from the south within twenty-four hours. Despite Rommel's best hectoring efforts, however, it still took two days and another confrontation with *Generalmajor* Streich to get 5 *Leichte* Division's widely scattered and fuel starved units to where they could strike against Tobruk, and as a result the German advance on the port was disjointed and piecemeal.

Von Prittwitz and his new command were the first to make contact, after Rommel returned to Derna on 9 April and ordered an attack on Tobruk from the west the following day. The attack was thus supposed to begin in the early hours of 10 April but the supporting bombardment did not begin until 09:00. The last gasp of the two day sandstorm came at 10:30, which reduced visibility to twenty feet, slowed matters yet further. Additional delay may also have arisen from von Prittwitz catching some much-needed sleep after his breakneck journey from Tripoli, given that Rommel rousted him from his bedroll and accused him of giving the British time to 'do another Dunkirk'.[37] Whatever the reason, the first contact with the Tobruk garrison came at approximately midday on 10 April 1941, when lead elements of *Maschinengewehr Bataillon* 8 approached a bridge carrying the *Via Balbia* across a wadi ten miles west of the port, on the 2/28th Battalion's frontage. A Lieutenant Bamgarten of the 2/3rd Field Company RAE blew the bridge, and the defenders called down artillery fire on the stalled Germans from the nearby 51st Field Regiment RA and the so-called 'Bush Artillery', a number of captured Italian guns manned by 2/28th Battalion personnel and commanded by the Battalion Transport Officer. The Germans withdrew briefly to reorganise and then launched a number of vehicles led by armoured cars in a charge toward the bridge, which was met with a wall of concentrated fire that knocked out seven vehicles and two armoured cars; von Prittwitz was moving up to get a better view of the fight in one of the latter, and was killed by an artillery round that disabled the vehicle and set it on fire. His men continued to exchange fire across the wadi for several hours before finally withdrawing out of range. *Generalmajor* von Prittwitz's sojourn in North Africa had thus lasted only a matter of days, and he paid a heavy price for Rommel's haste. He was not to be the last. The first clash on the Tobruk perimeter also cost the defenders two dead, thirty wounded, two guns and two Bren Carriers.[38]

Rommel appears to have reset his sights on more ambitious targets than merely bouncing the British out of Tobruk while von Prittwitz and his men were still preparing to move, and thus before they had 'failed' Rommel by paying the price for his substitution of haste and wishful thinking for reconnaissance and sober appreciation. According to his aide *Hauptmann* Heinz Schmidt, Rommel announced his intention of reaching the Nile on the morning of 10 April,[39] and a note in 5 *Leichte* Division's War Diary refers to orders to inform the troops that seizing Tobruk was merely a step on the way to securing the Suez Canal.[40] Perhaps the clearest evidence of the shift in Rommel's priorities comes from his indifferent reaction to the death of von Prittwitz. A meeting between Rommel, *Generalmajor* Streich and *Oberstleutnant* Olbrich on the track linking Acroma and El Adem in the afternoon of 10 April led to another angry exchange with Streich, who criticised the pointless death of von Prittwitz. Rommel replied offhandedly by admitting that 'We probably tried too much with too little. Anyhow, we are in a better position now.'[41] This was a blasé and callous reaction by any standard, and not only reinforces the impression that Rommel's primary motivation was self-glorification, but also that he was quite willing to sacrifice the lives of his subordinates in its pursuit. It also suggests that despite his lionisation as a scion of modern mechanised warfare, Rommel also had much in common with his First World War forebears like Erich von Falkenhayn; the latter had earned the dubious distinction of being the first modern practitioner of *Ermattungsstrategie*, ruthlessly using battlefield attrition as a deliberately calculated strategy at Verdun between February and July 1916.

Be that as it may, while all this was going on Rommel had despatched *Aufklärungs Abteilung* 3 and the spearhead of the still deploying 15 Panzer Division, *Oberstleutnant* Gustav Knabe's *Kradschützen Bataillon* 15, to El Adem via Acroma to scout the way for the *Brescia* Division; these were probably among the estimated 700 German vehicles spotted moving east from Gazala by British reconnaissance aircraft on the morning of 10 April. By nightfall the German advance had closed to within seven miles of El Adem, prompting Brigadier Gott's 7th Support Group to withdraw toward the Egyptian frontier.[42] This permitted *Oberstleutnants* von Wechmar and Knabe to loop around the Tobruk perimeter and cut the *Via Balbia* running east toward Bardia. The Australians manning the Tobruk perimeter noted this movement as a group of around 300 hundred vehicles moving east between their positions and El Adem, and the Bardia road was reportedly cut initially by just four tanks and a party of motorised infantry on the morning of Good Friday 11 April 1941.[43] This marked the encirclement of Tobruk and thus the official beginning of the siege, although it would be some time before that state was fully achieved. The eastern blocking position was subsequently taken over by *Maschinengewehr Bataillon* 2, which freed *Aufklärungs Abteilung* 3 and Knabe's unit to move east on Bardia and Sollum respectively.

In the afternoon of 11 April the Germans made their second and more determined attempt to penetrate Tobruk's defences, this time in the southern sector of the perimeter held by Brigadier John Murray's 20th Australian Brigade. The brigade was deployed along a frontage of just over ten miles straddling the El Adem road, with the 2/13th Battalion east of the road, the 2/17th Battalion to the west and the 2/15th Battalion in reserve. The initial contact came in the mid-afternoon with the appearance of a battalion's size of groups of enemy infantry in front of both the 2/13th and 2/17th Battalions, backed at the latter by about seventy tanks divided into four echeloned groups. The latter was a matter of some concern for the 2/17th Battalion, which had yet to receive its allocation of extra automatic weapons or anti-tank guns. An RHA observer officer attached to the

Australian Battalion called down artillery fire that drove the infantry
to ground but the tanks, estimated as numbering seventy and identified in an eye-witness account as a mixture of German Panzer IVs
and Italian M13/40s, came on until they reached the anti-tank ditch,
which was fortunately properly excavated and intact at this point
in the perimeter. Unable to cross the ditch the tanks paused before
turning east and moving parallel with it, firing on the Australian
defence posts as they went. At this point an erroneous report reached
the 9th Australian Division HQ that ten enemy tanks had broken
through the perimeter, and the mixed Squadron from the 1st RTR,
made up of five Cruiser and eight Light Tanks was ordered forward
from its position south of Pilastrino to deal with the interlopers.[44]
The German tactic of following the ditch backfired when the tanks
reached the El Adem road, where the 2/13th Battalion had emplaced
two captured Italian 47mm anti-tank guns that promptly knocked
out one M13/40 and scored hits on several other, prompting a hasty
withdrawal to the south.

The scratch Australian gunners were reinforced at this point
by the 1st RTR Squadron, who engaged the next wave of enemy
tanks in a thirty-minute gunnery duel from within the perimeter that knocked an M13/40 and three CV33 tankettes. Another
Panzer IV was knocked out by artillery and a CV33 was disabled by
concentrated small-arms fire; the crew abandoned the vehicle and
surrendered to a nearby Australian position. In all, the clash cost the
Germans seven vehicles in return for two of the 1st RTR's Cruiser
Tanks. One of the latter continued to fight after being immobilised
by a hit on its running gear but was then hit three times in quick
succession; all three penetrated the Cruiser's armour killing one
crewman, wounding another and setting the ammunition stowage
ablaze. The German infantry then put in a determined attack against
the 2/17th Battalion which succeeded in reaching the cover of the
anti-tank ditch due to a lack of Australian automatic weapons and
the gathering dusk. An Australian counter-attack at around 22:00
reached the ditch and found that the Germans had withdrawn, but
were then cut off by machine-gun and mortar fire that continued

sporadically throughout the night. To the east a number of German tanks approached the 2/13th Battalion's front after dark but withdrew when they were unable to locate a crossing point in the moonlight. A subsequent Australian fighting patrol intended to prevent German infiltration of the anti-tank ditch came upon preparations to bridge the ditch; the enemy retired without contact abandoning tools, explosives, a number of Bangalore torpedoes pre-positioned in the wire and a functioning field radio.[46] The 20th Australian Brigade thus held the attacks, but the situation was considered sufficiently serious for Major-General Lavarack to order the deployment of the garrison's tank and infantry reserve to cover the El Adem sector of the perimeter.[47]

The Australians defending the El Adem road sector would have been unaware of it, but their attackers were from *Oberstleutnant* Olbrich's Panzer Regiment 5, reinforced with a mixed group of approximately forty-five M13/40 medium tanks and CV33 tankettes from the *Ariete* Division, and *Oberstleutnant* Ponath's *Maschinengewehr Bataillon* 8. The Panzer Regiment had finally arrived at the front after its somewhat redundant diversion to Derna, and a captured report provides details of the German side of the engagement. By the early morning of 11 April Panzer Regiment 5 was laagered alongside the *Via Balbia* twenty miles west of Tobruk, and the order to sweep into Tobruk from the south via Acroma was received at 07:30. The move began an hour later, with an officer from *Deutsches Afrikakorps* HQ providing the precise route as the Regiment passed through Acroma. Olbrich's men reached their designated jump-off position at 15:00, where they linked up with *Maschinengewehr Bataillon* 8 and immediately came under artillery fire.

The attack, which involved the Regimental HQ and both Panzer *Abteilungen* with a reported twenty-five tanks in addition to the *Ariete* contingent, went in at 16:00. The presence of the anti-tank ditch came as an unexpected and unwelcome surprise as did the level of resistance, for the Germans had been under the impression that the defence would crumble before them. Instead the four-kilometre eastward sideslip along the ditch in search of a crossing point was done under constant artillery and small-arms fire, until the lead vehicles actually ran into a minefield beside the El Adem road at approximately 17:15. Faced by this and the fire from the 2/13th Battalion's Italian 47mm anti-tank guns Olbrich ordered a withdrawal to the south to regroup, leaving behind two knocked out M13s, one Panzer III and the CV33 whose crew had surrendered after their vehicle was disabled by small-arms fire. He then despatched a party from *Panzer Abteilung* II into the dusk under a *Leutnant* von Hulsen to reconnoitre east along the anti-tank ditch in search of a crossing point. This party were presumably responsible for the moonlight tank investigation noted by the Australians; the attempt to prepare a ditch crossing point thwarted by the fighting patrol from the 2/13th Battalion was an independent initiative by *Pionier Bataillon* 200, which specialised in breaching fixed defences.[48] What comes through clearly in the first part of the German report is a feeling that the attackers had been misled and thrown into battle without the most basic intelligence or preparation.[49]

While all this was going *Maschinengewehr Bataillon* 8 had been left stranded in front of the 2/17th Battalion's positions by the disappearance of its tank support to the east. Their woes were exacerbated by strafing attacks by Hurricanes from No. 73 Squadron, although the damage was not all one-way; two Hurricanes were shot down by German fire, another disappeared after a sudden sandstorm blanketed El Gubbi airfield; the latter obliged a fourth to divert to Mersa Matruh, almost 200 miles east of Tobruk.[50] After being expelled from their foothold in the ditch by the Australian counter-attack at 22:00, Ponath's men constructed a line of makeshift shell-scrapes and sangars about 400 yards from the ditch, where the 2/17th Battalion discovered them at dawn on Easter Saturday 12 April. Both sides maintained a wary watch, and the Germans harassed the arrival and emplacement of seven anti-tank guns from around 09:00 with small-arms fire. Once again the bulk of the action occurred to the east near the El Adem road, where Panzer Regiment 5 was re-arming and preparing to renew the attack in a large hollow about 3,000 yards south of the perimeter. Alerted to the German activity by the stirred

up dust, the defenders began to shell the hollow, with the RHA firing a ninety-minute, 500 round concentration on a group of sixty
German vehicles that positioned themselves within view. A number
of ambulance vehicles were subsequently observed removing casualties. The Australians also called in Blenheims from No. 55 Squadron
to bomb another enemy vehicle concentration in the hollow in the
afternoon.

The *Luftwaffe* was also active. Some aircraft flew low-level sorties
along the perimeter to gather information on the state of the anti-
tank ditch, while others scattered leaflets with the following rather
stilted message:

> The General Officer Commanding the German forces in Libya hereby
> requests that the British troops occupying Tobruk surrender their arms.
> Single soldiers waving white handkerchiefs are not fired on. Strong
> German forces have already surrounded Tobruk and it is useless to try
> and escape. Remember Mekili [sic]. Our dive-bombers and Stukas are
> awaiting your ships which are lying in Tobruk.[51]

The official response by Tobruk HQ was to drily point out that the
shortage of water meant there was a lack of white handkerchiefs
within the perimeter, while the daily situation report to GHQ Cairo
announced its response as a two-word epithet ending in 'off'. Other
German aircraft harassed the 1ˢᵗ RHA's gun positions, and a force of
fifteen Junkers 87 dive-bombers attacked Tobruk harbour. They were
fought off by the harbour's anti-aircraft defences, some of which had
only recently arrived, and Hurricanes from No. 73 Squadron. Three
German machines were claimed shot down.

The Germans appear to have spent much of 12 April waiting for
information from the *Luftwaffe* on the anti-tank ditch. This seems a
curious omission, for not only are such obstacles difficult to assess
accurately from the air, but even a cursory ground inspection would
have shown that in two places the ditch was unfinished and only
around eighteen inches deep, including a full four mile stretch east of
the El Adem road. Whichever, Panzer Regiment 5 prepared to renew

the attack with twenty-four tanks at 15:15 after an officer, probably from *Pionier Bataillon* 200, reported that there might be a break in the anti-tank ditch four kilometres west of the point where they had attacked the 2/17th Battalion's frontage the previous day. A party of engineers were attached to the Regiment as a precautionary measure, but they soon became separated from the tanks by British artillery fire that followed the move west. At 16:00 the tanks came within sight of Australian defence posts covering the attack point, and forty-five minutes later the Regiment's lead elements discovered that their target was indeed fronted by an impassable section of intact anti-tank ditch. Olbrich's tanks paused for fifteen minutes under increasingly heavy artillery and anti-tank fire and when the engineers failed to catch up to deal with the ditch, the Panzers pulled back out of range. The idea that the defenders of Tobruk could be easily bounced out of their positions or that they were likely to collapse at the mere approach of a Panzer withdrew with them, although Rommel was to take a little more convincing.

8

Tobruk Attacked:
12 April 1941 – 18 April 1941

By nightfall on Easter Saturday 1941, Rommel's *Deutsches Afrikakorps* had made three hasty attacks on the west and southern sectors of the Tobruk perimeter over the preceding seventy-two hours, all of which failed to make any impression on the defences. The strength of the latter and the resolute behaviour of the troops holding them came as an unpleasant surprise to their German counterparts, who appear to have become accustomed to sweeping all before them. It was an even more unwelcome setback for Rommel who had also expected opposition to crumble, in part on the erroneous assumption that the ships unloading personnel, equipment and supplies in Tobruk harbour were there to carry out an evacuation. More especially, he did not welcome the distraction from his self-imposed goal of pushing into Egypt to the Suez Canal and lost no time in apportioning blame.

Perhaps predictably, his chosen whipping boys were *Generalmajor* Streich and more especially *Oberstleutnant* Olbrich, who bore the brunt of Rommel's displeasure. Olbrich was lambasted for not pressing home his attacks against the Tobruk defences with sufficient vigour, although it is unclear if Rommel also advised him on how he was supposed to levitate his tanks across an intact anti-tank ditch, while Streich appears to have been in the firing line simply because he commanded 5 *Leichte* Division. To be fair, Rommel's criticisms may well have been justified to an extent. Neither Panzer Regiment 5, *Maschinengewehr Bataillon* 8 nor *Pionier Bataillon* 200 appear to have pressed their attacks especially hard, with tiredness if not outright exhaustion doubtless being a significant factor. Panzer Regiment 5, for example, had been almost constantly on the move or fighting for the whole of the three weeks since its road march from Tripoli to Nofilia on 23 March. It would therefore appear that by 12 April Rommel's men were reaching the end of their physical tether, a circumstance on which no amount of haranguing and harassment was likely to much effect. It is interesting to contrast Rommel's *modus operandi* with O'Connor's much less confrontational command style and the achievements of the latter's force during Operation COMPASS at Bardia, Tobruk and elsewhere under similar constraints and conditions. Be that as it may, the meeting ended with Rommel ordering Streich to carry out another attack on the night of 13–14 April, which was to be 'made with the utmost resolution under your personal leadership', and Rommel also detailed his aide *Hauptmann* Heinz Schmidt to remain at Streich's HQ to ensure the latter complied with his orders. This was a quite breathtaking example of double-standards given Rommel's own predilection for simply ignoring directives and explicit orders from his own superiors.[1] It is unclear what Streich made of this, but he set rapidly to work to make the most of the mere twenty-four hours or so he had been given to prepare.

By Easter Sunday 13 April the *Trento* Division had closed up to the south-west corner of the Tobruk perimeter, with the *Ariete* and 5 *Leichte* Divisions respectively deployed along the southern sector to just east of the El Adem road. Streich arranged for diversionary activity to be carried out along the whole of this ten-mile stretch of the perimeter, in an effort to mislead the defenders as to the precise location of the upcoming attack. This included movement east from Acroma noted by reconnaissance aircraft and a demonstration with tanks and motorised infantry against the western side of the Tobruk perimeter during a sandstorm, presumably by units from the *Ariete* and *Trento* Divisions.[2] The spot chosen was again on the

2/17th Battalion's frontage just west of the El Adem road, in the vicinity of defence post 33. The plan was a three phase affair. The first stage was to be an infantry night assault by *Maschinengewehr Bataillon* 8, which was intended to neutralise selected defence posts and secure a section of the perimeter. With that done, engineers from *Pionier Bataillon* 200 would move in to clear the wire and mines and prepare tank crossing points over the anti-tank ditch. Once the crossing points were complete, Panzer Regiment 5 would pass across the ditch, move through the gap and split into two and move to secure Tobruk proper and cut off any attempts by the defenders to escape from the perimeter. The *Ariete* Division was also warned to stand by to assist Panzer Regiment 5 in exploiting the break through.

The plan was therefore relatively straightforward, but the preparations and organisation were more problematic. *Oberstleutnant* Ponath's *Maschinengewehr Bataillon* 8 had been in near-constant contact for fourteen days by this point, and was still ensconced in its makeshift positions 400 yards in front of the 2/17th Battalion. As a result merely receiving the briefing for his new mission was far from straightforward for Ponath, as leaving his command post entailed a lengthy and stealthy crawl to avoid attracting potentially terminal attention from the watchful Australians. It is unclear who delivered the briefing, but a contemporary Australian account suggests that his efforts to avoid detection may have been ineffective. Major J. W. Balfe, one of the 2/17th Battalion's company commanders, noted the arrival of German staff cars and motor cycle combinations at what was assumed to be a battle HQ approximately 2,000 yards in front of his positions, and reported that the Battalion's newly-arrived anti-tank guns scored hits on one car and two motorcycles.[3] *Generalmajor* Streich's deception measures also appear to have been ineffective if not actually counter-productive. A circling *Luftwaffe* reconnaissance aircraft and vehicles manoeuvring and unloading infantry several thousand yards to their front convinced the 2/17th Battalion that a renewed attack was imminent and a Forward Observer Officer from the 1st RHA, Major Robert Loder-Symonds, called down fire on the German infantry.[4] Australian accounts refer to this as a rebuffed attack but it may have been either pre-attack reinforcement or part of Streich's diversion tactics, given that it does not figure in Panzer Regiment 5's report.

Major-General Morshead was certainly convinced of the target of the German attack, so much so that he ordered four batteries of 25-Pounder guns from the 1st RHA to be dug in on the Blue Line inner defensive perimeter just south of the junction of the El Adem and Bardia roads; the latter was commonly referred to as the El Adem crossroads or 'King's Cross'. From there the gunners were to provide fire support and act as a backstop position. A number of 2-Pounder portees and towed weapons from the 3rd RHA and 3rd Australian Anti-Tank Regiment were also moved up to the area of the junction and the commander of the 3rd Armoured Brigade, Lieutenant-Colonel H. D. Drew, was ordered to prepare to meet an enemy attack in the vicinity of the El Adem road.[5] Help was also summoned from further afield, with Bristol Blenheims from Nos. 45 and 55 Squadrons being called in from Egypt to bomb enemy vehicle concentrations; re-arming between missions at El Gubbi allowed the bombers to maximise their sortie rate.[6]

While all this was going on, shipping was still passing in and out of Tobruk harbour, and vital equipment was still being unloaded. Five new anti-aircraft units arrived in the six days between 6 and 12 April, along with eight 3.7-inch and twelve 40mm Bofors static guns and all the associated equipment. The Bofors guns were immediately deployed to protect the harbour, but setting up the 3.7-inch guns took a considerable period of time due to interference from the *Luftwaffe* and a shortage of labour, while plans to form two light anti-aircraft batteries armed with salvaged Italian Breda 20mm guns was stymied when the guns were issued to units on the perimeter instead.[7] On the morning of Easter Sunday 13 April a small convoy of five unfamiliar looking craft arrived. Dubbed 'A Lighters' as a security measure, the vessels were in fact the forerunners of an entire class that were to play a leading role in the Allied amphibious landings at Sicily, Salerno, Anzio and Normandy. Officially known as the Landing Craft Tank (LCT) Mk. 1, the first example was produced by Hawthorn Leslie shipbuilders of Newcastle-upon-Tyne in November 1940.

The first five prototypes, originally intended for a cancelled landing in the Dodecanese Islands, were shipped in sections as deck stowage to the Middle East, arriving in January 1941. After assembly at the shipyards at Port Fuad and Port Tewfik, they were pressed into service ferrying supplies west along the coast from Alexandria. With a length of 160 feet, a crew of fourteen and equipped with a blunt square bow that doubled as an unloading ramp for the well deck capable of accommodating five tanks, the LCT's flat bottoms and boxy hull shape made them poor sea boats, but the numerous voids and buoyancy tanks made them very difficult to sink. The LCT Mk.1's greatest weakness actually lay in its two 650 hp Hall-Scott petrol engines, for the 8,000 gallons of high-octane fuel stored in under-deck tanks were terribly vulnerable to battle damage, to the extent that subsequent marks used diesel rather than petrol engines. In all 864 LCTs were produced in Britain, and a further 965 were built in US shipyards. The five prototypes vessels were all marked with the letters WDLF, standing for Western Desert Lighter Force, although their crews claimed with macabre humour that the correct translation was 'We Die Like Flies'. They were nonetheless destined to play a role in running supplies into besieged Tobruk in a regular but hazardous shuttle service called the 'Spud Run'.

The first Spud Run, escorted by the anti-submarine trawler *Southern Maid* and the anti-aircraft sloop *Auckland* and carrying a combined cargo of eight Matilda Infantry Tanks, a number of Bren Gun Carriers, some 25-Pounders and assorted ammunition, thus arrived at the entrance to the swept channel through Tobruk's protective minefield in the early hours of Easter Sunday, 13 April 1941. An Axis bombing raid on the port was in full swing, and the *Southern Maid* shepherded her charges back out to sea to avoid them being spotted when the invisible bombers started dropping parachute flares. Another raid just after dawn delayed matters further, and it was almost midday before the little convoy finally passed through the boom. The A Lighters were unloaded across the beach in the north-east corner of the harbour, supervised by Army Lieutenant O'Shaughnessy, the Chief Movement Control Officer. After unloading, they moved to refuel in pairs from a tanker moored in the harbour, and were so engaged when an attack by approximately thirty Junkers 88 bombers came in at around 14:00. The tanker escaped damage despite a number of near misses but one merchantman was sunk out in the harbour and another, moored alongside the port's single quay, was hit and set on fire prompting a frantic but successful effort to tow it clear. In return the anti-aircraft guns protecting the port claimed seven aircraft shot down during the thirty minute raid. The A Lighters were unscathed and sailed out of the harbour at sundown.[8]

The German attack against the 2/17th Battalion's section of the perimeter began at around the same time the little convoy of A Lighters were leaving Tobruk harbour. At 17:00 Rommel personally directed a barrage from *Major* Hetch's *Artillerie Abteilung* 75 and a number of co-opted Italian guns onto defence Posts R31 and R32 which flanked the selected attack point; the latter was actually occupied by Post R33, the existence of which the Germans appear to have been unaware of. The infantry attack by Ponath's *Maschinengewehr Bataillon* 8 which followed the barrage was therefore stopped by small-arms fire from the platoon holding Post R33, commanded by twenty-three year old Lieutenant Austin Mackell. Mackell's fire was thickened with artillery support from the 1st RHA called down by Major Balfe from Post R32, who thus entered the record books as the first Australian infantry officer to control RHA guns in action.[9] There was then a pause while the attackers evaluated the situation and modified their plan. At 22:00 the forward defence positions came under heavy mortar and machine-gun fire, and German troops were spotted moving through the wire to the east of Post R33. Within an hour a party of around thirty men from *Maschinengewehr Bataillon* 8 armed with a reported eight machine-guns, mortars and two light guns had established a foothold inside the wire 100 yards east of R33. The guns were probably 75mm *leichtes Infanteriegeschütz* 18 pieces, and their crews and the rest of the party were busy digging in.

When the interlopers proved impervious to small-arms fire Lieutenant Mackell sallied forth from Post R33 to dislodge them at approximately 23:45, accompanied by Corporal Jack Edmondson and five volunteers armed with rifles, fixed bayonets and grenades. Under cover of fire from the remainder of his platoon Mackell's little party circled to take the Germans in the flank, lobbed a volley of grenades and then charged straight into the concentrated German machine-gun fire. Corporal Edmondson was hit in the stomach and neck in the final rush but nonetheless bayoneted two Germans on the way into the German position and killed two more who were wrestling with Lieutenant Mackell. The Germans fled into the darkness leaving all their weapons and equipment along with around a dozen dead and a lone prisoner, while Mackell and his party withdrew to Post R33. Corporal Edmondson made it back to safety but died of his wounds early the next morning; he was subsequently awarded a posthumous Victoria Cross, the first such award to an Australian serviceman during the Second World War and the only one of the siege. Mackell's little band were not the only Australians roaming the darkness for the commander of the 2/17th Battalion, Lieutenant-Colonel J. W. Crawford, had despatched two fighting patrols that made contact with the enemy before returning with a prisoner apiece and reports of German activity all along the Battalion frontage.[10]

Courageous though it was, the rebuff administered by Lieutenant Mackell and Corporal Edmondson gained only a temporary respite. Just after 02:15 *Maschinengewehr Bataillon* 8 returned with around 200 men and set about extending the penetration into the Australian positions. The interlopers were again not deterred by fire from Mackell's men in Post R33 or the artillery barrage called down via flares by Major Balfe, and were soon laying down heavy suppressive fire on Post R33 and its western neighbour to cover engineers from *Pionier Bataillon* 200 clearing the wire and mines and preparing crossing points across the anti-tank ditch. At 04:30 the latter work was complete and Panzer Regiment 5 received the order to begin passing its two battalions with their combined total of thirty-eight tanks and attached elements from *Maschinengewehr Bataillon* 8, *Panzerjäger Abteilung* 39 and *Luftwaffen Flugabwehr Abteilung* 33 through the gap. Within fifty minutes the lead tanks were approaching Post R32 in the inner defence line, half a mile inside the perimeter. The Australian infantry holding the perimeter defences had been briefed to allow enemy armour to pass unmolested, and the Panzers thus unwittingly passed within thirty yards of Major Balfe's company HQ in the darkness. The German advance was not unscathed, for at around this time the Panzers began to lose contact with their attached anti-tank and anti-aircraft gunners due to the 1st RHA's shelling; the gunners were able to track the dust raised by the advancing vehicles in the waning moonlight. Nonetheless, by 5:45 *Oberstleutnant* Olbrich's lead battalion was formed up in a convenient fold in the ground almost a mile inside the perimeter, ready to push on toward the El Adem crossroads as the first stage in the advance into Tobruk proper while the second battalion was moving through the gap in support.[11]

According to one source these initial stages of the attack were commanded by Rommel in person, who then handed over control to *Generalmajor* Streich. Streich then moved forward to lead the advance on Tobruk in person, still accompanied by the hapless *Hauptmann* Schmidt, but in the process strayed too close to an Australian position and became pinned down, remaining there for most of the rest of the battle.[12] When Streich failed to appear Panzer Regiment 5's lead battalion launched the attack at 06:00, ten minutes after first light, with the second battalion following close behind. The Regiment's line of advance ran north parallel with the El Adem road toward the King's Cross road junction, and thus straight into the 1st RHA's guns deployed on the embryonic Blue Line, which had maintained a steady barrage on the advancing armour. As the light grew and the range closed the Panzers began firing at the 25-Pounder's muzzle flashes with machine-guns and main armament. Sergeant-Major Reg Batten, a Gun Commander with the 1st RHA, likened the resultant pyrotechnic display of explosions and multi-coloured tracer rounds to the Blackpool illuminations. He also noted that the Panzers remained widely dispersed while employing fire and movement tactics, some vehicles providing covering fire while others leapfrogged forward before reversing roles, and that their advance also began to home in on the space between two RHA Troop positions although they may have been actually aiming for a gap in the Pilastrino escarpment. Whether or not, two Panzer IVs also began moving to outflank the gun-line to the west, which took them almost directly toward Sergeant-Major Batten's gun, which engaged them over open sights at a range of 600 yards, scoring a hit on the first. The gun was then hit on the shield by a 75mm HE round from the second Panzer IV that damaged the gun and killed or wounded every man in the crew apart from Sergeant-Major Batten. The latter nonetheless managed to fire off the round in the 25-Pounder's breech, at which both tanks began to retire toward the main group, seemingly unaware that they had actually put their opponent out of action.[13]

The main 1st RHA gun line engaged the main group of Panzers when they came within clear visual range. One Panzer III, struck simultaneously by two 25-Pounder rounds, had its 37mm gun turret blown clean off and six more tanks were knocked out in quick succession as the gun crews strove to keep the Panzers at arm's length, with one troop of four guns firing off over a hundred rounds in under twenty minutes. The volume of German return fire may have been visually impressive but it made little impression on the 25-Pounders, partly due to the low light conditions and dust which reduced visibility, and partly because the guns were dug into protective gun pits; the degree to which all this handicapped the German tank gunners is clear from the fact that the RHA gun crews suffered only six casualties in the whole of the action.[14] The Panzers pushed their attack home to within approximately 500 yards of the RHA gun line at which point the pounding became too much and the leading vehicles veered right toward the El Adem road. However, this ran across the path of the second Panzer battalion, which was echeloned to the right and behind the lead unit. The result was a confused melee of vehicles manoeuvring to avoid collision in the swirling dust thrown up by tracks and explosions. The move to the right also brought the lead Panzers within range of two 2-Pounder anti-tank guns from the 3rd Australian Anti-Tank Regiment dug in on the other side of the El Adem road to cover the 1st RHA flank. Firing into the confused mass of German vehicles, the anti-tank gunners scored several hits and claimed another four Panzers knocked out, but the 25-Pounders were still firing and there was some understandable confusion as to who had hit what and to what effect.

With forward momentum lost and still under an increasing volume of fire, Olbrich's Panzers started to withdraw out of range to regroup. In the process they came under attack from five of the 3rd RHA's 2-Pounder Portees, using what they dubbed 'mosquito' tactics', which amounted to the unarmoured Portees charging headlong at the enemy tanks, relying on speed for protection until within half a mile or so of the selected target. At that point the Portees would swing round to bring their rear-facing guns to bear and fire off as many aimed shots as possible before racing away to avoid retaliation. The first pass took the Germans by surprise but they swiftly adapted to meet the new threat and subsequent passes were met with concentrated machine-gun fire as the Panzer crews sought to counter the Portees' speed with volume of fire. This knocked out two Portees and the remainder suffered varying degrees of damage, one by what was probably a 37mm solid shot that passed clean through the vehicles reserve fuel tank located beneath the driver's seat, fortunately without igniting the petrol therein.[15] The 3rd RHA also lost one of their towed 2-Pounders after its stockpiled ammunition was detonated by a direct hit, killing or wounding its entire crew.[16] The efforts of the 3rd RHA, along with the continued shelling by the 1st RHA thus kept the Germans off balance as they sought to regroup, and the *Panzers'* discomfiture was also due in part to their isolation. Their initial assault had failed because the *Panzers*, most of which were equipped with 20mm or 37mm guns with relatively puny high explosive rounds, simply lacked the means to deal with field defences and dug-in field or anti-tank guns. Ordinarily the latter would have been suppressed and overrun by their accompanying guns and infantry, using the carefully worked out and exhaustively practiced battle drills that had carried the day in Poland and first stage of the Battle of France. On this occasion the Panzers were on their own, however, because the support elements were fighting their own battle two miles or more to the rear, in the perimeter defences.

As we have seen, the 2/17th Battalion had allowed Olbrich's Panzers and the lead elements of *Maschinengewehr Bataillon* 8 to pass unmolested in the pre-dawn darkness, but they did not extend the same courtesy to those who followed. The latter's confidently shouted demands that the defence posts overlooking the gap in the perimeter surrender were met with predictable obscenities and a hail of small-arms fire that drove most of them to take cover in the anti-tank ditch or among a number of shallow wadis just behind the perimeter defences; one large party sought refuge in a ruined building a few hundred yards north of Post R32. Attempts to move guns through the gap after dawn received similar treatment. Major Balfe allowed three anti-tank guns to be hauled to within fifty yards of his HQ before ordering his men to open fire, the German gun crews being killed to a man in the subsequent firefight and the crews of a number of larger guns suffered the same fate as they negotiated the anti-tank ditch without getting off a round in retaliation.[17] The first group were probably 37mm *PaK* 36/37 and/or 50mm *PaK* 38 pieces belonging to *Panzerjäger Abteilung* 39, and the second 88mm *FlaK* 18 weapons from *Luftwaffen Flugabwehr Abteilung* 33. This stalled the column of vehicles, guns and prime movers waiting to pass through the gap, which presented a juicy target for the 1st RHA, whose shelling reportedly damaged three more guns, destroyed or disabled two prime movers and inflicted numerous casualties. With the flow of enemy through the gap stymied, the defenders turned their attention to the group from *Maschinengewehr Bataillon* 8 which had taken refuge in the ruined building, and Lieutenant-Colonel Crawford despatched a force to deal with them at 06:30. While one section of his platoon laid down suppressive fire Sergeant R.M. McElroy used the same tactics successfully employed earlier by Lieutenant Mackell, using dead ground to get the other two sections within fifty yards of the German position before hurling a volley of grenades and going in with the bayonet. Eighteen Germans were killed in the brief hand-to-hand fight that followed, another eighteen were taken prisoner and a handful escaped toward the perimeter wire.

While all this was going on Panzer Regiment 5 was simultaneously trying to sort out the confusion created by the inadvertent collision of its two battalions and withdrawing to regroup out of range of the RHA's 25-Pounders. In the process, however, they ran into further trouble. Morshead had warned Lieutenant-Colonel Drew's 3rd Armoured Brigade to stand-by to counter attack in the event of an enemy assault the previous day, and once the German line of attack became clear in the early morning of 14 April Drew was ordered to deploy two of the 1st RTR's Squadrons, each equipped with around half a dozen Cruiser Tanks. C Squadron, commanded by Major Walter Benzie, was deployed just behind the perimeter defences and east of the El Adem road, from where they could take advantage of the concealment afforded by the glare of the rising sun, while Major George Hynes B Squadron also appears to have been deployed in that area before moving to the west of the German penetration, presumably in the course of the fight with Olbrich's *Panzers*.[18] Whatever the precise details, the deployment appears to have come in the nick of time, given that some and possibly all of the 1st RTR's vehicles moved up from their laager near Fort Pilastrino via the same gap in the escarpment that Panzer Regiment 5 had used to orient its advance. Thus by the time the Panzers withdrew the British tanks were in place, although it is unclear whether the RTR vehicles attacked the Panzers as they withdrew or after they were in the process of reorganising, and also whether their attack was pre-planned or impromptu; one source refers to an officer from the 1st RHA driving up to one of the RTR Squadrons and asking them to attack to take the pressure off the guns.[19]

Whichever, the Cruiser Tanks east of the attackers opened fire on the larger German force at a range of just over a mile and then proceeded to close to within half that distance, firing into the mass of manoeuvring *Panzers*. One British participant referred to the thick clouds of dust making it difficult to identify specific targets, and to discovering four abandoned Panzers in the area after the battle. For their part, the Germans reacted with characteristic speed and do not appear to have been handicapped by the conditions to the same extent, with B Squadron taking the initial brunt. Major Hynes' A9 Cruiser was immobilised by a hit on the suspension, and then received three more hits in quick succession which wounded the gunner, detonated ammunition stored in the turret and killed a Trooper Knapton manning one of the small machine-gun turrets at the front of the vehicle; according to one source the latter was the first member of the RTR killed in the siege of Tobruk.[20] C Squadron received similar treatment. Major Benzie's tank was disabled by two direct hits, as was another to which he moved to control his Squadron from the engine deck.[21] This may have been the incident referred to by Captain Rea Leakey, also of C Squadron, who saw a tank on his left receive numerous hits before starting to burn and German machine-gun fire hit the crew as they bailed out. Leakey's own A9 Cruiser then became a target while providing covering fire to the other crew and a German armour-piercing shot penetrated the turret, killed his gunner and set the vehicle on fire. On abandoning the burning tank Leakey discovered that another of his crewmen had also been killed after bailing out, while another's right leg had been almost severed by machine-gun fire.[22]

With hindsight the engagement can be divided into the neat, step-by-step sequence of events cited above, but the reality for the participants was far less clear cut. For the crewmen of Panzer Regiment 5 the thrill of the 06:00 advance swiftly degenerated into a nightmare of dust-reduced visibility and attendant confusion, explosions, muzzle flashes, burning tanks, radio calls for medical assistance and fire from all sides including the air; British fighter aircraft made at least one low-level attack with machine-guns and bombs. One of the Regiment's tank commanders, *Leutnant* Joachim Schorm, aptly described the conditions as a 'witches' cauldron' in his diary.[23] By the time the Regiment made its tactical withdrawal to regroup Schorm's tank was suffering from brake and transmission trouble as well as a malfunctioning engine after almost an hour of maximum demand on powerplant and running gear, and it is unlikely that his was an isolated example. The appearance of British tanks on top of the pounding from the field and anti-tank guns caused understandable consternation, especially when two were identified as Matilda Infantry Tanks, or Mk.II Heavies as Panzer Regiment 5's after-action report referred to them;[24] in fact all four of the 7th RTR's Matildas were present.[25] The appearance of the Matildas was doubtless a matter of concern in itself, given that at that time they enjoyed a similar reputation to that of the Tiger tank later in the war and not merely due to their recent performance against the Italians in Egypt and Cyrenaica. On 21 May 1940 the 4th and 7th RTR had carried out a counter-attack near Arras that included sixteen Matilda IIs. The latter proved impervious to the standard German 37mm *PaK* 36/37 used against them by the SS *Totenkopf* Division, and only succumbed to hastily redeployed 88mm *FlaK* 18 and 105mm *leFH* 18 field guns.[26] As the British attack threatened the flank of 7 Panzer Division and indeed held up the German formation's advance for several hours, Rommel was personally involved in these emergency artillery. The experience at Arras was probably the reason *Luftwaffen Flugabwehr Abteilung* 33 was attached to Panzer Regiment 5 for the attack on Tobruk.

Be that as it may, the British tank attack seems to have been the final straw, and just after 07:00 Olbrich ordered his isolated and increasingly beleaguered Panzers to withdraw to the gap in the perimeter defences. Initially the withdrawal appears to have been made in good order, with crewmen from disabled and knocked out vehicles being carried on the outside of the runners. Interestingly, the German official report refers to shepherding 200 prisoners, although it is unclear where and when these can have been taken and they are conveniently referred to as all having escaped in the confusion when the withdrawal reached the perimeter. The orderly start degenerated under the concentrated fire from the British tanks and the anti-tank guns dug in to cover the perimeter defences, which knocked more vehicles and killed and wounded several of the rescued crewman from the outside of the tanks; Major Balfe, still observing from his command post, reported seeing two Panzers knocked out and burning just outside the perimeter wire. *Leutnant* Schorm noted passing abandoned 88mm guns and almost becoming stuck in the anti-tank ditch before clearing the perimeter and making his way back to the pre-attack concentration area; a post-battle inspection revealed an armour-piercing shot wedged in the armoured side of a auxiliary petrol tank, which had fortunately drained to empty without igniting. As Schorm's account suggests, the tanks of Panzer Regiment 5 were intent only on escaping from the battle. Major Balfe described the retreating Germans as a 'rabble', although he also noted that three Panzers coolly halted to hitch up artillery pieces, which they hauled for a thousand yards or more before abandoning them to hasten their escape from the pursuing British fire.[27] According to the German after-action report, the British artillery fire followed the retreating German tanks for a full two kilometres beyond the perimeter.[28]

The precipitate withdrawal of the Panzers left a large proportion of *Maschinengewehr Bataillon* 8 pinned down where they had sought cover, and the defenders quickly set about mopping them up. A detachment from B Company 2/17th Battalion led by Captain C. H. Wilson overran a large group sheltering in a wadi near Post 28, killing several and taking seventy-five prisoners.[29] The process was assisted by several Light Tanks from B Squadron 1st RTR, which Major Hynes sent forward when two of his Cruisers became stuck in a ditch while moving to cut off the retreating *Panzers*, and patrols from the 2/15th Battalion and the 18th Indian Cavalry Regiment. Lance-Sergeant Hulme, an RTR tank commander, was shot dead after dismounting to take the surrender of a group Germans, his killer being subsequently despatched by accompanying Australian infantrymen, and a patrol from A Company 2/15th Battalion led by a Sergeant Keyes captured a group of ninety-four, including five officers. The 14 April battle thus saw *Maschinengewehr Bataillon* 8 virtually wiped out, with 250 men becoming POWs in addition to 150 dead including *Oberstleutnant* Ponath; the latter appears to have been killed by Sergeant Keyes' group, which a post-battle intelligence report credited with killing a German lieutenant-colonel. Perhaps the clearest indicator of the damage sustained by the *Bataillon* comes from its ration returns, which dropped from 1,400 pre-battle to a mere 300 afterward.[30] Panzer Regiment 5 also paid a heavy price for its involvement in the battle. Seventeen of the thirty-eight tanks with which the Regiment had started the battle had been knocked out or abandoned, along with twenty-two men missing or killed and seventeen wounded, an overall loss of around fifty per cent.[31] The fighting cost the Tobruk garrison twenty-six dead, sixty-four wounded, two Cruiser Tanks and one 25-Pounder – presumably Sergeant-Major Batten's – damaged.[32]

The psychological impact of all this on the attackers appears to have been at least as great as the physical reality, if not more so. In the immediate term the rebuff on Tobruk perimeter was the first failure the *Deutsches Afrikakorps* had experienced in the invasion of Cyrenaica that began on 31 March 1941, and indeed since the first successful clash between *Aufklärungs Abteilung* 3 and the 1st King's Dragoon Guards near El Agheila almost two months earlier, on 24 February. Rommel's force was therefore used to easily overcome whatever resistance did not simply crumble before them, an expectation reinforced in this instance by pre-attack briefings. Panzer Regiment 5, for example, had been told that their opponents' morale was low, that they were on the brink of withdrawal and were also weak in artillery; the latter stipulation cannot have done other than render the presence and accuracy of the 1st RHA's 25-Pounders an even more unwelcome surprise.[33] Similarly, *Maschinengewehr Bataillon* 8 was so confident that enemy resistance would be perfunctory that the *Bataillon* HQ truck, complete with all the unit's administrative paperwork, was among the vehicles trapped by the 2/17th Battalion queuing up to access the gap in the perimeter.[34] The shock of the reverse was exacerbated yet further by the fact that the abortive assault on the Tobruk perimeter was also the first time the Germans' so-called *Blitzkrieg* tactics had failed to work as expected. The latter failure is perhaps best summed up by a comment attributed to a German medical officer taken prisoner during the action: 'I cannot understand you Australians…in Poland, France and Belgium once the tanks got through the soldiers took it for granted that they were beaten. But you are like demons. The tanks break through and your infantry still keep fighting.'[35]

The latter point should not be pushed too far as there were some extenuating circumstances in this instance. The Panzer force was not really configured nor intended for deliberate attacks against prepared defences, which is why specially trained and equipped assault troops were used to clear the way for 9 Panzer Division to cross the Albert Canal and other watercourses in the Low Countries, and why the main Panzer assault was made across the River Meuse in order to outflank of the Maginot Line in May 1940. Tobruk's coastal location meant there were no flanks to exploit, neither was Rommel's force really large enough for the task it was assigned. Ideally the assault would have employed multiple break-in points to stretch the defenders and prevent them responding effectively, a tactic that would have worked well given that Morshead was obliged to deploy most of his mobile reserve to counter the advance of Panzer Regiment 5. Making a single break-in point sufficiently wide to prevent flanking defensive positions from interfering with movement would have helped, or at least eliminating the ones close enough to do so. This rather basic omission was doubtless exacerbated by the unwarranted German overconfidence cited above, which may also explain why *Sturtzkampfgeschwader* 3's dive-bombers were not deployed against the 2/17th Battalion's defensive posts in the 'flying artillery' role used with some success in Poland, France and Belgium. Neither does much attempt appear to have been made to expand the attack force by involving Italian units, although the evidence is somewhat contradictory. One source refers to Rommel ordering the *Brescia* and *Ariete* Divisions to expand the width of the break-in but being obliged to go ahead alone when the former failed to turn up and the latter demanded more preparation time.[36] On the other hand, a contemporary account cites enemy POWs and captured documents suggesting that the Italians were supposed to launch a simultaneous attack on the western sector of the perimeter but did not translate the orders from German in time,[37] while a more recent

Italian-oriented account refers to the *Ariete* Division being merely warned to stand by to exploit in the wake of 5 *Leichte* Division.[38]

Whatever the truth of the Italian situation, *Generalmajor* Streich's units were also still facing the factors that had undermined the earlier attacks on 11 and 12 April. Foremost among these were physical exhaustion, insufficient time for proper reconnaissance and planning, and poor to non-existent co-ordination between units. According to one source Panzer Regiment 5 had only two maps of the area which turned up too late for the tank crewmen to actually look at, and no access to aerial photographs of the area either.[39] Given the outstanding nature of their achievements hitherto, it is interesting to speculate as to what Streich's men might have achieved had some of these basic requirements been fulfilled. In the event, the end result was yet another demonstration for Rommel that a commander's ambition-driven will was no substitute for the basics of military operations; it cost him a large portion of his armoured strength and one of his precious mechanised units – losses that the *Deutsches Afrikakorps* could ill afford in the prevailing circumstances. Characteristically, the blame was adroitly placed elsewhere. Ponath was criticised for wasting time filling in the perimeter anti-tank ditch, while Streich and Olbrich were accused of failing to ensure their Panzers performed to the required standard.[40] The former was of course beyond such unfair censure, but the latter were not and in mid-May 1941 Streich was replaced by *Generalleutnant* Karl Böttcher as commander of 5 *Leichte* Division. In the meantime *Generalmajor* Heinrich Kirchheim, the visitor who had been co-opted to oversee the *Brescia* Division's advance on Derna at the beginning of April, was placed in command of part of the division, presumably as a means of circumventing Streich's authority in the period leading up to his replacement.[41]

For all that, the fact still remains that 14 April 1941 was the very first occasion on which a full-scale *Blitzkrieg* assault of the type that had overwhelmed armies in Poland, Belgium, France and Holland had been stopped, and the episode showed that such tactics could be thwarted by troops capable of holding their nerve and their positions. The lesson appears to have been absorbed better by the

British and their Commonwealth Allies than the Germans, the latter being presumably misled by their continued successes in Yugoslavia, Greece and the Soviet Union. For example, on the night of 8–9 June 1944 the Canadian Regina Rifles Regiment successfully repulsed an attack by the Panther-equipped SS Panzer Regiment 12 and elements of SS *Aufklärungs Kompanie* 15 on the Normandy village of Bretteville l'Orgueilleuse, a few miles inland from the JUNO landing area; the veteran command cadre of the SS units was reportedly surprised at the failure of the shock tactics they had employed with some success in Russia.[42]

Be that as it may, the events of 14 April at Tobruk had a rather different effect on the defenders. The series of defeats, delaying actions and hasty withdrawals fought across Cyrenaica dubbed the 'Benghazi-Tobruk Handicap' or the 'Tobruk Derby' had inevitably sapped the spirit of those involved, and the sight of the much-vaunted and supposedly unstoppable Panzers being not just stopped but forced into an unceremonious retreat both 'cemented the determination and boosted the morale' of the Tobruk garrison.[43] The now rather optimistically titled GOC Cyrenaica Command Major-General John Laverack, who had flown into Tobruk on 8 April with Wavell and remained to oversee preparations for the defence, marked the occasion with a Special Order of the Day with a suitably stirring ending that neatly contrasted the approach and performance of defenders and attackers: 'Stern determination, prompt action and close co-operation by all arms ensured the enemy's defeat, and we can now feel more certain than ever of our ability to hold TOBRUK in the face of any attacks the enemy can stage. Every one can feel justly proud of the way the enemy has been dealt with. Well done TOBRUK!'[44] In fact this was also Laverack's farewell to the garrison, for he left Tobruk by sea on the night of 15 April for Maaten Baggush in Egypt, where his staff and function were absorbed into Lieutenant-General Sir Noel Beresford-Peirse's Western Desert Force HQ. Command of what became known as the Tobruk Fortress thus passed to Morshead, who wasted no time in making his intentions known to his subordinate commanders in an address that bluntly informed them that 'There'll be no Dunkirk here. If we should have to get out, we shall fight our way out. There is to be no surrender and no retreat.'[45] Laverack's departure and Morshead's bellicose address thus arguably marked the beginning of the siege of Tobruk proper.

In addition to the attack on the perimeter, 14 April also marked the first massed air attacks on Tobruk harbour and the anti-aircraft positions protecting it, an event that was to become all too familiar in the coming months. The first attack began between dawn and 07:30 and involved between forty and seventy Junkers 87 dive-bombers, Messerschmitt 110 twin-engine fighters and Fiat G50 *Freccia* (Arrow) single-engine fighters.[46] The first two were drawn from *Sturtzkampfgeschwader* (StG) 3 and *Zestörergeschwader* (ZG) 26 respectively, while the latter may have been from either 12° *Gruppo Autonomo CT* or 160° *Gruppo Autonomo* CT. Attacks later in the day may have included Junkers 88 and Heinkel 111 bombers from *Kampfgeschwader* (KG) 4 and 26 and *Lehrgeschwader* 1 based at Catania and Comiso in Sicily. No. 73 Squadron at El Gubbi scrambled all its remaining eight Hurricanes to meet the attackers and the resultant dogfights ranged across the Tobruk perimeter, with some downed aircraft crashing into the battle to contain Panzer Regiment 5. *Leutnant* Schorm referred to two Italian machines crashing among his vehicles before the Regiment began its withdrawal to the perimeter for example, and Captain Leakey of C Squadron 1st RTR saw a Hurricane dive into the ground within yards of his A9 Cruiser shortly before his unit attacked.[47]

The air attacks went on throughout the day, with No. 73 Squadron making thirty-eight separate sorties that claimed a Heinkel 111, two Fiat G50s and six Junkers 87s shot down for the loss of a reported three Hurricanes and five pilots. Flight-Lieutenant Smith was killed in a fight with five G50s and was credited with downing two and damaging a third. Pilot-Officers Goodman and Millist were also killed and Pilot-Officer Lamb failed to return; he was found dead with his aircraft the following day. The fifth pilot, Flight-Sergeant Webster, was killed when his Hurricane was hit by friendly Bofors fire while pursuing a German machine. The guns protecting the harbour claimed a further three Junker 87s, with the sixteen 3.7-inch guns of the 51st Heavy Anti-Aircraft Regiment firing 1,200 rounds in the course of the day. The damage was not all one-way. The commander of the 152nd Heavy AA Battery, Lieutenant-Colonel McIntyre, was wounded sufficiently seriously by a bomb splinter to require evacuation.[48] More seriously, during the last raid of the day a number of Junker 87s attacked the Hospital Ship *Vita*, en route to Haifa with over 437 wounded aboard, just outside Tobruk harbour. The *Vita* was not hit but a near miss disabled her engines and she had to be towed back to Tobruk by the destroyer *Moorhen* where the casualties were disembarked. The *Vita* was eventually towed back to Alexandria on 21 April before being despatched to Bombay for major repairs.

Despite the severity of the 14 April rebuff, Rommel had not quite given up on the idea of breaching the Tobruk perimeter and seizing the port. With his German units rendered unfit for battle he turned to the Italians, forming an ad hoc attack force by marrying up the armoured component of the *Ariete* Division with the 62° *ReggimentoFanteria* from the *Trento* Division. The target this time was the western sector of the perimeter held by Brigadier Raymond Tovell's 26th Australian Brigade, and particularly the south-western corner where the defences ran across the Ras El Medauar, a commanding height also known as Hill 209.[49] The action began on the morning of Tuesday 15 April and while most sources refer to a single Italian infantry attack that day, a contemporary account refers to a two-pronged assault. A force of several hundred Italian infantry approached the elements of the 2/48th Battalion holding Hill 209, and was driven off by small-arms and artillery fire from 51st Field Regiment RA. Further north another Italian force, estimated in excess of battalion strength, advanced toward a mile-wide gap between Posts S13 and S17; the latter were held by the 2/24th Battalion and were located just south of the Derna Road near the boundary with the neighbouring 2/48th Battalion. British artillery again drove the closely-packed attackers to ground, but they resumed their advance after a delay of an hour or so when a shortage of ammunition caused the artillery fire to slacken. The attackers penetrated the barbed wire apron before being stopped by fire from the flanking defence posts that drove the majority back, leaving behind at least thirty dead while a further 111 subsequently surrendered to Australian patrols. A twenty-two strong patrol from the 2/48th Battalion led by Lieutenant Claude Jenkins captured a further seventy-five Italians in a wadi just under a mile west of their Battalion frontage.[50]

Rommel took personal control for the continued attacks the following day, although the Australians got in first. An early morning patrol by the 2/24th Battalion along the *Via Balbia* captured sixty-nine Italians, and a later patrol from the 2/48th Battalion led by a Lieutenant Wardle came upon ninety-eight Italians sheltering in a wadi who also surrendered after the Australians shot one of their number; both groups may well have been stragglers from the previous day's action.[51] The Italian attack did not begin until the late afternoon of 16 April, when six M13/40 medium tanks and twelve CV33 tankettes from the *Ariete* Division supported by the 1st *Battaglione*, 62° *Reggimento Fanteria* advanced on a subsidiary peak on the Ras El Medauar dubbed Point 187.[52] The armoured vehicles passed through the perimeter wire and defence posts without difficulty and reached their objective, but the infantry were pinned down by artillery fire while passing through the barbed wire.[53] At this point Lieutenant O. H. Isaksson of the 2/48th Battalion was ordered to take his three-vehicle Bren Carrier Platoon out to investigate the situation at the wire. After a brief exchange of fire during which a Carrier circled out onto each flank while one charged straight through the middle of the Italians, a group of ninety-seven laid down their arms. When they were fired upon by an observing German armoured car another 400 or so promptly surrendered, including the battalion commander; according to one of Isaksson's men, they were hurried on their way by shelling from unidentified Axis armoured vehicles.[54] The Italian battalion commander was apparently so incensed by being fired on by his supposed allies that he helped Tobruk HQ draft a leaflet calling on his countrymen to follow his example, copies of which was subsequently dropped on the Italian positions by the RAF. A foot patrol commanded by a Lieutenant Brocksopp took another 150 prisoners, raising the 2/48th Battalion's bag for the day to 803, almost the whole of the 1st *Battaglione*. The action cost the Australians just two casualties, one of whom was killed. Meanwhile the *Ariete* tanks remained on Point 187 under artillery fire until dusk, when they withdrew unmolested through the perimeter wire.[55]

Stubbornly refusing to accept defeat, Rommel spent the night of 16–17 April preparing yet another attack on the Ras El Medauar for the following day. The assault force was assembled behind a terrain feature known as Carrier Hill, approximately a mile west of the Ras El Medauar, and consisted of at least two M13/40s and eight CV33s supported by a battalion of motorised infantry; some accounts refer to the armoured component numbering twelve or even thirty-two vehicles.[56] The attack was preceded by an artillery bombardment on the 2/48th Battalion's positions, augmented by Italian machine-guns and mortars that had stealthily moved into concealed positions forward of Carrier Hill during the night.[57] The assault force emerged from behind Carrier Hill at 10:00, and the infantry dismounted from their troop-carrying vehicles before reaching the perimeter wire. Events then began to repeat themselves, with the infantry being pinned down by artillery fire from the 51st Field Regiment RA while the armoured vehicles forged on through the wire into the perimeter on the northern side of the Ras El Medauar. On this occasion however, the Italian vehicles encountered more resistance and displayed more aggression and initiative.

The Italian tanks advanced straight at the position held by Lieutenant Bryant's platoon, possibly defence Post R2. One CV33 was destroyed by a mine but the rest opened fire on the Australian positions in an attempt to suppress them from firing at the Italian infantry pinned down just outside the perimeter wire. The Australians responded by redirecting some of their fire onto the armoured intruders, and knocked out two more CV33s with their Boys anti-tank rifles. Although the Italian vehicles' machine-guns and two

47mm guns failed to make much impression on the concrete defence works, they shot up a number of sangars and wounded Lieutenant-Colonel Douglas, commander of the 51st Field Regiment who was directing his guns from a front line position; it is unclear whether this was one of the defence posts or a separate observation post of some kind. One of the M13/40s closed up to one of the defence posts but inadvertently drove into the circular anti-tank ditch surrounding it. The driver succeeded in reversing back out of the trap and withdrew, but with a length of concertina wire tangled in the vehicle's running gear.[58] The Italian tanks then split up into two groups, with one moving back to join the infantry pinned down at the perimeter wire while the other pushed deeper into the Australian positions, pursued by artillery fire controlled from a number of observers in the defence posts.[59]

The latter group overran the 2/48th Battalion's reserve company position almost a mile inside the perimeter, destroying weapon pits and trenches; one Australian infantryman barely escaped being crushed and had the epaulette torn from his shirt by one vehicle's tracks. The occupants of the position opened up on the tanks with everything they had and succeeded in knocking out another CV33, but were unable to prevent the rest pushing on for another mile or so.[60] They were finally stopped by an old Italian anti-tank obstacle, combined with thickening artillery fire and the arrival of seven Cruiser Tanks, although it is unclear how many if any of the interlopers succeeded in withdrawing all the way back to safety at the perimeter.[61] At least one vehicle was disabled in some way en route and the crew captured; on interrogation they proved to be labouring under the same optimistic illusion as their German counterparts three days earlier, that the enemy would surrender once the armour penetrated the perimeter.[62] In all, of the ten vehicles deployed for the attack, one M13/40 and four CV33s were knocked out, a further four CV33s were abandoned by their crews after suffering mechanical breakdown of some kind and only a lone M13/40 escaped back through the perimeter wire to safety.[63] It remained with the infantry under throughout the night, pinned down by artillery and small-arms fire until the morning of Friday 18 April, when fresh tanks from the *Ariete* Division came forward to cover their withdrawal.[64]

The rebuff on 17–18 April marked the end of Rommel's initial attempts to overcome Tobruk's defences, and was dictated by the fact that he had simply run out of battleworthy units to continue the fight. 5 *Leichte* Division had lost over half its combat power, with *Maschinengewehr Bataillon* 8 virtually wiped out and Panzer Regiment 5 reduced to around half its original complement of men and machines The *Ariete* Division had only ten tanks remaining from the eighty with which it had begun the campaign in February 1941.[65] Rommel therefore had little choice but to cool his heels and wait for replacement men, machines and reinforcements, the latter in the shape of 15 Panzer Division which was en route from Tripoli. However, OKH had been keeping a jaundiced eye upon Rommel's activities in Libya, and his freedom of action was about to be constrained.

9
Tobruk Assailed:
19 April 1941 – 4 May 1941

While Rommel's two strongest formations were expending their strength in repeated but fruitless attempts to break through the Tobruk perimeter, other German and Italian units were continuing their advance on the Egyptian border. In an effort to keep his opponents off balance, Rommel had despatched the units briefly commanded by the ill-fated *Generalmajor* von Prittwitz, *Aufklärungs Abteilung* 3, the *Ariete* Division's 8° *Reggimento Bersaglieri* and *Kradschützen Bataillon* 15 from the still deploying 15 Panzer Division eastward, and on 13 April they occupied Bardia, Fort Capuzzo and Sollum, and seized the Halfaya Pass.[1] The only British unit in the area was Brigadier William 'Strafer' Gott's 7th Armoured Division Support Group, which had fallen back from El Adem on 10 April. Despite the weakness of his force Gott nonetheless managed to prevent the Germans advancing beyond Sollum, assisted by gunfire from the destroyers HMS *Griffin*, HMAS *Stuart* and the Gunboat *Gnat*; the latter was damaged by return fire. This was not the first or only instance of the Royal Navy attempting to alleviate the pressure on their army colleagues where the enemy came within range. The gunboats *Aphis* and *Gnat* had bombarded Gazala airfield and enemy transport on the nights of 10 and 11 April, and on the night of 15 April the cruiser *Gloucester* and destroyer *Hasty* shelled transport concentrations near Bardia and Fort Capuzzo while the gunboat *Ladybird* hit Gazala airfield again.[2]

RN involvement at this time was not confined solely to providing gunfire support. On the night of 19–20 April, No. 7 Commando carried out a raid on Bardia from the Landing Ship *Glengyle*, escorted by the cruiser *Coventry* and three destroyers. The raid, already postponed by bad weather, did not run smoothly from the outset. The submarine carrying the canoe party assigned to set out navigation markers for the attack force was late on station after being strafed by a British aircraft, and the delay was compounded when one of the party's craft was damaged during launch and yet further by one of the *Glengyle's* LCAs becoming entangled in the davits. The raiders nonetheless gained the shore unopposed after a forty minute run and split up to attack a number of objectives. The party assigned to attack the Italian barracks inflicted an estimated forty-five casualties on the Italian troops billeted there and destroyed twenty-five assorted vehicles although they lacked the means to do much damage to the stone buildings, but the rest of the raiders were less successful. The group assigned to destroy the water pumping station were unable to locate their target for example, although the raiders did disable a number of Italian naval guns covering the beach before making their way back to the *Glengyle* without incident. Overall the raid appears to have been handicapped by the initial two hour delay. This rendered the timetable-based plan, which was founded on the absolute necessity for raiding force to be well away from Bardia by dawn in order to avoid unwelcome attentions from the *Luftwaffe*, largely unachievable.[3] As a result 'no worthwhile objectives were found and only trifling damage was done,' in part because the earlier sea bombardment had persuaded the Germans and Italians to relocate their vulnerable transport and supply facilities further inland.[4]

After being reinforced with the 22nd Guards Brigade and some additional tanks Gott counter-attacked on 15 April, and recaptured Sollum and the Halfaya Pass.[5] By 19 April his force was deployed with part of the 22nd Guards Brigade in forward posts to protect the latter, and a company from the Free French Motor Battalion holding the Halfway House Pass further east along the Sollum Escarpment. The remainder of the 7th Armoured Division Support Group was divided up into four all-arms Jock Columns made up of a few armoured cars or Light Tanks, a motorised infantry company and a troop or two of 25-Pounder guns to provide fire support, operating from Buq Buq, Halfaya, Sidi Barrani and Sofafi. The 11th Hussars reverted to the scouting and reconnaissance role they had carried out against the Italians in the same area in the latter half of 1940. They also reverted to their previous practise of expanding their reconnaissance activities to include raiding and general harassment, although they rapidly discovered that their new enemy was far less passive that their earlier Italian opponents. The mark was overstepped on 24 April, when three complete troops of Hussars raided Fort Capuzzo and harassed enemy traffic on the road linking Fort Capuzzo and Sidi Azeiz.

The local German commander was *Oberstleutnant* Maximilian von Herff, who had succeeded *Oberstleutnant* Gustav Knabe as CO of *Kradschützen Bataillon* 15. Herff obtained armoured reinforcements from Rommel by exaggerating the potential threat Gott's forces presented to himself and the units investing Tobruk, and then launched his own counter-strike on 25 and 26 April. The attack drove back the 22nd Guards Brigade's forward posts, recaptured Sollum, seized the Halfaya Pass, advanced along the Sollum Escarpment as far as the post at Halfway House Pass and effectively obliged the British to operate thereafter from a line running south from Buq Buq to Sofafi, twenty miles or more inside the Egyptian border.[6] The Germans also extracted retribution specifically from the 11th Hussars. Two troops were badly shot up by Messerschmitt 110s from *Zestörergeschwader* (ZG) 26, and on 29 April two Hussar armoured cars were lost in a fight with a German *Sdkfz* 231 8-*rad* armoured car in the Halfaya Pass, in the course of which Lieutenant Vyvyan Gape MC was killed. Perhaps surprisingly given the amount of action the unit had seen, Lieutenant Gape was the first 11th Hussars officer to be killed in the Second World War.[7]

Back at Tobruk, the withdrawal of the Italian survivors on the morning of Friday 18 April was followed by a pause while the ground forces on both sides took stock. Prompted by enemy activity along the 26th Australian Brigade's frontage, Brigadier Raymond

Tovell broke the hiatus by launching two sorties on 22 April. The 2/23rd Battalion, which had not been involved in the attacks that ended on 18 April, despatched ninety two men in two groups to attack an Italian position straddling the *Via Balbia* running west to Derna. The attackers were to outflank the position from north and south before attacking from the rear; according to one account this was a feint to distract attention from the larger effort against Carrier Hill to the south.[8] The northern group, commanded by Captain Rupert Rattray, ran into in heavy automatic fire from Italian troops entrenched in sangars at the head of a wadi running parallel with the road a mile from the perimeter. When Italian mortar fire followed the group up a smaller branch wadi Rattray ordered his men over the lip of the wadi and rushed the enemy sangars, killing a number of Italians with bayonets, grenades and machine-gun fire and taking forty prisoners. Rattray's men were then obliged to withdraw after coming under heavy fire from surrounding Italian positions.

South of the *Via Balbia* Lieutenant J. A. Hutchinson's group also ran into concentrated fire from mortar and machine-gun posts covering a number of Italian anti-aircraft and artillery positions, and the two lead Sections under Lieutenant R. W. James were pinned down on an exposed forward slope. The rest of the group led by Hutchinson and supported by four Bren Carriers overran the anti-aircraft position but not before most of James' party had been killed or wounded. Hutchinson then pushed on to attack the enemy artillery position, assaulting one field piece in person with grenades accompanied by Lance-Corporal W. Crumney; the latter was killed and Hutchinson badly wounded in the leg. Another group of ten men led by the already wounded Sergeant J. W. Barnard attacked a neighbouring gun pit supported by the Bren Carriers, but two of the latter were knocked out and Barnard's party were pinned down and then obliged to withdraw due to the weight of Italian fire. The fight went of for four hours, and four-fifths of the southern group became casualties; Lieutenant Hutchinson was captured while trying to make his way to friendly lines. In total the attack cost the 2/23rd Battalion one killed, twenty-two wounded and twenty-three missing, most of whom were later confirmed killed. The toll would doubtless have been higher had the two surviving Carriers not made multiple trips to collect the wounded in spite of the heavy enemy fire. The raiders also brought in a total of eighty-seven prisoners and killed or wounded an estimated equal number.[9]

Events unfolded somewhat more successfully to the south, where the 2/48th Battalion put in a raid on Carrier Hill. Commanded by Captain Bill Forbes, the raid began at dawn and was intended to clear Italian guns emplaced behind the Hill that were harassing the Australian perimeter positions, and to discourage the enemy from using the area as a forming -up area for future attacks. A force of ninety men, supported by a troop of three Matilda Infantry Tanks from the 7th RTR, was to loop south around Carrier Hill, sweep the area behind the feature and destroy any enemy located before withdrawing. There was to be no friendly artillery preparation to maximise surprise and a strict time-limit of two hours on the objective was imposed, presumably to ensure the raiders were back inside the perimeter before the *Luftwaffe* were abroad. Flank protection was provided by a troop of 2-Pounder Portees from the 3rd RHA and the 2/48th Battalion's organic Bren Carriers. The attackers moved off at first light with Lysanders from No. 6 Army Co-operation Squadron flying overhead to mask the noise of tracks and engines and under cover of early morning mist, although the latter caused the Matildas to become separated shortly after leaving the perimeter.

Forbes pressed on without the tanks and closed to within 500 yards of Italian artillery positions before being spotted by their cover force, which opened up a heavy but poorly directed fire with machine-guns, mortars and anti-tank guns. Seeing the infantry's predicament Sergeant L. W.C. Batty charged the Italian positions from the left with his section of Bren Carriers and literally overran one gun pit but was then wounded when an Italian anti-tank gun disabled his vehicle. His gunner, Private R.G. Daniells continued to lay down covering fire until he too was wounded after which driver Private J.L. Spavin took over the Bren. The distraction afforded by the carrier charge allowed the infantry to reach the gun positions largely unmolested, at which the Italians promptly surrendered in large numbers. The raiders rounded up 370 prisoners and herded them back to the perimeter, along with a number of motorcycles, vehicles, anti-tank guns, automatic weapons and ammunition. They also sabotaged the guns they were unable to haul away by dropping grenades down their barrels after stripping off the sights for use on the motley collection of captured weapons that had been pressed into service on the perimeter. The action cost Forbes' force two dead, seven wounded and a damaged Bren Carrier.[10]

In all, the raids by the 2/23rd and 2/48th Battalions cost a total of fifty-four casualties, approximately twenty-eight of which were killed. In return the raiders inflicted around a hundred casualties, captured 457 prisoners along with a number of weapons, vehicles and guns, and a quantity of ammunition and ancillary equipment; Morshead referred to the episode as 'an epic worthy of the finest traditions of the AIF '.[11] The troops involved certainly merited such acclaim, but the necessity or indeed wisdom of their employment is less certain. The general opinion of the raids was that they were good for morale,[12] and Morshead made it clear that he considered dominating the space between the opposing forces an important factor in his defensive scheme, ordering his Brigade commanders to send out patrols every night.[13] Unsurprisingly given his background, this was a continuation of the First World War policy of dominating no-man's land with which most, if not all the 9th Australian Division's senior commanders would have been familiar.[14]

However, despite the fulsome praise the fact remains that the 2/23rd Battalion's raiders paid a heavy price for a feint attack that failed to achieve its objective, and in total the raids cost the already manpower-strapped garrison almost an infantry company for not much return, apart from burdening Tobruk's administrative and logistic system with more POWs. The latter was a not inconsiderable point, given that the 22 April haul brought the number of POWs captured by the 2/48th Battalion alone to around 1,700.[15] Neither do the 22 April raids appear to have particularly overawed the Italians. On the night of 23–24 April a large force of Italian infantry infiltrated into the gap between two of the 2/48th Battalion's defence posts on the Ras El Medauar from where they either launched an attack at 08:45 or engaged at dawn in a fifteen-minute long firefight, depending on the source. The episode ended with the 2/48th Battalion taking another 107 Italians prisoner and burying a further forty.[16] Perhaps more seriously, there was another fight with a group of German infantry on the 2/48th Battalion's frontage later on the morning of 24 April, their first appearance on the western sector of the perimeter since the ill-fated attack down the *Via Balbia* by *Generalmajor* von Prittwitz on 10 April. The defenders hit the interlopers with machine-gun fire 300 yards beyond the wire, and a subsequent Australian patrol found several bodies and took seven prisoners including an officer.[17]

While the Italians were making their presence known on the ground the German were doing the same in the air. The *Luftwaffe* was a near-constant presence in the air over the Tobruk perimeter after the first mass raid on 14 April. On 17 April a formation of fifty Junkers 87 dive-bombers hit targets inside the perimeter assisted by a localised dust storm that prevented No. 73 Squadron scrambling its five remaining Hurricanes to interfere. The following day smaller formations attacked targets throughout the day from 03:00, with many attacking El Gubbi airfield, and on 19 April *Sturtzkampfgeschwader* 3's Junkers 87 dive-bombers returned *en masse* to Tobruk harbour.[18] They may have been reinforced with Junkers 88 bombers from *Lehrgeschwader* 1, eleven of which carried out a dive-bombing attack on the harbour and town on their own account on 20 April. The attack was not a success. RAF fighters shot down four of the big twin-engine machines and the harbour anti-aircraft defences accounted for another three and possibly two more. This mauling was probably responsible for the Junkers 88 unit reverting to high-level attacks shortly thereafter.[19] On 22 April No. 73 Squadron's Hurricanes were scrambled on six separate occasions to meet attacks involving up to sixty *Luftwaffe* and *Regia Aeronautica* aircraft, five of which were brought down. The traffic was not all one-way, and RAF units based in Egypt caused German ground units considerable concern. *Leutnant* Schorm of Panzer Regiment 5 complained in his diary of undergoing ten separate attacks in a day as well as night raids, and bemoaned the lack of protection from *Flak* or *Luftwaffe*, for example.[20]

For the outnumbered RAF contingent operating from Tobruk matters reached a climax on 23 April, with eight separate attacks between 10:00 and 19:28, again involving up to sixty Axis aircraft. No. 73 Squadron mustered seven Hurricanes to meet the attackers and brought down seven but the latter's numeric superiority meant they were able catch the Hurricanes landing or on the ground between sorties. Thus Pilot Officer Haldenby was killed when his Hurricane was shot up and crashed in flames while landing, and Sergeant Marshall was badly wounded when his aircraft was strafed on the ground while waiting to be refuelled. At least two more Hurricanes were also shot down, although their pilots parachuted to safety.[21] By 24 April the writing was on the wall and No. 73 Squadron was ordered to leave Tobruk perimeter for Sidi Haneish the next day.[22] A number of ground crew and non-essential personnel had already left on 14 April, and No. 6 Army Co-operation Squadron had pulled out on 19 April, apart from a small reconnaissance force of two Hurricanes and the requisite pilots and ground crew; the aircraft were ensconced in specially prepared underground shelters.[23] No. 73 Squadron flew its eight worn and repaired Hurricanes out of El Gubbi on 25 April, and the senior RAF officers in the perimeter were supposed to follow in a Bristol Blenheim on 28 April. Unfortunately the unescorted Blenheim was attacked by enemy fighters just after take off and crashed into the sea just outside Tobruk harbour; there were no survivors. Thereafter, apart from the detachment from No. 6 Army Co-operation Squadron, the only RAF personnel inside the Tobruk perimeter were a sixteen-strong party commanded by Flying Officer Mathies. Their task was to locate the fifteen Hurricane wrecks scattered across the perimeter and cannibalise them of any parts that might be reused, especially wings, which were in short supply. The parts were shipped back to Egypt by sea via the Spud Run.[24]

The reason for German quiescence on the ground was that Rommel was busy gathering his strength for another effort to capture Tobruk. The process was delayed by the temporary diversion of some Panzers to *Oberstleutnant* von Herff for his seizure of the Halfaya Pass, the need to make good the losses suffered by Panzer Regiment 5 and the drawn out arrival of 15 Panzer Division. The latter's Panzer Regiment 8 was still absent, but by the end of April *Schützen Brigade* 15, consisting of *Infanterie* Regiments 104 and 115, had arrived or were en route to Tobruk along with *Pionier Bataillon* 33. Rommel worked these fresh units into a new scheme entrusted to *Generalmajor* Kirchheim, who was brought out of convalescence at Tripoli for the wound he suffered in an RAF strafing attack on or around 9 April.[25] The first stage of the scheme was the seizure of the Ras El Medauar with a three-pronged assault. After a prepara-tory artillery bombardment and dive-bombing along a 7,000 yard frontage, *Pionier Bataillon* 33 was to go in under cover of darkness to clear the mines and obstacles at the break in points, one on either side of the feature and one atop it, which would then be widened by *Infanterie* Regiments 104 and 115 while *Maschinengewehr Bataillon* 2 secured the hill; the *Ariete* and *Brescia* Divisions were then to move in and roll up the perimeter defences to the north and south respec-tively. While this was going on Panzer Regiment 5 and its supporting elements would pass through the resulting gap, regroup atop the Ras El Medauar and launch the second stage of the plan, a dawn advance on Tobruk via Fort Pilastrino.[26]

Preparations for the attack were well in hand by the end of April, with a provisional start time of the late afternoon of Wednesday 30 April. However, launching it proved to be a less than straightfor-ward matter. As we have seen, Rommel's blatant exploitation of personal links with Hitler and his high-handed behaviour as com-mander of 7 Panzer Division in France in 1940 had secured him a poor reputation with many of his peers and superiors, and as a result *Oberkommando des Heeres* (OKH) placed strict limitations on his autonomy as commander of the *Deutsches Afrikakorps*; for exam-ple he was initially forbidden from undertaking any offensive action until his force was fully up to strength and was ordered to clear any plans with OKH in person, as well as being placed nominally under

Italian command.[27] Rommel was able to circumvent these strictures through a combination of wilful disobedience and Hitler's 3 April declaration of personal support following his first prohibited incursion into Cyrenaica, but a plea from an alarmed *Comando Supremo* to *Oberkommando der Wehrmacht* (OKW) and the series of failures between 10 and 17 April 1941 presented an opportunity for the head of OKH, *Generaloberst* Franz Halder, to bring Rommel back under control.

Halder had been monitoring Rommel's activities and does not appear to have been particularly impressed. On 23 April he complained in his diary that despite clear and repeated orders Rommel had failed to send a single clear report, that his 'senseless' air transport demands could not be met, that he was needlessly wearing out his tank engines and motor vehicles. More importantly, was frittering away his strength in costly reconnaissance probes and piecemeal attacks.[28] Halder's criticisms are frequently dismissed as the product of snobbery and the pique of a bureaucrat and military theoretician toward the upstart, man-of-action Rommel, who got things done by discarding the rule book and refusing to be overawed by the *Junker* aristocracy that still ran the *Heer*.[29] While there may have been an element of truth in this, it conveniently overlooks the fact that Halder's points were fully justified from a purely pragmatic military perspective. Rommel had wilfully and repeatedly disobeyed direct orders and he had squandered a major portion of his combat power for no return, not least because he had deliberately ignored some of the most basic requirements for military operations, such as reconnaissance, concentration of force and sufficiency of supply. Halder's diary comments might equally therefore have reflected the exasperation of a career military professional at the behaviour of a subordinate who was allowing personal ambition to override duty, and putting his overall mission in jeopardy in the process.

Be that as it may, by the latter of half of April 1941 Halder had decided that Rommel had pushed his luck too far and that it was time to send out an OKH representative to bring him to heel. *Generalleutnant* Friedrich Paulus was selected as 'perhaps the only man with enough influence to head off this soldier gone stark mad' and despatched to Cyrenaica with orders to ascertain Rommel's intentions and to impress upon him that few if any additional resources would be available in the future; although he was not at liberty to say so, this was due to the upcoming invasion of the Soviet Union, which was at this time was scheduled to begin in mid-May 1941. He was also to clarify the situation in Cyrenaica and assess whether the province would be defensible should the British counter-attack to retake Sollum and secure access to the Cyrenaican road and track network. Paulus arrived at Rommel's HQ on 27 April and immediately suspended the planned attack until he had ascertained the situation for himself. He appears to have discussed the plan with the senior Italian commander in Libya, *Generale d'Armata* Italo Gariboldi, who visited Rommel's HQ on 28 April and informed Rommel that his plan was approved the following day. Approval was only granted on the strict understanding that the attack would be suspended immediately if progress failed to meet expectations and because Tobruk was too valuable an installation to leave in British hands; grandiose ideas of extending the advance to seize the Suez Canal or conquering Egypt in its entirety were quietly dropped. The timing of the approval meant the existing 30 April deadline could be maintained, and Paulus elected to stay and observe even though his mission had been completed.

At the end of April the Ras El Medauar sector of the Tobruk perimeter was held by the 2/24th Battalion, commanded by Lieutenant-Colonel Allan Spowers. The Battalion occupied a front of around 7,000 yards encompassing twenty-two defence posts running south from S11 to R10, occupied by A, C and D Companies, with B Company in reserve a mile or so east of the hill. Spowers' men were supported by a number of Vickers medium machine-guns from the 1st Northumberland Fusiliers, anti-tank guns from the 3rd RHA, 24th and 26th Australian Anti-Tank Companies, backed by part of the 2/48th Battalion working on the inner Blue Line defences in the Wadi Giaida two miles further back. Artillery support was provided by the nearby 51st Field Regiment RA. Australian suspicion was doubtless aroused by the appearance of German troops on the western side of the perimeter on the morning of 24 April, and this was confirmed when the enemy spent 29 April shelling and dive-bombing the perimeter defences along with artillery positions and dumps to the rear.

The bombardment continued on 30 April, with observers noting larger than average amounts of dust being thrown up by vehicles west of the perimeter. Artillery fire was called down on the billowing dust clouds but to little discernible effect, and all doubt that something was afoot was removed when observers saw trucks unloading infantry, and tanks and guns manoeuvring south of the *Via Balbia* two miles or so outside the perimeter. The positions on the Ras El Medauar were heavily shelled and dive-bombed in the afternoon and toward dusk the 51st Field Regiment returned the favour to a large number of Axis tanks and infantry spotted moving within 3,000 yards of the perimeter. At 19:00 enemy infantry and guns were again seen moving toward the perimeter and at 19:15 twenty-one Junkers 87s came out of the setting sun and bombed and strafed the defence posts on and to the north of the Ras El Medauar, with artillery taking over when the aircraft left. As darkness fell the infantry were seen still moving toward the perimeter but despite this and the night being exceptionally dark no special alarm was given; according to the 9th Australian Division Report this was because the advancing troops were thought to be Italians.[30] The Germans were also active in a diversionary role on the southern sector of the perimeter. A patrol from the 2/15th Battalion ambushed a group of fifty German troops approaching the perimeter wire near the El Adem road, taking six prisoners and capturing a quantity of engineering equipment including Bangalore torpedoes and other explosives. A group of enemy tanks that approached the perimeter wire in the same area just before dawn were driven off by artillery, and at 08:30 group of twenty vehicles manoeuvred close to the perimeter wire under cover of a smokescreen.[31]

Back to the west at the real focus of the German attack, *Leutnant* Schorm and the rest of Panzer Regiment 5 had moved up to their

assembly area at 17:45 and witnessed the start of the pre-attack barrage at 20:00 before snatching some rest; Schorm was asleep under
his tank by 22:00 despite the racket from the guns. The Panzer crews
were roused at 03:30 and moved off for the perimeter an hour later,
although progress was jerky as tanks lost and regained contact in the
darkness.[32] *Pionier Bataillon* 33 were the first to reach the anti-tank
ditch on either side of the Ras El Medauar and set about lifting mines
and blowing half a dozen separate lanes through the shellfire-dam-
aged wire on schedule.[33] Their work was covered by an intensified
barrage which lifted onto the defence posts either side of the breach
to cover Major Heinrich Voigtsberger and *Maschinengewehr Bataillon*
2, who infiltrated around the hill and were on its rearward slope by
around 21:30. Voigtsberger's men then signalled their guns to lift the
barrage with a flare before setting about clearing the crest of the hill
bringing the 2/24th Battalion's reserve company position, almost a
mile inside the perimeter, under machine-gun fire. Other parties of
Germans appear to have attempted to clear additional paths through
the minefield; a Sergeant Kierle of the 3rd RHA, whose gun was
dug covering the minefield, noted some German troops firing their
weapons into the ground in an attempt to detonate mines. As he was
drastically outnumbered Kierle decided that discretion was the better
part of valour and stealthily withdrew after stripping the sight from
his gun, but a combination of the shelling, darkness and German
activity meant he and crew did not reach friendly positions until the
early morning of 1 May.[34]

According to communications reaching *Deutsches Afrikakorps* HQ,
by midnight *Maschinengewehr Bataillon* 2 was not alone inside the
perimeter. *Infanterie* Regiments 104 had reportedly achieved its initial
objective, and a party under *Generalmajor* Kirchheim had secured a
spot height east of the Ras El Medauar. Not all went according to plan.
The British counter-barrage interfered with movement as far afield as
the roads to Derna and El Adem, the group from the *Brescia* Division
assigned to widen the breach to the north were reportedly tardy in
moving up to the perimeter, and some of the defence posts stubbornly
refusing to yield. The latter forced a postponement at 03:00 to allow

Maschinengewehr Bataillon 2 more time to overcome the defences on the Ras El Medauar, and at 04:00 Rommel personally urged the commander of the *Brescia* Division to begin widening the northern side of the breach .[35] By this time Panzer Regiment 5 and its supporting units were passing through the gap onto the Ras El Medauar, and by dawn the attackers had secured seven posts and taken around a hundred Australian defenders prisoner.[36] At this point the German plan had received another set back, however. By 05:30 the Ras El Medauar was shrouded in heavy fog that not only hampered the effort to extend the width of the breach but also obliged Rommel to postpone Panzer Regiment 5's first light attack until visibility improved.[37]

Little if any of this was apparent to Lieutenant-Colonel Spowers. The field telephone lines linking him with his companies and Tovell at 26th Australian Brigade HQ were cut repeatedly by German shells or infiltrators, and many signallers sent to effect repairs simply disappeared. Patrols despatched to ascertain what was happening on the perimeter became lost because there had been little time for the Battalion to familiarise itself with the local geography; the Battalion Carrier Platoon was unable to locate the safe lane through a minefield between the 2/24th Battalion's reserve position and the Ras El Medauar, for example.[38] Spower's first inkling that there were Germans inside the perimeter appears to have come from Captain Clapham of the 51st Field Regiment, who was fired on by German troops while attempting to restore the telephone line linking the Regiment's gun line and observation post on the Ras El Medauar sometime after 20:45. He promptly reported the incident to 2/24th Battalion HQ, but Spowers was unable to pass the information on because the line to Brigade HQ was down. Confirmation of Clapham's warning came at 05:15, when B Company reported several enemy tanks and a number of infantry east of the Ras El Medauar; the information may have come from a B Company patrol that took five prisoners at some point during the night and somehow passed the information up the chain to Morshead.[39]

For his part, Morshead had been aware that something was going on in the area of the Ras El Medauar from the late evening, and he began to orchestrate countermeasures immediately. At 23:50 a warning order explaining that enemy infantry were probably inside the perimeter and that a tank attack was likely at dawn was sent out to the 1st and 107th RHA and 51st Field Regiment, who responded by sending forward additional observer parties. The 24th Australian Anti-tank Company was ordered to dig in at Maccia Bianca, a track junction three miles east of the Ras El Medaur, and just after midnight two troops of Matildas from 7th RTR were ordered to a position south-west of Fort Pilastrino, from where they could attack any armoured penetration in the flank. Once these were in position at 04:15 the remainder of 7th RTR was ordered to Fort Pilastrino to act as a reserve. The rest of the garrison's armoured units were dispersed to pre-arranged patrols or covering positions covering the west and southern sectors of the perimeter, the 3rd Hussars were ordered to attach two Light Tanks to the 2/48th Battalion in readiness for a local counter-attack at dawn and the 18th Australian Brigade was also placed on stand-by.[40] The scale of the German penetration was finally revealed when the fog began to lift after 07:00 on Thursday 1 May. One of the 1st RHA's forward observers, Captain Hay, reported the presence of up to thirty Panzers on a ridge east of the Ras El Medauar at 07:17, while Lieutenant-Colonel Spowers made a similar report fifteen minutes later; their estimates were was soon increased to sixty vehicles, and air reconnaissance confirmed this and also spotted additional groups of vehicles totalling over 200 approaching the perimeter.[41]

Panzer Regiment 5 launched its attack as scheduled at 08:00 along two separate axes, with approximately half the Regiment's tank strength moved east along either side of the track running from the Ras El Medaur to Fort Pilastrino, pursued by British artillery fire. This took the northern group of approximately eighteen Panzers straight at the reserve position occupied by B Company 2/24th Battalion, commanded by Captain Peter Gebhardt, and a smaller group of around a dozen tanks south of the track toward 2-Pounder guns of the newly arrived 24th Australian Anti-tank Company dug in at the Maccia Bianca. The latter made first contact; Corporal F.

C. Aston set a Panzer III on fire and scored hits on two more before his gun was knocked out along with two others. Both groups of Panzers then ran straight onto a supplementary minefield just over a mile inside the perimeter that stretched roughly a mile and a half either side of the track; it had been laid in response to the penetration by the *Ariete* Division's tanks on 17 April. At least a dozen Panzers were immobilised in quick succession among them *Leutnant* Schorm's vehicle, which damaged its right track and then lost the other attempting to manoeuvre away from the danger. Schorm bailed out and took over another nearby *Panzer*, noting that the mines had claimed nine heavy and three light tanks, presumably referring to Panzer IV and Panzer IIs.[42] The stranded vehicles were engaged by Gebhardt's men with Boys anti-tank rifles and small-arms as all the anti-tank guns within range had been disabled; they were unable to call down artillery because shelling was banned inside the minefield to avoid disrupting it. A barrage was called down on the undamaged Panzers lurking on the edge of the minefield however, which were eventually driven off by the 26th Australian Anti-Tank Company. Brought up to replace the 24th Company, the latter scored several hits that prompted the Panzers to withdraw into the dust cloud thrown up by the shelling.[43]

It is unclear whether the second strand of Panzer Regiment 5's attack went in simultaneously with the main effort toward Pilastrino and Tobruk or succeeded it. Whichever, between twenty and forty tanks angled south-east from the Ras El Medauar in company with infantry and assault engineers and began widening the breach in the perimeter. As with the eastward thrust this force also split in two, half moving between and parallel with the perimeter defences and the new minefield to roll up units positioned to support the perimeter defences. Several 2-Pounder anti-tank guns from the 3rd RHA were thus taken in the flank by Panzers and the crew of one was machine-gunned by German infantry after turning their gun to face the threat. They did not go quietly, however; the commander of the latter gun reported seeing another disable five German tanks before being overcome.[44] The other half concentrated their attention on the perimeter defences, working to what appears to have been a pre-arranged drill. A group of four to six tanks would concentrate their fire on an individual post to suppress the defenders and allow the infantry and assault engineers to close in with explosives and in some instances flame-throwers, probably Italian *Carro Lanciaflamme*, a version of the CV33 tankette mounting a flamegun and towing a specially configured 500-litre fuel trailer.[45] Despite this the Australians resisted obstinately, aided by the fact that their positions had been reworked to allow all-round defence. Some defied all attempts to dislodge them throughout the day, obliging their attackers to desist and mask them off for reduction at a later date, and up to a dozen Panzers were also claimed disabled or knocked out in the process. A smaller scale attempt to widen the gap north of the Ras El Medauar by Italian infantry with German support did not fare well either. Three posts were taken but were recaptured in the afternoon of 1 May by Captain Malloch of the 2/23rd Battalion.[46]

Rommel's main eastward thrust had thus been stopped cold by the unexpected minefield by 09:00, and the south-eastern drive along the perimeter thus became the focus of the German attack by default. By 09:30 this force had advanced almost three miles from the Ras El Medauar, bringing the Panzers into contact with B Squadron 1st RTR commanded by Major George Hynes which had been ordered up from the southern sector in response to the German drive. The fire from Hynes' fourteen Cruisers held up the German advance and forced the lighter Panzers to shelter under a smoke-screen until they were reinforced by heavier vehicles, possibly those that had avoided running into the minefield in front of the 2/24th Battalion's position. Despite these reinforcements, which expanded the Panzer force up to an estimated thirty-four vehicles, the Germans remained reluctant to resume their advance and instead continued to exchange fire at range of around half a mile. One Cruiser was knocked out and another damaged while the Germans lost what were probably one Panzer III and two Panzer IIs before withdrawing back into the smoke. Hynes then led his tanks along the edge of the minefield in search of a better firing position. In the process they were attacked by dive-bombers and joined by Major Walter Benzie and C Squadron 1st RTR at around 10:15 and the combined force eventually found a hull-down position from where they could fire on the Panzers stranded in the minefield. This was a successful ploy until Hynes decided to relocate and in so doing expose some of his vehicles to German return fire. Hynes' own Cruiser took a hit in the turret that wounded two of his crew and set the vehicle ablaze, and the next tank in line was also hit. Its commander, Sergeant Cornish, was wounded in both legs but was awarded the Military Medal for a third wound received while warning his driver that they were running into the minefield. A member of Hynes' crew, Lance-Corporal Maconnachie, was also awarded the MM for braving enemy fire to retrieve a first aid kit from the burning tank.[47]

By late morning the Panzers making up the cutting edge of the German attack had been in near-continuous contact for several hours and needed to replenish their fuel and ammunition. The need to rotate vehicles back for resupply was presumably the rationale for an order issued at 11:45 that instructed the Panzers south of the Ras El Medauar to move up and reinforce the point of the drive along the perimeter, although the redeployment may also have been because the strength deployed for the attack was proving insufficient to carry it out. Orders issued by Rommel at 14:00, possibly with input from Paulus, clearly acknowledged this reality and that the attack schedule had been derailed beyond repair. All thought of reaching Fort Pilastrino and thence Tobruk proper were abandoned. Instead a new objective was set, of establishing a defensible line roughly three miles long, running around the base of the Ras El Medauar where *Leutnant* Schorm and his companions were working to tow disabled vehicles clear of the mines,[48] north to Post S7 and south to Post R14.

However, the advance along the perimeter was still some distance from the latter and at the time Rommel issued his order his men were still fighting for Posts R8 and R9 and were not making much progress. The problem was a combination of the obstinacy of the Australian infantrymen and the constant British artillery fire, which prevented the German infantry and engineers from keeping up with the *Panzers*. Small-arms fire from the garrison of R8, for example, kept the infantry at bay and forced the engineers riding on the Panzers to dismount. While two Panzer IIIs closed to within fifty yards, their fire was insufficient to suppress the defenders even when the Panzer crewmen resorted to hurling stick-grenades from their hatches. The stand-off continued until the Panzers finally withdrew under heavy shelling in the late afternoon at which point the Australians, low on ammunition and with several wounded to consider, evacuated to Post R10. From there they were still able to prevent the Germans occupying their erstwhile position.[49] Repeated attempts to silence or at least suppress the British artillery with dive-bombing attacks were unsuccessful, and guns were credited with breaking up several attacks before they could get properly underway. The Panzers also appear to have been reluctant to push ahead on their own. The two Panzer IIIs that attacked R8 were part of a force of twenty-four vehicles for example, and an Australian observer noted that a group of over fifty tanks massed near R6 remained in place until withdrawing to the Ras El Medauar in the late afternoon. This reticence was doubtless due to a combination of the experience of 14 April and the under-standable fear of running into additional mines and anti-tank guns in the restricted cockpit between the perimeter defences and the sup-plementary minefield, but overall it had the effect of stultifying the advance and Rommel's plans.

Morshead had been monitoring the situation while all this was going on, and in the early afternoon began to make preparations for launching counter-attacks before the Germans consolidated their gains. Thus at 13:00 the commander of the 7th RTR was ordered to despatch a troop of three Matildas along the inside of the sup-plementary minefield, to engage the Germans salvaging the Panzers in the minefield in front of the 2/24th Battalion's reserve position and more importantly, prevent them from clearing the mines. The remaining two troops of Matildas were to support an infantry coun-ter-attack in the same area, with the aim of cutting off the German troops pushing south-east between the perimeter defences and the supplementary minefield. In the event, Morshead's intentions were overtaken by events. The move to tackle the Panzers in the minefield had to be abandoned because two of the Matildas broke down on the way, while the other two troops were diverted to assist Majors Benzie and Hynes and their survivors from B and C Squadrons 1st RTR in countering the renewed German push against Posts R8 and R9. One Matilda was lost to a dive-bombing attack en route, but at 15:30 the combined force of between three and six Cruisers and five Matildas began working its way along the perimeter posts, ascertaining which were still held by friendly forces as they went.

All went well until one of the Cruisers moved forward to investigate a lone, supposedly knocked out Panzer near Post R4. The German tanks crews may have been reticent at advancing against possible mines and other hidden dangers but they were more than willing to take on their opposite numbers and the Cruiser came under heavy fire at 1,000 yards' range from an additional fourteen Panzers previously out of view. The Cruiser retired hastily to Post R6 where a troop of Matildas was waiting, and a firefight ensued during which a further eight Panzers appeared on the British left against the perimeter wire along with fourteen more on the right flank. It is unclear whether this was a deliberate ambush or simply that the British tanks ran into a developing German advance, but the upshot was that they came under heavy and accurate German fire from three sides and rapidly began to get the worst of the encounter. Three of the 1st RTR's Cruisers were knocked out and burned, one of them Major Hynes' second vehicle of the day, another was damaged and the 7th RTR lost two Matildas destroyed, two were obliged to withdraw with damaged guns and another broke down but appears to have been repaired; four Panzers were reported badly damaged in the exchange.[50] The encounter was the first between Panzers and Matildas in North Africa and the fact that the latter suffered multiple full penetrations effectively demolished the latter's reputation for invulnerability and raises the question as to what exactly did the damage. One account suggests, not unreasonably given the presence of such weapons among Panzer Regiment 5's supporting attachments on 14 April, that 88mm *FlaK* 18 weapons were responsible.[51] If so, this would support the suggestion that the encounter was a deliberate ambush using the Panzers as bait to draw the British tanks into the 88's field of fire, a tactic that was to become a German staple of the desert war.

Be that as it may, the Panzers did not press their advantage, but withdrew into the fading light to assist their infantry in reducing Posts R6 and R7, which held out until mounting casualties obliged them to surrender at around 19:30. Had the Germans been aware, there was actually very little to stop a determined thrust, and pushing on to Post 14 as Rommel ordered would have carried the German advance past the end of the supplementary minefield. For his part, Morshead has been criticised for committing his armour in so-called 'penny-packets' that left them at a numeric disadvantage, but this glosses over at least two salient points. First, concentrating the Tobruk garrison's entire Matilda and Cruiser Tank strength of only thirty-one vehicles – the twelve Light Tanks would have been of limited use in the tank-versus-tank role – would still have left the British tanks outnumbered by a ratio of over two to one, given that Panzer Regiment 5 began the 1 May attack with eighty-one tanks. Furthermore, Morshead could not afford such a concentration in any case as he had to hold back a reserve to counter additional German attacks elsewhere on the perimeter. Consequently he had little choice but to deploy his armour as he did. Secondly and arguably more importantly, the British tanks appear to have had a significant psychological impact on the Germans irrespective of their numbers and outcomes. The appearance of the 1st RTR in the morning must have been a contributing factor in the reticence displayed in the German push south-east from the Ras El Medauar, and it was certainly a factor in the Panzers breaking off the action after mauling the 7th RTR's Matildas. A German report captured later referred to the Panzers holding off a British counter-attack by twenty tanks at 17:10, and to the attack being renewed with tanks and infantry at 18:00.[52]

The outcome of Morshead's second counter-attack, orders for which went out at 16:45 while the tank fight near Posts R6 and

R7 was still underway, was rather less successful. Lieutenant-Colonel
W. J. V. Windeyer's 2/48th Battalion, located on the Blue Line near
the Wadi Giaida, was ordered to attack at 19:15 and retake the Ras
El Medauar and defence posts lost to the enemy. Reinforced with
Captain Gebhardt's B Company from the 2/24th Battalion, the
attack was oriented along the Acroma Track that ran west from Fort
Pilastrino to the northern edge of the Ras El Medauar. Captain H.A.
Woods' D Company moved to the north, Gebhardt's B Company
straddled the Track and Major J. Loughrey's A Company moved along
a rough parallel trail nicknamed Pirie Street half a mile to the south,
which led directly to the Ras El Medauar's peak. Understandably
concerned over the short lead time, lack of tank support and near-
total lack of information of the German dispositions, Windeyer
requested a delay until first light on 2 May but Morshead, arguably
justifiably, was eager to strike before the Germans had sufficient time
to consolidate their gains. The request for postponement denied, the
2/48th Battalion moved off from its forming up point at the Maccia
Bianca track junction at 19:30, fifteen minutes behind schedule.

Assisted by the gathering darkness, the attackers closed to with a
thousand yards or so before coming under German fire, the latter
possibly being alerted by the covering bombardment. A Company's
move up the Pirie Street track was disrupted by six Panzers that
appeared to the south *inside* the supplementary minefield moving west toward the Ras El Medauar and machine-gunned the
advancing infantrymen in passing and after turning across their line
of advance. The Panzers were presumably part of the group from
Panzer Regiment 5 that became trapped in the minefield during
the morning that succeeded in moving forward rather than back
although *Leutnant* Schorm, who spent the day covering attempts
to salvage the trapped vehicles, does not refer to any such development. Whatever their origin, there were numerous eye-witnesses
to the incident including the commander of the left flank platoon.
Fire from the mystery Panzers kept Major Loughrey's men pinned
down until dark, and an attempt to resume the advance thereafter
was stopped by heavy machine-gun fire 500 yards in front of the

objective, while Major Gebhardt's advance down the Acroma Road was stymied by a blocking position made up of three Panzers and numerous machine-guns that cost B Company numerous casualties. On the right flank Captain Woods' D Company lost contact and reoriented on a water tower just west of the perimeter. This drew the line of advance north of its intended track, and more seriously within range of the Germans holding defence Posts S4 and S6 at last light. The latter thwarted an attempt to continue the advance in bounds under covering fire by pulling the back and drawing the advance into a crossfire from flanking positions. The Australians nevertheless pressed on to within 250 yards of the German positions before being pinned down, with Captain Woods being mortally wounded while scouting forward with a small party in an attempt to pinpoint the German machine-gun positions for attack.[53]

Morshead called off the attack at 21:30 and the three battalions broke contact in the darkness, losing more casualties in the process although the Germans do not appear to have been aware that the Australians were withdrawing. The attack cost B Company 2/24th Battalion fourteen dead and twenty-five wounded, while the two companies from the 2/48th Battalion lost a total of fifteen dead and thirty-seven wounded. The attack also left the perimeter vulnerable, for the 2/48th Battalion withdrew all the way back to its original position on the Blue Line, while Gebhardt's company did not reoccupy its pre-attack reserve position either. As a result the supplementary minefield was left uncovered and there was virtually nothing in place to counter a renewed German attack. Fortunately for the Tobruk garrison, their opponents had also had enough for the moment, as graphically illustrated by *Leutnant* Schorm's diary. The latter remained in a covering position west of the Ras El Medauar until 23:30, when he withdrew back through the gap in the perimeter defences. Even then it was 03:00 before he was able to leave his tank for a snack and some rest. Apart from the hurried move from his disabled Panzer in the early morning he had spent twenty-three and a half continuous hours under armour; unsurprisingly he also reported suffering from 'frightful' cramp and thirst as a result.[54] In a sense Schorm was lucky, for the fighting had reduced the tank strength of Panzer Regiment 5 by over half. In return, as of midnight on Thursday 1 May the *Deutsches Afrikakorps* had secured the Ras El Medauar in its entirety and pushed a three-mile wide salient up to a mile deep into the perimeter that included fifteen defence posts, eleven of which were in the outer ring.[55] There the matter rested, for Paulus decided that progress had failed to meet expectations and thus ordered Rommel to desist. His decision was made official on 2 May, when he informed OKH that the May Day attack had failed to yield anything more than 'inconclusive, local gains', and that the Tobruk operation had been terminated as a result. The following day he added a rider recommending that Rommel's standing orders be modified to oblige him to seek explicit permission for any future attack on Tobruk even after 15 Panzer Division had arrived in Libya in its entirety.[56]

None of this was apparent to Morshead and the men manning the western perimeter, however, who fully expected the Germans to resume the attack at first light if not before. As their best full strength efforts had been barely sufficient to prevent a full-scale German breakthrough, this was not an attractive prospect and at least some thought the next day would bring the Tobruk saga to a bloody end. This appears to have been foremost in the minds of the garrison's surviving tank crewmen, many of whom destroyed their personal papers in anticipation of a fight to the finish.[57] Mobile patrols from the 3rd Hussars and King's Dragoon Guards (KDG) kept watch on the German positions through the night until nature took a hand in the early hours. Dawn on Friday 2 May saw the battlefield blanketed by a fierce sandstorm that cut visibility and severely impeded vehicle movement. For a time the only force standing between the Germans and Fort Pilastrino was an observation party from the 51st Field Regiment, a single anti-tank gun and two Vickers guns from the 1st Northumberland Fusiliers located on a small rise near the Maccia Bianca track junction. This little band drove off at least one German foot patrol that penetrated as far as the track junction under cover of the storm before the 26th Australian Anti-tank Company and

Lieutenant-Colonel Arthur Drummond Verrier's 2/10th Battalion from the 18th Australian Brigade came up to seal the gap and block larger and more determined German infantry probes through the morning.

When the sandstorm ceased abruptly in the afternoon it revealed a conglomeration of German tanks, vehicles and foot soldiers in plain view on the eastern slopes of the Ras El Medauar, a juicy target that the 51st Field Regiment's forward observers quickly brought under fire until the enemy withdrew out of sight over the crest or into concealment in dead ground. Artillery fire was also instrumental in foiling German attempts to clear paths through the supplementary minefield and repairing and improving their new positions, in spite of attempts to suppress the guns with dive-bombing and strafing attacks from the *Luftwaffe* which was active over the Tobruk perimeter throughout the day. The Germans were also busy recovering vehicle casualties of the previous day's fighting; *Leutnant* Schorm reported being involved in salvaging two Panzer IIs that were for some reason carrying 800,000 *Reichsmarks*.[58] This was a not inconsiderable task, for only twelve of the forty-six Panzers damaged or knocked out had been totally destroyed. This recovery activity may have been responsible for reports of up to 300 German vehicles massing outside the perimeter at 17:30 that sparked a major alarm inside the perimeter, leading to the 3rd Armoured Brigade being deployed in readiness for a last ditch defence; the British tanks remained on alert throughout the night before being finally stood down at 09:00 on 3 May when it became clear that no German attack was forthcoming.

In the absence of a renewed German assault and on the advice and urging of his subordinates, Morshead set about organising another counter-attack intended to eliminate the German salient and restore the perimeter. Scheduled for Saturday 3 May, the attack was assigned to Brigadier George Wootten's 18th Australian Brigade, and involved all three of its constituent battalions. Lieutenant-Colonel Verrier's 2/10th Battalion was tasked to carry out a number of fighting patrols against the German troops holding the Ras El Medauar proper as a diversion from the main effort, which consisted of full-scale attacks by the other two battalions on either side of the feature. Lieutenant-Colonel John Field's 2/12th Battalion, supported by four Matildas from the 7th RTR and half a dozen or so Light Tanks from the 3rd Hussars were to attack and capture Posts S6 and S7 to the north of the Ras El Medauar, while Lieutenant-Colonel James 'Sparrow' Martin's 2/9th Battalion with three Matildas and another group of Light Tanks secured Posts R7 and R8 to the south. Once these posts had been secured the attackers were to pinch off the salient by turning inward and rolling up the defences from the flank all the way up to Point 209 atop of the Ras El Medauar. The Light Tanks were detailed to accompany the infantry while the Matildas stood off to the rear, and the attacks were also supported by a total of thirty-nine guns from the 1st and 104th RHA and 51st Field Regiment. These were to lay down rolling barrages for each attack set to advance at a rate of eleven yards per three minutes.

Given the degree of resistance encountered by the 2/48th Battalion's counter-attack on 1 May and indeed put up by the Australians from the same positions against stronger assaults, this was optimistic to say the least, and so it proved. Zero hour had to be postponed until after it was fully dark at 20:45 because German observers on Point 209 called down accurate artillery fire on the 2/9th and 2/12th Battalions as they moved up to their start lines in the late afternoon, putting the former thirty-five minutes behind schedule. That was just the beginning. The Light Tanks, with no training or experience in operating with infantry at night had to be withdrawn, and the pace of the rolling barrage proved to be too fast for the infantry to keep up with and ran ahead to no effective purpose. The preparatory artillery concentration on Posts S6 and S7 had little noticeable effect and the 2/12th Battalion advanced into concentrated machine-gun, mortar and artillery fire controlled with the aid of parachute flares. The attack began to falter when the lead companies lost their way in the darkness and unfamiliar terrain, and eventually faded away in the darkness and confusion. The 2/10th Battalion's fighting patrols enjoyed rather more success, with at least two enemy positions being overrun and temporarily occupied by the attackers, killing an estimated twenty-four Germans in the process.[59]

The 2/9th Battalion's attack to the south also fared better than the northern attack, despite heavy Axis shelling on the start line and machine-guns and heavier weapons firing on fixed lines along the Battalion's line of advance. For some reason *Maggiore* Gaggetti's battalion from 8° *Reggimento Bersaglieri* had not manned R8 but were occupying a stone wall to the rear of the post instead. Lieutenant W.H. Noyes' platoon from A Company ran into them after overshooting R8 in the darkness and cleared the wall in a vicious and confused hand-to-hand fight that cost the attackers around a third of their strength. As Noyes' platoon reorganised they were approached by three CV33 tankettes, which were stalked and knocked out with hand grenades by Noyes, Sergeant R.W. Hobson and three others; at least one of the tankettes caught fire, drawing a storm of small-arms fire from Australians in the surrounding darkness.[60] Noyes then moved on toward R6, overrunning several incomplete defence works including a partly finished anti-tank ditch reportedly held by a mixture of Italian and German troops. By this point his platoon was out of touch with friendly forces and had been reduced to around section strength so Noyes pulled back in an effort to re-establish contact with Captain E.W. Fleming and the remainder of A Company. In so doing he literally stumbled upon the empty R8, which he then occupied. While all this was going on Captain F.E.C Loxton's D Company had attacked R7 and managed to occupy its anti-tank ditch before being driven back and apparently succeeded by Captain B.H. Lovett's company, which joined the fight for R7 after becoming lost en route to R6. The Australians appear to have penetrated into the post but were ejected by *Maggiore* Gaggetti's *Bersaglieri* supported by an M13/40 tank, three armoured cars of some description and possibly flame-throwers as well. At 00:45 Lieutenant-Colonel Martin ordered a tactical withdrawal to R14 to regroup and reorganise, a process that took over two hours.[61]

Nonetheless, the activities of the 2/9th Battalion certainly appears to have unsettled their opponents. *Leutnant* Schorm's portion of Panzer Regiment 5 were stood to at 22:00 and ordered forward through the gap in the perimeter despite having no clear picture of the situation apart from reports of an enemy penetration in the region of Posts R1 to R7 that reached the Panzers at 01:15. After passing the burning CV33 knocked out by Noyes and his party, Schorm found Gaggetti's *Bersaglieri* holding R7 under heavy British artillery fire, having suffered over a hundred casualties in the fight to defend and then retake their post, two-thirds of their original strength. Schorm also referred to the Australians leaving behind twenty-six dead. This was hardly the work of troops in confusion, and Schorm may therefore have been exaggerating when he described the *Bersaglieri* as such but his description of the British artillery was accurate.[62] The latter fired over 10,000 rounds in two and a half hours, and one of the 51st Field Regiment's guns alone fired 375 rounds after which it was hot enough to fry eggs, according to one of the Regiment's officers.[63] In the event, *Leutnant* Schorm remained in his covering position near R7 until ordered back before first light at 05:30, but his vigil proved to be uneventful apart from the shelling. Concerned that his men would be caught in the open by the *Luftwaffe* come daylight, Morshead halted the attack and ordered a withdrawal shortly after 03:00 on 4 May, just as the 2/9th Battalion were moving forward to renew the attack.

In total the counter-attack cost the 18th Australian Brigade between 152 and 155 casualties depending on the source.[64] While the 2/10th Battalion escaped relatively lightly, with its fighting patrols suffering just fifteen men wounded, the heaviest burden was borne by the 2/12th Battalion which lost five dead, fifteen missing and fifty-seven wounded in its abortive assault on S6 and S7. The 2/9th Battalion, whose capture of the unmanned Post R8 was the only gain from the operation, was not far behind with a total of three dead, three missing and fifty-one wounded. Axis casualties from this specific action are unclear apart from a reported 150 suffered by *Maggiore* Gaggetti's battalion from 8° *Reggimento Bersaglieri*, a figure two-thirds higher than that suffered by the attackers.[65] While a proportion of the Italian casualties were doubtless due to British artillery fire, the total casualty figure of over 200 not only illustrates the ferocity of the fight for R7 but provides a further example of the sidelining of the Italian role in the fighting in North Africa. Contemporary and more recent accounts of the 3 May counter-attack refer to them in passing at best, or in disparaging terms or with no mention at worst, and the casual reader could be forgiven for not realising that there were any Italian troops involved, let alone that they actually played the key role part in stopping and then rebuffing the southern prong of the Australian counter-attack.[66]

Portrayal of the Italians aside, the fighting on the western side of the Tobruk perimeter between 1 and 4 May reiterated the lesson of 13–14 April with another clear demonstration that the so-called *Blitzkrieg* operational technique was not an automatic guarantee of success but could be thwarted by steady troops that were not over-awed by tanks, and that the key countermeasure was to separate the Panzers from their support elements. The point was not an absolute, for the Germans were handicapped to an extent by the abnormally restricted and tactical nature of the battlefield and more crucially, by a lack of numbers. On both occasions the attackers proved they were perfectly capable of piercing the defensive perimeter, the prob-lem was that after doing so they lacked the tanks and men necessary to exploit the breach properly. Responsibility for this lies almost solely with Rommel, whose overconfidence and impatience trans-lated into a lack of basic preparation and reconnaissance. This in turn exacerbated the numeric weakness of the *Deutsches Afrikakorps* to the point where it is difficult to see how they could realistically have prevailed without the Tobruk garrison totally collapsing after token resistance, a highly unlikely scenario given the calibre of the opposi-tion. It is interesting to speculate how the siege of Tobruk might have developed had Rommel waited and launched the 1 May assault with all the resources squandered in his earlier piecemeal attacks on the perimeter.

Be that as it may, Rommel was doubtless quite willing to simply ignore the order from Paulus to desist, but had run down his force to the point where continuing the attacks on Tobruk was simply unfea-sible. By the beginning of May the various attacks on Tobruk had cost the *Deutsches Afrikakorps* a total of 1,240 casualties, a considerably significant proportion of its manpower and a serious matter for a force barred from receiving significant reinforcement.[67] The materiel toll had also been heavy. Panzer Regiment 5 had made up its losses earlier in April to begin the 1 May attack with eighty-one tanks. Within two days forty-six of these had been knocked out or disabled by mines, artillery fire or British tanks, of which twelve were totally destroyed with the remainder requiring varying degrees of repair.[68] Rommel therefore had little choice but to rein in his ambitions for Tobruk, a position that OKH was about to make official in unambiguous terms.

10
Tobruk Besieged:
4 May 1941 – 25 October 1941

By the beginning of May 1941 the situation on the Egyptian border, the losses incurred in the recent attack and more crucially supply problems ruled out further German attempts to seize Tobruk in the immediate future. German and Italian forces in Libya required an estimated 30,000 tons of supplies per month purely to remain operational, with an additional 20,000 tons to build up stocks for future operations. However, there was only sufficient coastal shipping capacity to move 29,000 tons per month, the bulk of which had to be unloaded at Tripoli and then moved the remaining 1,000 miles or more to eastern Cyrenaica by road. Damaged docks, RAF bombing and Royal Navy activity meant Benghazi could handle only small coastal vessels on an intermittent basis, Buerat and Sirte were too small and Derna could only be accessed relatively safely by submarines carrying ammunition. Rommel's activities had strained this tenuous logistic linkage to breaking point; as *Generaloberst* Halder, head of the *Oberkommando des Heeres* (OKH), noted in his diary: 'By overstepping his orders Rommel has brought about a situation for which our present supply capabilities are insufficient.'[1] Rommel became aware of OKH's displeasure with the Libyan situation on 3 May, after *Generalleutnant* Paulus had rendered his initial report. As well as reprimanding him for his reckless and wasteful conduct to date, OKH explicitly forbade Rommel from renewing the attack on Tobruk or anywhere else and specifically ordered him to hold in place. Rommel's reaction to this can be well imagined, but the news came as a considerable relief to the Tobruk garrison; Morshead received an intercepted copy of the signal, hand carried by a destroyer captain, on 6 May.[2] Rommel therefore had no option but to resort to the more traditional siege tactics of containing the Tobruk garrison while starving the fortress of supplies and reinforcements. Responsibility for carrying out the process thus passed to *Fliegerführer Afrika, Generalmajor* Stefan Fröhlich.

The *Luftwaffe* had been active over the Tobruk perimeter in support of ground forces from early April 1941 reconnoitring the perimeter defences and dropping leaflets urging the garrison to surrender, while dive-bombers from *Sturtzkampfgeschwader (StG)* 3 had engaged in harassing artillery positions and attacking the harbour. Mass raids on 14 and 17 April were followed by smaller, sustained attacks on 18 April on a variety of targets inside the perimeter including El Gubbi airfield.[3] In all, between 11 and 30 April twenty-one separate dive-bombing attacks were recorded, involving a total of 386 aircraft.[4] Luftwaffe activity followed a similar pattern in support of Rommel's May Day attack, with eight separate attacks on British artillery positions in the vicinity of Fort Pilastrino between 28 April and 2 May. Attacks on targets in what was dubbed the forward area of the perimeter then fell away, apart from reprisal attacks in response to damage inflicted by the garrison's artillery.[5] This was due to the *Luftwaffe* shifting its attention to Tobruk harbour, although this was not a totally new departure. The harbour had been attacked on 12 and 13 April, sinking one merchantman and damaging another, and again on 18 and 19 April. It is unclear whether these attacks were part of a deliberate effort to alternate attacks between the perimeter and Tobruk proper or provoked by the presence of shipping in the harbour, but the latter was where the bulk of Tobruk's anti-aircraft (AA) strength was concentrated; three aircraft were claimed shot down on 12 April and three more and two probables on 20 April, for example. The statistics gathered by the defenders illustrate the intensity of the struggle between the *Luftwaffe* and the AA gunners at this early stage

of the siege. Between 10 and 30 April 1941 Tobruk's AA guns claimed
to have downed thirty-seven attackers, sixteen probables and to have
damaged a further forty-three for the expenditure of 8,230 rounds of
3.7-inch and 25,881 rounds of 40mm and 20mm ammunition.[6]

While the 4th AA Brigade and *Luftwaffe* were fighting their own
war over Tobruk and the adjacent harbour, the Tobruk garrison was
becoming accustomed to existence within the perimeter. A billet in
Tobruk meant relatively comfortable and fairly civilised living conditions but with the ever present danger from the Axis air attacks
that came in day and night. Troops on the perimeter, on the other
hand, were rarely troubled by aircraft but had to be constantly on the
alert for enemy patrols and the like while enduring extremely primitive and uncomfortable living conditions. The greatest trial was the
fine, powdery dust that permeated food, weapons, vehicle engines
and moving parts, clothing and living quarters to the extent that the
men ended up eating and breathing it as a matter of course. This was
especially troublesome for the troops stationed on the Blue Line and
inward, due to the constant passage of vehicles, and matters were
exacerbated overall by the dust storms that occurred every few days
that reduced visibility to near zero and made movement difficult if
not impossible. The dust was exacerbated on the perimeter and in
units stationed in the open desert by large numbers of voracious fleas
and clouds of flies. One NCO from an AA crew claimed the former
were more of a tribulation than enemy bombs,[7] and the latter were
attracted to refuse, food, bare flesh and broken skin with manic tenac-
ity, clogging eyes, ears and nostrils and making eating a one-handed
trial.[8] The arid conditions meant there were no mosquitoes and thus
no malaria, and generally the health of the garrison remained good.
The exception was the occasional outbreak of dysentery caused by
failure to observe sanitary arrangements and drinking unchlorinated
water, but this was largely eliminated with rigorous enforcement of
the rules following an outbreak in June that laid low 226 men in a
single week. The lapses with regard to water were understandable if
not excusable, given that the daily water ration up to 19 June was four
pints per man for all purposes; after that date it increased to six pints.[9]

There was little wildlife in the perimeter apart from a species of small brown mouse and the odd jackal or gazelle, but the troops adopted a number of starving dogs and cats that had belonged to Tobruk's evacuated civilian population. There was also a lone, aged sheep nicknamed 'Larry the Lamb' by the AA unit that adopted him as a mascot; the gunners had to post extra guards to prevent Larry augmenting the rations of some prowling Australian.[10] The latter threat was not an idle one, and not merely because bully beef was the staple ration item for the first three months of the siege and beyond, occasionally replaced with canned bacon, herrings and M&V stew. The canned rations were augmented with bread from the ex-Italian bakery in Tobruk, margarine, sugar and jam, although the latter two were in short supply. The rations were barely adequate and nutritionally deficient even with the issue of concentrated vitamin C tablets in lieu of fresh fruit and vegetables, and the limited diet eventually began to take its toll, most markedly in the shape of ugly and painful desert sores. The ration situation improved from mid-July 1941, with fresh meat being served to troops in reserve positions once a month, fresh fruit and vegetables on a weekly basis and more regular issues of the latter in cans. Even so, when the 9th Australian Division's infantrymen were examined after being relieved it was discovered that each man had lost up to twenty-eight pounds in weight.[11]

The garrison routine settled into a pattern that would have been instantly recognisable to the First World War veterans in its ranks, with units being rotated regularly between the perimeter, the Blue line, reserve and manning the exposed positions facing the Ras El Medauar salient. Troops in the perimeter split their time between patrolling, and maintaining their positions, while units in the Blue Line were not only employed in digging defensive positions, but in laying mines, erecting and maintaining barbed wire entanglements and creating a third line of defence dubbed the Green Line. While in reserve the troops were allowed a few days' rest by the sea, where they could launder their clothing, swim and simply soak up the sun in relative safety. It was not unusual for units in reserve to suffer more casualties from air raids than they incurred while manning the perimeter; on one occasion a platoon from the 2/43rd Battalion lost two killed and three wounded to bombs while engaged in road repairs, for example.[12] There was thus no real escape from danger and the concomitant mental stress anywhere within the Tobruk perimeter, although significant efforts were made to maintain morale primarily via the provision of cigarettes, comforts and mail. A weekly issue of fifty cigarettes per man was made from the beginning of the siege, augmented with another fifty from unit canteens to those with the funds to pay for them from June. Additional cigarettes were distributed for free by the Australian Comfort Fund (ACF), an organisation set up during the First World War to support the troops by providing canteens, clubs, hostels and the comforts to stock them. The ACF also provided the Tobruk garrison with pre-stamped air-mail letter cards, writing paper, envelopes and stamps, with £3,200 of the latter being sold in one month alone. The mail was handled by an Australian postal unit located in what had been Tobruk's bank which received an average of 700 bags of mail and despatched half that number per week through the siege, equivalent to 5,000 parcels and 50,000 letters; by August 1941 the unit was moving fifty tons of assorted mail per week.[13]

The infantry were not employed solely in standing watch and maintaining their positions during their stints on the perimeter. Morshead implemented a policy of aggressive action and patrolling, partly to offset the enervating effects of boredom and partly to tie down as many Axis troops as possible to relieve the pressure on the Egyptian border. In essence Morshead's policy amounted to a revival of the First World War practise of dominating no-man's land, and this was literally the case on the southern and eastern sectors where the enemy positions were rarely more than a mile from the perimeter. Patrols up to twenty strong, carrying only weapons, ammunition and grenades leavened with Thompson guns and usually a single Bren for support were despatched almost every night, with socks over their leather-soled boots for stealth; special rubber-soled footwear and camouflage clothing became available in the later stages of the siege. If the target was an enemy position the patrol would navigate their way on compass bearings in the darkness, picking their way stealthily through the protective barbed wire, booby-traps and mines without alerting the sentries before attacking from the flank or rear. As well as inflicting casualties and unsettling the enemy a frequent objective for the patrols was to capture a prisoner for intelligence, often by penetrating beyond the enemy front line. On one occasion a patrol from the 2/23rd Battalion led by Captain Rattray captured a lone Italian sentry near the Bardia road after attracting his attention with a combination of low whistles and calling him comrade in his native tongue as they drew close enough to seize him. Among the most adept at this hazardous nocturnal activity were the dismounted armoured crewmen from the 18th Indian Cavalry Regiment, who gained a fearsome reputation among friend and foe alike. Many moved silently on rubber sandals fashioned from discarded vehicle tyres, and one group is reputed to have presented their commander with two sacks of severed enemy ears when the veracity of their post-patrol reports was questioned.[14]

The most intense activity took place facing the Ras El Medauar. The creation of the salient added an additional five and a half miles to the perimeter that had to be built from scratch under the noses of *Infanterie Regiment* 115 holding the hill. The extra frontage obliged Morshead to press personnel from support units stationed in Tobruk into service as substitute infantry; the 2/1st Pioneer Battalion held a section of the line until mid-May, for example. Initially the new line was sketchy, with random patrolling by both sides between front lines to half a mile apart, but on 13 May the 18th Australian Brigade was ordered to take over the salient and push forward until in close contact with the German line. Conditions on the salient were the worst in the entire Tobruk perimeter, not least because the terrain was almost completely solid rock under a thin layer of fine sand. This meant that the troops were unable to dig in properly and had to make do with makeshift positions that were part sangar, part shell scrape, with no overhead cover. The latter deficiency was especially grievous because the presence of German observers on the Ras El Medauar made daylight movement impossible, and the troops

holding the line were obliged to remain totally motionless throughout the hours of daylight, totally exposed to the sun and enemy
artillery or mortars.

Allied activity on the front line in the salient thus became totally
nocturnal, revolving largely around the arrival of rations from the
rear. Breakfast was served at 21:30, hot meals at midnight and just
before dawn, the latter being accompanied by hard rations for
consumption during the coming day. Units could not bear such
conditions for long, and men emerged from a week long tour on the
salient undernourished, weak and frequently racked with dysentery.
The traffic was not all one-way. On 12 May the 2/13th Battalion shot
up a number of Germans who had taken up the habit of taunting
the previous unit by walking around and shaking their bedding in
the open, and A and B Companies from the same battalion sprang
a successful hasty night ambush on German troops attempting to
occupy some partly-completed positions in no man's land fourteen
days later. The Germans had to bring up five ambulances after first
light to remove the resulting casualties, and the Australians made
good use of the brief truce to openly examine their surroundings
from a standing position in daylight.[15]

The salient was also where Morshead's strategy to keep the maximum number of Axis troops occupied on the perimeter was most
successful, not least because Rommel had to keep hold of it as a
springboard for future attacks into the Tobruk perimeter. The order
for the 18th Australian Brigade to close up to the German front line
on 13 May was part of a ploy to persuade Rommel that the garrison were about to attempt a break-out, in order to draw German
troops away from an upcoming British attack on the Egyptian border. Throughout 14 May vehicles were driven back and forth near
the south-western sector of the perimeter to simulate a pre-attack
concentration, supported by spurious radio traffic. The following morning three Cruiser tanks and two platoons from the 2/12th
Battalion attacked positions held by elements of the *Pavia* Division
near defence Post S15, and in the afternoon the 2/10th Battalion
launched another limited attack further north to straighten out its

section of the line. The attacks succeeded in their intent. The *Pavia* Division infantry abandoned their positions, and RAF reconnaissance on 15 May noted German mechanised units moving toward Tobruk from Sollum to the east, and Axis armour concentrating west of Tobruk near Acroma.

In one way the deception succeeded rather too well, insofar as it provoked a strong German pre-emptive strike. After a two hour preparatory artillery and mortar bombardment the Germans attacked Posts S8, S9 and S10 in the late evening of 15 May supported by five *Panzers*, while the Italians counter-attacked S15. The attack was well organised, using coloured tracer ammunition to guide the troops toward their objectives, and went on throughout the night. One party penetrated into S9's anti-tank ditch before being forced back by a counter-attack. The Germans did succeed in overrunning S10 with the aid of flame-throwers and close support from the *Panzers*, taking a number of the Australian defenders prisoner and cutting off S8 and S9. The Panzers withdrew before first light but German infantry held onto S10 and beat off a counter-attack by a platoon from the 2/12th Battalion just after dawn. Another attack at midday finally retook the post, capturing twenty-eight Germans and liberating three wounded Australians. Contact was re-established with S8 and S9 after dark on 16 May and in the nick of time; the posts had beaten off numerous attacks through the day, but by dusk were running dangerously short of ammunition.[16]

Having gained the Germans' attention, Morshead set about keeping it with a larger attack on 17 May that had the secondary intent of eroding the size of the German salient by taking S6 and S7, and S4 and S5 as secondary objectives. The attack was assigned to the 2/23rd Battalion, supported by nine Matildas, and began at 05:27 with an artillery bombardment from thirty-nine guns, thickened with indirect fire from twelve Vickers medium machine-guns from the 1st Royal Northumberland Fusiliers, a smoke barrage on the Ras El Medauar to blind German observation posts and a fortuitous early morning mist. Things did not go according to plan from the outset. The Matildas failed to reach the start line in time, lost touch with the infantry despite the efforts of the reserve platoons to attract their attention and abandoned attempts to find their way forward after becoming disoriented by a German counter-smokescreen. The Germans hit the attacking infantry with every weapon they could bring to bear, with AA guns firing shells fused to detonate overhead being especially troublesome. S7 was seized by Captain Ian Malloch's Company in spite of this, but the troops could not be reinforced and by 07:30 the Germans had retaken it using *Panzers*. To the left Major W. H. Perry's Company secured S6 and moved on to take S4, taking a total of twenty-three Germans prisoner, but were then cut off by the weight of German defensive fire. An attempt to reach them at 07:40 was driven off despite support from four Matilda tanks, although two Bren Carriers succeeded in delivering ammunition and rations to S6 under cover of the mist and dust.

With no further contact, 2/23rd Battalion HQ wrote off Perry and his men after Panzers were seen in the vicinity of the recaptured posts at around 09:00, until the Company Clerk, Corporal Fred Carleton, succeeded in reaching Battalion HQ three hours or more later. By this time Sergeant-Major W.G. Morrison and twenty-three men were holding out in sangars 200 yards from S6, and Morrison was able to break up several attacks during the course of the afternoon by calling down artillery fire via a field telephone line repaired by Private H.P Clark under heavy German fire; at one point Morrison was obliged to call down fire virtually on top of his own position. The little band was finally ordered to withdraw from their embattled outpost at dusk after a relieving attack was abandoned for want of tank support and Panzers were seen advancing on the sangars. Despite being ordered to abandon his five wounded after an attempt to lift them with two Bren Carriers was thwarted by a German anti-tank position, Morrison brought them and his fourteen able-bodied survivors out after a hair-raising crawl along an old Italian pipeline trench under constant German machine-gun fire; his was the only organised sub-unit to survive the day's action. Only two of the ten officers from the two companies that spearheaded the attack escaped injury. Of the remainder, four were killed, one was seriously wounded and three were wounded and taken prisoner. In all the 2/23rd Battalion suffered twenty-five dead, fifty-nine wounded and eighty-nine missing, at least half of whom were believed killed.[17] The Tobruk garrison thus paid a heavy price, and arguably one it could ill afford, for the privilege of diverting Axis attention from events on the Egyptian border, which did not meet expectations either.

The attack the Australian diversionary operation was intended to assist was Operation BREVITY, commanded by Brigadier Gott. Contemporary accounts cite the Operation as an attempt to relieve Tobruk, but Wavell's typically wide-ranging and arguably contradictory instructions for the attack show this was not the case.[18] Gott was ordered to recapture Sollum and Fort Capuzzo, inflict as much damage as possible on the enemy while not endangering his own force, and to exploit any success as far toward Tobruk as the logistic chain would permit. With large-scale reinforcements en route from the UK, Wavell allotted Gott all the armour and mechanised forces that could be mustered; two Squadrons of Cruiser Tanks from the 2nd RTR totalling twenty-nine vehicles, and two Squadrons of Matildas from the 4th RTR totalling twenty-four vehicles, along with the 22nd Guards Brigade mounted in vehicles borrowed from the 4th Indian Division, and the 7th Armoured Division Support Group. Artillery support was provided by the 8th Field Regiment RA, air cover by Hurricanes from No. 274 Squadron, and close air support by fourteen Blenheims from No. 14 Squadron. The attack began in the early hours of 15 May, and was initially successful. The Halfaya Pass, lost to *Oberstleutnant* Maximilian von Herff at the end of April, was retaken by the 2nd Scots Guards and a Squadron from the 4th RTR, the 1st Durham Light Infantry and more tanks captured Fort Capuzzo and the 7th Armoured Division Support Group made good progress toward Sidi Azeiz, ten miles north-west of Fort Capuzzo. Progress had not been easy or universal, however. The attackers were unable to clear enemy forces from the crucial approaches to the Halfaya Pass, and the various actions cost Gott's force nine tanks destroyed or otherwise put out of action.

However, BREVITY had been compromised by poor signal security which allowed Rommel to send the *Ariete* Division to El Adem as a backstop, and more pertinently permitted the local German commander, *Oberstleutnant* von Herff, sufficient time to organise a response in advance. Thus after initially giving ground Herff launched a counter-attack with a battalion from Panzer Regiment 5 that recaptured Fort Capuzzo, from where he launched a second attack on 17 May after receiving reinforcements including another battalion of tanks from the newly arrived Panzer Regiment 8 from 15 Panzer Division. The reinforcement was not straightforward for Panzer Regiment 8 ran out of fuel after reaching Sidi Azeiz at 03:00 on 16 May and remained stranded for fourteen hours but Herff was able to begin his counter-attack in the early afternoon of 17 May, which forced the 7th Armoured Division Support Group back toward Bir El Khireigat, over ten miles south of Fort Capuzzo. Herff halted as ordered on a line running south and west from of Sollum, which efficiently screened and further British moves toward Tobruk. Overall BREVITY yielded only the recapture of the Halfaya Pass in return for six RAF aircraft lost, five Matildas destroyed and thirteen damaged. This was equivalent to the loss of three-quarters of the Matildas committed, while the 1st Durham Light Infantry suffered a total of 160 casualties in the fight for Fort Capuzzo. On the other side of the ledger German losses totalled three Panzers destroyed, twelve killed, sixty-one wounded and 185 missing, along with an unknown number of Italians taken prisoner. There matters rested, with a small British all-arms force built around the 3rd Battalion The Coldstream Guards holding the Halfaya Pass, for nine days while the Germans organised fuel supplies for their *Panzers*. Von Herff then retook the Pass with an attack that began on 26 May and forced the British back with the loss of five Matildas, twelve assorted guns and 173 casualties.[19]

With the end of the fighting on the western sector of the perimeter the struggle for Tobruk shifted to the sky, most intensely over the harbour. Tobruk's AA defences grew out of a relative handful of guns deployed to protect the harbour after Operation COMPASS, augmented with reinforcements brought in by sea. Between 6 and 12 April 1941 the 4th AA Brigade HQ and five fresh AA units arrived

by ship, along with an additional twelve 40mm Bofors and eight
3.7-inch guns configured for static emplacement; all the latter were
immediately co-opted for harbour defence despite a shortage of
personnel to construct the necessary emplacements and man them.
By 11 April the commander of the Brigade, Brigadier John Nuttall
Slater, had at his disposal the 51ˢᵗ Heavy AA Regiment with two batteries of 3.7-inch guns, the 14ᵗʰ Light AA Regiment with a total of
seventeen 40mm Bofors, the 306ᵗʰ Searchlight Battery and a number
of signal and workshop units. These were supplemented with forty-
two Breda 20mm automatic cannon, one twin 37mm Breda, four
102mm guns and two searchlights, all captured from the Italians; the
static 3.7-inch guns were later formed into a third battery.

Within fifteen days of the 4ᵗʰ AA Brigade's arrival, the 3.7-inch guns
had been deployed around the harbour in six Sites labelled A, B, C, D,
G and H, with B and D Sites being equipped with predictor apparatus for use against high-level targets and for night barrages.[20] The
newcomers soon found themselves directly targeted as the *Luftwaffe*
attempted to suppress Tobruk's AA defences. On 14 April 1941, for
example, six to eight Junkers 87s attacked a 3.7-inch Site, killing two,
wounding nine and destroying two battery vehicles. As a result of this
4ᵗʰ AA Brigade HQ ordered all gun positions and control posts to be
dug in and reinforced, the preparation of alternate gun positions and
purely dummy positions to confuse the high-level and dive-bombers; the former tended to make pre-planned attacks based on aerial
photography, while the latter identified targets visually during their
attacks. The dummy gun positions were sophisticated affairs carefully
constructed to be indistinguishable from the real thing, complete
with mocked-up guns, flash and dust simulators, vehicle tracks and
dummy ammunition dumps. A defensive tactic nicknamed the 'porcupine' was also formulated, which involved attacked gun positions
pointing all guns outward and firing at maximum rate at an eleva-
tion of sixty-five degrees or above. The wisdom and effectiveness of
these precautions was to become apparent in due course.

Axis aircraft were an almost permanent feature in the skies above
Tobruk during the siege, with high-level bombing raids a daily

occurrence from the outset. Their frequency increased markedly from the end of May 1941, with ten to fifteen raids per day on some occasions, and fell off abruptly in October with only four in the first ten days of that month. In all, between 9 April and 10 October a total of 301 separate attacks were recorded reaching a peak with eighty-seven raids during July. The vast majority were directed against the harbour, Tobruk town and surrounding dumps and installations, although at least two high-level attacks were made against troops in the western side of the perimeter. Most were made from 18,000 to 25,000 feet, sometimes in formation and sometimes independently. Bombing from such altitude permitted most attacks to deliver their loads before the AA defences were aware of their presence, which was exacerbated by the location of most of the 3.7-inch gun Sites. While accuracy did not compare to that achievable by dive-bombing they did enjoy some success. The tail end of a stick of bombs destroyed a large dump of captured Italian ammunition four miles south-west of Tobruk town at the beginning of August, for example. For a while the bombers were able to confuse the AA fire control system by attacking in spaced increments; this was overcome by devolving fire control instructions from battery to gun section level, and the handicap of poor early warning was offset to some extent by authorising all guns to engage any target within range without waiting for permission.

There was no respite during the hours of darkness. The port was on the receiving end of a total of 908 night bombing raids between 9 April and 9 October, the peak month being August with 205. For the first two months raids averaged between one and three raids per night, and apart from a handful of aircraft dropping mines into the harbour, involved scattering Italian AR-4 anti-personnel devices across the town and harbour side. The devices were nicknamed 'Thermos Bombs' due to their resemblance to the vacuum flask of the same name and were dropped from low level, often in a tight pattern of thirty to forty at a time. The attackers launched a concerted attempt to block the harbour and approaches with mines on the nights of 21, 27 and 30 July, coming in at a variety of heights and directions to confuse the AA defences; this was the first time that the night attacks presented a serious threat to Tobruk. The raids refocused on the town and harbour installations in August, while the bulk of attacks in September took place on moonlit nights and were more balanced between mining missions and attacks on the town; the latter alternated between dropping Thermos devices and larger bombs, with some raids also dropping very large, parachute-delivered aerial mines. On 1 October the attackers dropped incendiary bombs on the town for the first time, but to little effect; as the official report dryly noted, by this point there was little left in the town to burn. The incendiaries nonetheless set parts of the town ablaze, but other enemy aircraft did not appear to make much use of the resulting illumination. Overall the night attacks did not present the AA defences with any special problems, apart from some minor modifications to fire control procedures. By the end of the siege the night barrage was employing twelve Bofors, seventeen 3.7-inch guns along with the five ex-Italian 102mm guns and twin 37mm Bredas.

However, the most intense struggle in the sky above Tobruk took place in daylight, between the AA defences and *Sturtzkampfgeschwader* 3's dive-bombers. The contest began on 27 April with an attack on the AA positions covering the harbour by approximately fifty Junkers 87s, with twelve dive-bombers targeting each site. The gun positions went into porcupine mode, engaging all visible targets, and the tactic worked well for the A and C Sites; no bombs landed closer than fifty to a hundred yards and the newly dug gun pits effectively shielded guns, crews and ancillary equipment; only one man was killed and another wounded another. The B and D Sites were not so fortunate. The guns were not manned, the lookouts failed to spot the dive-bombers approaching from out of the sun, and the guns were not properly dug in, with flimsy parapets made of empty oil drums. The attack killed five, wounded over forty and put four of the 3.7-inch guns out of action for forty-eight hours; in addition the cables linking the individual guns to the predictor gear were shredded and the predicting equipment at both Sites was damaged. The B Site was hit again on 12 May, along with the G Site. According to the official report, the latter failed to defend itself with sufficient vigour while the B Site personnel panicked instead of manning their guns. Two men were wounded, one of whom died later, and four guns were put out of action for between twelve and twenty-four hours.

The process of measure and counter-measure set in these early encounters continued in the months that followed. The poor performances of 27 April and 12 May led 4th AA Brigade HQ to order all personnel in gun positions under attack to take part in the fight using small-arms, with only the unarmed being permitted to seek cover. Each gun pit was issued a Breda machine-gun for this purpose, although these had to be sited some distance away to avoid being unsighted by the dust kicked up by the larger guns. In addition, all gun pits and control posts were modified to withstand the impact of a 1,000 pound bomb landing within ten yards, and after members of a gun crew were injured by a primed 3.7-inch shell detonating after being struck by shrapnel, ammunition storage was modified so that stored shells faced outward. Observation showed that dive-bombing attacks were most accurate when delivered at a seventy to eighty degree angle, but this left them vulnerable to fire from light AA guns when pulling out at low level. Many attacks were thus made at shallower angles in the region of forty to fifty degrees, which allowed the dive-bombers to retain the safety of altitude at the cost of reduced bombing accuracy; bomb releases at altitudes as high as 6,000 to 8,000 feet were noted over Tobruk harbour, for example. It was also noted that accurate AA fire could provoke attackers to opt for the shallow angle attacks, and gun crews were encouraged to assist this tendency whenever possible.

By June 1941 the dive-bombers were becoming noticeably reluctant to press home their attacks. All of the Junkers 87s involved in attacks on AA positions on 1 and 2 June stayed above 3,000 feet, for example, with none of their bombs coming within 150 yards of their targets as a result; eyewitnesses also reported some aircraft jettisoning their bombs into the sea. The 2 June attack was accompanied by three Henschel 129 observation aircraft, presumably to gather information on the AA defences, and their presence was noted in subsequent raids too. The *Luftwaffe* tried a number of innovations during July. Some raids were preceded by small groups of Junkers 88s as a diversion, and on 4 July the dive-bombers avoided the 3.7-inch barrage by approaching from the west rather than south. Unfortunately this took them directly over a Bofors emplacement which promptly shot down five with a sixth being downed by a direct hit from a 3.7-inch shell. On 10 August Tobruk's AA defences deployed a new weapon against an attack by eighteen dive-bombers, the Unrotating Projectile Rocket Barrage, consisting of salvos of 3-inch rockets containing contact-fused parachute mines on 400-foot cables. The mines were ejected automatically when the rocket reached an altitude of 1,000 feet, and the attacking aircraft were supposed to obligingly snag the cables and pull the mines onto themselves. Overall the system was not a success, although on this occasion its spectacular firing disrupted the incoming formation, two dive-bombers detonated mines with unknown results and another ended up with a mine parachute wrapped around its tail.

Over the next two weeks the attackers tried attacking through low cloud, approaching simultaneously from three different directions and preceding the latter with a diversionary gliding attack on the harbour. On the other side of the fence, the presence of the Henschel 126 prompted the AA defence to amend the porcupine defence by ordering only half the guns in any Site to fire at any one time; the reduction in the intensity of the barrage was considered worthwhile in order to avoid revealing the true gun strength of the defences. On 1 September the *Luftwaffe* roped in the *Regia Aeronautica* to assist in an attempt to overwhelm the AA defences by sheer weight of numbers. An estimated mixed force of 120 Junkers 87s, Fiat BR20s and Savoia Marchetti SM.79s attacked the harbour and surrounding AA positions, while additional aircraft bombed positions on the perimeter; this was the single heaviest air raid on Tobruk during the siege. The AA gunners claimed one Junkers 87 shot down, three probables and a number damaged in return for one killed, six wounded and up to five 3.7-inch guns put out of action by shrapnel, all of which were back in action by 16:30. In the event, this mass raid proved to be the penultimate major dive-bombing attack on Tobruk. The last, on 9 September, turned out to be something of an anti-climax, with only one Junkers 87 making a shallow angle attack on the harbour. The remainder of the formation were seen to jettison their bombs on finding no worthwhile shipping targets. Altogether Tobruk withstood sixty-two separate dive-bombings in the course of the siege, and over the same period the AA defences suffered a total of 158 casualties, forty of which were killed in action. In return they claimed ninety enemy aircraft shot down, seventy-four by light AA, a further seventy-seven probables and 183 damaged.[21]

An aspect of the struggle between the Tobruk garrison and the *Luftwaffe* that has gone virtually unremarked is the role played by camouflage and deception. The man behind it was Captain Peter Proud RE, who arrived at Tobruk after an eventful journey from Cyrenaica during the Benghazi-Tobruk Handicap. He was appointed 'G3 (Camouflage) Desert Force Attached to the 9th Australian Division' at some point shortly before 16 April 1941, and on that date wrote to a Major Barkas at GHQ Middle East explaining the importance of his work and recommending the formation of a dedicated force to help him carry it out; at the time of writing he was co-opting Indian Sikh troops in increments of 200 on a day-to-day basis. The latter were employed gathering and preparing a stock of materials that included approximately 2,000 coloured nets, 20,000 yards of natural Hessian, 250 gallons of assorted paint, a number of stirrup pumps for use as improvised sprayers, and an ex-Italian workshop with tools and an electrically powered band saw among other equipment. The nets were modified with strips of Hessian referred to as 'garnish' and part painted to match the terrain, the colour of which was likened to the shade of the foundation cosmetic Max Factor No.9. The nets were then configured for specific applications, such as covering pre-manufactured metal frames artillery gun pits. Sufficient equipment was provided to permit artillery sites to place all gun pits, crew bivouacs, slit trenches, ammunition storage and latrines under camouflage.

The latter idea was adapted for other purposes, with smaller frames being manufactured in the workshop to suit positions and even individual slit trenches out on the perimeter, and not just there. A large net was made to cover the gunboat *Gnat* when occupying her berth in a narrow cove on the south side of the harbour, the vessel's mast and searchlight top being removed to ease its deployment, and a similar expedient was employed to protect A Lighters while berthed in the harbour. The Lighters were run into the shore bow first near a small headland projecting into the harbour and covered with garnished nets pegged to the shore. The open end of the net was then draped over cables stretched taut behind the Lighters and allowed to dangle down to the water; from the air the camouflaged vessels looked like an innocuous extension of the headland. A system for camouflaging aircraft was also formulated, using three thirty-five foot square camouflage nets linked in a T-shape, pegged out over specially made support posts mounted in sand-filled petrol cans. Blast walls and slit trenches for ground crew were constructed under the netting.

Many of Proud's initiatives were equally simple but effective. A drive-through paint-spray booth was set up for vehicles at the building Proud had commandeered as a combined store house and workshop. To stretch the limited supply of paint, vehicles were sprayed with used engine oil scrounged from the garrison's REME vehicle workshops before being driven outside for a second coat of sand and dust that blended perfectly with the surrounding terrain; instructions, oil and other kit were available for units to camouflage their own vehicles on request. The booth was later augmented with a mobile spray unit, using a captured Italian compressor mounted on a 15 cwt truck, equipped with fifty gallon oil drums as a paint reservoir and a folding ladder for spraying tall buildings and tents. Fuel dumps were concealed by distributing the fuel cans in irregular linked patterns stacked only one or two cans high to avoid casting tell-tale shadows. These were then flanked by berms formed from supply boxes filled with sand and then coated with oil and more sand to protect the fuel cans from shrapnel.

In addition to merely hiding things from enemy view, Proud supervised the construction and execution of a number of novel and in some instances highly sophisticated deception measures. At the lower end of the scale wrecked vehicles were positioned to the south of weapon pits in order to cast them in shadow, and discarded Italian uniforms were stuffed to create dummy personnel to man dummy positions. Decoy tanks were constructed from camouflage nets covering a stone sangar to the front surmounted by a wooden frame and pole to simulate the turret and gun. Proud's workshops also produced a more sophisticated version of wood and canvas with painted running gear and folding mudguards fashioned from petrol cans along with a 3 ton truck of similar construction, some mounted on wheels to ease movement. There was also a plan to produce dummy fighter aircraft of similar construction, complete with compressors to simulate propeller wash, although it in unclear if they were actually produced. Convoy movements were simulated by single vehicles towing a number of weighted sledge-like devices, while sea water was used to damp down the dust created when moving guns between locations.

On a grander scale, a fake fuel dump was constructed, complete with a convoy of wrecked Italian vehicles towed into position on the supposed approach road. The dummy AA positions with gun-fire simulators and other equipment constructed in the vicinity of the harbour have been mentioned above, and a similar site was constructed 1,000 yards from one of the 51st Heavy AA Regiment's positions facing the Ras El Medauar in mid-May. The dummy incorporated four unserviceable guns and was sufficiently convincing to draw German artillery fire directed by a Henschel 126, while the real site was left unmolested. Perhaps the most spectacular was a scheme to deceive the enemy into thinking that Tobruk's coal-fired power station had been damaged and put out of action. During a daylight raid smoke bombs were set off near the station and one of its tall chimneys was brought down by a demolition charge, empty crates were scattered in the vicinity along with pieces of corrugated iron and other bits of scrap metal; sheets of hessian painted to represent bomb holes were hung on the building itself later.[22]

Unfortunately camouflage and deception was of limited value to the vessels carrying supplies into the besieged port and evacuating the wounded and prisoners on the return trip. Air attacks thus took an increasing toll on shipping in the approaches to Tobruk and the harbour itself. On 1 May the minesweeper *Milford Countess* was machine-gunned while picking up the crew of a downed Blenheim, and a high-level bombing attack on two A Lighters being reloaded for the return trip on their designated beach in the north-east corner of the harbour killed one crewman and wounded another; other A Lighters nearby beneath Captain Proud's camouflage netting remained unnoticed. As a result of the incident it was recommended that A Lighters only be used for embarkation at Tobruk in an emergency.[23] On the afternoon of 2 May a dozen *Stukas* attacked shipping therein and two days later, in a rerun of the events of 14 April, another dive-bombing attack set the engine-room of the Hospital Ship *Karapara* ablaze on the vessel's second trip to the port after being redirected from Aden; she was towed out of danger and reached the safety of Alexandria on one engine and with jury-rigged steering. On 12 May another mass afternoon raid by thirty *Stukas* and eight Junkers 88s caught the gunboat *Ladybird* at the western end of the harbour. One bomb hit a 2-Pounder AA gun on the vessel's stern, killing its crew and wounded two men manning Italian 20mm weapons mounted nearby, and another detonated in her boiler room blowing out the ship's bottom and setting her fuel oil tanks ablaze. As the *Ladybird* listed heavily to starboard her captain, Lieutenant-Commander Jack Blackburn, ordered the wounded evacuated while the forward 3-inch and 2-Pounder guns continued to engage the attackers; the latter remained in service after the gunboat had settled upright in ten feet of water.[24]

In all eight ships were lost during May, and not all of them in Tobruk harbour or its environs. The sloop HMS *Grimsby* and merchantman SS *Helka*, carrying a cargo of water and petrol into Tobruk, were sunk after being caught by dive-bombers forty miles north-east of the port on 25 May; the anti-submarine trawler *Southern Maid* which was also accompanying the *Helka* shot down one of the attackers and damaged another before ferrying the survivors to Mersa Matruh. By the end of May it was virtually impossible to use Tobruk harbour in daylight, and vessels were instructed to avoid approaching the port before dusk and to be well clear before first light. Matters were complicated yet further by Axis aircraft assiduously sowing the harbour and approaches with mines, usually at night, which had to be painstakingly cleared by the minesweepers *Arthur Cavanagh*, *Bagshot*, and *Milford Countess*. Axis torpedo bombers also proved adept at attacking at night, and the movement of petrol and water carriers like the ill-fated *Helka* was restricted to no-moon periods as a result. A variety of small craft were pressed into service as supply carriers by the Inshore Squadron, and warships visiting Tobruk invariably carried supplies in and wounded out.

Thus by the end of May 1,688 men had been carried into Tobruk and 5,198 lifted out, the latter including wounded, POWs and unnecessary administrative personnel. In addition, 2,593 tons of assorted supplies had also been delivered, a daily average rate of eighty-four tons and fourteen tons above the estimated daily requirement.[25] Even so, at the beginning of June the loss rate had become prohibitive and Eastern Mediterranean Fleet HQ in Alexandria temporarily decreed that only destroyers should be employed on Tobruk supply runs because their speed permitted them to make the round trip in darkness. The wisdom of this decision was highlighted on 24 June, when an attempt to get another cargo of water and petrol into Tobruk aboard the SS *Pass of Balmaha*, escorted by the sloops HMS *Auckland* and HMAS *Paramatta*, again ended in disaster. The little flotilla was attacked by torpedo bombers approximately twenty miles north-east of Tobruk, and then by a total of forty-eight Junkers 87s in three groups. The *Auckland* was abandoned after being badly hit and sank after almost breaking in two while the *Paramatta* was picking up survivors. The *Pass of Balmaha* was also badly damaged and temporarily abandoned, but was eventually towed into Tobruk after dark by the destroyer HMAS *Waterhen*.[26] Even then, night runs provided insufficient protection for the destroyers as Axis aircraft proved adept at locating them and attacking with the aid of moonlight, and the fast runs had to be further restricted to no-moon periods. Runs were made by up to three destroyers per night and the fast minelaying cruisers *Abdiel* and *Latona* once a week; during the no-moon period in August 1941 the minelayers made seven round trips to Tobruk and the destroyers twenty-seven.

The regular Spud Runs by the A Lighters and other small vessels continued throughout. The latter, consisting of a number of small, aged merchantmen and four captured Italian fishing schooners, were responsible for carrying in most of Tobruk's food. The schooner *Maria Giovanni*, commanded by Lieutenant Alfred Palmer RNR, was perhaps the most famous, making runs into Tobruk loaded to capacity with assorted victuals, sometimes including live sheep and bristling with jury rigged weaponry. She was lost after a German decoy lured her onto the shore in mistake for the light marking the entrance to Tobruk harbour; Palmer was shot and wounded trying to escape and was repatriated to his native Australia two years later. The A Lighters were based at Mersa Matruh from June 1941, carrying vehicles, ammunition and fuel into Tobruk and, time and enemy activity permitting, returning with cargoes of damaged equipment for repair in Egyptian workshops, wounded and prisoners. Attack could come at any time. One A Lighter was sunk by a magnetic mine as it approached its unloading point inside Tobruk harbour, and on another occasion two more were attacked by dive-bombers off Sidi Barrani. A four hour fight ensued during which the A Lighters fired off over 1,000 rounds, in the course of which one was sunk by multiple bomb hits. Only one crewman survived, after forcing himself through a small scuttle as the vessel went down, breaking all his ribs in the process. The second was taken in tow by a tug from Tobruk, but was so badly damaged she broke up and sank en route.

Neither were mines and aircraft the only threat. In the evening of 9 October a convoy of three A Lighters, A2, A7 and A18, left Mersa Matruh loaded with tanks, intending to rendezvous with an anti-submarine trawler and air cover at around noon the following day. At 04:00 on 10 October they were attacked by a U-Boat on the surface, whose gunfire damaged the A18's bridge, cut her degaussing cable, carried away her mast and badly wounded her navigator.[27] The A Lighter responded with its own armament and A7, commanded by Sub-Lieutenant Dennis Peters, part lowered her bow ramp with the intention of ramming but the U-Boat disappeared. The convoy then became split, with A18 limping back to Mersa Matruh while the other two A Lighters pushed on to Tobruk. The remainder of the voyage was far from uneventful. The air and sea cover failed to materialise and the A Lighters came under attack from a dozen aircraft at 17:00, from two more at 22:00 and from enemy coastal guns at around midnight; to round things off Tobruk was undergoing a heavy air raid when they finally arrived at 01:30 on 10 October.[28] After unloading A2 and A7 sailed back out of Tobruk harbour at dusk on 11 October. They were ambushed at around midnight by U-75 lurking inshore, again using guns rather than torpedoes. A7 suffered several hits that set her engine room and mess deck on fire, while return fire forced the U-Boat to submerge. The A2 took the A7's wounded aboard and put the vessel in tow when the latter's commander, Sub-Lieutenant Bromley, declined to scuttle her. The U-75 then reappeared and sank both vessels with gunfire. Only one crewman of the thirty-seven men aboard the two vessels survived, being picked up by the same U-Boat after twenty-four hours in the water.[29] Eleven days later the gunboat *Gnat* was torpedoed by the U-79 off Bardia; she was towed back to Alexandria by the destroyer *Jaguar* where she was beached and written off.

The first attempt to relieve Tobruk came in mid-June, using recently arrived equipment from the UK. When the presence of 15 Panzer Division in Libya was confirmed in mid-April 1941 Lieutenant-General Wavell had appealed to London for reinforcements, and on 21 April Churchill and the Defence Committee authorised the despatch of a special convoy. Codenamed TIGER, the convoy consisted of five fast merchant vessels, the *Clan Chattan*, *Clan Lamont*, *Clan Campbell*, *Empire Song* and *New Zealand Star*, carrying a total of 295 tanks and forty-three Hurricane fighters. By mid-May Wavell's need had grown even more acute, as the failure of Operation BREVITY reduced the Western Desert Force's armoured strength to a single Squadron of Cruiser Tanks located at Mersa Matruh and up to forty vehicles undergoing workshop repair. Arriving at Gibraltar on

5 May, TIGER was directed through the Mediterranean rather than taking the longer Cape route in order to cut forty days from the journey time; this was the first convoy to run the gauntlet since January 1941 when *Fliegerkorps X* had badly mauled Operation EXCESS, sinking the cruiser *Southampton* and seriously damaging the cruiser *Gloucester* and aircraft-carrier *Illustrious*. Virtually the entire strength of H Force and the Mediterranean Fleet operating from Gibraltar and Alexandria respectively was mobilised to protect TIGER, including the battleships *Barham*, *Queen Elizabeth*, *Valiant* and *Warspite*, and the aircraft carriers *Ark Royal* and *Formidable*. The convoy docked in Alexandria on the morning of 12 May, after fighting off numerous day and night air attacks and accompanied by a telegram from Churchill quoting Scripture: 'For he saith, I have heard thee in a time accepted, and in the day of Salvation have I succoured thee; behold now is the day of salvation.' The TIGER convoy did not escape totally unscathed. The *New Zealand Star* and *Empire Song* detonated mines at around midnight on 8 May. The former suffered minor damage but the latter caught fire, blew up and sank at 04:00 on 9 May, taking fifty-seven tanks and ten Hurricanes with her.[30]

The Western Desert Force thus received a total of 238 tanks: twenty-one Mark VIC Light Tanks, thirty-two Cruisers, fifty of the latest Mark VI Cruisers dubbed 'Crusaders' and 135 Matildas.[31] These were immediately earmarked for Operation BATTLEAXE, for which Wavell issued his orders on 28 May. The attack was to be commanded by Lieutenant-General Sir Noel Beresford-Peirse, and carried out by Major-General Frank Messervy's 4th Indian Division and the ubiquitous 7th Armoured Division, commanded by Major-General Sir Michael O'Moore Creagh. The first phase was to be a three-pronged attack to recapture the frontier area with the 4th Indian Division and the 4th Armoured Brigade securing the Halfaya Pass, Sollum, Bardia and Fort Capuzzo, while the 7th Armoured Division looped around to the south to deal with the Panzers believed to be concentrated in the vicinity of the Hafid Ridge, just west of Fort Capuzzo. With this done the attack force was to relieve Tobruk and destroy any enemy forces in the region of El Adem before exploiting as far west as possible toward Mechili and Derna. Although the TIGER convoy arrived on 12 May, it took some time to unload the new vehicles, disperse them to workshops and modify them for desert service, and 10 June 1941 was earliest possible date for launching BATTLEAXE. In the event several days were added to allow the crews time to train with their new tanks, and for the 7th Armoured Division to train as a formation, having not operated as such for several months. In parallel with this the RAF stepped up its day and night attacks upon Axis airfields, the port of Benghazi and the columns carrying supplies and munitions up to the border area, right up to the point where the BATTLEAXE force left its concentration areas for its start lines near Buq Buq and Sofafi on the afternoon of 14 June. It was going up against a number of fortified positions strung out between Sidi Azeiz and Halfaya, equipped with mines and anti-tank guns. The line had been ordered by Rommel as a precaution after BREVITY and was backed by newly arrived *Generalleutnant* Walther Neumann-Sylkow's 15 Panzer Division, with the *Trento* Division under command; 5 *Leichte* Division was held in reserve south-east of Tobruk.

The attack began at dawn on 15 June. The 7th RTR had taken Fort Capuzzo by the early afternoon, and after being reinforced by the 22nd Guards Brigade, succeeded in repelling a series of small counter-attacks by elements of Panzer Regiment 8. Other elements subdued a German position atop a height to the south known as Point 206, after a hard fight that saw one Squadron from the 4th RTR reduced to a single Matilda, while a battalion from the 22nd Guards Brigade occupied Musaid to the south-east. However, the attack to secure the Halfaya Pass was stopped by a combination of mines, anti-tank guns and armoured cars despite numerous attempts by tanks and infantry to push forward. The 7th Armoured Brigade reached the Hafid Ridge at around 09:00, but then ran into dug-in German anti-tank guns that the Cruisers lacked the firepower to deal with; at least four of the German guns were 88mm pieces. An attempt to outflank the guns from the west in the late morning was halted when the complexity of the enemy positions became apparent, losing a number of tanks in the process. At around 17:30 the Crusader-equipped

6th RTR launched a hasty attack after receiving reports that the German anti-tank screen was withdrawing; the withdrawal was a ploy and eleven Crusaders were knocked out in a well-executed ambush. The British withdrew under cover of long-range gunnery and the action tapered off with the onset of darkness despite the arrival of a number of Panzers from the north. By nightfall the attack had achieved only one of its initial objectives, and at some cost. The 7th Armoured Brigade had thus been reduced to forty-eight tanks, and the 4th Armoured Brigade had only thirty-seven Matildas left of the hundred or so it had begun the battle with. Many of these were repairable but the withdrawal made retieval difficult.

The pendulum swung to some extent on 16 June. Panzer Regiment 8 launched a pincer attack on Fort Capuzzo at 06:00, led by *Generalleutnant* Neumann-Sylkow in person. The attack was fought off by dug-in Matildas and 25-Pounder guns brought up during the night; by 10:00 approximately fifty Panzers had been put out of action, and Neumann-Sylkow broke off the attack at around midday. British attempts to renew the attack on the Halfaya Pass were stymied again, while the 7th Armoured Brigade, 7th Armoured Support Group fought a day-long running battle with 5 *Leichte* Division that ran south for the fifteen miles from Hafid Ridge to Sidi Omar, and then east toward the Cyrenaica–Egypt border. The Panzers skilfully orchestrated the superior range of their 50mm and short 75mm guns, using the latter to knock out the British 25-Pounders to clear the way for the Panzer IIIs, which then exploited the superior range and penetrating power of the former against the 2-Pounder armed Cruisers Tanks. By evening the 7th Armoured Brigade had been pushed well east of the border, and only darkness saved it from a strong German attack launched at 19:00. Rommel, meanwhile, had decided to concentrate his force to encircle and destroy the 7th Armoured Brigade, and at 16:00 ordered 15 Panzer to leave a screen at Fort Capuzzo and move south-east through the night to join 5 *Leichte* Division.

The redeployment of 15 Panzer Division threatened to leave the 4th Indian Division and 4th Armoured Brigade high and dry

in the vicinity of Fort Capuzzo and Sollum. Fortunately for them
Messervy learned of the German move during the night of 16–17
June and ordered a withdrawal on his own initiative, instructing the
surviving Matildas to form a protective screen to cover the infantry.
The Panzers resumed their advance at 04:30, and by 08:00 5 *Leichte*
Division had reached Sidi Suleiman, twenty miles or so inside Egypt
and due south of the Halfaya Pass. Two hours later they made contact with the armoured screen protecting the withdrawal of the 11th
Indian Brigade and the 22nd Guards Brigade, sparking a battle that
went on for the rest of the day. The British armour held the Panzers
back until 16:00, by which time Messervy's infantry had successfully
evaded the developing trap.

Thus by 17 June Egypt lay virtually undefended once again, and
Rommel was once again incapable of exploiting his advantage, having overtaxed his tenuous supply line. Operation BATTLEAXE cost the
British 122 dead, 588 wounded and 259 missing, along with sixty-
four Matildas and twenty-seven assorted Cruisers and Crusaders;
many of the tanks were only damaged or broken down but had to
be abandoned on the battlefield during the withdrawal. Overall,
Afrikakorps tank losses were substantially lower for although a total
of fifty Panzers were put out of action in the course of the battle,
only twelve were totally destroyed. The remainder were returned to
service by recovery and repair crews, underscoring the importance
of retaining control of the battlefield. There was less disparity in the
human cost with German units suffering a total of ninety-three
killed, 350 wounded and 235 missing, while the *Trento* Division lost
an additional 592 casualties. The failure of BATTLEAXE also prompted
a major reshuffle among the British senior commanders. Dissatisfied
with Wavell but unable to simply remove him for political reasons,
Churchill arranged a sideways exchange with the Commander-in-
Chief India, General Sir Claude Auchinleck, with effect from 1 July
1941. Beresford-Peirse was replaced as Commander Western Desert
Force by Lieutenant-General Alfred Reade Godwin-Austen, and
Creagh was supplanted as commander of the 7th Armoured Division
by newly promoted Major-General William Gott.[32]

While the Ras El Medauar salient saw the most intense fighting of the siege, matters were far from quiescent elsewhere on the
perimeter due to Morshead's First World War policy of dominating
no-man's land. On a day-to-day basis this consisted of maintaining
outposts forward of the main defence line, manned by two or three
men equipped with a field telephone during daylight and carrying
out aggressive patrols during the night, with larger raids to pre-empt
enemy action or keep him off balance being mounted where necessary. On 13 May, for example a company from the 2/43rd Battalion,
supported by eight Matilda tanks and seven Bren Carriers launched
a dawn attack on an Italian strongpoint straddling the Bardia Road
a mile east of the perimeter, and on 30 May a clash between a patrol
of three Light and four Cruiser Tanks and a force of enemy tanks on
the southern side of the perimeter sparked a roving skirmish that
lasted most of the day. The garrison also disrupted the largely Italian
construction of minefields and defences along the southern sector,
not least by lifting and stealing newly laid enemy mines. On 1 July
Lieutenant-Colonel Colonel Allan Spowers of the 2/24th Battalion
led a party of fifty with three trucks that returned with 500 German
anti-tank mines, and exactly a month later a patrol from the 2/13th
Battalion occupied a partly built position during darkness and
ambushed the Italian working party as it came forward to work, killing four, taking one prisoner and scattering the remainder.[33] It was
not all ambushes and hostility on the perimeter, and in another echo
of the First World War a live-and-let-live system developed between
friend and foe. Local truces to allow the dead and wounded from
clashes to be evacuated were common, and on the sector straddling
the El Adem road both sides observed a daily semi-official cease-fire
for the two hours before midnight, the end of which was signalled
by a burst of tracer fired vertically into the air.[34]

Such niceties were not unknown on the Ras El Medauar sector,
but relations between the Australians and the German units manning the salient had an edge not apparent in the formers' relatively
benign attitude to the Italians. Sniping was a popular pastime, and
the commander of 2 *Bataillon*, *Infanterie* Regiment 115 referred to

the remarkable marksmanship of his opponents, who he credited with killing a number of NCOs doing their rounds in front-line positions.[35] Morshead launched another attempt to reduce the Ras El Medauar salient at 03:30 on 3 August, after intensive reconnaissance patrolling had mapped out the defences. The attack was again a two-pronged affair intended to envelop the feature carried out by the 2/28th Battalion to the north and the 2/43rd Battalion to the south. The latter failed to get beyond the anti-tank ditch protecting Post R6, and while the former managed to secure S7 the small party holding it were again cut off and overwhelmed by a German counter-attack the following night. The attack cost the attackers a total of 188 casualties from the 264 men involved, while the defenders from *Infanterie* Regiments 104 and 115 lost twenty-two killed and thirty-eight wounded. The 3 August attack proved to be the final Australian attempt to retake the Ras El Medauar.[36]

In the event, the 9th Australian Division was not to see Tobruk relieved either. Sir Robert Menzies' Government had despatched the 2nd AIF to the Middle East in 1940 as a complete Corps, and on the understanding that its constituent divisions and sub-formations would continue to serve in that capacity. To this end the commander of the 2nd AIF, Lieutenant-General Thomas Blamey, reported directly to the Australian Minister of Defence and was tasked to ensure the integrity of his command. With the exception of the 18th Australian Brigade's temporary posting to the UK in the wake of Dunkirk, the understanding was respected until circumstances conspired against it in 1941, with Blamey's Corps HQ and the 6th Australian Division joining the Greek expedition while the 7th Australian Division fought the Vichy French in Lebanon and Syria and the 9th Division went to Cyrenaica before being trapped at Tobruk. Blamey began agitating for the reassembly of his Corps after the Greek evacuation, and officially requested Wavell relieve the 9th Australian after the failure of BATTLEAXE, to join its sister divisions in Palestine. He was supported in this by Menzies and the Australian Government from at least 20 July 1941, when Menzies raised the matter with Churchill, which he did again on 7 August.[37] The Australian Government's interest was driven at least in part by public opinion, which gained the erroneous impression from news reports and German propaganda that Morshead's men were fighting the Desert War single-handed, and there was also widespread and exaggerated concern over the privations they were suffering. The resulting furore forced Menzies to resign on 28 August. By that time Auchinleck, loath to lose seasoned units on the front line, had reluctantly agreed to the relief of part of the garrison and the operation had been going on for nine days.[38]

The first lift of the relief was codenamed Operation TREACLE, allegedly because the RN personnel charged with carrying it out thought it would be a 'sticky business'. The lift was carried out across the no-moon period beginning on 19 August in order to avoid moonlight air or surface attack. The RAF bombed Axis airfields after dark, loitering to prevent the airfields operating their runway lights, while the RN and the garrison's own guns bombarded enemy artillery positions near Bardia. The latter was also intended to suppress 'Bardia Bill', the garrison's nickname for a heavy gun or guns that had taken to dropping shells into Tobruk harbour. Most sources are vague on the details with the weapon or weapons being described as being of 8-inch calibre of possibly German or Italian provenance. The guns may have belonged to *Artillerie Kommand* 104, a siege artillery train despatched to Libya on Hitler's orders to assist with the reduction of Tobruk. Commanded by *Generalmajor* Karl Böttcher, the unit was deployed around Belhammed, five miles south-east of the perimeter and was equipped with almost 200 assorted guns, including nine 210mm pieces.[39] In Tobruk the harbour defences were strengthened by moving mobile 3.7-inch AA guns back from the perimeter, and two wrecked vessels were pressed into service as improvised jetties; according to one account they were connected to the shore by pontoon bridge. In addition the small vessels and A Lighters from the Inshore Squadron in the harbour on the nights of the lift were held back to assist with unloading. The lift was carried out by the minelaying cruisers *Abdiel* and *Latona* and the destroyers *Encounter*, *Havoc*, *Jarvis*, *Jaguar*, *Kimberley*, *Kipling*, *Latima* and *Nizam*.

For ten consecutive nights two destroyers, carrying 350 troops apiece and one of the cruisers, carrying an additional 400, entered

Tobruk harbour, accompanied by a third destroyer carrying up to 200 tons of supplies. The cruiser was unloaded at anchor out in the harbour by the A Lighters and small vessels, and the supply destroyer moored alongside the permanent quay while the troop-carry-ing destroyers exchanged their human cargo over the improvised jetties. According to an eyewitness, the destroyers completed their exchange in ten minutes, and all four vessels were underway again with their new passengers within thirty minutes. This was not an arbitrary time period, for if the ships spent any longer in Tobruk harbour they would not be clear of Sollum and thus the clutches of the *Luftwaffe* by dawn.[40] By 29 August General Stanislaw Kopański's 1st Independent Carpathian Brigade had been delivered safely to Tobruk. Formed in 1940 from Polish regular troops who elected to continue the fight with the French, the Brigade had been posted to Syria and defected to the British in preference to serving the Vichy French regime after the fall of France in 1940. In exchange Brigadier George Wootten's 18th Australian Brigade had been carried to Alexandria, along with the 16th Anti-Tank Company, the 2/4th Field Company, the 2/4th Field Ambulance, the 51st Field Regiment RA and the 18th Indian Cavalry Regiment.[41] The lift did not go totally unscathed. The destroyer *Nizam* was damaged by an air attack, and the cruiser HMS *Phoebe*, part of the TREACLE covering force, was so badly damaged by an Italian torpedo bomber on 27 August that she had to be sent to the US for repair.

Churchill and the British senior command appears to have hoped that returning the 18th Australian Brigade to its parent 7th Australian Division in Palestine would placate the Australian Government, but it soon became apparent that only the relief of the 9th Australian Division in its entirety would do. Menzies' successor Arthur Fadden took up the gauntlet with Churchill within days of taking office, and reiterated the Australian position in no uncertain terms to the Dominions Office ten days later.[42] Auchinleck appears to have been resigned to the fact by 10 September, given that he was discuss-ing options with the War Office on that date.[43] In the event, the 9th Australian Division left Tobruk in two lifts. Operation SUPERCHARGE ran from 19 to 27 September, and saw the 24th Australian Brigade and the 2/4th Field Park Company carried to Alexandria in exchange for the 16th Infantry Brigade and the 32nd Army Tank Brigade Forward HQ. The latter was augmented by four Light Tanks and forty-eight Matildas from the 4th Armoured Brigade, carried into Tobruk by A Lighter. C Squadron 4th RTR came in aboard Lighter A7, part of the convoy with A2 and A18 that ran into the unknown U-Boat on the night of 9–10 October. The tank crews were sleeping on the tarpaulins covering their vehicles, and when the gunfire began they unshipped their Matildas' co-axial Besa machine-guns and went on deck to join the fray. A Trooper Weech was credited with scoring hits on the U-Boat when it appeared fifty yards off the Lighter's port side, along with Sub-Lieutenant Peters wielding a Thompson gun on the bridge. According to one account C Squadron's commander talked Peters out of trying to ram the U-Boat by pointing out the importance of delivering his tanks intact, and the two shared a celebratory whisky on the bridge after the U-Boat finally disappeared.[44]

The third and final lift, codenamed CULTIVATE, ran for thirteen days beginning on 12 October, the extension being necessary because the lift had been expanded to include the remaining two-thirds of Morshead's Division. Thus the 9th Australian Division HQ, Australian 4th Field Hospital, 20th and 24th Australian Brigades were taken off and replaced with the 14th and 23rd Brigades, the 62nd General Hospital and the 11th Czechoslovak Infantry Battalion, which was attached to General Kopański's 1st Independent Carpathian Brigade. Moving the Australian infantry off the front line and getting the newcomers in place without weakening the defences or alerting the enemy was a complex and fraught business, and the timetable and organisation was a triumph of staff work in its own right.[45] The Operation nonetheless proceeded as smoothly as its two predecessors until the final individual lift scheduled to move the 20th Australian Brigade HQ and the 2/13th Battalion on the night of 25–26 October. The convoy, consisting of the cruisers *Abdiel* and *Latona* and destroyers *Encounter* and *Hero* were spotted on the inbound leg near Bardia, possibly by a U-Boat, and underwent fifteen attacks by aircraft between 19:00

and 23:00. The *Latona* was hit in the engine room and the resulting fire grew out of control. The *Hero* closed in to take off the cruiser's troops and crew and suffered structural damage from three bomb near-misses in the process. The *Latona* sank two hours later after a magazine explosion, possibly with the assistance of *Encounter*; thirty seven of *Latona's* crew died in the attack. By the time all this was over it was too late to proceed safely to Tobruk and the convoy thus returned to Alexandria leaving the 2/13th Battalion stranded in Tobruk, a victim of its battalion number according to some of its men. The unit therefore returned to its positions within the perimeter where it remained until Tobruk was relieved by ground forces at the end of the following month; through this accident the 2/13th Battalion thus earned the distinction of being the only Australian unit to serve with the Tobruk garrison throughout the siege.

In all Operations TREACLE, SUPERCHARGE and CULTIVATE successfully shuttled in the region of 15,000 men out of Tobruk and carried a similar number into the port over a total of thirty-one nights. The shortest, SUPERCHARGE, took out 5,444 men and in excess of 500 wounded, and brought in 6,308 and 2,100 tons of supplies in just eight nights.[46] Apart from the stranded 2/13th Battalion, the Australian role in the story of Tobruk now came to an end, although a large number of Morshead's men would not be leaving under any circumstances. Between April and October 1941, the 9th Australian Division lost 744 men killed, along with 1,974 wounded and a further 476 missing.[47] In the process they and their comrades established a legendary reputation based on standing firm in the face of stifling heat, sandstorms, thirst, hunger and everything Rommel could throw at them. It was now up to their replacements to carry out the final act in the siege.

11
Tobruk Relieved:
25 October 1941 –
10 December 1941

The 9th Australian Division was replaced in the Tobruk perimeter by Major-General Ronald Mackenzie Scobie's 70th Division, to whom Morshead handed over command of the Tobruk Fortress on 19 October. Scobie had been commissioned into the Royal Engineers in 1914 and after serving as the Deputy Director of Mobilisation at the War Office at the outbreak of war had held staff appointments in Sudan and the Middle East. Originally the 6th Division before being renumbered on 10 October 1941, the 70th Division was a new formation raised from units in Cyprus, Egypt and Palestine. By the time of arrival in Tobruk the division was made up of three infantry brigades: Brigadier Brian Chappel's 14th Brigade, the 16th Brigade commanded by Brigadier Cyril Lomax, and Brigadier Walter Brooks' 23rd Brigade. Scobie also had General Stanislaw Kopański's 1st Independent Carpathian Brigade under command, along with an expanded and revamped armoured force in the shape of Brigadier Arthur Willison's 32nd Army Tank Brigade. The latter consisted of the newly arrived 4th RTR and incorporated the 1st RTR, D Squadron 7th RTR and C Squadron King's Dragoon Guards (KDG) which were already present. By 19 October Tobruk's tank strength totalled 131 vehicles, consisting of thirty four Light Tanks, six A9 Cruisers, nine A10 Cruisers, thirteen A13 Cruisers and sixty-nine Matilda IIs.[1] Scobie also inherited a small but useful aerial reconnaissance capability. Concerned at the lack of intelligence on enemy activities and dispositions in the run up to the relief, Morshead had ordered the creation of a new runway and camouflaged shelters adjacent to El Gubbi airfield, which were occupied by two stripped down Hurricanes from No. 451 Squadron RAAF. One of these flew a reconnaissance mission to Acroma on 27 September, the first Allied aircraft to operate from the Tobruk perimeter since the end of April.[2]

As Operation BATTLEAXE had seriously depleted both sides, the period after June 1941 was one of reinforcement, resupply and reorganisation. For Rommel, this meant gathering the reinforcement and more importantly the supplies to finally capture Tobruk. His single-minded pursuit of this objective has been characterised as obsessive but the simple fact was that Rommel had little option if he wished to push further into Egypt. Tobruk presented a constant threat to the *Deutsches Afrikakorps'* tenuous supply line, denying the convoys use of the only decent surfaced road in the region and forcing Rommel to route his supply convoys over rough tracks to the south. Securing the port would ease the Axis supply position immensely by removing the need to truck supplies the 1,000 miles or so from Tripoli, and also remove the possibility of Tobruk forming an anvil against which Rommel's forces could be pinned by British attacks across the Egyptian border. Gathering the necessary supplies was no easy feat, however, for the Royal Navy and RAF were becoming increasingly adept at interdicting Axis shipping. One small coastal convoy into Tripoli was attacked by the RAF seven times in a three-day voyage between 11 and 13 September, losing four of its six vessels in the process. Between June and October 1941 forty Axis cargo vessels were sunk carrying supplies to North Africa by aircraft, submarines and mines, totalling 178,577 tons.[3] The *Luftwaffe* attempted to alleviate the situation by establishing an air bridge between Crete and Derna using transport aircraft and gliders which carried in up to 400 tons of supplies per day, equivalent to a fifth of the daily requirement for the Axis forces in Cyrenaica. The RAF countered this with patrols by long-range Bristol Beaufighters and night bombing the landing grounds around Derna, which destroyed a large proportion of the supplies.[4]

On 14 September Rommel embarked on a novel initiative to expand his supply stocks. Prompted by intelligence reports of a major British supply dump twenty miles south of Sollum and fifteen miles inside the Egyptian border, he launched *Unternehmen Sommernachstraum* (Operation Summer Night's Dream) to capture and carry off the stocks therein. The Operation despatched *Aufklärungs Abteilung* 3 south along the border wire as a diversion while *Kampfgruppe* Schütte and *Kampfgruppe* Stephan both drawn from 21 Panzer Division, as 5 *Leichte* Division had been renamed on 1 August 1941, executed a ten-mile wide pincer movement to secure the alleged supply dump, each trailed by a number of tucks to carry away the booty. *Kampfgruppe* Schütte was accompanied by Rommel in person, riding in his captured AEC Mammoth Command Vehicle. A flanking patrol captured a truck carrying the 4th South African Armoured Car Regiment's HQ records en route but the dump proved to be non-existent; the force pressed deeper into Egypt at Rommel's prompting until finally coming to a stop for want of fuel in mid-afternoon near Sofafi, where the interlopers remained under air and artillery attack until dusk when they made a hurried withdrawal to the border, during which Rommel's AEC suffered a flat tyre. Unwilling to risk attracting unwelcome attention with a radio call for assistance, Rommel and his high-ranking companions effected repairs by torchlight and passed back through the frontier wire to safety without further mishap.[5]

Rommel had also come up with an equally novel way of circumventing the stricture on receiving reinforcements placed upon him by *Oberkommando des Heeres* (OKH) on 3 May. The *Afrika* Division *zur besondern Verfügung* (zbV), roughly 'Africa Division for Special Purposes' was formed in late July-August from units already serving in Libya including *Aufklärungs Abteilung* 580, *Panzerjäger Abteilung* 190, *Panzergrenadier* Regiment *Afrika*, *Infanterie* Regiments 155 and

200, and *Infanterie* Regiment *Afrika* 361; the latter unit included a contingent of German nationals with prior service in the Légion Étrangère. Commanded by *Generalmajor* Max Sümmermann, the *Afrika* Division *zbV* increased Rommel's contingent of German Divisions to three alongside 15 and 21 Panzer Divisions commanded by *Generalmajor* Walter Neumann-Sylkow and *Generalmajor* Johannes von Ravenstein respectively. The two Panzer Divisions remained grouped as the *Deutsches Afrika Korps*, commanded from 17 September by *General* Ludwig Crüwell, formerly of 11 Panzer Division; at the same time Rommel was in command of *Panzerarmee Afrika*, with responsibility for all three divisions. In addition to *Panzerarmee Afrika* there were two Italian formations in the Tobruk/Egyptian border region. These were *Generale* Enea Navarinni's 21° *Corpo d'Armata*, consisting of the *Bologna, Brescia, Pavia* and *Savona* Divisions and the 20° *Corpo d'Armata Manovra* (CAM). Headed by *Generale* Gastone Gambara, the latter was made up of the *Ariete* armoured and *Trieste* motorised divisions and was officially independent of Rommel's command.

Rommel determined to use the bulk of this force in his final operation to take Tobruk, and he also changed his tack with regard to the location. Instead of the Ras El Medauar salient, the new attack was to target the south-eastern corner of the Tobruk perimeter, and preparatory work went on throughout October 1941. The outposts from which the Australians had monitored and harassed the Italians east of the El Adem road were rendered untenable, and the besiegers established new forward positions close enough to bring the perimeter defences under small-arms fire.[6] Rommel also established a series of four strongpoints between the perimeter and El Duda, set on a rise twenty miles or so to the south-east as a precaution against a breakout by the Tobruk garrison toward Bardia. Precisely what Rommel knew of British intentions is a matter of dispute. One source claims that the failure to locate any evidence of British preparations during *Sommernachstraum* led Rommel to deduce that the threat was minimal, whereas another claims he was well aware of British intentions from decrypts of intercepted signals from the US Military Attaché in Cairo and concludes that Rommel simply ignored the risk due to a fixation on capturing Tobruk.[7] Whatever the truth of the matter, Rommel left 21 Panzer and the *Savona* Divisions to cover the Egyptian frontier and allotted the remainder of his force roles in the attack on Tobruk, which was scheduled to begin on 20 November.

The British intentions revealed by Colonel Fellows' signals to Washington were the preparations for Operation CRUSADER, which was to be carried out by the 'best-equipped army Britain had managed to put into the field so far in the Second World War'.[8] This was Lieutenant-General Sir Alan Cunningham's 8th Army, formed in September 1941 from the 13th and 30 Corps and totalling 115,000 men, 5,000 vehicles and 600 tanks; the latter included numbers of Crusaders, the new and faster Valentine Infantry Tank and US-produced M3 Stuart Light Tanks dubbed 'Honeys' by their British crews on account of their reliability and ease of maintenance. To maintain this force and its estimated daily battle requirement of 2,500 tons of food, water, fuel and munitions vast forward supply dumps had been established as for Operation COMPASS, fed by a coast railway that now extended eighty-five miles west of Mersa Matruh and a water pipeline from Alexandria that had been stretched twelve miles beyond that. There was also a substantial deception effort in support of CRUSADER in the area of Jarabub, far to the south of the real attack, involving large numbers of dummy vehicles and spurious radio traffic.[9]

Two diversionary operations were also planned. A raid involving five Bristol Bombay transports and fifty-seven parachutists was launched on the night of 16–17 November. Intended to destroy *Luftwaffe* aircraft on airfields in the vicinity of Gazala and Tmimi, the Bombays flew into unexpected heavy cloud and turbulence. One was shot down on the way in and while the remainder dropped their sticks the raiders were widely scattered and unable to recover their equipment. The raid was therefore abandoned and twenty-two survivors walked out to a prearranged rendezvous with the Long Range Desert Group. The second operation involved fifty-nine men from No. 11 Commando, led by Lieutenant-Colonel Geoffrey Keyes, delivered by canoe from the submarines *Talisman* and *Torbay* to attack a number of targets on the night of 13–14 November. Deployment from the submarines was complicated by bad weather that swept away eleven men and came close grounding the *Torbay*, and cut the force to half. As a result only one target, a German HQ at Beda Littoria where Rommel was believed to be quartered, was attacked on the night of 16 November. Rommel was not there, Keyes was killed in a firefight at the HQ building, and all but two of the raiders were subsequently killed or captured trying to evade back to British lines after the *Torbay* failed to see their pick-up signal. The raid killed four Germans, destroyed the generator lighting the HQ and demolished an electricity pylon; Keyes was awarded a posthumous Victoria Cross.[10]

The main crusader attack was a two-pronged affair. The 13th Corps, commanded by Lieutenant-General Godwin-Austen, consisted of the 4th Indian Division, the recently arrived 2nd New Zealand Division and the 1st Army Tank Brigade while 30 Corps, commanded by Lieutenant-General Charles Willoughby Norrie, comprised of the 7th Armoured Division, the also newly arrived 1st South African Division and the 22nd Guards Brigade. The overall plan, informed by accurate information on Axis dispositions from ULTRA decrypts, tasked the 13th Corps to cross into Cyrenaica south of Sidi Omar before swinging north to take the fortified Axis positions strung out between Sidi Azeiz and Halfaya in the rear along with Fort Capuzzo while pushing north to cut off Bardia. 30 Corps meanwhile was to despatch the 4th Armoured Brigade in a loop west and north in support of 13th Corps, the 7th Armoured Brigade and 7th Armoured Division Support Group north-west toward Sidi Rezegh while the 22nd Armoured Brigade moved on a shallower angle toward Bir El Gubi. Finally the 1st South African Division was to advance almost due west toward El Cuasc and Elwet El Hamra, in preparation for a subsequent thrust across the middle of Cyrenaica. The overall objective was to draw the German armour out into the open where it could be overwhelmed by the 7th Armoured Division with its superior numbers, after which Tobruk was to be relieved.

Operation CRUSADER began in an overcast dawn on 18 November, after the attacking units had suffered a torrential rainstorm on the start line. The weather prevented the RAF from initially providing close air support and attacking Axis airfields, supply dumps and communications as planned, but its effects were more severe on the Germans, whose coastal airfields were turned into quagmires. As a result the *Luftwaffe* remained effectively grounded for forty-eight hours, and as this included reconnaissance aircraft CRUSADER achieved complete surprise; it was the afternoon before word of the British advance reached Rommel's HQ. The British formations attained their initial objectives without incident apart from the 22nd Armoured Brigade, whose reconnaissance screen fought a skirmish with armoured cars from *Generale* Gambara's CAM before leaguering for the night ten miles or so short of Bir El Gubi. The latter was occupied by the *Trieste* Division and at midday on 19 November the 22nd Armoured's Crusaders clashed sixteen M13/40s, sparking a fight that lasted for two days and which seriously upset the British formation's timetable. Meanwhile the 7th Armoured Brigade and Support Group had reached the Sidi Rezegh Ridge and airfield while in the evening the 4th Armoured became embroiled with elements of 21 Panzer Division moving south to meet the British advance. The struggle between the latter two continued on the morning of 20 November, while to the north-west the 7th Armoured Brigade repulsed a counter-attack by elements of the *Afrika* Division *zbV* and *Bologna* Division at Sidi Rezegh.

The 4th Armoured Brigade resumed its fight with 21 Panzer Division on 20 November, and reports received through the day indicated that 15 and 21 Panzer Divisions were concentrating. This was precisely what the original British plan had called for, but by this point 7th Armoured Division's combat power had become dispersed as its constituent Brigades fought their individual and widely separated battles. The 4th Armoured Brigade was particularly hard pressed when 21 Panzer Division withdrew to refuel and rearm in the late afternoon, and was replaced by 15 Panzer Division. Panzer Regiment 8 from the latter came up against the 4th Armoured ensconced in a defensive position on a slight rise at around 16:30 and after a thirty-minute gunnery duel began to push the British tanks back. The situation was saved by the arrival of the 22nd Armoured Brigade's Crusaders at dusk, which allowed the 4th Armoured to break contact. The former had been ordered to leave the 1st South African Brigade to mask the Italians still stubbornly holding out at El Gubi.[11] By nightfall the 4th Armoured Brigade had lost forty of its Honey Light Tanks, over a third of its tank strength, while the 22nd Armoured Brigade had been reduced to 100 Crusaders.[12] Once again many repairable vehicles were lost when the battlefield was ceded to the Germans.

It was at this point that the Tobruk garrison entered the fray. Major-General Scobie had been instructed to prepare for a break-out, which began at dawn on 21 November after an order from Norrie at 30 Corps HQ the previous day. Launched from the south-east corner of the perimeter and spearheaded by the 32nd Army Tank Brigade, the attack came as a considerable surprise as the Axis troops encircling the port were unaware that the Australians had been replaced or that the garrison harboured such a powerful armoured force. The first stage of the break-out was to overcome the five enemy strongpoints barring the way to El Duda, which was only two miles from Sidi Rezegh. The first strongpoint, codenamed BUTCH, was secured by the 7th RTR by 09:00 but the parallel attack on the adjacent JILL strongpoint by the 4th RTR and 2nd Battalion, The Black Watch, did not start well, with the tanks being delayed and then losing several vehicles to mines. Undaunted, the Black Watch carried the position with a bayonet charge and their momentum carried both units on to the next strongpoint (JACK), which was secured by 10:30. The most westerly strongpoint, TUGUN, took rather more effort to overcome as did strongpoint TIGER and fighting was still going on at 14:30, when the final push for El Duda, codenamed PLUM, was scheduled to begin. Expecting the strongpoints to be manned by Italian troops from the *Bologna* Division, the attackers were surprised in turn to discover they were facing German personnel from the *Afrika* Division *zbV* who made up a large proportion of the 1,000 or more prisoners taken in the fight for the strongpoints. The presence of the latter became apparent through a series of aggressive and persistent counter-attacks; according to one source these were controlled by Rommel in person.[13] It was thus perhaps fortunate that 30 Corps cancelled PLUM at around 16:00, for the day's fighting had also taken a heavy toll on Scobie's force. Brigadier Willison's 32nd Army Tank Brigade had only forty serviceable vehicles remaining from the 158 with which it had begun the breakout,[14] and casualties among the accompanying infantry battalions were also heavy. The 2nd Battalion, The Black Watch suffered the greatest loss, with only eight officers and 196 men still fit for duty by nightfall.[15]

PLUM was cancelled because the 7th Armoured Brigade and Support Group had run into even more trouble on the Sidi Rezegh Ridge than experienced by Scobie's breakout force. The 1st KRRC and 2nd Rifle Brigade set about clearing the airfield and feature of enemy positions at 08:30 with tank and artillery support, and had completed the task by midday after a series of stiff fights that cost the attackers eighty-four casualties in exchange for approximately 400 enemy casualties and 600 prisoners. In the process Rifleman John Beeley of the 1st KRRC earned a posthumous Victoria Cross for single-handedly storming an enemy machine-gun position. With the Ridge secured the 6th RTR's Cruiser Tanks swept forward toward El Duda and ran headlong into *Aufklärungs Abteilung* 3 and four 88mm *FlaK* 36 guns lurking on a reverse slope; all the Cruisers were knocked out in short order. Rommel had redeployed 15 and 21 Panzer Divisions during the night of 20–21 November, leaving the 4th and 22nd Armoured Brigade's high and dry, and set them loose on the British force on the Sidi Rezegh Ridge. Thus while the infantry were clearing the Ridge the 2nd RTR and 7th Hussars were being mauled by the oncoming *Panzers*, which then turned their attention to the British infantry on the newly captured Ridge. By nightfall the 7th Armoured Brigade and 7th Armoured Division Support Group had been driven back to their start point and were fighting for their very existence despite the 4th and 22nd Armoured Brigades playing catch-up. The battle for Sidi Rezegh went on through 22 November while Willison's 32nd Army Tank Brigade received a series of orders authorising and then cancelling PLUM until the attack was again cancelled for the day at 12:05. The break-out force spent the afternoon and early evening clearing enemy positions that posed a threat to the eastern flank of any advance toward El Duda.

On 23 November Rommel launched a co-ordinated attack with both Panzer and the *Ariete* Divisions to encircle and destroy 30 Corps, sparking a three day fight that pushed the 7th Armoured Division away from Tobruk and ranged as far east as the Egyptian border. In the process 30 Corps was split, 13th Corps came close to being cut off and the German advance provoked a rerun of the Benghazi-Tobruk Handicap by the rear echelon and support units; by the afternoon of 24 November thousands of vehicles were making all speed eastwards for the safety of the border wire. The situation was stabilised by the arrival of Auchinleck at 8th Army HQ at Maddalena on the evening of 24 November, after Cunningham had broached breaking off the offensive and ordering a withdrawal. After reviewing the situation Auchinleck forbade this and explicitly instructed Cunningham to continue the attack with a written order to that effect.[16] Even this does not appear to have done the trick, for Cunningham was replaced by the newly promoted Lieutenant-General Neil Ritchie on 26 November, on the grounds that he (Cunningham) 'was unduly influenced by the threat of an enemy counterstroke against his communications.';[17] on arrival in Cairo Cunningham was hospitalised with severe exhaustion.[18] A signal was despatched to Scobie the same day, informing him that the 2nd New Zealand Division had been instructed to regain Sidi Rezegh forthwith, and that the Tobruk break-out force was to do its bit by seizing El Duda as soon as possible.

The New Zealanders had actually been on their way since the previous day, and by daybreak on 25 November the 4th and 6th New Zealand Brigades, supported by Matildas from the 144th RTR, had secured Zaafran after a battle to secure a nearby strongpoint. While they reorganised, the 46th Battalion was despatched to probe across Sidi Rezegh airfield, which was littered with burned out aircraft and detritus from the fighting between the 7th Armoured Division

Support Group and *Kampfgruppe* Knabe from 21 Panzer Division four days earlier. This placed the New Zealanders on the eastern end of the Sidi Rezegh Ridge, less than ten miles from the designated rendezvous point at El Duda. The instruction to press on for the latter was passed on by 13th Corps HQ in the late morning, apparently with a few additions from Lieutenant-General Godwin-Austen. The 2nd New Zealand Division was thus ordered to not only link up with the Tobruk garrison at El Duda, but also to clear and occupy the whole of the Sidi Rezegh Ridge and adjacent high ground at Belhammed. The attack began at 21:00, Major-General Freyberg having decided to go in under cover of darkness with all six of his infantry battalions in the lead, but he became bogged down due to a combination of the broken terrain, lack of reconnaissance and stiff enemy resistance. 4th New Zealand Brigade HQ became separated from its battalions fighting with *Kampfgruppe* Böttcher for Belhammed, the two battalions tasked to advance along the crest of the Sidi Rezegh Ridge slipped off the crest to the south after running into stiff resistance from the 9° *Reggimento Bersaglieri*, while the remaining two battalions of New Zealanders became pinned down while attempting to traverse Sidi Rezegh airfield. As a result the fighting was still in progress at first light and went on through 26 November with the New Zealanders making little progress.

The timing of the New Zealanders' thrust toward El Duda was fortuitous for the Tobruk break-out force, which had spent two days consolidating and defending the corridor it had pushed toward El Duda while the 32nd Army Tank Brigade maintained and repaired its vehicles. Two preparatory attacks for PLUM were mounted on the night of 25–26 November in concert with the New Zealanders. The 2nd Battalion, The Leicestershire Regiment and D Squadron 7th RTR assaulted a position near BUTCH to reinforce the base of the corridor, while A and B Squadrons, 4th RTR and the 2nd Battalion, The York and Lancaster Regiment attacked the last enemy strongpoint, code-named WOLF and held by elements of the *Bologna* Division, which barred the way to El Duda. The initial frontal assault on WOLF stalled when four of A Squadron's Matildas ran onto mines and the infantry suffered a number of casualties, but other tanks from B Squadron succeeded in breaching a flank and by 22:30 the much of the strong-point had been cleared. The remainder was taken after first light with support from C Squadron 4th RTR, the original tanks having withdrawn to rearm and refuel. The attackers bagged over 200 pris-oners including the Italian divisional commander along with twelve Italian 37mm guns and two German 88mm pieces, but the 2nd York and Lancaster's were reduced to only forty-two men in the process. With WOLF secured El Duda lay only five miles away, and the order to launch PLUM was given at 10:48.

The attack began at 11:46 and was carried by the 1st and 4th RTRs, which mustered a combined strength of sixteen Light Tanks, fourteen Cruisers and thirty-four Matildas, supported by the 1st Battalion, The Essex Regiment and the 1st Battalion, The Northumberland Fusiliers. Despite suffering a number of casualties to anti-tank fire the tanks were atop the El Duda escarpment at 13:20, although their supporting infantry were embroiled in suppressing enemy posi-tions on the flanks, for which Captain James Jackman from the 1st Northumberland Fusiliers was awarded a posthumous Victoria Cross. By 14:50 the flanks of the corridor had been secured, and the infan-try battalions repulsed enemy counter-attacks at around 15:00 and 17:00 that cost the 1st Essex sixty-three casualties and reduced on of the 1st Northumberland Fusiliers' companies to twenty-five per cent of its original strength. Word that Willison's tanks were finally at El Duda was quickly relayed to the 2nd New Zealand Division, many of whom were actually in sight of the escarpment. At 16:20 the 19th Battalion and 44th RTR were ordered to push on to El Duda after dark, using green Very lights as a recognition signal. First contact came at 18:30, when Major Gibbon's Squadron from the 44th RTR and part of the 19th Battalion accompanied by its com-mander, Lieutenant-Colonel Sydney Hartnell, entered the 32nd Army Tank Brigade's perimeter on the escarpment; the event was captured by a Captain Keating, who photographed Hartnell and Willison shaking hands, the former in steel helmet and greatcoat and the latter resplendent in his black RTR beret. The Tobruk garrison thus made its first physical contact with external ground forces for the 230 days since 10 April 1941, when the siege is generally considered to have begun. Contact did not equate with relief however, and Tobruk's land link with the outside world was extremely tenuous. When Hartnell and Willison were exchanging salutations the corridor linking the Tobruk perimeter and El Duda was in the region of nine miles in length and between one and five miles wide, tapering in at the base and head. The latter was only as wide as the wolf strongpoint and was also the point of maximum danger, with enemy counter-attacks on the flanks only being held at bay by the mobility of the handful of Cruiser Tanks which were almost constantly on the move between danger points. The situation did not improve in the short term, for on 27 November Willison was informed that the New Zealanders would be temporarily unable to render any further assistance and that the Tobruk garrison would have to take responsibility for maintaining the corridor. The grim news was accompanied by torrential rain that severely restricted visibility and the orphaned 2/13th Battalion, which had been left stranded at Tobruk at the end of October when the remainder of the 9th Australian Division had been evacuated, was pressed into service to reinforce El Duda. The New Zealanders were fully occupied by the Germans, who employed 15 and 21 Panzer and the *Ariete* Divisions in a determined attempt to encircle and destroy the New Zealand Division that lasted until 1 December. In the course of this the *Afrika Korps* lost the services of *Generalmajor* von Ravenstein, who inadvertently drove into a 21st Battalion outpost at Point 175, four miles east of Sidi Rezegh airfield at 08:00 on 28 November. 15 Panzer Division came close to overrunning El Duda on 29 November, and cut the corridor for a time on 1 December after Panzer Regiment 8 overran the New Zealand positions atop the Belhammed escarpment.

Despite a series of German tactical victories the level of attrition eventually became too great, however. By 4 December the CRUSADER fighting had cost *Panzerarmee Afrika* 4,000 casualties, 142 tanks and a large number of guns including four 88mm pieces and 34 assorted anti-tank guns.[29] Rommel launched his final attempt to recapture

El Duda and thus sever Tobruk's tenuous contact with friendly forces the same day. The attack began at 06:45 with German infantry infiltrating broken ground from the south-west on the 1st Essex, followed by another attack from the south-east just before 07:30. Both were rebuffed by mid-morning, but were followed by a heavier attack just west of El Duda by *Maschinengewehr Bataillon* 8 during while another German force with several anti-tank guns managed to infiltrate the British line nearby and establish themselves astride the road running onto the feature from the east. The interlopers repelled several British counter-attacks and by just after 15:00 had knocked out a total of ten of the Matildas involved with their 88mm guns. Assuming the German incursion was the precursor for another full-scale attack the thinly stretched British units holding El Duda had an anxious time through the night of 4–5 December. However, the incursion was in fact a defensive measure intended to prevent the Tobruk break-out force interfering with German troop movements as Rommel shuffled his units to meet the growing threat from British forces to the east.

German fears were confirmed when Scobie renewed the Tobruk breakout at 20:30 on 7 December with a successful attack on the German positions fronting El Duda that netted 150 prisoners from the *Pavia* Division and four 75mm guns. The next day, 8 December, the 4th Battalion, The Border Regiment and the 7th RTR pressed on to El Adem. There was no resistance, for Rommel had finally if reluctantly recognised that he had no option but to abandon the investment of Tobruk. His units, reduced to a total of forty *Panzers*, were in the process of withdrawing to a new line near Gazala, to reorganise and shorten his badly stretched supply lines. The simple fact was that Auchinleck had beaten Rommel, and while the latter succeeded in avoiding the fate suffered by *Generale* Tellera's 10° *Armata* at Beda Fomm, the former nonetheless became the first British general to inflict a defeat upon the Germans in the Second World War. For Tobruk, the siege was lifted on the eastern side of the perimeter, and the process was completed on the night of 9–10 December, when General Kopański's 1st Independent Carpathian

Brigade attacked and secured the Ras El Medauar at the western side. Tobruk was thus finally relieved after 244 days of siege, the longest in British military history, and largely by the garrison's own efforts. As Brigadier Willison is alleged to have put it to the men manning his command vehicle, 'I'll shoot the next man I hear say that Tobruk has been relieved. It was the Eighth Army that was relieved and it was the men from Tobruk who relieved it.'[20]

The relieving did not come without a price, however. In its fifty-two days in Tobruk Scobie's 70th Division suffered a total of 1,953 casualties, the bulk of them incurred during the nineteen-day brea-kout battle. The intensity of this fighting is clear from the fact that this was almost half the number of casualties suffered by the garrison during the 9th Australian Division's six month tenure. Between April and November 1941 the Australian, British, Indian and latterly Polish troops at Tobruk suffered 855 dead, 2,487 wounded and 494 missing, totalling 3,863 casualties overall. To this figure has to be added at least ten RAF pilots and up to a dozen air and ground crew, and there was also the cost of running supplies and reinforcements into Tobruk and carrying the wounded out; 468 RN and RAN personnel were killed along with seventy members of the Merchant Navy, along with 186 and fifty-five wounded respectively. The maritime side of the siege was also costly in materiel terms, with a total of twenty-six RN ships sunk including two destroyers, seven anti-submarine trawlers and minesweepers and six A Lighters, along with six merchantmen. A further thirty-six RN and Merchant Navy vessels were damaged.[21] In a sense part of the Tobruk perimeter is still being held. The Tobruk War Cemetery, located five miles east of the port, contains 2,282 graves tended by the Commonwealth War Graves Commission. The graves contain the remains of servicemen from Australia, Britain, India, New Zealand, Poland, South Africa and Sudan, 171 of whom remain unidentified.

The occupants of the Tobruk Cemetery and their comrades who survived the siege endured thirst, hunger, primitive living condi-tions and stood firm in the face of sustained and intensive air attack. They also proved on several occasions that the German Panzers and their much vaunted *blitzkrieg* technique were neither invincible nor unstoppable. Their tenacious refusal to give up Tobruk also arguably shaped the course of the Desert War. Denied use of the port, the Axis had no option but to truck their supplies for the 1,000 miles from Tripoli, a process that consumed a large proportion of the materiel that reached North Africa before it got anywhere near the fighting front. Perhaps more importantly, possession of Tobruk also thwarted Rommel's personal ambition to conquer Egypt. Rommel could not simply ignore the port because its geographic position posed a threat to any further eastward advance and to his lines of communication, and the resultant diversion of his attention and resources not only derailed his designs on Egypt but also permitted the British forces there to repeatedly regroup and re-equip. It would probably be stretching things too far to say that possession of Tobruk would have allowed Rommel to conquer Egypt, given the relative paucity of his forces and the slenderness of his logistical support, but there can be no doubt that the *Deutsches Afrikakorps* could and would have caused far more damage to the British in Egypt without Tobruk acting as a brake on Rommel's intentions and freedom of manoeuvre. It should also be noted that to an extent that brake was self inflicted. The *Deutsches Afrikakorps* might have inflicted a great deal more dam- age with what they had if Rommel had simply sealed off Tobruk, rather than repeatedly squandering his men, tanks and supplies in ill- advised attempts to storm the port that flew in the face of military logic, direct orders from his superiors and advice from high-ranking subordinates.

Be that as it may, while Rommel may have been obliged to break his siege on 10 December 1941, he had not yet finished with Tobruk.

12
Epilogue: Tobruk Taken:
10 December 1941 –
21 June 1942

For the garrison, the relief of Tobruk was something of an anti-climax after the anxious days of the breakout. There was no triumphal entry by the relieving force, or ecstatic reception by the garrison, just an almost instant shift back to business as usual as the tide of battle swept past the Tobruk perimeter and away to the west. The men who had run the port and its defences were replaced almost overnight by fresh-faced incomers from Egypt and Tobruk reverted to the supply depot it had been before 10 April 1941. As one garrison veteran put it, '[the] moment the siege was over Tobruk reverted to what it had always been – a hideous, smelly North African port' with the air of a graveyard that had been neglected, desecrated and abandoned.[1] Benign as it seemed, the seeds of what came later were actually contained in this low-key shift. In the meantime the 8th Army attacked Rommel's defence line at Gazala, almost forty miles west of Tobruk, on 13 December, and within two days the *Deutsches Afrikakorps* had been reduced to eight serviceable *Panzers*, bolstered by a further thirty tanks belonging to the *Ariete* Division. Rommel's force began another withdrawal the same night, screened by the *Brescia* Division, and the 4th Armoured Brigade missed a chance to encircle 15 Panzer Division on the afternoon of 16 December. By

27 December *Panzerarmee Afrika* was concentrated near Agedabia, over 200 miles from Tobruk, where Rommel fought a three-day battle with the 22nd Armoured Brigade before withdrawing to prepared defensive positions at El Agheila at the base of the Gulf of Sirte. Rommel was thus back where he had started in April 1941, with the weather conspiring to provide respite as torrential rain turned the desert into a vast bog. Rommel's withdrawal also left a large number of Axis troops marooned in defensive positions on the Egyptian border. The garrisons at Bardia, Sollum and Halfaya surrendered on 2, 12 and 17 January 1942 respectively, and over 12,000 Axis troops went into Allied captivity.

However, the strategic pendulum had now reached its stop and began to swing back, and the logistic limitations that had handicapped Axis operations on the Egyptian border began to dog his opponents once again. In addition, the flow of supplies into Tripoli to rebuild *Panzerarmee Afrika* and build up stocks for offensive action was assisted by a series of mishaps that effectively reduced the British Mediterranean Fleet to three cruisers and a handful of destroyers; the aircraft carrier *Ark Royal* and battleship HMS *Barham* were sunk by U-Boats on 14 and 25 November respectively, the battleships *Queen Elizabeth* and *Valiant* were seriously damaged by Italian frogmen in the harbour at Alexandria on 18 December, and two cruisers were damaged and another sunk after running into a minefield off Tripoli the following day. On 21 January Rommel was able to launch a surprise attack at El Agheila involving 21 Panzer Division, 90 *Leichte* Division, as the *Afrika* Division *zbV* had been renamed in November 1941, and the *Ariete* Division. Events rapidly began to devolve into a near rerun of the events of April 1941. Within six days Rommel had taken Msus, mauling Major-General Frank Messervy's inexperienced 1st Armoured Division at Agedabia in the process, and three days after that Benghazi was once again in German hands. Spearheaded by *Aufklärungs Abteilung* 33, the 90 *Leichte*, *Ariete* and *Trieste* Divisions pursued the 5th and 11th Indian Brigades around the bulge of Cyrenaica through Barce, Derna and Martuba, while 15 and 21 Panzer Divisions cut across its base to Mechili in pursuit of the

7th Indian Brigade and the remnants of the 1st Armoured Division. This time, however, mutual exhaustion brought matters to a stop on 4 February forty miles further west than hitherto, at Gazala rather than Tobruk.

There followed a four month hiatus while both sides gathered the strength to make their next move. The British established a defensive line behind a string of minefields running forty miles south from Gazala to Bir Hacheim, behind which the 1st South African Division, 50th Division and Free French Brigade occupied a number of defended locations called 'boxes'. These were roughly a mile square, surrounded with mines and barbed wire and capable of all-round defence with codenames that included Retma, Knightsbridge and Commonwealth Keep. Deployed among the boxes were the 1st Army Tank Brigade and 2nd and 4th Armoured Brigades, in readiness to mount counter-attacks against any enemy penetration of the forward zone. With his defence line established, Auchinleck set about making preparations for resuming the offensive, setting up and stocking forward supply dumps and extending the Egyptian coastal railway forward to El Adem, aimed at a limited push to seize landing grounds in the vicinity of Derna and Mechili with a tentative start date of 1 June 1942. This, however, did not suit Churchill, and Auchinleck found himself fielding a stream of chiding telegrams, demands for clarification and calls for action from Whitehall just as Wavell had done before him.

In the event Rommel pre-empted his opponents by launching his own offensive on 27 May 1942, after moving in the region of 10,000 vehicles up to the start line under cover of a severe sandstorm. The attack looped south around the end of the Gazala line before pushing north between the Bir Hacheim Box held by Brigadier-General Pierre Koenig's Free French Brigade and the 3rd Indian Motor Brigade commanded by Brigadier Anthony Filose in the Retma Box to the east. The latter was overwhelmed after a courageous defence by the 15 and 21 Panzer and 90 *Leichte* Divisions, which moved on to overrun and destroy the 4th Armoured Brigade and 7th Armoured Division HQ. The latter was now commanded by Messervy who escaped after being captured in his pyjamas, and by 11:00 a feint attack by 90 *Leichte* Division using dust making apparatus had reached the El Adem crossroads. On 29 May a fierce armoured battle around the Knightsbridge Box led to the area being dubbed 'the Cauldron', and the following day the 150th Brigade Box fell after running short of ammunition, with the loss of 3,000 men, 124 guns and over a 100 tanks. By 14 June Rommel's forces were pressing north behind the Gazala Line, prompting a hurried withdrawal by the three South African brigades holding the northern sector along the *Via Balbia* and into the Tobruk perimeter. The latter was now occupied by Major-General Hendrik Klopper's 2nd South African Division, with an outpost held by a number of units including the 2nd Transvaal Scottish and 8th RTR on a small height nicknamed 'the Pimple' just west of Acroma. The outpost held out for three days against attacks by 15 Panzer Division and at one point had Rommel himself trapped in a defensive minefield before being ordered back into the Tobruk perimeter with loss of a single casualty.[2] Meanwhile 21 *Panzer*, 90 *Leichte* and elements of the *Ariete* Divisions were pressing westward past Tobruk. El Adem fell on 16 June and the site of the hard fought breakout at Sidi Rezegh and Belhammed was taken the following day. 21 Panzer Division then veered north through Gambut and reached the coast twenty miles east of the Tobruk perimeter at 00:45 on 18 June 1942.

Tobruk was thus cut off once more, and on this occasion events developed rather differently than had been the case fourteen months earlier. On the surface the situation was similar. There were approximately 35,000 troops in the Tobruk perimeter, along with two understrength field artillery regiments, sixty-nine anti-tank guns and fifty-four assorted tanks. The primary difference appears to have been a lack of application, determination and competence at the top. The head of the 8th Army, Lieutenant-General Neil Ritchie, was willing to simply abandon Tobruk and had begun making arrangements to that effect before Auchinleck expressly forbade him from doing so on 14 June with an order that stated 'Tobruk must be held and the enemy must not be allowed to invest it.'; Auchinleck was receiving similar signals from Churchill literally at the same time.[3] Ritchie may in turn have been misled by reports on the state of Tobruk's defences from Lieutenant-General Gott, recently promoted to command 30 Corps, even though both men met with Klopper at Tobruk on 16 June. For his part, Klopper was misled by Ritchie, who ordered him to concentrate his forces at the western end of the perimeter, and he also appears to have fully grasped the implications of his new mission, given the tone of a telegram he sent to a friend in Cairo on the same day as Ritchie's visit.

This may have been due to lack of experience for unlike his predecessor 'Ming the Merciless' Morshead, Klopper had no First World War experience to draw on. Neither did he have the same level of grip on his subordinates. There was good deal of argument at a meeting at Kloppr's HQ in the Pilastrino Caves on 18 June, something Morshead is highly unlikely to have tolerated. Neither does Klopper appear to have transmitted his intentions to the men on the perimeter, or to have implemented a co-ordinated programme of renovation and improvment of the perimeter defences. Some sources make the point that the defences were also in a dilapidated state when the 9th Australian Division occupied the perimeter in April 1941. However, it took a Herculean effort to return the defences to usable condition at that time after less than three months' neglect, whereas in June 1942 the period was over six months with some deliberate dismantling thrown in for good measure; a large proportion of the mines employed on the Gazala Line had been lifted from the Tobruk perimeter minefields.

Be all that as it may, Rommel launched his attack on Tobruk at 05:20 on 20 June, supported by what one source claims to have been the '…most concentrated bombardment the Western Desert had ever seen' from artillery and Junkers 87 dive-bombers.[4] The assault went in at the south-eastern corner of the perimeter, ironically in the same place the 6th Australian Division had made its break in back in January 1942. As Klopper was expecting the threat to materialise on the western side of the perimeter the defence was caught wrong footed, and never really recovered. By 07:45 ten defence posts had been taken and within forty-five minutes vehicles from 21 Panzer Division were pushing into the perimeter. By 11:00 the Panzers had reached the King's Cross road junction. Five hours later the Panzers were in the vicinity of Klopper's HQ near Pilastrino, and an hour after that the ships in Tobruk harbour were ordered to prepare for evacuation while the AA gunners began to disable their weapons and other troops began to destroy motor transport on the south side of the harbour. Rommel entered the Tobruk perimeter at 05:00 the next day, 21 June, while the Tobruk garrison began spiking its guns and burning fuel stockpiles and the RN personnel stationed in the harbour sabotaged the refrigeration and distillation plants there. The end came at 09:40 when Klopper met Rommel three miles or so from Tobruk proper and formally surrendered; in return he received a tongue-lashing from Rommel, who was annoyed with the destruction wrought by the garrison on the supplies and infrastructure he had intended to use for the advance to the Egyptian border.[5]

After fourteen months Rommel had finally taken the port of Tobruk.

Notes

Chapter 1: Lines in the Sand and Black Shirts

1 Cited in Barrie Pitt, *The Crucible of War Volume III: Montgomery and Alamein*, p. 217
2 Sometimes rendered as Tel el Aqqakir or Aqqaqir
3 Sometimes rendered Tewfik
4 Figures cited in Field Marshal Lord Carver, *The Seven Ages of the British Army* (London: Grafton, 1986), p. 169
5 Sometimes rendered as Aduwa or Adwa
6 *Askari*: East African term for soldier or policeman
7 All figures cited in Greg Blake, '[The] First Italo-Abyssinian War: Battle of Adowa', *Military History Magazine* http://www.historynet.com/magazines/military_history/3028431.html
8 Sometimes rendered Umar al Mukhtar
9 Ian W. Walker, *Iron Hulls Iron Hearts: Mussolini's Elite Armoured Divisions in North Africa* (Marlborough: The Crowood Press, 2003), p. 36
10 Ibid., p. 36
11 MacGregor Knox, *Hitler's Italian Allies: Royal Armed Forces, Fascist Regime and the War of 1940-1943* (Cambridge: Cambridge University Press, 2000)
12 For figures and details of the *Luftwaffe* effort see Captain F.O. Miksche, *Paratroops: The History, Organisation and Tactical Use of Airborne Formations* (London: Faber & Faber, 1943), p. 22
13 Figures cited in Walker, p.17
14 Figures from Knox, p. 11

Chapter 2: Down the Slippery Slope, Ready or Not

1 E.R. Hooton, *Luftwaffe at War: Gathering Storm 1933-1939,* Volume I (Hersham, Surrey: Classic, 2007), p. 91; cited at http://en.wikipedia.org/wiki/Invasion_of_Poland_(1939)#_note-18
2 Knox, op cit., p. 16
3 Ibid., p. 16
4 Walker, op cit., p. 37
5 See Lt. Colonel T.B.H. Otway DSO, *Airborne Forces* (London: Imperial War Museum, 1990), pp. 16-17; for a contemporary view see 'Notes of the Week', *The United Services Review* (16 June 1938), p. 3
6 Knox, pp. 24-25, and especially Table 2.1, p. 24
7 Ibid., pp. 42-45
8 Quoted from ibid., p. 42
9 Ibid., pp.52-53
10 See Brian R. Sullivan, *The Italian Soldier in Combat, June 1940-September 1943: Myths, Realities and Explanations*, pp. 184-185; in Paul Addison and Angus Calder (eds), *Time to Kill: The Soldier's Experience of War in the West 1939 – 1945* (London: Pimlico, 1997), pp. 177-205

11 See for example National Archive File *FO 916/158 Sulmona*, Doc. 2, letter from Red Cross to Foreign Office dated 08/01/1941 and attached 'Report on [Sulmona] Camp' dated 12/12/1940; and Doc. 22, covering letter from Foreign Office to US Ambassador, London dated 21/03/1941, and attached 'Report on [Sulmona] Camp Dated 6 March 1941 from US Embassy Rome'

12 Sullivan, pp. 180-183

13 For details see Cajus Bekker, *The Luftwaffe War Diaries* (New York: MacDonald, 1966), pp. 58-59, 97-113

14 For a detailed account see *Militärgeschichliches Forschungsamt* (Research Institute for Military History) (Ed), *Germany and the Second World War* Volume II, pp. 254, 275-276; and Bekker, pp. 58-59

15 Dunkirk figures cited in Hugh Sebag-Montefiore, *Dunkirk: Fight to the Last Man* (London: Viking, 2006), Appendix B, *Number of Soldiers Evacuated from Dunkirk During Operation Dynamo, 26 May-4 June 1940*, pp. 540-541; for subsequent lifts see for example Major L.F. Ellis, CVO CBE DSO MC, *The War in France and Flanders 1939-1940* (London: HMSO, 1953), pp. 244-246, 305

16 Cited in Alistair Horne, *To Lose a Battle: France 1940* (London: Papermac, 1990), pp. 647-648

17 Ibid., p. 648

18 For details of the No. 10 Squadron raid see Max Hastings, *Bomber Command* (London: Pan, 1999), pp. 86-87; for details of the deployment by Nos. 99 & 149 Squadrons, see http://www.raf.mod.uk/bombercommand/h3gp.html

19 For details see Derek Wood and Derek Dempster, *The Narrow Margin: The Battle of Britain and the Rise of Air Power 1930-1940* (London: Tri-Service Press, 1990), pp. 308, 311; and Stephen Bungay, *The Most Dangerous Enemy: A History of the Battle of Britain* (London: Aurum Press, 2000), p. 348

20 See Spencer di Scala, *Italy: From Revolution to Republic, 1700 to the Present* (Boulder, Colorado: Westview Press, 2004), p. 234; cited at http://en.wikipedia.org/wiki/Italo_Balbo

21 Higher figure taken from Major-General I.S.O. Playfair, *The Mediterranean and Middle East: Volume I: The Early Successes against Italy* (London: HMSO, 1954; facsimile Naval & Military Press, 2004), p. 95; the lower is cited in Philip S. Jowett, *The Italian Army 1940-45 (2)* (Oxford: Osprey Publishing, 2001), p. 8

22 Playfair, writing in 1954, refers to a total of fifteen divisions, Pitt refers to fourteen and a more up to date internet based source cites thirteen; see *Playfair*, p. 92; Barrie Pitt, *The Crucible of War* Volume I: *Wavell's Command* (London: Cassell, 2001), p. 24; and *Regio Esercito Order of Battle 10 June 1940* at http://niehorster.orbat.com/019_italy/40-06-10_army/_re_40.html

23 Pitt, op cit., (Volume I), p. 27

24 Italian estimate from ibid., pp. 21-22; the two thirds inflation is based on a British strength of 36,000 cited in *Playfair*, Volume I, p. 93

25 80,000 figure cited in *Playfair*, Volume I, p. 4

26 see for the air drops see Pitt, Volume I, pp.28, 49-50; for the Italian eyewitness testimony on Balbo's death, see for example http://www.comandosupremo.com/Balbo.html

27 Figures cited in Pitt, Volume I, p. 47

28 Figures and performance details from *Playfair*, pp. 95-96

29 Quoted from Pitt, Volume I. p. 49

30 Types and figures from Walker, p. 62

31 For a detailed account of the invasion, see Pitt, Volume I. pp. 50-54

Chapter 3: Stroke and Counter-Stroke

1 Cited in Pitt, op cit., Volume I, p. 49

2 John Ellis, *The Sharp End: The Fighting Man in World War II*, p. 27

Notes

3 NA File *AVIA 15/2376*, Doc. 1B, 'Report on Lessons Learned During Air Operations in the Western Desert August 1940 – February 1941

4 Quoted from Malcolm Smith, *British Air Strategy Between the Wars*, p. 28

5 For details of Force Z see David Omissi, *Air Power and Colonial Control: The Royal Air Force, 1919-1939* (Manchester: Manchester University Press, 1990) pp. 14-17; for details of Air Control in Iraq, see Jafna L. Cox, 'A Splendid Training Ground: The Importance to the Royal Air Force of its Role in Iraq, 1919-32', *The Journal of Imperial and Commonwealth History*, Volume 13 No. 1 (October 1984)

6 Omissi, pp. 60-63; and W. Michael Ryan, 'The Influence of the Imperial Frontier on British Doctrines of Mechanised Warfare', *Albion*, Volume 15, No. 2 (1983), p. 136

7 Ibid., p. 21

8 Quoted from Brian Bond, *British Military Policy Between the Two World Wars* p. 106

9 For details of this and subsequent RAF air ambulances, see Roderick Grant and Christopher Cole, *But Not in Anger*, pp. 91-94

10 Ibid., p. 54

11 NA File *AIR 5/1253*, Chaps. 9 & 12; *AIR 5/1255*, Chap. 35; and Captain J. R. Kennedy MC, RA (Ret'd), *This, Our Army* , pp. 149-150

12 Grant & Cole, p. 80

13 Quoted from Bond, p. 24

14 For the Army cuts and expansion of commitments see Bond, pp. 15-25, 33; for details of the naval cuts see Alan Ereira, *The Invergordon Mutiny*, pp. 31-37

15 Quoted from 'Statement Relating to Defence, 1935', *Cmd. 4827*; cited in Kennedy, *This, Our Army*, p. 18.

16 *Playfair*, op cit., Volume I, pp. 33, 63

17 For a copy of the Army Councils instructions to Wavell on his appointment, see ibid., pp. 457-459

18 For a detailed account of Wavell's career, see for example John Connell, *Wavell: Soldier and Scholar*

19 Details from John Terraine, *The Right of the Line*, p. 311

20 For overall figure and O'Connor's arrival see *Playfair*, Volume I, pp. 93, 97; for Western Desert Force composition, see Anthony Heckstall-Smith, *Tobruk: The Story of a Siege*, p. 12

21 Pitt, Volume I, pp. 13-14

22 Quoted in Kenneth Macksey, *Armoured Crusader*, p. 157

23 Pitt, Volume I, pp. 18-22

24 Macksey, p. 173

25 In addition to Maitland Wilson, Hobart's Staff College course Alan Brooke, Lord Gort and Montgomery; see ibid., pp. 71-72

26 For a full if rather pro-Hobart account of the incident, see ibid., pp. 169-170

27 Ibid., p. 173

28 Ibid., pp. 111-112

29 For a detailed account of Hobart's involvement see ibid., Chaps. 9 though 12

30 Terraine, pp. 311-312

31 Quoted from Pitt, Volume I, p. 38

32 See Brigadier Dudley Clarke, *The Eleventh at War* pp. 105-106; cited in Pitt, Volume I, pp. 44-45

33 See G.L. Verney, *The Desert Rats*, p. 23; cited in Ellis, *The Sharp End*, p. 273

34 Clarke, p. 107

35 *Playfair*, Volume I, pp. 205, 209-210

36 Pitt, Volume I, pp. 46-47

37 For a full breakdown see *Playfair*, Volume I, Footnote 1, p. 190

38 Pitt, Volume I, p. 54

39 Ibid., p. 54

40 *Playfair*, Volume I, p. 257
41 Ibid., p. 257
42 Ibid., pp. 195, 251
43 For the make up of Nos. 6 & 208 Squadrons see Terraine, p. 314; for the consequences of losing the forward landing grounds see *Playfair*, Volume I, pp. 212-213
44 *Playfair*, Volume I, pp. 211-212
45 Ibid., p. 259
46 for a detailed account of the evolution of the Jock Columns and the Maktila raid see Pitt, Volume I, pp. 69-71
47 *Playfair*, p. 258
48 Supply details cited in *Playfair*, Volume I, pp. 262-263
49 Connell, p. 277
50 *Playfair*, Volume I, p. 258
51 Quote and response from Connell, pp. 288-289
52 Quoted from ibid., p. 286
53 For O'Connor's instructions in full, see Pitt, Volume I, p.90
54 For details of the Matilda, see for example Peter Chamberlain and Chris Ellis, *British and American Tanks of World War II*, pp. 56-59
55 Terraine, pp. 315-316
56 *Playfair*, Volume I, p. 274
57 NA File *DEFE 2/822*, 'Naval Operations: Mediterranean Area: Report on Naval Operations in Support of the Army Off the Western Desert 7 December 1940 – 3 May 1941'
58 figures cited in *Playfair*, Volume I, p. 268
59 POW figures cited in *Playfair*, Volume I, p. 268 and Pitt, Volume I, p. 104 respectively
60 Cited in Alan Moorehead, *African Trilogy*, p. 68; cited in Pitt, Volume I, p. 109
61 See Pitt, Volume I, p. 115
62 16th Infantry Brigade casualty figures from *Playfair*, Volume I, p. 270; 6th RTR losses cited in Pitt, Volume I, p. 115
63 See Lt.-Col. G.R. Stevens, *Fourth Indian Division* p. 23; cited in Pitt, Volume I, p.116
64 Figures cited in Pitt, Volume I, p. 116; and *Playfair*, Volume I, p. 273

Chapter 4: Tobruk Captured

1 For Wavell's instructions in full see Connell, op cit., p. 286
2 Figures cited in Pitt. Op cit., Volume I, p. 120
3 B.H. Liddell Hart, *The Tanks, Volume Two*; cited in Pitt, Volume I, p. 120
4 Pitt, Volume I, pp. 121-123
5 Captain Hobart was Percy Hobart's nephew. For a detailed account of the fight at Sidi Omar with participant accounts see Pitt, Volume I, pp. 126-127
6 Ibid., Volume I, pp. 123-124
7 NA File *WO 201/2586* Middle East Training Pamphlet No. 10, Lessons of Cyrenaica Campaign, Dec. 1940-Feb. 1941; and *WO 201/352* General Staff, XIII Corps, Operations Western Desert, Dec. 40, Lessons from, 18 Jan. 1941; cited in French, *Raising Churchill's Army*, p. 214
8 Major-Gen. G.P.B. Roberts, *From the Desert to the Baltic*, p. 29; cited in French, p. 214
9 Figures cited in *The Army at War: Destruction of an Army, The First Campaign in Libya Sept. 1940 – Feb. 1941* (London: HMSO, 1941), p. 44
10 *Playfair*, op cit., Volume I, pp. 279-281
11 Pitt, Volume I, p. 133
12 Pitt, Volume I, p. 128
13 *Playfair*, p. 278

Notes

14 For contemporary details of Bardia and the Italian defences see *The Army at War: Destruction of an Army*, pp. 38-39

15 *Playfair*, Volume I, p. 282; and Pitt, Volume I, pp. 124-125

16 Bangalore Torpedo: five-foot lengths of metal tubes filled with explosives capable of being linked together to blow breaches in barbed wire obstacles. Invented in 1912 by Captain McClintock of the Bombay and Madras Sappers and Miners based in Bangalore, India

17 Sometimes rendered as the 6th Australian Division Cavalry Regiment

18 Figures cited in Pitt, Volume I, p. 141

19 See Ellis, *The Sharp End*, p. 126

20 Portee was the British term for a standard truck, usually a Bedford QLT 3-ton or Morris 15-CWT, with a 2-Pounder, 6-Pounder or 20mm gun mounted in the load bed; incident cited in Pitt, Volume I, p. 136

21 Heckstall-Smith, op cit., p. 22

22 Tobruk details from James W. Stock, *Tobruk: The Siege* (New York: Ballantine Books, 1973), pp. 10-12; Heckstall-Smith, *Tobruk: The Story of a Siege*, p. 21; and Frank Harrison, *Tobruk: The Great Siege Reassessed*, pp. 28-29

23 Sometimes rendered as Mannella

24 Stock, *Tobruk: The Siege*, p. 48

25 See *The Army at War: Destruction of an Army*, pp. 45-46

26 NA File *DEFE 2/822*, 'Naval Operations: Mediterranean Area: Report on Naval Operations in Support of the Army Off the Western Desert 7 December 1940 – 3 May 1941'

27 Ibid.

28 Pitt, Volume I, p. 133

29 See Gavin Long, *To Benghazi*, pp. 233-234; cited in Pitt, Volume I, p. 155

30 NA File *DEFE 2/822*, 'Naval Operations: Mediterranean Area: Report on Naval Operations in Support of the Army Off the Western Desert 7 December 1940 – 3 May 1941'

31 Pitt, Volume I, p. 156

32 For Hennesy's personal account see Chester Wilmot, *Tobruk 194: Capture-Siege-Relief*, p. 44; cited in Pitt, Volume I, p. 156; final surrender time cited in *Playfair*, Volume I, p. 293.

33 Figures cited in *Playfair*, Volume I, p.293; and Pitt, Volume I, p.157

34 For the observer's account see Long, p.239; cited in Pitt, Volume I, p. 158

35 Details from NA File *DEFE 2/822*, 'Naval Operations: Mediterranean Area: Report on Naval Operations in Support of the Army Off the Western Desert 7 December 1940 – 3 May 1941'

Chapter 5: COMPASS Concluded

1 Walker, op cit., p. 63

2 *Playfair*, op cit., Volume I, p. 353; and Pitt. Op cit., Volume I, pp. 160-161

3 Walker, p. 63

4 Quoted from Pitt, Volume I, p. 162

5 Quotes from O'Connor's report cited in Pitt, Volume I, p. 162

6 Long, op cit., p. 252n; cited in Pitt, Volume I, p. 163

7 *Playfair*, Volume I, p. 357

8 Antill, P. (8 October 2005) *Operation Compass: The First Campaign of the Desert War, 1940-1941 (Part Two)*, articles/battles_compass2.html

9 *The Army at War: Destruction of an Army*, p. 52

10 Figure cited in Pitt, Volume I, p, 174

11 Account by Trooper 'Topper' Brown, in George Forty, *Desert Rats at War*, p. 69; cited in Pitt, Volume I, pp. 174-175

12 Order cited in Pitt, Volume I, p. 178

13 Figures cited in *Playfair*, Volume I, p. 360

14 Account by Trooper 'Topper' Brown, in Forty, *Desert Rats at War*, pp. 69-70; cited in Pitt, Volume I, p. 180

15 See Moorehead, op cit., p. 106; cited it Pitt, Volume I, p. 184

16 The account of the Battle of Beda Fomm was drawn from *The Army at War: Destruction of an Army*, pp. 50-55; Pitt, Volume I, pp. 160-193; *Playfair*, Volume I, pp. 356-362; and Stock, op cit., pp. 66-72

17 Figures cited in *The Army at War: Destruction of an Army*, p. 55

18 Pitt, Volume I, p. 190

19 Quoted in Pitt, Volume I, p.189

20 Tank figures cited in Pitt, *Vol. I*, p. 190; POW and gun figures cited in *The Army at War: Destruction of an Army*, p. 55

21 RAF and *Regia Aeronautica* cited in Terraine, op cit., pp.317-318

22 Figures cited in *Playfair*, Volume I, p. 362

Chapter 6: Tobruk Menaced

1 Pitt, op cit., Volume I, pp. 191-192

2 Quoted from *Playfair*, op cit., Volume I, pp. 338 & 365

3 Ibid., pp.365-366

4 Ibid., p. 398

5 Pitt, Volume I, p. 195

6 Aircraft figures from Terraine, op cit., p. 320

7 Field-Marshal Sir William Slim, *Unofficial History* p. 140; cited in Terraine, p. 321

8 For a detailed account of the Gallabat operation, see *Playfair*, Volume I, pp. 398-399; and The War Office, May 1946, 'Operations in the Middle East from August 1939 to November 1940; Despatch to the Secretary of State for War on 10 December 1940 by General Sir Archibald P. Wavell KCB CMG MC, Commander in Chief Middle East', in *The London Gazette*, Third Supplement, dated 13 June 1946, pp. 6-7; for the air perspective see Terraine, pp. 320-321

9 Figures cited in Gian Spagnoletti, 'Italian East Africa and the Battle of Keren', at the *Commando Supremo: Italy at War* website, http://www.comandosupremo.com/KerenBattle.html

10 Quoted from Compton Mackenzie, *Eastern Epic*, Volume I: *September 1939 – March 1943, Defence* (London: Chatto & Windus, 1951) p. 64

11 The awards were to Second-Lieutenant Premindra Singh Bhagat of the Corps of Indian Engineers near Metemma on the night of 31 February-1 March 1941; Subedar Richhpal Ram of the 6th Rajputana Rifles at Keren on 7 February 1941; and Sergeant Nigel Gray Leakey of the 1/6th Battalion, King's African Rifles at Colito on 19 May 1941. The latter two were awarded posthumously

12 *Playfair*, Volume I, pp. 228-229

13 Terraine, pp. 327-331

14 ULTRA was…. ; see Terraine, pp. 325-326; for a detailed account of the attack on the *Illustrious*, see '*Der Blitzkrieg im Süden: Malta im Kreuzfeuer*' (The Blitzkrieg in the South: Malta in the Crossfire), *Aero Illustrated Magazine*, Volume 56, p. 1544, c.1984

15 For a detailed account of the meeting and a copy of the 4 March Agreement, see *Playfair*, Volume I, pp. 374-381, and Appendix 7, p. 470

16 figures from *Playfair, The Mediterranean and Middle Eat* Volume II: *The Germans Come to the Help of their Ally* (1941), pp. 102-103

17 figures cited in Fraser, *And We Shall Shock Them*, pp. 145-146

18. ibid., p. 132

19 *Playfair*, Volume II, p. 6

20 *Playfair*, Volume I, pp. 207, 209

21 *Playfair*, Volume I, p. 257

22 figures cited in Samuel .W. Mitchell Jr, *Rommel's Greatest Victory: The Desert Fox and the Fall of Tobruk, Spring 1942*, p. 15

23 See Heinz Werner Schmidt, *With Rommel in the Desert* (London: Harrap & Co., 1972), p. 89; cited in Mitchell, p. 14

24 Horne, op cit., pp. 274, 309-312

25 Figures cited in Mitchell, p. 15.

26 Ibid., p. 16; and Pitt, Volume I, pp. 368-369.

27 Quoted in Pitt, Volume I, p. 241

28 Schmidt, pp. 243-244

29 *Playfair*, Volume II, pp. 10, 14

30 Pitt, Volume I, pp. 245-246

31 Ibid., pp. 252-253; and *Playfair*, Volume II, pp. 15-16

32 *Playfair*, Volume II, p. 16

33 sometimes rendered Mersa el Brega

34 *Playfair*, Volume II, pp. 2-3; and Pitt, Volume I, pp. 217-219

35 Pitt, Volume I, p. 249.

36 *WO 201/353*, '9th Australian Division: Report on Operations in Cyrenaica, March-October 1941 Including the Defence of Tobruch [sic]'.

37 See *Playfair*, Volume II, pp. 6-7; and Connell, *Wavell, Scholar and Soldier*, pp. 385-386. Interestingly the 9th Australian Division official report does not mention the withdrawal although precise dates are provided for the division's arrival

38 Connell, pp. 385-386

39 Connell, pp. 385-386

40 Pitt, Volume I, p. 255

41 Ibid., Volume I, p. 256; and *Playfair*, Volume II, p. 20

42 *Playfair*, Volume II, p. 21

43 See Pitt, Volume I, p. 262

44 Mitcham, *Rommel's Desert Commanders*, pp. 18-19

45 *Playfair*, Volume II, p. 29

46 Pitt, Volume I, pp. 261, 265

47 *Playfair*, Volume II, pp. 22-24

48 Walker, p. 71; and *Playfair*, Volume II, p. 30

49 Major Rajendrasinhji went on to a distinguished career and was appointed Commander-in-Chief of the Indian Army on 14 January 1953

Chapter 7: Tobruk Invested

1 *WO 201/353*, '9th Australian Division: Report on Operations in Cyrenaica, March-October 1941 Including the Defence of Tobruch [sic]'

2 Quoted from Chester Wilmot, *Tobruk 1941: Capture-Siege-Relief* , p. 69

3 *Playfair*, op cit., Volume II, pp. 6-7; and Connell, op cit., pp. 385-386. Interestingly the 9th Australian Division official report does not mention the withdrawal although precise dates are provided for the division's arrival

4 Wilmot, p. 69

5 See *WO 201/353*

6 The official history merely refers to O'Connor issuing the withdrawal order in Neame's name, while the 9th Australian Division report refers to a conference at El Abiar; see *Playfair*, Volume II, p. 23; and *WO 201/353*

7 For a detailed account of the battle see Wilmot, pp. 71-74

8 According to the Official History, the order was to withdraw to the Wadi Cuff, fifty miles north-east of Barce, but the 9th Division report clearly states the destination was the Wadi

Derna, As the Wadi Cuff would still leave the Australians in danger of being cut off by the German advance on Mechili, the divisional report is cited; see *Playfair*, Volume II, p. 28; and *WO 201/353*

9 The four were Nos. 3 RAAF and 73 Squadrons (Hawker Hurricanes), No. 55 Squadron (Bristol Blenheim VIs) and No. 6 Army Co-operation Squadron (Westland Lysanders); see Terraine, op cit., p. 335

10 Wilmot, p. 79

11 Ibid., p. 79; figures from *Playfair*, Volume II, p. 31

12 *Playfair*, Volume II, p. 28

13. Wilmot, pp. 77-78; and Pitt, op cit., Volume I, p. 28

14 Harrison, op cit., pp. 23-24

15 Wilmot, p. 81

16 Pitt, Volume I, pp.271-272

17 Ibid., p. 272; and Heckstall-Smith, op cit., pp.45-47

18 David Coombes, *Australian Army History Series: Morshead: Hero of Tobruk and El Alamein*, pp. 5-22

19 Harrison, p. 27

20 Wilmot, p. 84

21 Ibid., pp. 85-86; and Heckstall Smith, pp. 50-51

22 For details of the British First World War system see for example Martin Middlebrook, *The Kaiser's Battle 21 March 1918: The First Day of the German Spring Offensive*, pp. 74-75

23 Figures from *WO 201/353*; and Wilmot, Appendix I: Tobruk Garrison, p. 320. The former source cites the slightly higher overall figure of 38,000

24 *WO 201/353*

25 Wilmot, p. 85

26 Harrison, p. 23

27 Wilmot, p. 86

28 gun types and numbers from *WO 201/354* 'The Anti-Aircraft Defences of Tobruck [sic] Fortress (1 April to 10 October 1941)

29 For details of the journey to Tobruk see Harrison, pp. 24-25; figures from Wilmot, Appendix I: Tobruk Garrison, p. 320

30 For aircraft figures see *WO 201/353*; and Harrison, p. 25

31 Harrison, footnote 12, p. 331

32 Wilmot, p. 88; the 18th Indian Cavalry Regiment's full title was the 18th King Edward VII's Own Cavalry Regiment: the former title is used hereafter for brevity

33 Quoted from Pitt, Volume I, p. 267

34 Harrison, p. 40

35 For von Prittwitz's arrival, see Pitt, Volume I, p. 266; and Harrison, p. 40; for details of his career see Samuel W. Mitcham, *The Panzer Legions: A Guide to the German Army Tank Divisions of WWII and Their Commanders*, p. 126

36 Harrison, p. 40

37 Ibid., p. 41

38 Wilmot, pp. 92-93; and Harrison, p. 41

39 Schmidt, op cit., p. 11

40 Cited in Harrison, p. 43

41 Quoted from A. J. Barker, *Afrika Korps*, p. 30; cited in Harrison, p. 43

42 Wilmot, p. 93

43 Ibid., p. 93

44 Harrison, p. 46

45 Wilmot, p. 95

46 For a detailed account of the 20th Australian Brigade's fight on 11 April, see ibid., pp. 93-95

47 Harrison, p. 48

48 *WO 201/353*, Appendix F: Captured Documents 'Colonel Olbrich's Report on the Assault

on Tobruk by the 5th Tank Regiment, 11-14 April 1941'

49 Harrison, p. 48

50 Wilmot, p. 95

51 *WO 201/353*, entry for 12 April 1941; leaflet text quoted from Wilmot, p. 96

Chapter 8: Tobruk Attacked

1 Quote from Schmidt, op cit., p. 44; cited in Harrison, op cit., p.49

2 See *WO 201/353*, 9th Australian Division: Report on Operations in Cyrenaica, March-October 1941 Including the Defence of Tobruch [sic], entry for 13 April 1941

3 Wilmot, op cit., p. 96; Major Balfe is referred to as Captain in some accounts

4 This was not to be the last siege for Major Loder-Symonds; promoted to Lieutenant-Colonel, he served as Commander Royal Artillery, 1st Airborne Division at Arnhem in September 1944

5 Harrison, p. 50

6 *Playfair*, op cit., Volume II, p. 38

7 *WO 201/354* The Anti-Aircraft Defence of Tobruck [sic] Fortress (1 April to 10 October 1941) entries for 6-12 April 1941

8 For a detailed account of events see Heckstall-Smith, op cit., pp. 54-60. Interestingly the air raids do not figure in the official reports in the 9th Australian Division or Anti-Aircraft Defence reports, presumably because they were considered routine and due to more dramatic events on the perimeter

9 Harrison, p. 51

10 Wilmot, pp. 97-99

11 *WO 201/353*, Appendix F: Captured Documents 'Colonel Olbrich's Report on the Assault on Tobruk by the 5th Tank Regiment, 11-14 April 1941'; and Wilmot, pp. 100-105

12 Harrison, p. 53

13 For Sergeant-Major Batten's personal account see Wilmot, p. 101

14 Casualty figures from *The Royal Artillery Commemoration Book, 1939-1945* (London: G. Bell on behalf of The Royal Artillery Benevolent Fund, 1950), p. 186; cited in Harrison, p. 54

15 Wilmot, p. 102

16 Harrison, p. 57

17 Wilmot, p. 103

18 Wilmot refers to both Squadrons being deployed east of the El Adem road, and Oberstleutnant Olbrich's after action report supports this, referring to fourteen British tanks attacking his Regiment from the right, rear whereas Harrison refers to C Squadron 1st RTR being deployed east of the road and B Squadron on the west side of the penetration; see Wilmot, p. 104; *WO 201/353*, Appendix F: Captured Documents 'Colonel Olbrich's Report on the Assault on Tobruk by the 5th Tank Regiment, 11-14 April 1941'; and Harrison, map on p. 51

19 Harrison, p. 55

20 Ibid., p. 47

21 Wilmot, p. 104

22 Harrison, pp. 55-56

23 *WO 201/353*, Appendix F: Captured Documents 'Colonel Olbrich's Report on the Assault on Tobruk by the 5th Tank Regiment, 11-14 April 1941'; Schorm diary entry cited in Wilmot, p. 105

24 Ibid. (*WO 201/353*, Appendix F)

25 Wilmot, p. 104

26 See for example Hugh Sebag-Montefiore, *Dunkirk: Fight to the Last Man*, pp. 142-155

27 Participant accounts by Schorm and Balfe cited in Wilmot, pp. 105-106.

28 *WO 201/353*, Appendix F: Captured Documents 'Colonel Olbrich's Report on the Assault on Tobruk by the 5th Tank Regiment, 11-14 April 1941'

29 Wilmot, p. 106
30 Details and figures cited in Harrison, pp. 58-59
31 Panzer Regiment 5 loss/casualty figures cited in *Oberstleutnant* Olbrich's after action report; see *WO 201/353*, Appendix F: Captured Documents 'Colonel Olbrich's Report on the Assault on Tobruk by the 5th Tank Regiment, 11-14 April 1941'
32 Figures cited in *Playfair*, Volume II, p. 38
33 *WO 201/353*, Appendix F: Captured Documents 'Colonel Olbrich's Report on the Assault on Tobruk by the 5th Tank Regiment, 11-14 April 1941'
34 Wilmot, p. 107
35 Quoted from ibid., p. 107
36 Harrison, p. 63
37 Wilmot, pp. 116-117
38 Walker, op cit., p. 72
39 Harrison, p. 63
40 Ibid., p. p. 63
41 *Playfair*, Volume II, p. 153; and Pitt, op cit., Volume I, p. 269
42 For details see Michael Reynolds, *Steel Inferno: I SS Panzer Corps in Normandy*, pp. 75-80
43 *WO 201/353*, entry for 14 April 1941
44 For the Special Order of the Day in full see Wilmot, p. 108
45 Quoted in Wilmot, p. 87
46 Forty figure cited in Wilmot, p. 106; seventy figure cited in Harrison, p. 59
47 Schorm account cited in Wilmot, p. 105; Leakey in Harrison, p. 55
48 Harrison, pp. 59-60
49 Sometimes rendered as Ras el Medawar or Ras El Medauur
50 Wilmot, p. 117; and *WO 201/353*, entry for 15 April 1941
51 Wilmot, p. 117
52 Details of tank types, numbers and other details from Walker, p. 73
53 Walker, p. 73. According to Wilmot the Italian tanks were dispersed by artillery fire, while Harrison claims that the Italian armour commander withdrew as soon as his vehicles came under fire and refused point-blank to move up again; see Wilmot, p. 117, and Harrison, p. 60
54 Surrender sequence and numbers from Harrison, p. 60; other details from testimony of Private R.G. Daniells, 2/48th Battalion Carrier Platoon cited in Wilmot, p. 118
55 *WO 201/353*; Harrison, p. 60; Wilmot, p. 118; and Walker, p. 73. The text of the leaflet drawn up by the commander of the 1st *Battaglione* is reproduced in full in Wilmot, p. 118
56 Tank type and numbers cited in Walker, p. 74. Wilmot's contemporary account refers to twelve and claims several were German, while Harrison cites thirty-two, all from the *Ariete* Division; see Wilmot, p. 119, and Harrison, p. 61. However, the official 9th Division report refers to five Italian vehicles being knocked out and the *Ariete* Division was down to ten vehicles at the end of the action, and Harrison may therefore have confused the designation of the Italian armoured unit cited in the 9th Division Report ('32 Tank Regiment, Ariete Division') for the number of vehicles involved; see *WO 201/353*, entry for 17 April 1941. Wilmot's reference to twelve tanks presumably arises from miscounting in the dust and confusion of battle
57 Wilmot, pp. 118-119
58 Testimony from Lieutenant D. Bryant cited in Wilmot, p. 119
59 Harrison, p. 61
60 Wilmot, p. 119
61 Arrival of Cruiser Tanks cited in Walker, p. 74.
62 Wilmot, p. 119
63 Details from Walker, p. 74
64 *WO 201/353*, entry for 17 April 1941
65 figures from Walker, p. 74

Notes

Chapter 9: Tobruk Assailed

1 Wilmot, op cit., p.115

2 *Playfair*, op cit., Volume II, p. 40

3 James D. Ladd, *Commandos and Rangers of World War II*, pp. 114-117

4 Quote from *Playfair*, Volume II, p. 40

5 Wilmot, p. 115

6 *Playfair*, Volume II, p. 36

7 Pitt, op cit., Volume I, pp. 269-270; Lieutenant Warren Vyvyan Hamilton Gape interred in Plot
   1.E.10, Halfaya Sollum War Cemetery, and is commemorated on the Caxton War Memorial
   in his home village in Cambridgeshire

8 Harrison, op cit., p.76

9 Wilmot, pp. 121-123

10 *WO 201/353*, '9th Australian Division: Report on Operations in Cyrenaica, March-October
   1941 Including the Defence of Tobruch [sic]', entry for 22 April 1941; and Wilmot, pp. 120-
   121

11 Quoted from Wilmot, p. 123

12 See for example Stock, op cit., p. 105

13 Harrison, p. 75

14 See for example Richard Holmes, *Tommy: The British Soldier on the Western Front 1914-1918*,
   pp. 311-314 ; and Denis Winter, *Death's Men: Soldiers of the Great War*, pp. 92-95

15 Figure cited in Wilmot, p. 123

16 *WO 201/353*, , entry for 24 April 1941; and participant testimony from Lieutenant D.G.
   Kimber, cited in Wilmot, p. 123

17 Wilmot, p. 123

18 Harrison, p. 69

19 *WO 201/354* The Anti-Aircraft Defence of Tobruck [sic] Fortress, 1 April to 10 October
   1941

20 Leutnant Schorm's diary entries for 16 & 17 April, cited in Wilmot, p. 124

21 Harrison, pp. 69-70

22 *Playfair*, Volume II, p. 39

23 Wilmot, p. 126

24 Harrison, p. 71

25 Ibid., p. 40

26 *Playfair*, Volume II, pp. 153-155; and Harrison, pp. 77-78

27 See for example Mitchell, *Rommel's Greatest Victory*, p. 16; and Pitt, Volume I, pp. 368-369

28 Extracts from Halder's diary cited in *Playfair*, Volume II, p. 41

29 See for example Pitt, Volume I, pp.274-275

30 *WO 201/353*, entry for 30 April 1941

31 Wilmot, p. 132

32 *WO 201/353*, Appendix G, 'Diary of Leutnant Schorm, 5 Tank Regiment'

33 Wilmot, p. 129

34 Harrison, p. 81

35 Ibid., pp.81-82

36 Wilmot, p. 130

37 Harrison, p. 85

38 Testimony from Lt-Col. Spowers, cited in Wilmot, p. 129

39 See testimony from Lt-Col. Spowers, cited in ibid., p. 129; and Harrison, p. 81

40 Harrison, p. 83

41 Ibid., pp. 85-86; and testimony from Lt-Col. Spowers cited in Wilmot, p. 129

42 *WO 201/353*, Appendix G, 'Diary of Leutnant Schorm, 5 Tank Regiment', entry for 1 May
   1941

43 See testimony from Capt. Gebhardt and general account in Wilmot, pp. 131-132

44 Testimony from Sergeant Bettsworth, J Battery 3rd RHA; cited in Wilmot, pp. 133-134

45 *WO 201/353*, Appendix G, 'Diary of Leutnant Schorm, 5 Tank Regiment', entry for 1 May 1941; for details of the *Carro Lanciaflamme* see for example George Forty, *Second World War Tanks*, pp. 183-185

46 Harrison, p. 88

47 Ibid., pp. 88-89

48 *WO 201/353*, Appendix G, 'Diary of Leutnant Schorm, 5 Tank Regiment', entry for 1 May 1941

49 Testimony from Sergeant Ernest Thurman, cited in Wilmot, p. 137

50 British tank casualty figures cited in ibid., p. 147

51 Harrison, pp. 96-97

52 Extracts cited in ibid., p. 95

53 *WO 201/353*, entry for 1 May 1941; Wilmot, pp. 142-144; and Harrison, pp. 97-98

54 *WO 201/353*, Appendix G, 'Diary of Leutnant Schorm, 5 Tank Regiment', entry for 1 May 1941

55 Figures cited in Harrison, p. 99

56 Ibid., p. 104

57 *WO 169/1278*, 3rd Armoured Brigade HQ, 1941 January – September, Report by Brigade-Major A.J. Lascelles

58 *WO 201/353*, Appendix G, 'Diary of Leutnant Schorm, 5 Tank Regiment', entry for 2 May 1941

59 Wilmot, p. 150

60 Testimony from Lieutenant W.H. Noyes, cited in ibid., p. 150

61 Wilmot, p. 150; and unreferenced testimony from *Maggiore* Gaggetti, cited in Walker, pp. 75-76; and Harrison, pp. 102-103

62 *WO 201/353*, Appendix G, 'Diary of Leutnant Schorm, 5 Tank Regiment', entry for 3 May 1941

63 Figures and comment cited in Wilmot, p. 151

64 152 figure from *WO 201/353*, entry for 3 May 1941; 155 figure total from individual battalion figures for killed, wounded and missing cited in Wilmot, p. 151

65 See unreferenced testimony from *Maggiore* Gaggetti, cited in Walker, pp. 75-76

66 See for example Harrison, pp. 102-103; Wilmot, pp. 149-151, and *WO 201/353*, Appendix G, 'Diary of Leutnant Schorm, 5 Tank Regiment', entry for 3 May 1941

67 Casualty figures from Wolf Heckmann, *Rommel's War in Africa*, p. 116; cited in Harrison, p. 104

68 German tank loss figures cited in Wilmot, p. 147

Chapter 10: Tobruk Besieged

1 Quoted in See *Playfair*, op cit., Volume II, p. 157

2 Wilmot, op cit., p. 154

3 Harrison, op cit., p. 69

4 Figures cited in *WO201/354*, The Anti Aircraft Defence of Tobruck [sic] Fortress (1 April to 10 October 1941), table entitled 'JU 87 Attacks'

5 Ibid

6 *WO201/354*, Appendix Tables entitled 'Enemy Aircraft Losses' and 'Ammunition Expenditure'.

7 Heckstall-Smith, op cit., p. 80

8 See for example Ellis, *The Sharp End*, pp. 80-81

9 Wilmot, pp. 169, 173

Notes

10 Ibid., p. 169

11 Ibid., pp. 169-170, 175

12 Ibid., p. 172

13 Figures cited in ibid., pp. 174-175

14 Heckstall-Smith, pp. 85-87

15 Ibid., pp. 81-84

16 Wilmot, pp. 184-186

17 Figures cited in ibid, pp. 192-193

18 See for example Wilmot, caption to map, p. 162; for Wavell's orders to Gott, see *Playfair*, Volume II, p. 160

19 *Playfair*, Volume II, pp. 162-163

20 Weapon details cited in *WO201/354*

21 *WO201/354*, various sections and appendices

22 *WO201/2840* Camouflage in the Tobruk Fortress April-July 1941, various sections and appendices

23 *WO201/2840*, Naval Situation Report, dated 1 May 1941

24 For a detailed account with eyewitness and participant testimony, see Heckstall-Smith, pp. 107-109

25 Figures cited in *Playfair*, Volume II, p. 157

26 Ibid., p. 158

27 A degaussing cable was means of counter-acting German magnetic mines; a current passed through a copper coil cable encircling a vessel's hull virtually neutralised its magnetic field, thus nullifying the triggers fitted to magnetic mines

28 Harrison, p. 159

29 For a detailed account including testimony by the survivor, see Heckstall-Smith, pp. 154-163; the latter claims the first attack was carried out by the U-34, but according to the records that vessel was assigned to a training unit in the Baltic at that time

30 *Playfair*, Volume II, pp. 114-118

31 Figures and details from Pitt, op cit., Volume I, p. 294

32 For a detailed account of Operation BATTLEAXE and all figures cited see *Playfair*, Volume II, pp. 163-173; and Pitt, Volume I, pp. 294-310

33 Wilmot, pp. 220-224

34 Cited in Pitt, *The Crucible of War* Volume II: *Auchinleck's Command*, p. 21

35 Pitt, Volume II, p. 20

36 For a detailed account see Wilmot, pp. 190-203

37 *PREM 3/63/2* Aggregate Australian Troops and the Relief of Tobruk 1941, July-November, Doc. 94, Telegram from Australian Prime Minister Menzies to Prime Minister Churchill, dated 20/7/1941; and Doc. 89, Telegram from Australian Prime Minister Menzies to Prime Minister Churchill, dated 7/8/1941

38 See for example Wilmot, pp. 281-283, and Heckstall-Smith, pp. 138-139

39 Pitt, Volume II, pp. 23-24

40 Heckstall-Smith, p. 147

41 Wilmot, pp. 282-283

42 *PREM 3/63/2*, Doc. 85, Telegram from Australian Prime Minister Fadden to Prime Minister Churchill, dated 5/9/1941; and Doc. 66, Telegram from Australian Prime Minister Fadden to Dominions Office, dated 15/9/1941

43 *PREM 3/63/2*, Doc. 78, Telegram from C-in-C Middle East to War Office, dated 10/9/1941

44 Harrison, p. 159

45 For the timetable see *WO 201/353*, Table 'Progress of Battalion Reliefs'

46 Figures cited in Harrison, p. 160

47 Figures cited in Harrison, Appendix 3, 'Tobruk: The Account Rendered', p. 338

Chapter 11: Tobruk Relieved

1 Tank strength figures cited in Harrison, op cit., Table 3, p. 163
2 Harrison, pp. 160-161
3 Figures from *Playfair*, op cit., Volume II, Table p. 281
4 Wilmot, op cit., pp. 290-291
5 Pitt, op cit., Volume II, pp. 24-25
6 For a detailed account of this process see for example Harrison, pp. 279-185
7 Pitt, Volume II, p. 27; and Harrison, pp. 175-178
8 Quoted from Pitt, Volume II, p. 29
9 Wilmot, pp. 292-293; and Pitt, Volume II, pp. 30-31, 43
10 Ladd, *Commandos and Rangers of World War II*, pp. 120-121; for a detailed account see Gordon Landsborough, *Tobruk Commando: The Raid to Destroy Rommel's Base* (London: Greenhill, 1989
11 For a detailed account of the fighting at El Gubi from an Italian perspective, see Walker, op cit., pp. 82-87
12 Pitt, Volume II, p. 62
13 Ibid., p. 67
14 Harrison, p. 217
15 J.A.I. Agar-Hamilton & L.C.F. Turner, *The Sidi Rezeg Battles 1941* (Cape Town: Oxford University Press, 1957, p. 64; cited in Pitt, Volume II, p. 67
16 For the order in full see Pitt, Volume II, pp. 117-118
17 Quoted from Heckstall-Smith, op cit., p. 173
18 Pitt, Volume II, pp. 124-125
19 Figures cited in Harrison, p. 291
20 Quoted from ibid., p. 294
21 Figures cited in ibid., Appendix 3, 'Tobruk: The Account Rendered', p. 338

Epilogue: Tobruk Taken

1 Heckstall-Smith, op cit., p. 181
2 Ibid., pp. 231-232
3 Quoted from ibid., p. 220
4 Quoted from Pitt, op cit, Volume II, p. 247
5 Ibid., p. 264

Illustrations

All illustrations are from the author's collection unless stated otherwise.

1 British convoy on the move in the desert near Bardia. The tell-tail dust trail illustrates the problem inherent in moving large numbers of vehicles unnoticed, and the crucial importance of aerial reconnaissance.

2 A British vehicle, possibly a Chevrolet 8–cwt truck, illustrates the difficulty of moving without creating dust, and the threat the latter posed to engines and mechanical parts.

3 Desert brew up: the crew of a British Vickers Light Tank prepare tea and a meal over a makeshift fire. The crewman on the right is using a 5-gallon can, dubbed 'flimsies' due to their fragility, as a seat; flimsies were the primary containers for carrying fuel and water before the adoption of the German 'Jerry can'. The cooking vessel on the fire is also fashioned from a flimsy.

4 Vickers Light Tanks moving across the type of rocky terrain that rapidly wore out tracks and running gear. The tanks are painted in the so-called 'Caunter Scheme' formulated by the commander of the 4th Armoured Brigade, Brigadier John Caunter. Used in Egypt in 1940-41 the Scheme was intended to make vehicles blend with the desert horizon, and utilised a near-horizontal splinter pattern in light stone, light grey-green and dark slate grey. The individual vehicle names beginning with the letter A show the vehicles belong to A Squadron of their Regiment.

5 Logistic lifeline: 5-gallon flimsies full of water, as indicated by the 'W' markings, being unloaded for distribution.

6 Universal Carriers, possibly from the 6th Australian Division Cavalry Regiment, manoeuvring at speed. The latter unit was the first Australian unit to see action in the Second World War during Operation COMPASS and were involved in the capture of Bardia in January 1941.

7 A Morris CS9 Light Armoured Car crossing the border wire into Cyrenaica from Egypt, probably from the 11th Hussars, who deployed thirty in the Western Desert fitted with special sand tyres. Based on the Morris Commercial 15 cwt truck chassis, the CS9 weighed four and a half tons and was armed with a .55 Boys Anti-tank Rifle in the turret and a Bren gun for close and anti-aircraft defence on a pintle mount at the rear of the turret.

8 Universal Carriers mounting Boys Anti-tank Rifles and Bren Guns in the ruins of Fort Capuzzo after the latter's capture in December 1940.

9 Hawker Hurricane fighters taking off from a forward airstrip; the machines could belong to a number of units including No.3 Squadron RAAF and RAF No. 33 and 73 Squadrons.

10 A formation of Bristol Blenheim Mk. IV bombers *en route* to attack Italian targets during the initial stages of the fighting in the Western Desert.

11 Italian trucks, probably from the 1st *Libica* or *Cirene* Divisions escorted by a *Bersaglieri* motor cyclist passing through the Sollum Escarpment, possibly at the Halfaya Pass, during the Italian advance into Egypt in mid-September 1940. The tank is a British A10 Cruiser, probably lost during one of the delaying actions fought by the British at the time.

12 British artillery observers controlling artillery fire on the Italian advance into Egypt in September 1940.

13 Italian infantry advancing near Sidi Barrani during the Italian invasion of Egypt in

September 1940. The men at the extreme left and right of the front file are carrying 6.5mm Breda *Modello* 30 light machine guns, which featured a permanently attached twenty-round box magazine with an integral cartridge oiler to ease extraction.

14 On the brink: British tanks, possibly from the 7th Royal Tank Regiment, move forward to the start line for Operation COMPASS on the night of 8-9 December 1940.

15 Italian troops seek cover from RAF bombing. The weapon on the anti-aircraft mounting is an 8mm Schwarzlose medium machine gun obtained from the Austro-Hungarians as reparations at the end of the First World War.

16 British warships bombarding Fort Capuzzo during Operation COMPASS.

17 Italian stone-built artillery sangar with abandoned gun; note the raised platform in the centre of the sangar to allow the gun to clear the sangar wall.

18 British 60-Pounder gun shelling Axis positions in Libya; the breech mechanism appears to have been blanked out by the censor.

19 Bombardment of Bardia in preparation for the assault on the port by the 6th Australian Division on Friday 3 January 1941.

20 Infantrymen from the 6th Australian Division move up to the start line for the attack on Bardia, 2 January 1941.

21 Aerial view of some of the 40,000 Italian troops captured at Bardia, corralled in a makeshift compound.

22. A partly burned *Regia Aeronautica* Fiat CR42 *Falco* fighter. Armed with two 12.7mm machine-guns and with a top speed of 268 mph (430 kph), the Falco was the most numerous Italian fighter in North Africa and continued in production until 1944, by which time 1,782 had been built.

23 Booty: captured Breda *Cannone-Mitragliera da 20/65 Modello* 35 20mm anti-aircraft guns.

24 Hard living: a Royal Artillery gun crew snatch some sleep in front of their 25-Pounder gun, which is carefully covered to protect it from wind-blown sand and dust

25 The *Regia Marina* cruiser *San Giorgio* burning in Tobruk harbour after an attack by RAF Blenheim bombers on 21 January 1941. Damaged by RAF bombing on 11 June 1940, the cruiser had been a key part of Tobruk's anti-aircraft defences and was scuttled by her crew when the port garrison surrendered to the 6th Australian Division on 22 January 1941.

26 The scuttled *San Giorgio* in Tobruk harbour; the British vessel in the foreground may be part of Commander W. P. Carne's naval clearance party, which was tasked to return the harbour to service as quickly as possible after the Italian surrender on 22 January 1941.

27 Destroyed Italian aircraft at El Adem airfield, twenty miles south of the Tobruk perimeter.

28 *Regia Marina* personnel march to captivity through the streets of Tobruk after the Italian surrender on 22 January 1941.

29 Booty: captured Italian motor transport gathered south of Tobruk harbour after the Italian surrender on 22 January 1941, with smoke from burning fuel and supply dumps nearer the town and harbour in the background.

30 British or Australian troops manning a .303 Vickers Medium Machine Gun in the fighting near Derna in January 1941.

31 Into the bag: some of the 27,000 Italian troops who surrendered at Tobruk on 22 January 1941 marching into captivity.

32 A Chevrolet 30 cwt truck of the Long Range Desert Group (LRDG) on patrol in Libya. The LRDG carried out patrols and raids over a 1,000 miles behind Axis lines. The vehicle is armed with a Boys anti-tank rifle in the truck bed and a .303 Lewis Gun mounted by the front passenger seat.

33 Map of Cyrenaica and the Egyptian border.

34 Map of the Tobruk perimeter.

35 El Adem Road Sector, scene of Rommel's first attempt to take Tobruk, 14 April 1941.

36 Ras El Medavar Sector, scene of Rommel's second attempt to take Tobruk, 30 April – 2 May 1941.

Bibliography

Primary Sources

AVIA 15/2376, Doc. 1B, 'Report on Lessons Learned During Air Operations in the Western Desert August 1940 – February 1941'

CAB 106/372 Report on Visit to Tobruk Fortress 1941 Aug

CAB 106/530 War Office Memo Regarding Tobruk Demolitions 1942 – June 1943

DEFE 2/822, 'Naval Operations: Mediterranean Area: Report on Naval Operations in Support of the Army Off the Western Desert 7 December 1940 – 3 May 1941'

FO 916/158 Sulmona

PREM 3/63/2 Aggregate Australian Troops and the Relief of Tobruk 1941, July-November

PREM 3/313/3 Western Desert 1940 Dec – 1941 Feb – 1941 Aug

PREM 3/311 Tobruk 1941 Apr – 1942 Nov

WO 106/2171 Units in Tobruk During Siege of 1941, Nov 1941

WO 106/2188, Middle East – System of Defence of Tobruk 25/10/41 – 12/12/41

WO 169/1278, 3rd Armoured Brigade HQ, 1941 January – September, Report by Brigade-Major A.J. Lascelles

WO 201/2840 Camouflage in the Tobruk Fortress April – July 1941

WO 201/347 Operations Inshore Squadron 1941 Jan.

WO 201/352 General Staff, XIII Corps, Operations Western Desert, Dec. 40, Lessons from, 18 Jan. 1941

WO 201/353, '9th Australian Division: Report on Operations in Cyrenaica, March-October 1941 Including the Defence of Tobruch [sic]'

WO 201/354 'The Anti-Aircraft Defences of Tobruck [sic] Fortress (1 April to 10 October 1941)'

WO201/2840 Camouflage in the Tobruk Fortress April-July 1941

WO 201/2586 Middle East Training Pamphlet No. 10, Lessons of Cyrenaica Campaign, Dec. 1940-Feb. 1941

Published Sources

Addison, Paul and Angus Calder (eds), *Time to Kill: The Soldier's Experience of War in the West 1939 – 1945* (London: Pimlico, 1997)

Agar-Hamilton , J.A.I. & L.C.F. Turner, *The Sidi Rezeg Battles 1941* (Cape Town: Oxford University Press, 1957)

Barker, A. J., *Afrika Korps* (London: Bison, 1978)

Bekker, Cajus, *The Luftwaffe War Diaries* (New York: MacDonald, 1966)

Bond, Brian, *British Military Policy Between the Two World Wars* (Oxford: Clarendon Press, 1980)

Bungay, Stephen, *The Most Dangerous Enemy: A History of the Battle of Britain* (London: Aurum Press, 2000)

Carver, Field Marshal Lord, *The Seven Ages of the British Army: The Story of Britain's Arm from 1625 to the 1960s* (London: Grafton Books, 1986)

Chamberlain, Peter and Chris Ellis, *British and American Tanks of World War II: The Complete Illustrated History of British, American and Commonwealth Tanks, 1939-1945* (New York: Arco Publishing, 1981)

Clarke, Brigadier Dudley, *The Eleventh at War* (London: Michael Joseph, 1952)

Connell, John, *Wavell, Scholar and Soldier* (London: Collins, 1964)

Coombes, David, *Australian Army History Series: Morshead: Hero of Tobruk and El Alamein* (Oxford: Oxford University Press, 2001)

Cox, Jafna L, 'A Splendid Training Ground: The Importance to the Royal Air Force of its Role in Iraq, 1919-32', *The Journal of Imperial and Commonwealth History*, Volume 13 No. 1 (October 1984)

di Scala, Spencer, *Italy: From Revolution to Republic, 1700 to the Present* (Boulder, Colorado: Westview Press, 2004)

Ellis, John, *The Sharp End: The Fighting Man in World War II* (London: Pimlico, 1993)

Ellis, Major L.F., CVO CBE DSO MC, *The War in France and Flanders 1939-1940* (London: HMSO, 1953)

Ereira, Alan, *The Invergordon Mutiny* (London: Routledge and Kegan Paul, 1981)

Forty, George, *The Desert Rats at War* (London: Ian Allan, 1975)

Fraser, David, *And We Shall Shock Tem: The British Army in the Second World War* (London: Hodder & Stoughton, 1983)

French, David, *Raising Churchill's Army: The British Army and the War Against Germany 1919 – 1945* (Oxford: Oxford University Press, 2000)

Grant, Roderick and Christopher Cole, *But Not in Anger: The RAF in the Transport Role* (London: Ian Allan, 1979)

Harrison, Frank, *Tobruk: The Great Siege Reassessed* (London: Brockhampton Press, 1999)

Hartshorn, E.P., DSO DCM ED, *Avenge Tobruk* (Cape Town: Purnell & Sons (SA) (PTY.) Ltd, 1960)

Hastings, Max, *Bomber Command* (London: Pan, 1999)

Heckmann, Wolf, *Rommel's War in Africa* (New York: Doubleday, 1981

Heckstall-Smith, Anthony, DFC, *Tobruk: The Story of a Siege* (Bristol: Cerberus Publishing Limited, 2004 – originally published 1959)

HMSO, *The Army at War: Destruction of an Army, The First Campaign in Libya Sept. 1940 – Feb. 1941* (London: HMSO, 1941)

Holmes, Richard, *Tommy: The British Soldier on the Western Front 1914-1918* (London: Harper Collins, 2004)

Hooton, E. R., *Luftwaffe at War: Gathering Storm 1933-1939* Volume I (Hersham, Surrey: Classic, 2007)

Horne, Alistair, *To Lose a Battle: France 1940* (London: Papermac, 1990)

Humble, Richard, *Crusader: The Eighth Army's Forgotten Victory, November 1941 – January 1942* (London: Leo Cooper, 1987)

Jowett, Philip S., *The Italian Army 1940-45 (2)* (Oxford: Osprey Publishing, 2001)

Kennedy, Captain J. R. MC, RA (Ret'd), *This, Our Army* (London: Hutchinson, 1935)

Knox, MacGregor, *Hitler's Italian Allies: Royal Armed Forces, Fascist Regime, and the War of 1940-1943* (Cambridge: Cambridge University Press, 2000)

Ladd, James D., *Commandos and Rangers of World War II* (London: BCA, 1978)

Landsborough, Gordon, *Tobruk Commando: The Raid to Destroy Rommel's Base* (London: Greenhill, 1989)

Liddell Hart, B.H., *The Tanks*, Volume I (London: Cassell, 1959)

Long, Gavin, *To Benghazi* (Canberra: Australian War Memorial, 1952)

Mackenzie, Compton, *Eastern Epic* Volume I: *September 1939 – March 1943 Defence* (London: Chatto & Windus, 1951)

Bibliography

Middlebrook, Martin, *The Kaiser's Battle 21 March 1918: The First Day of the German Spring Offensive* (London: Allen Lane, 1978)

Mitcham, Samuel .W. Jr, *Rommel's Greatest Victory: The Desert Fox and the Fall of Tobruk, Spring 1942* (Novato: Presidio Press, 1998)

Id, *Rommel's Desert Commanders: The Men Who Served the Desert Fox, North Africa 1941-1942* (Mechanicsburg, Pennsylvania: Stackpole Books, 2007)

Id., *The Panzer Legions: A Guide to the German Army Tank Divisions of WWII and Their Commanders* (Mechanicsburg, Pennsylvania: Stackpole Books, 2007)

Militärgeschichliches Forschungsamt (Research Institute for Military History) (Ed), *Germany and the Second World War* Volume II: *Germany's Initial Conquests in Europe* (Oxford: Clarendon Press, 1991)

Macksey, Kenneth, *Armoured Crusader: The Biography of Major-General Sir Percy 'Hobo' Hobart* (London: Grub Street, 2004)

Montgomery, Dennis, *An Innocent Goes to War* (Sussex: The Book Guild Ltd., 1999)

Moorehead, Alan, *African Trilogy* (London: Hamish Hamilton, 1944)

Omissi, David, *Air Power and Colonial Control: The Royal Air Force, 1919-1939* (Manchester: Manchester University Press, 1990)

Otway, Lieutenant-Colonel T.B.H., DSO, *The Second World War 1939-1945 Army: Airborne Forces* (London: War Office, 1950; facsimile Imperial War Museum, 1990)

Pitt, Barry, *The Crucible of War,* Volume I: *Wavell's Command* (London: Cassell & Co., 2001)

Id., *The Crucible of War,* Volume II: *Auchinleck's Command* (London: Cassell & Co., 2001)

Id., *The Crucible of War,* Volume III: *Montgomery and Alamein* (London: Cassell & Co., 2001)

Playfair, Major-General I.S.O., *The Mediterranean and Middle East:* Volume I: *The Early Successes against Italy* (London: HMSO, 1954; facsimile Naval & Military Press, 2004)

Id., *The Mediterranean and Middle East:* Volume I: *The Germans Come to the Help of their Ally (1941)* (London: HMSO, 1956; facsimile Naval & Military Press, 2004)

Reynolds, Michael, *Steel Inferno: I SS Panzer Corps in Normandy* (Staplehurst: Spellmount, 1997)

Roberts, Major-General . G.P.B., *From the Desert to the Baltic* (London: Kimber, 1987)

Ryan, W. Michael, 'The Influence of the Imperial Frontier on British Doctrines of Mechanised Warfare', *Albion,* Volume 15, No. 2 (1983)

Schmidt, Heinz Werner, *With Rommel in the Desert* (London: Harrap & Co., 1972)

Sebag-Montefiore, Hugh, *Dunkirk: Fight to the Last Man* (London: Viking, 2006)

Slim, Field Marshal Sir William, *Unofficial History* (London: Cassell, 1959)

Smith , Malcolm, *British Air Strategy Between the Wars* (Oxford: Clarendon Press, 1980)

Stevens, Lieutenant.-Colonel G. R., *Fourth Indian Division* (Toronto: McLaren, n.d.)

Stock, James W., *Tobruk: The Siege* (New York: Ballantine Books, 1973)

Sullivan, Brian R., *The Italian Soldier in Combat, June 1940-September 1943: Myths, Realities and Explanations,* in Paul Addison and Angus Calder (Eds.) *Time to Kill: The Soldiers Experience of War in the West 1939-1945* (London: Pimlico, 1997)

Terraine, John, *The Right of the Line: The Royal Air Force in the European War 1939 – 1945* (London: Wordsworth Originals, 1997)

Verney, G.L., *The Desert Rats* (London: Hutchinson, 1954)

Walker, Ian W., *Iron Hulls, Iron Hearts: Mussolini's Elite Armoured Divisions in North Africa* (Marlborough, Wilts: Crowood Press, 2006

War Office by The Ministry of Information, *The Army at War Series: Destruction of an Army: The First Campaign in Libya: Sept. 1940-Feb. 1941* (London: HMSO, 1941)

Wilmot, Chester, *Tobruk 194: Capture-Siege-Relief* (London: Angus & Robertson Ltd., 1944)

Winter, Denis, *Death's Men: Soldiers of the Great War* (London: Penguin, 1979)

Wood, Derek and Derek Dempster, The Narrow Margin: The Battle of Britain and the Rise of Air Power 1930-1940 (London: Tri-Service Press, 1990)

Index

Aalborg 38

Abbassia 122, 148

Abyssinia 17, 19, 22, 24, 27, 29, 34, 37, 61

Acroma 100, 101, 197, 198, 205, 208, 209, 211, 216, 261, 262, 277, 304, 322

Addis Ababa 17, 19, 24, 32, 145

Aden 15, 42, 44, 45, 46, 48, 143

Adowa 18, 19, 22, 23

Agedabia 140, 161, 165, 166, 167, 168, 169, 320

Agordat, 145

Al Jaghbub 22

Alam el Dab 83

Alexandria 13, 15, 57, 62, 69, 74, 80, 99, 100, 104, 114, 150, 204, 235, 289, 290, 292, 293, 300, 301, 302, 307, 320

Algiers 19

Algoa Bay 14

Allen, Brigadier A.S. 93

Antelat 126, 128, 129, 133, 167, 169

Aosta, Duke of 41, 42, 43, 48, 56, 143, 145

Arras 153, 228

Auchinleck. General Sir Claude 297, 299, 301, 312, 316, 321, 322

Azziziya 77, 82, 83

Babini, *Generale di Divisione* Valentino 117, 118, 119, 120, 130

Badoglio, *Maresciallo* Pietro 21, 24, 39

Balbo, *Maresciallo d'Italia* Italo 48, 49, 50, 51, 52, 57, 142

Balfe, Major J.W. 217, 220, 221, 222, 225, 228, 229

Baratieri, *Generale* Oreste 18

Barce 123, 124, 125, 134, 142, 148, 166, 167, 175, 176, 193, 320

Bardia 51, 69, 71, 88, 89, 90, 92, 94, 95, 96, 97, 98, 99, 101, 104, 105, 107, 112, 116, 119, 150, 198, 200, 209, 216, 218, 240, 241, 275, 292, 293, 297, 299, 302, 306, 308, 320

Batten, Sergeant-Major Reg 222, 223, 230

BATTLEAXE, Operation 293, 294, 296, 299, 304

Beda Fomm 129, 131, 137, 138, 140, 193, 316

Benina 74, 79, 94, 105, 176

Benghazi 11, 20, 21, 22, 25, 50, 74, 99,
101, 116, 118, 120, 122, 123, 124, 125, 134, 135, 137, 140, 142, 143, 149, 157, 163, 164, 168, 169, 173, 175, 176, 194, 206, 233, 270, 286, 294, 312, 320

Benzie, Major Walter 226, 227, 257, 259

Bera Bera 42, 43, 44, 45, 46, 47, 145

Berberis, *Generale di Divisione* Umberto 108

Beresford-Peirse, Lieutenant-General Sir Noel 79, 83, 148, 233, 293, 297

Bergonzoli, *Generale di Corpo* Annibale 95, 98, 112, 130, 131, 137, 138

Bertello, *Generale di Brigata* 43, 45

Berti, *Generale d'Armata* Mano 50, 53

Bertoldi, *Generale di Corpo d'Armata* 43, 45

Bir el Gubi 308, 309, 310

Bir el Kenayis 79

Bir el Khireigat 280

Bir Enba 55, 76

Bir Hacheim 321

Birks, Lieutenant-Colonel Horace 88, 90

Blackburn, Lieutenant-Commander Jack 289

Blamey, Lieutenant-General Thomas DSO 92, 148, 298

Böttcher, *Generalleutnant* Karl 232, 299

Brauchitsch, Generalfeldmarschall Walter von 156, 160, 161

Brenner Pass 28, 37, 73, 150

BREVITY, Operation 279, 280, 293, 294

Briggs, Brigadier Harold Rawdon/ Brigg's Force 145

British, Commonwealth and Allied Army:

1st Australian Imperial Force 92, 200

2nd Australian Imperial Force 92, 160, 173, 201, 298

British Expeditionary Force (BEF) 39, 148, 202,

Western Desert Force 67, 78, 87, 99, 116, 138, 139, 169, 233, 293, 297

Armies

8th Army 307, 312, 317, 319, 322

Corps

1st Australian Corps 92, 148

13th Corps 99, 102, 104, 113, 116, 118, 119, 121, 124, 137, 138, 139, 141, 142,
148, 169, 307, 308, 312, 313

30 Corps 307, 308, 310, 311, 312, 323

Royal Tank Corps 64

Divisions

1st Armoured Division 11, 320, 321

1st South African Division 144, 308, 321

2nd African Division 46, 308, 322

2nd Armoured Division 122, 148, 149, 161, 162, 163, 166, 170, 171, 172, 173, 175, 176, 193, 194, 195

2nd New Zealand Division 11, 147, 308, 312, 313, 314

3rd Australian Division 200

4th Indian Division 62, 63, 76, 77, 79, 80, 83, 87, 93, 144, 145, 148, 149, 279, 293, 296, 308

5th Indian Division 46, 144

6th Australian Division 87, 92, 93, 98, 102, 110, 111, 112, 116, 117, 118, 121, 124, 130, 134, 140, 147, 148, 149, 160, 161, 163, 173, 174, 201, 206, 298, 323

7th Armoured Division 11, 63, 67, 73, 76, 77, 79, 80, 83, 86, 118, 120, 122, 124, 125, 126, 133, 140, 142, 148, 163, 293, 294, 297, 298, 308, 312, 321

7th Australian Division 92, 174, 198, 300

9th Australian Division 162, 163, 172, 173, 174, 175, 193, 194, 196, 201, 203, 210, 245, 251, 273, 286, 298, 299, 300, 301, 303, 315, 317, 323

10th Armoured Division 11

11th African Division 144

11th Armoured Division 67

12th African Division 144

50th Division 321

70th Division 303, 317

79th Armoured Division 67

Mobile Division 65, 66, 67

New Zealand Division 93

Brigades:

1st Armoured Brigade 162

1st Army Tank Brigade 308, 321

1st Independent Carpathian Brigade 300, 301, 303, 317

1st South African Brigade 310

2nd Armoured Brigade 321

3rd Armoured Brigade 148, 162, 163, 164, 165, 166, 170, 196, 198, 204, 218, 226, 264

3rd Indian Motor Brigade 171, 172, 173

4th Anti-Aircraft Brigade 272, 281, 284
4th Armoured Brigade 67, 71, 77, 82,
    83, 86, 88, 89, 90, 99, 117, 118, 119,
    122, 126, 129, 131, 132, 133, 134, 135,
    170, 293, 295, 296, 301, 308, 309, 310,
    311, 319, 321
4th New Zealand Brigade 93, 312, 313
5th Indian Brigade 82, 320
6th Infantry Brigade 63
6th New Zealand Brigade 312
7th Armoured Brigade 67, 71, 77, 86,
    88, 90, 99, 117, 118, 119, 122, 133, 295,
    296, 308, 309, 311
10th Indian Brigade 143, 145
11th Indian Brigade 62, 80, 296, 320
14th Brigade 301, 303
14th Light Anti-Aircraft Brigade 204
16th Australian Brigade 87, 92, 93, 94,
    95, 97, 99, 104, 106, 107, 108, 111, 112
16th Brigade 83, 84, 87, 91, 94, 174,
    301, 303
17th Australian Brigade 92, 93, 94, 95,
    96, 97, 103, 104, 105, 111, 121, 125
18th Australian Brigade 92, 93, 173, 174,
    198, 200, 201, 205, 254, 264, 267, 275,
    276, 298, 300
19th Australian Brigade 93, 96, 97, 99,
    102, 104, 107, 111, 118, 120, 121, 123,
    125, 134, 137
20th Australian Brigade 174, 175, 197,
    200, 205, 209, 211, 301, 302
22nd Armoured Brigade 309, 310, 311
22nd Guards Brigade 63, 198, 200, 241,
    242, 279, 294, 296, 308
23rd Brigade 301, 303
24th Australian Brigade 174, 175, 200,
    205, 301
25th Australian Brigade 173, 174
26th Australian Brigade 174, 175, 195,
    196, 197, 198, 200, 205, 235, 243, 253
32nd Army Tank Brigade 301, 303, 310,
    311, 312, 313, 314
235th Heavy Anti-Aircraft Brigade 204
Cairo Cavalry Brigade 64, 65
Infantry Units
1st Battalion, The Argyll and Sutherland
    Highlanders 83, 85
1st Battalion, Durham Light Infantry
    279, 280
1st Battalion, The Essex Regiment
    314, 316
1st Battalion, King's Royal Rifle Corps
    65, 67, 94, 195, 197, 311
1st Battalion The Northern Rhodesian
    Regiment 44, 47
1st Battalion, 2nd Punjab Regiment 44
1st Battalion, 6th Rajputana Rifles 81
1st Battalion The Royal Fusiliers 82
1st Battalion, The Royal
    Northumberland Fusiliers 77, 82, 96,
    107, 250, 263, 277, 314
1st Battalion, The Tower Hamlets Rifles

165, 166
2/1st Battalion 96, 107
2/2nd Battalion 94, 97, 106, 113
2/3rd Battalion 94, 96, 97, 98, 106
2/4th Battalion 107, 108, 109, 110, 112
2/5th Battalion 97, 105
2/6th Battalion 97, 107
2/7th Battalion 113
2/8th Battalion 97, 107, 108, 109, 110,
    111, 125, 135, 137
2/9th Battalion 265, 266, 267
2/10th Battalion 264, 265, 267, 276
2/11th Battalion 97, 107, 108, 109, 110,
    111, 114, 121
2/12th Battalion 265, 267, 276, 277
2/13th Battalion 175, 176, 193, 195, 197,
    209, 211, 212, 213, 276, 297, 302, 315
2/15th Battalion 196, 209, 229, 251
2/17th Battalion 209, 210, 212, 216, 217,
    220, 221, 225, 229, 230, 231
2/23rd Battalion 243, 244, 245, 256, 275,
    277, 278, 279
2/24th Battalion 175, 235, 236, 250, 252,
    253, 254, 256, 258, 261, 262, 297
2/28th Battalion 207, 250, 254, 298
2/43rd Battalion 274, 297, 298
2/48th Battalion 235, 236, 237, 238, 244,
    245, 246, 261, 262, 265
2nd Battalion, The Black Watch 46, 48,
    310, 311
2nd Battalion, The Leicestershire
    Regiment 313
2nd Battalion, The Queen's Own
    Cameron Highlanders 75, 81
2nd Battalion, The Scots Guards 279
2nd Battalion, The Transvaal Scottish
    Regiment 322
2nd Battalion, The York and Lancaster
    Regiment 313, 314
2nd (Nyasaland) Battalion The King's
    African Rifles 44
2nd Battalion, The Rifle Brigade 67,
    81, 88, 126, 127, 128, 130, 132, 135,
    136, 311
3rd Battalion, The Coldstream Guards
    54, 71, 72, 77, 280
3rd Battalion, 1st Punjab Regiment 84
3rd Battalion, 15th Punjab Regiment
    44, 46, 47
4th Battalion The Border Regiment
    316
4th Battalion, 6th Rajputana Rifles 82
11th Czechoslovak Infantry Battalion
    301
44th (New Zealand) Battalion 314
46th (New Zealand) Battalion 312
74th Regiment of Foot 14
Armoured Units:
1st King's Dragoon Guards 125, 126,
    127, 139, 159, 161, 204, 230, 263, 303
1st Battalion, Royal Tank Regiment 65,
    67, 90, 133, 134, 198, 204, 210, 226,

229, 234, 256, 257, 259, 260, 303, 314
2nd Royal Lancers (Gardner's Horse)
    171
2nd Battalion, Royal Tank Corps 64,
    88, 89
2nd Battalion, Royal Tank Regiment
    72, 83, 127, 128, 129, 130, 131, 132,
    133, 134, 279, 311
3rd King's Own Hussars 72, 88, 131, 132,
    133, 204, 254, 263, 265
4th South African Armoured Car
    Regiment 305
4th Battalion, Royal Tank Regiment
    198, 228, 279, 294, 303, 310, 313, 314
5th Battalion, Royal Tank Regiment 97,
    166, 169, 170, 171
6th Australian Cavalry Regiment 97,
    107, 108, 112, 121, 125, 134, 135, 168
6th Battalion, Royal Tank Regiment 65,
    67, 84, 143, 163, 170, 295, 311
7th Queen's Own Hussars 65, 67, 68,
    71, 77, 82, 89, 127, 128, 129, 131,
    132, 311
7th Battalion, Royal Tank Regiment
    72, 79, 80, 81, 82, 84, 96, 98, 104, 106,
    109, 204, 228, 244, 254, 258, 259, 260,
    265, 294, 303, 310, 313, 316
8th King's Royal Irish Hussars 65, 67,
    75, 83, 88
8th Royal Tank Regiment 322
11th Hussars 64, 65, 67, 68, 69, 70, 71,
    72, 73, 75, 76, 82, 86, 88, 89, 94, 117,
    119, 121, 123, 125, 126, 127, 131, 140,
    159, 167, 170, 198, 242
18th Indian Cavalry Regiment 171, 205,
    229, 275, 300
44th Royal Tank Regiment 312, 314
Other Units
1st Australian Anti-Tank Regiment 173
1st East African Light Battery RA
    44, 47
1st Regiment, Royal Horse Artillery
    213, 217, 218, 220, 222, 223, 224, 225,
    230, 252, 254, 265
2nd Armoured Division Support Group
    162, 163, 164, 165, 166, 170, 171
2/1st Machine Gun Battalion 173
2/1st Pioneer Battalion 275
2/3rd Field Company RAE 207
2/4th Field Company RAE 300
2/4th Field Ambulance RAAMC 300
2/8th Field Ambulance 196
2/12th Field Regiment RAA 204, 265
3rd Australian Anti-Tank regiment 171,
    203, 218, 224
3rd Regiment, Royal Horse Artillery
    65, 66, 67, 71, 107, 109, 110, 126, 203,
    218, 244, 250, 255
4th Regiment, Royal Horse Artillery
    67, 126, 127, 128, 130, 133, 134, 136
7th Armoured Division Support Group
    67, 68, 71, 72, 73, 75, 84, 86, 87, 96,

103, 111, 126, 137, 140, 197, 198, 199, 200, 209, 240, 242, 279, 280, 295, 308, 309, 311, 313
No.7 Commando 241
8th Field Regiment RA 279
No.11 Commando 307
14th Light AA Regiment 281
23 Battery, Hong Kong and Singapore Brigade RA 44, 48
24th Australian Anti-Tank Company 250, 254, 255
26th Australian Anti-Tank Company 250, 255, 264
51st Field Regiment RA 175, 176, 204, 207, 235, 237, 238, 251, 253, 254, 263, 264, 265, 267, 300
51st Heavy AA Regiment 235, 281, 288
104th Royal Horse Artillery 165, 204, 265
106th Regiment, Royal Horse Artillery 126
107 Regiment (South Notts Hussars) RHA 197, 204, 205, 254
152nd Heavy Anti-Aircraft Battery RA 135
306th Searchlight Battery 281
Mobile Force 64, 65
Somaliland Camel Corps 44
Sudan Defence Force 43
British Somaliland 26, 42, 48, 56, 57, 143, 145
Brooks, Brigadier Walter 303
Brown, Group-Captain L.O. 149, 194
Buerat 11, 159, 270
Buq Buq 54, 72, 77, 82, 83, 86, 88, 92, 242, 294
Burao 43, 45
Burrows, Lieutenant-Colonel F.A. 176, 193
Buscaglia, Tenente Carlo Emanuele 74

Cairo 16, 61, 64, 65, 67, 75, 103, 105, 122, 137, 142, 197, 198, 199, 213, 307, 312, 323
Campbell, Lieutenant-Colonel J.C. 75
Carne, Commander W.P. RN 113, 114, 115
Castel Benito 79, 94
Caunter, Brigadier J.R.L. 79, 89, 118, 127, 128, 129, 131, 132, 133, 134, 137
Chappel, Brigadier Brian 303
Charruba 169, 170, 176, 193, 195
Chater, Brigadier Arthur Reginald RM 44, 46
Chaulan 121, 123
Churchill, Prime Minister Winston 59, 67, 72, 77, 78, 100, 142, 292, 293, 296, 299, 300, 301, 321, 323
Cirene 117
Collishaw, Air Commodore Raymond 63, 68, 124
Combe, Lieutenant-Colonel later

Brigadier John/ Combe Force 70, 71, 88, 89, 125, 126, 127, 129, 130, 132, 133, 135, 136, 137, 138, 140, 141, 167, 195, 196
Compagnie Universelle du Canal Maritime de Suez 13
COMPASS, Operation 76, 77, 78, 79, 84, 85, 86, 91, 93, 138, 139, 142, 143, 148, 169, 196, 216, 280, 307
Cona, Generale di Corpo d'Armata Ferdinando 117
Crawford, Lieutenant-Colonel J.W. 221, 225
Creagh, Major-General Michael O'Moore MC 66, 76, 79, 118, 121, 124, 126, 133, 140, 293, 297
Crete 12, 100, 146, 147, 304
Crüwell, General Ludwig 306
CRUSADER, Operation 307
CULTIVATE, Operation 301, 302
Cunningham, Lieutenant-General Sir Alan 51, 104, 144, 307, 312,
Cunningham, Admiral Sir Andrew 197
Cyprus 15, 60, 147, 303
Cyrenaica/Cyrenaica Command 19, 20, 21, 22, 25, 50, 99, 102, 120, 121, 123, 140, 141, 142, 143, 146, 147, 148, 149, 150, 159, 160, 162, 163, 164, 167, 172, 173, 174, 175, 193, 194, 195, 196, 197, 198, 199, 228, 230, 233, 249, 250, 270, 286, 298, 305, 308, 320
Cyrene (see also Cirene) 120, 125

D'Albiac, Air Vice Marshal J.H.D. 146
D'Annunzio 193
Dalmazzo, Generale di Corpo d'Armata Lorenzo 53
Dardanelles 20
De Bono, Maresciallo Emilio 23, 24
Della Bona, Generale di Divisione Guido 117
Della Mura, Generale Vincenzo 111
Dembeguina Pass 23
Derna 11, 20, 21, 111, 117, 118, 120, 121, 123, 149, 168, 169, 171, 173, 175, 195, 196, 205, 206, 207, 211, 232, 235, 243, 252, 270, 294, 304, 305, 320, 321
de Simone, Generale di Divisione Carlo 44, 46, 48
Dill, Field Marshal Sir John 78, 149, 163, 164, 174, 197
Djibouti 42
Dogali 17
Dorman-Smith, Brigadier Eric 121, 122, 123, 141, 142
Drew, Lieutenant-Colonel H.D. 169, 218, 226
Durazzo 31

Eather, Lieutenant-Colonel Kenneth DSO 111
Eden, Secretary of State for War

Anthony 78, 197
Edmondson, Corporal Jack VC 221
Egypt 11, 12, 13, 15, 16, 21, 25, 26, 29, 46, 48, 49, 51, 54, 57, 58, 59, 61, 62, 63, 64, 67, 70, 71, 73, 74, 75, 77, 79, 90, 92, 93, 99, 117, 122, 123, 124, 143, 148, 150, 162, 195, 198, 199, 201, 204, 215, 218, 228, 233, 247, 250, 296, 303, 304, 305, 318, 319
El Abiar 122, 134, 175, 176, 193
El Adem 51, 68, 99, 101, 103, 104, 106, 108, 111, 163, 168, 171, 197, 198, 199, 201, 204, 208, 209, 210, 211, 212, 213, 214, 216, 217, 218, 222, 223, 226, 240, 251, 252, 280, 294, 297, 306, 316, 321, 322
El Agheila 11, 22, 141, 158, 159, 160, 161, 164, 166, 230, 320
El Alamein 10, 12
El Duda 306, 310, 311, 312, 313, 314, 315, 316
El Gubbi 101, 204, 212, 218, 234, 246, 247, 271, 304
El Magrun 137
Enba Gap 76, 77, 80, 84, 86
Er Regima 169, 175, 193
Eritrea 17, 19, 23, 24
EXCESS, Operation 29

Fabris, Tenente Colonello Gino 168, 169, 171
Fadden, Australian Prime Minister Arthur 300
Field, Lieutenant-Colonel John 265
Forbes, Captain Bill 244, 245
Fort Capuzzo 54, 68, 69, 71, 76, 90, 91, 92, 95, 97, 240, 242, 279, 280, 294, 295, 296, 308
Fort Harrington 43, 46
Fort Maddalena 68, 71
Fort Pilastrino 101, 109, 111, 210, 226, 248, 254, 255, 257, 261, 263, 271, 323, 324
Fort Solaro 101, 109, 110
Freyberg, Major-General Bernard VC 93, 313
Fröhlich, Generalmajor Stefan 151, 152, 158, 194, 271
Fuka 11
Fuller, Colonel J.F.C. 64, 65

Gaggetti, Maggiore 266, 267
Gallabat 43, 143, 144
Gallina, Generale di Corpo Sebastiano 83
Gambara, Generale di Corpo d'Armata Gastone 306, 309
Gambier-Parry, Major General Michael 162, 165, 166, 171, 172, 195, 206
Gape, Lieutenant Vyvyan MC 242
Gariboldi, Generale d'Armata Italo 50,

Index

123, 157, 160, 161, 164, 166, 167, 250
Gazala 111, 175, 193, 197, 209, 240, 241, 307, 316, 319, 321, 322, 323
Gebhardt, Captain Peter 254, 255, 261, 262
Geissler, *Generalleutnant der Flieger* Hans 151, 157

German Armed Forces:
Oberkommando des Heeres (OKH) 151, 156, 157, 160, 168, 239, 248, 249, 263, 269, 270, 305
Oberkommando der Luftwaffe (OKL) 151
Oberkommando der Wehrmacht (OKW) 73, 150, 157, 249
Army Groups & Armies
4 Armee 155
Armee Gruppe Süd 153
Heeresgruppe B 38
Panzerarmee Afrika 10, 11, 306, 315, 320
Panzergruppe Kleist 155, 156
Corps:
15 Panzerkorps 153, 155, 156,
Deutsches Afrika Korps 10, 11, 152, 162, 173, 206, 211, 215, 230, 232, 248, 252, 263, 268, 269, 296, 304, 306, 315, 318, 319,
Divisions:
2 Leichte Division 153
3 Panzer Division 73, 74, 150
5 Leichte Division 151, 157, 158, 160, 161, 165, 167, 168, 206, 207, 208, 215, 216, 232, 239, 294, 295, 296, 205
5 Panzer Division 155
7 Panzer Division 153, 154, 155, 156, 228, 248
9 Panzer Division 231
11 Panzer Division 306
15 Panzer Division 151, 157, 161, 206, 209, 239, 240, 248, 263, 280, 292, 294, 296, 306, 309, 311, 315, 319, 320, 321, 322
21 Panzer Division 11, 305, 306, 307, 309, 311, 313, 315, 320, 321, 322, 324
90 Leichte Division 320, 321, 322
Afrika Division *zur besonderen Verfügung* 305, 306, 309, 310, 320
SS *Totenkopf* Division 228
Armoured Units:
Panzer Regiment 5 151, 161, 165, 166, 168, 171, 172, 206, 207, 211, 213, 214, 216, 217, 218, 221, 222, 226, 227, 228, 229, 230, 231, 232, 234, 239, 247, 248, 252, 253, 254, 255, 260, 261, 263, 267, 269, 280
Panzer Regiment 8 248, 280, 294, 295, 315
SS *Panzer* Regiment 21 233
Infantry Units:
Infanterie Regiment 104 248, 252, 298
Infanterie Regiment 115 248, 275, 298
Infanterie Regiments 155 305
Infanterie Regiments zbV 200 151, 306

Infanterie Regiment *Afrika* 361 306,
Panzergrenadier Regiment *Afrika* 305
Schützen Brigade 15 248
Other Units:
Artillerie Abteilung 75 220
Artillerie Kommand 104 299
Aufklärungs Abteilung 3 151, 158, 159, 161, 165, 166, 167, 168, 169, 176, 206, 207, 209, 230, 240, 305, 311
Aufklärungs Abteilung 33 320
Aufklärungs Abteilung 580 305
Aufklärungsstab Rommel 151, 160
Führerbegleitbataillon 153, 154
Kampfgruppe Böttcher 313
Kampfgruppe Schütte 305
Kampfgruppe Stephan 305
Kampfgruppe Knabe 313
Kradschützen Bataillon 15 209, 240, 242
Luftwaffen Flugabwehr Abteilung 33 222, 225, 228
Maschinengewehr Bataillon 2 165, 168, 209, 248, 252, 253
Maschinengewehr Bataillon 8 165, 169, 171, 173, 195, 196, 206, 207, 211, 212, 216, 217, 220, 221, 225, 229, 230, 239, 316
Panzerjäger Abteilung 39 151, 158, 222, 225
Panzerjäger Abteilung 190 305
Panzerjäger Abteilung 605 207
Pionier Bataillon 33 248, 252
Pionier Bataillon 200 212, 214, 216, 217, 221
Sperrverband 150, 151, 156, 161
SS *Aufklärungs Kompanie* 15 233
Luftwaffe:
X *Fliegerkorps* 146, 151, 157, 293
Fallschirmjäger Regiment 2 147
Jagdgeschwader (JG) 27 152
Kampfgeschwader 4 152, 234
Kampfgeschwader 26 152, 234
Lehrgeschwader 1 152, 246
Sturtzkampfgeschwader (StG) 3 152, 165, 231, 234, 246, 271, 283
Zestörergeschwader (ZG) 26 152, 205, 234, 242
Ghemines 122, 135, 137
Giof el Matar 167
Giovanni Berta 123
Godfrey, Brigadier Arthur 200
Godwin-Austen, Major-General Arthur Reade 46, 47, 297, 308, 313
Gordon-Finlayson, Lieutenant-General Sir Robert 65, 66
Gott, Brigadier later Major-General William 71, 151, 197, 198, 209, 240, 241, 242, 279, 297, 323
Graziani, *Maresciallo* Rudolfo 22, 24, 25, 29, 52, 53, 54, 57, 72, 73, 74, 75, 76, 77, 83, 94, 120, 123, 124, 157
Greece 12, 77, 78, 146, 148, 149, 160, 198, 233

Guzzoni, *Generale* Alfredo 31, 39, 157

Haile Selassie, Emperor 24, 25, 144, 145
Halder, *Generaloberst* Franz 156, 161, 249, 270
Halfaya, Halfaya Pass 11, 54, 72, 76, 89, 240, 241, 242, 248, 279, 280, 293, 294, 295, 296, 308, 320
Handley, Captain E.A. 176, 193
Harding, Brigadier Allan 195, 197, 198
Harding, Brigadier John 121
Hargeisa 44, 45, 46
Hartlieb-Walsporn, *Generalleutnant* Max von 155
Hartnell, Lieutenant-Colonel Sydney 314, 315
Harwich 40, 41
Hennessy, Lieutenant E.C. 112
Herff, *Oberstleutnant* Maximilian von 242, 248, 279, 280
Hickling, Captain H. RN 103, 104, 114
Hitler, *Führer* Adolf, 10, 28, 29, 30, 31, 37, 38, 49, 57, 73, 74, 150, 151, 168, 248, 249, 299
Hobart, Major-General Percy Cleghorn Stanley DSO MC 64, 65, 66, 67, 77
Hobart, Captain Patrick 89
Hoth, *Generaloberst* Hermann 155, 156
Hutchinson, Lieutenant J.A. 243
Hynes, Major George 226, 227, 229, 256, 257, 259
Ironside, General Sir Edmund 66
Ismailia 16

Italian Armed Forces:
Army Groups, Armies & Corps
Gruppo Dell'Esercito Ad Ovest (Army Group West) 39
1° *Armata* 39
4° *Armata* 39
5° *Armata* 50, 53, 123
10° *Armata* 50, 53, 54, 64, 69, 76, 117, 123, 124, 137, 138, 140, 149, 193, 316
20° *Corpo d'Armata Manovra* (CAM) 117, 306, 309
21° *Corpo d'Armata* 53, 306
Divisions:
Ariete Division 158, 160, 168, 170, 171, 206, 211, 216, 217, 231, 235, 237, 238, 239, 240, 248, 255, 280, 306, 312, 315, 319, 320, 322
1° *Libica* Division 53, 54, 72, 76, 84, 87
1° MVSN (23 *Marzo*) Division 54, 73, 76, 88, 89, 95
2° *Libica* Division 53, 54, 76, 84, 87
2° MVSN Division 76, 88, 90, 95, 119
4° MVSN Division 76, 84, 87
17° *Pavia* Division 117, 158, 276, 277, 306, 316
27° *Brescia* Division 117, 158, 167, 168, 169, 173, 206, 209, 231, 232, 248, 252, 253, 306, 319

40° *Cacciatori d'Africa* Division 41
60° *Sabratha* Division 117, 118, 119, 120, 121
62° *Marmarica* Division 53, 54, 75, 76, 95
63° *Cirene* Division 53, 54, 72, 76, 84, 86, 95
64° *Catanzaro* Division 76, 88, 95
65° *Granatieri Savoia* Division 41
Bologna Division 306, 309, 310, 313
Littorio Division 28
Savona Division 306, 307
Sirte Division 102, 111
Trento Division 216, 235, 294, 296
Trieste Division 306, 309, 320
Other Units:
3° *Battaglione del Carro Armato* 117
5° *Battaglione del Carro Armato* 117
8° *Reggimento Bersaglieri* 240, 266, 267
9° *Reggimento Bersaglieri* 313
10° *Reggimento Bersaglieri* 127
62° *Reggimento Fanteria* 236
67° *Reggimento Fanteria* 235
Brigata Corazzata Speciale (Special Armoured Brigade) 117, 118, 119, 124, 130
Raggruppamento Maletti 53, 54, 76, 80
Regimento Misto Motorizzato (Mixed Motorised Regiment) 32
Regia Aeronautica
Avazione Legionaria 27
Corpo Aereo Italiano 40
12° *Gruppo Autonomo CT* 234
18° *Gruppo CT* 40, 41
20° *Gruppo CT* 40, 41
13° *Stormo BT* 40
43° *Stormo BT* 40
160° *Gruppo Autonomo CT* 234
172ª *Squadriglia* 40
240ª *Squadriglia Aerosiluranti* 74
410ª *Sezione CT Autonomo* 45
Regia Marina:
Flotilla Del Mare Rosso 42, 87
Evangelista Toricelli (submarine) 42
Francesco Nullo (destroyer) 42, 87
Guglielmo (submarine) 42, 87
Leone 87
Liguria 114
Marco Polo 114
Pantera 87
San Giorgio 51, 52, 111, 114
Italian East Africa 24, 26, 41, 48, 56, 87, 143, 150
Italian Somaliland 17, 22, 23, 24, 42

Jackman, Captain James VC 314
James, Lieutenant R.W. 243
Jarabub 71, 307
Jebel Akhdar 22, 120, 122, 123, 125, 135, 169
Jenkins, Lieutenant Claude 235

Kassala 43, 46, 144, 145
Keyes, Lieutenant-Colonel Geoffrey VC 307, 308
Kirchheim, *Generalmajor* Heinrich 168, 169, 206, 232, 248, 252
Klopper, Major-General Hendrik 322, 323, 324
Kluge, *Generaloberst* Hans von 155, 156
Knabe, *Oberstleutnant* Gustav 209, 242
Kopa ski, General Stanislaw 300, 301, 303, 317
Kufra 20, 21, 22

Lastucci, *Generale di Corpo* 69
Latham, Brigadier Harold Cecil 164
Laverack, Major-General John 198, 199, 200, 205, 211, 233, 234
League of Nations 22, 23, 26, 28, 61
Leakey, Captain Rea 227, 234
Lesseps, Vicomte Ferdinand Marie de 13
Libya 12, 25, 26, 32, 48, 49, 52, 56, 57, 63, 64, 67, 73, 88, 91, 92, 116, 117, 120, 156, 157, 158, 159, 160, 161, 162, 168, 239, 250, 263, 270, 292, 299
LIGHTFOOT, Operation 10
Lloyd, Colonel Charles 198
Loder-Symonds, Major Robert 217
Lomax, Brigadier Cyril 83, 84, 303
Longmore, Air Chief Marshal Sir Arthur 52, 149, 197
Loughrey, Major J. 261
LUSTRE, Operation 147

Maaten Baggush 51, 67, 233
Maccia Bianca 254, 255, 261, 263
McIntyre, Lieutenant-Colonel 235
Mackay, Major-General Iven 93, 94, 95, 97, 102, 103, 111, 118, 140
Mackell, Lieutenant Austin 220, 221, 225
Maddalena 312
Maitland Wilson, Lieutenant-General Henry 66, 75, 76, 142, 147, 148, 164
Maktila 54, 73, 75, 76, 83, 88
Maletti, *Generale* Pietro 53, 80, 81,
Malloch, Captain Ian 256, 278,
Malta 15, 62, 74, 79, 94, 124,
Mannella, *Generale di Corpo d'Armata* Enrico Petassi 102, 110
Maraua 170, 194, 195
Mareth Line 12
Marlan, Lieutenant-Colonel R.F. 196
Martel, Lieutenant-Colonel Sir Gifford 59
Martin, Lieutenant-Colonel James 265, 266
Martuba 117, 118, 195, 197, 308
Massawa 17, 42, 145
Mechili 117, 118, 119, 122, 123, 125, 126, 163, 167, 168, 169, 170, 171, 172,

173, 175, 193, 194, 195, 203, 205, 206, 294, 320, 321
Menelik II, King of Abyssinia 17, 18, 19
Menzies, Australian Prime Minister Sir Robert 298, 299, 300
Mersa Brega 161, 162, 163, 164, 168, 174, 175
Mersa Matruh 11, 54, 62, 64, 65, 67, 71, 72, 73, 74, 75, 76, 77, 79, 87, 91, 92, 93, 104, 114, 138, 150, 212, 290, 291, 292, 293, 307
Messervy, Major-General Frank 145, 293, 296, 320, 321
Metemma 143, 144
Meuse, River 18, 153, 155, 156
Milan 32, 40
Mills, Sergeant G.M. 112, 121
Mitchell, Lieutenant-Colonel John, DSO & Bar 135, 137
Montemurro, *Colonello* Ugo 169, 171, 172, 206
Morrison, Sergeant-Major W.G. 278
Morshead, Major-General Sir Leslie 174, 175, 193, 194, 197, 198, 200, 201, 202, 203, 204, 205, 206, 218, 226, 231, 233, 234, 245, 253, 254, 258, 259, 260, 261, 262, 263, 264, 267, 271, 274, 275, 276, 277, 297, 298, 299, 302, 303, 304, 232
Msus 122, 124, 125, 126, 133, 167, 168, 169, 170, 175, 194, 320
Mugtaa 160
Muhammad Ali Pasha 12, 13
Murray, Brigadier John 174, 200, 209
Mussolini, *Duce* Benito 21, 24, 25, 26, 28, 31, 32, 37, 38, 39, 40, 49, 50, 52, 53, 56, 57, 61, 73, 77, 95, 123, 150, 158

Nasi, *Generale di Corpo d'Armata* Guglielmo 43, 46, 145
Navarrini, *Generale di Corpo d'Armata* Enea 306,
Neame, Lieutenant-General Philip VC 148, 149, 163, 164, 166, 167, 171, 174, 175, 193, 194, 195, 196, 197, 198, 306
Neumann, Major Eduard, 152
Neumann-Sylkow, *Generalleutnant* Walther 294, 295
Nibeiwa 76, 77, 79, 80, 81, 82, 83, 86
Nile, River 13, 208
Nofilia 158, 159, 160, 161, 215
Norrie, Lieutenant-General Charles Willoughby 308, 310

O'Connor, Major-General Richard 63, 66, 67, 69, 70, 71, 72, 73, 76, 78, 79, 80, 86, 87, 89, 90, 96, 97, 98, 99, 103, 116, 117, 118, 119, 120, 121, 123, 124, 125, 126, 137, 138, 139, 140, 141, 142, 143, 148, 149, 167, 175, 193, 195, 196, 216

Index

Olbrich, *Oberstleutnant* Dr Friedrich 165, 168, 169, 171, 172, 206, 207, 208, 211, 212, 214, 215, 217, 222, 224, 225, 226, 228, 229, 232

Pact of Steel 29, 31, 40
Palestine 59, 60, 63, 75, 91, 92, 93, 147, 148, 174, 299, 300, 303
Palmer, Lieutenant Alfred RNR 291
Passerone, *Generale* 45
Paulus, *Generalleutnant* Friedrich 250, 257, 263, 268, 270
Perry, Major W. H. 278
Peters, Sub-Lieutenant Dennis RNVR 292, 301
Pintor, *Generale* Pietro 39
Platt, Lieutenant-General William 144, 145
Ponath, *Oberstleutnant* Gustav 169, 171, 173, 195, 206, 211, 212, 220, 232
Port Said 13, 15, 59, 104, 125
Prittwitz und Gaffron, *Generalmajor* Heinrich von 206, 207, 208, 240, 246
Proud, Captain Peter RE 286, 287, 288, 289

Qasaba 77

Rabia 76, 77, 83, 84, 86, 91
Rajendrasinhji, Major Maharaj K.S. 171
Ras El Medauar 101, 235, 236, 237, 246, 248, 250, 251, 252, 253, 254, 255, 256, 257, 258, 260, 261, 262, 263, 264, 265, 273, 275, 276, 277, 288, 297, 298, 306, 317
Rattray, Captain Rupert 243, 275
Ravenstein, *Generalmajor* Johannes von 306, 315
Rawson, Commander Wyatt RN 16
Red Sea 13, 17, 26, 42, 62, 145
Renton, Lieutenant-Colonel Callum 126
Rimington, Brigadier Reginald 196
Rintelen, *Generalmajor* Enno von 150, 157
Ritchie, Lieutenant-General Neil 312, 322, 323
Robertson, Brigadier Horace 107, 109, 112, 118, 125, 134, 137, 174
Rome 52, 53, 61, 150, 157
Rommel, *Generalfeldmarschall* Erwin 10, 11, 12, 152, 153, 154, 155, 156, 157, 158, 159, 160, 161, 162, 164, 165, 166, 167, 168, 169, 170, 171, 172, 173, 194, 196, 206, 207, 208, 209, 214, 215, 216, 220, 222, 228, 230, 231, 232, 235, 236, 237, 239, 240, 242, 248, 249, 250, 253, 256, 257, 258, 260, 263, 268, 269, 270, 271, 276, 280, 294, 295, 296, 302, 304, 305, 306, 307, 308, 309, 311, 312, 316, 318, 319, 320, 321, 322, 323, 324

Royal and Commonwealth Air Force:
No. 202 Group 63, 68, 74, 79, 124, 149
No.1 Squadron SAAF 143
No.3 Squadron RAAF 107, 149, 194
No. 6 Army Co-operation Squadron 74, 103, 117, 149, 199, 204, 205, 244, 247
No. 8 Squadron 45
No. 11 Squadron 45
No. 14 Squadron 279
No.17 Squadron 41
No. 30 Squadron 146
No.33 Squadron 63, 74
No.37 Squadron 105
No.38 Squadron 105
No.39 Squadron 45
No. 45 Squadron 63, 68, 107, 171, 218
No. 46 Squadron 41
No.47 Squadron 143
No.53 Squadron 63
No.55 Squadron 107, 149, 171, 213, 218
No.70 Squadron 74, 96
No. 73 Squadron 107, 149, 204, 212, 213, 234, 246, 247
No.80 Squadron 146
No.84 Squadron 146
No. 94 Squadron 45
No.112 Squadron 143, 146
No.113 Squadron 63, 74, 107
No. 203 Squadron 45
No. 208 Army Co-operation Squadron 63, 74, 103, 111, 117, 124
No.211 Squadron 63, 68, 146
No. 216 Squadron 79
No. 219 Squadron 96
No. 237 (South Rhodesian) Squadron 42, 144
No.257 Squadron 41
No. 274 Squadron 107, 279
No. 451 Squadron RAAF 304
Royal Navy & Royal Australian Navy:
H Force 293,
Inshore Squadron 103, 104, 290, 300,
Far Eastern Fleet 42,
Mediterranean Fleet 61, 290, 293, 320,
Western Desert Lighter Force (WDLF) 219,
Ships:
HMS *Abdiel* 291, 300, 302
HM Gunboat *Aphis* 74, 80, 92, 94, 104, 240
HMS *Ark Royal* 293, 320
HMS *Arthur Cavanagh* 114, 290
HMS *Auckland* 219, 290
HMS *Bagshot* 80, 104, 105, 114, 290
HMS *Barham* 97, 293, 320
HMS *Birkenhead* 14
HMS *Coventry* 241
HMS *Eagle* 51

HMS *Encounter* 300, 302
HMS *Formidable* 293
HM Gunboat *Gnat* 104, 105, 240, 287, 292
HMS *Griffin* 240
HMS *Grimsby* 289
HM Landing Ship *Glengyle* 241
HMS *Gloucester* 240, 293
HMS *Hasty* 240
HMS *Havoc* 300
HMS *Hero* 302
HMAS *Hobart* 46, 47
HMS *Illustrious* 74, 80, 293
HMS *Jaguar* 292
HMS *Jarvis* 300
HMS *Kent* 74
HMS *Khartoum* 42
HMS *Kimberley* 300
HMS *Kipling* 300
HM Gunboat *Ladybird* 74, 80, 92, 104, 105, 241, 289
HMS *Latima* 300
HMS *Latona* 291, 300, 302
HMS *Magnet* 114
HMS *Malaya* 51
HMS *Milford Countess* 114, 289, 290
HMS *Moorhen* 245
HMS *Nizam* 300
HMAS *Paramatta* 290
HMS *Phoebe* 300
HMS *Queen Elizabeth* 293, 320
HMS *Southampton* 293
HMS *Southern Maid* 114, 219, 290
HMAS *Stuart* 111, 240
HM Submarine *Talisman* 308
HM Monitor *Terror* 80, 92, 94, 104, 105, 115, 149
HM Submarine *Torbay* 308
HMS *Valiant* 97, 293, 320
HMAS *Vampire* 111
HMAS *Voyager* 104, 111
HMS *Warspite* 51, 97, 293
HMAS *Waterhen* 291
Hospital Ship *Karapara* 289
Hospital Ship *Vita* 235
Maria Giovanni 291
SS *Clan Campbell* 292
SS *Clan Chattan* 292
SS *Clan Lamont* 292
SS *Empire Song* 292, 293
SS *Helka* 289, 290
SS *New Zealand Star* 292, 293
SS *Pass of Balmaha* 290
SS *Thurland Castle* 204
Russell, Brigadier H.E. 86, 133

St. Giovanni de Medua 31
Sandford, Brigadier Daniel 144
Santamaria, *Maggiore* Nicolini 168
Savige, Brigadier S.G. 94
Scarpe, River 155
Sceleidima 126, 131, 166

Tobruk: The Great Siege 1941–42

Schmidt, *Hauptmann* Heinz 208, 216, 222

Schorm, *Leutnant* Joachim 227, 229, 234, 247, 252, 255, 257, 261, 262, 263, 264, 267

Schwerin, *Oberst* Graf von 167, 168, 169, 206

Scobie, Major-General Ronald Mackenzie 303, 304, 310, 311, 316, 317

Seelöwe, Operation 73, 150

Sedan, 156

Selby, Brigadier A.R./ Selby Force 76, 80, 83, 84

Senussi 19, 20, 21, 22

Senussi, Sheikh Muhammad bin Ali al 19

Sfax 99

Sidi Azeiz 68, 242, 279, 280, 294, 308

Sidi Barrani 51, 53, 54, 55, 73, 74, 75, 76, 77, 80, 82, 83, 84, 86, 88, 90, 91, 92, 116, 118, 242, 291

Sidi Omar 54, 71, 76, 88, 89, 295, 308

Sidi Rezegh 308, 309, 310, 311, 312, 313, 315, 322

Sidi Saleh 126

Sidi Suleiman 296

Sirte/Gulf of Sirte 123, 140, 157, 158, 159, 270, 320

Slater, Brigadier John Nuttall 281

Slim, Brigadier William 143, 144, 145

Slonta 117, 119, 125, 193

Smith, Commander F.M. R.NR. 113

Sofafi 76, 77, 83, 84, 86, 91, 242, 294, 305

Sollum 11, 53, 54, 57, 71, 72, 73, 74, 76, 88, 90, 91, 92, 93, 94, 95, 101, 104, 114, 116, 119, 199, 209, 240, 241, 242, 250, 277, 279, 280, 293, 296, 300, 305, 320

Soluch 122, 138, 167

Sommernachtstraum, Operation 151, 305, 306

Spowers, Lieutenant-Colonel Allan 250, 253, 254, 297

Streich, *Generalmajor* Johannes 151, 160, 161, 162, 165, 166, 167, 168, 169, 171, 206, 207, 208, 215, 216, 217, 218, 222, 232

Sudan 42, 43, 56, 78, 93, 143, 303

Suez, Suez Canal 13, 14, 15, 16, 26, 56, 58, 61, 124, 134, 148, 150, 208, 215, 250

Suluq 22

Sümmermann, *Generalmajor* Max 306

SUPERCHARGE, Operation 10, 11, 301, 302

Tel el Aqaqir 11

Tel el Kebir 16

Tellera, *Generale d'Armata* Guiseppe 123, 137, 149, 193, 316

Tembien 24

Thoma, *Generalleutnant* Wilhelm Ritter von 11, 73, 74, 150

TIGER, Operation 292, 293, 294

Tilly, Major-General Justice Crosland 162

Tmimi 122, 124, 125, 168, 195, 196, 197, 307

Tobruk 11, 12, 20, 21, 29, 50, 51, 52, 69, 88, 89, 90, 94, 95, 97, 98, 99, 100, 101, 102, 103, 104, 105, 109, 110, 111, 112, 113, 114, 115, 116, 117, 118, 120, 121, 122, 123, 124, 142, 143, 156, 160, 162, 164, 168, 174, 175, 194, 197, 198, 199, 200, 201, 203, 204, 205, 206, 207, 208, 209, 211, 212, 213, 214, 215, 216, 217, 218, 220, 222, 230, 231, 233, 234, 235, 236, 239, 240, 242, 245, 246, 247, 248, 250, 255, 257, 262, 263, 268, 269, 270, 271, 272, 273, 274, 275, 277, 279, 280, 282, 283, 286, 288, 289, 290, 291, 292, 294, 298, 299, 300, 301, 302, 303, 304, 306, 307, 310, 312, 313, 315, 316, 317, 318, 319, 320, 321, 322, 323, 342

TORCH, Operation 12

Tovell, Brigadier Raymond 195, 197, 200, 235, 243, 253

TREACLE, Operation 299, 300, 302

Tripoli 19, 20, 25, 50, 52, 53, 79, 124, 141, 151, 157, 158, 159, 161, 206, 215, 239, 248, 270, 304, 318, 320

Tripolitania 19, 20, 21, 22, 25, 50, 123, 141, 143, 150, 159, 160

Tug Argan 43, 44, 45, 46, 47, 48

Tummar 77, 82, 83

Tunis 19

Tunisia 12, 25, 49, 99

Turin 40

Umberto, Prince of Savoy 39

Valona 31

Vaughn, Brigadier Edward 171

Ventimilli 26, 120

Verrier, Lieutenant-Colonel Arthur Drummond 264

Via Balbia 25, 49, 69, 89, 100, 101, 104, 105, 106, 107, 108, 120, 121, 122, 125, 126, 127, 129, 132, 133, 136, 137, 158, 165, 167, 168, 169, 173, 195, 197, 207, 209, 211, 236, 243, 246, 251, 322

Victor Emmanuelle III, King 24, 31

Vietina, *Ammiraglio* Massimiliano 112, 121, 174

Voigtsberger, *Major* Heinrich 252

Wadi Belgassem 100

Wadi Derna 120, 121, 193

Wadi Giaida 250, 261

Wadi Sehel 100, 101, 105, 197

Wadi Zeitun 100, 101

Walwal 22

War Office 58, 159, 164, 301, 303

Wavell, Lieutenant-General Sir Archibald 46, 63, 66, 67, 70, 75, 77, 78, 86, 87, 93, 116, 122, 123, 125, 138, 141, 143, 146, 147, 149, 159, 161, 163, 164, 165, 166, 167, 170, 174, 175, 197, 198, 199, 200, 206, 233, 279, 292, 293, 296, 299, 321

Wechmar, *Oberstleutnant* Freiherr von 168, 176, 206, 209

Weiss, Operation 30

Weserübung, Operation 38

Wightman, Squadron-Leader W.T.F. 45

Wilkie, Lieutenant David 89

Willison, Brigadier Arthur 303, 311, 312, 314, 315, 317

Wilson, Captain C.H. 229

Windeyer, Lieutenant-Colonel W.J.V. 261

Wingate, Lieutenant-Colonel Charles Orde 144

Wolseley, Lieutenant-General Sir Garnet GCMG KCB 15, 16

Woods, Captain H.A. 261, 262

Wooten, Brigadier Frederick 200, 264, 300

Wynter, Major-General Henry 173

Z Squadron 59

Zamboni, *Generale di Divisione* Bertolo 167, 168

Zuetina 166